All About Language

(Неделя языка: наука, теория, практика)

All About Language
Science, Theory, and Practice

(Неделя языка: наука, теория, практика)

edited by

Elena L. Grigorenko, Ph.D.
University of Houston and Baylor College of Medicine, Houston, Texas
St. Petersburg State University, St. Petersburg, Russia
Moscow State University of Psychology and Education, Moscow, Russia

Yury Shtyrov, Ph.D.
Aarhus University, Denmark
St. Petersburg State University, St. Petersburg, Russia
Higher School of Economics, Moscow, Russia

and

Peggy McCardle, Ph.D., M.P.H.
Peggy McCardle Consulting, LLC, Tarpon Springs, Florida
Haskins Laboratories, New Haven, Connecticut

with invited contributors

· PAUL · H ·
BROOKES
PUBLISHING CO®

·P A U L·H·
BROOKES
PUBLISHING CO.®

Paul H. Brookes Publishing Co.
Post Office Box 10624
Baltimore, Maryland 21285-0624
USA
www.brookespublishing.com

Typeset by BMWW, Baltimore, Maryland.
Manufactured in the United States of America by
Sheridan Books, Inc., Chelsea, Michigan.

The symposium and this resulting volume were supported primarily by two laboratories led by Elena Grigorenko (the Laboratory of Translational Developmental Science, grant contract No. 14.A50.31.0027) and Yury Shtyrov, (the Laboratory of Behavioral Neurodynamics, grant contract No. 14.W03.31.0010), both established at the St. Petersburg University, Russia, within the framework of so-called "Mega-grant projects" aimed at giving a major boost to Russian sciences (http://www.p220.ru/en/) and by philanthropic organizations, including The Dyslexia Foundation (USA), the Association for Children and Parents with Dyslexia (Russian Federation), and the Way Out Foundation (Russian Federation). This volume in the Extraordinary Brain Series is sponsored by the University of St. Petersburg, particularly the Laboratory of Translational Developmental Science and the Laboratory of Behavioural Neurodynamics; the Russian Federal P220 program (grant contracts No. 14.Z50.31.0027 to ELG and No. 14.W03.31.0010 to YS, respectively); The Dyslexia Foundation (TDF), co-sponsor of the symposium and initiator of the Extraordinary Brain Symposium; the Way Out Foundation (Russian Federation); and the Association for Children and Parents with Dyslexia (Russian Federation).

Library of Congress Control Number: 2019946275

ISBN-13: 978-1-68125-355-8

2023 2022 2021 2020 2019

10 9 8 7 6 5 4 3 2 1

Contents

About the Editors

Elena L. Grigorenko, Ph.D., Head of the Laboratory of Translational Sciences of Human Development, St. Petersburg State University, St. Petersburg, Russia; Professor of Psychology, University of Houston, Texas; and Professor of Molecular and Human Genetics and Pediatrics at Baylor College of Medicine, Houston, Texas

Dr. Grigorenko received her Ph.D. in general psychology from Moscow State University, Russia, her Ph.D. in developmental psychology and genetics from Yale University, USA, and her re-specialization in clinical (forensic) psychology from Fielding University, USA. Dr. Grigorenko is affiliated with five universities: Baylor College of Medicine, University of Houston, and Yale University in the USA, and Moscow State University for Psychology and Education and St. Petersburg State University in Russia. Dr. Grigorenko has published more than 500 peer-reviewed articles, book chapters, and books. She has received multiple awards for her work; obtained funding for her research from numerous federal and private sponsoring organizations in the USA and other countries; supported multiple nonprofit organizations, including as a board member; and served as editor-in-chief for professional journals. Dr. Grigorenko has worked with children and their families in the United States as well as in Africa (Kenya, Tanzania and Zanzibar, the Gambia, and Zambia), India, Saudi Arabia, and Russia.

Yury Shtyrov, Ph.D., Professor, Center of Functionally Integrative Neuroscience (CFIN), Institute for Clinical Medicine, Aarhus University/Aarhus University Hospital, Aarhus, Denmark; and Visiting Professor, St. Petersburg State University, St. Petersburg, Russia, and the Higher School of Economics, Moscow, Russia

Dr. Shtyrov is a professor in the Department of Clinical Medicine at Aarhus University, Denmark, where he is Head of the magnetoencephalography/electroencephalography (MEG/EEG) group. He is also a visiting professor at St. Petersburg State University and the Higher School of Economics, Moscow. He majored in neurophysiology at St. Petersburg State University in 1994, and, after working in clinics and industry, obtained his Ph.D. in cognitive neuroscience at the University of Helsinki, Finland. Following this, he worked for many years at the Medical Research Council (Cambridge,

United Kingdom), leading research into brain bases of the language function. His main research focuses on delineating the neural dynamics of spoken language processing, its automaticity and interactions with other cognitive systems, and the brain bases of language learning.

Peggy McCardle, Ph.D., M.P.H., President/Consultant, Peggy McCardle Consulting, LLC, and Affiliated Research Scientist, Haskins Laboratories, New Haven, Connecticut

Dr. McCardle is President/Consultant, Peggy McCardle Consulting, LLC, and an affiliated research scientist at Haskins Laboratories in New Haven, Connecticut. As former Branch Chief at the *Eunice Kennedy Shriver* National Institute of Child Health and Human Development (NICHD), U.S. National Institutes of Health (NIH), she developed and directed the research program in language, bilingualism, and biliteracy and various literacy and child development initiatives. Dr. McCardle is a linguist, former speech-language pathologist, and former university faculty, and she currently works as a private consultant, science writer, and editor (including volume and thematic journal issue design and implementation). Her publications address various aspects of public health, developmental psycholinguistics, and human development. She is currently involved in various projects related to literacy, English language learners, early childhood, education and learning difficulties, and human–animal interaction.

About the Contributors

Leonard Abbeduto, Ph.D., Professor of Psychiatry and Behavioral Sciences, University of California, Davis

Dr. Abbeduto is Director of the UC Davis Medical Investigation of Neurodevelopmental Disorders Institute (UC Davis MIND), and he is Tsakopoulos-Vismara Endowed Chair and Professor of Psychiatry and Behavioral Sciences at the University of California, Davis. He conducts research focused on differences in language development across neurodevelopmental disorders such as autism spectrum disorder (ASD) and fragile X syndrome, the determinants of within-disorder variation in language development, methods of measuring language development, and language intervention. His research increasingly includes the use of telehealth distance-based technologies and other digital technologies. Dr. Abbeduto has participated in several National Institutes of Health (NIH) working groups on outcome measures for treatment trials in neurodevelopmental disorders and is a frequent consultant on clinical endpoints for industry trials testing the efficacy of new targeted pharmaceuticals. He also directs the National Institute of Child Health and Human Development (NICHD)–funded MIND Institute Intellectual and Developmental Disabilities Research Center, which provides scientific support to more than 60 projects and 40 scientists at the UC Davis MIND Institute.

Tatiana Akhutina, Ph.D., Chief Researcher, Laboratory of Neuropsychology, Psychology Department, Lomonosov Moscow State University, Russia

Dr. Akhutina is the chief researcher of the Laboratory of Neuropsychology, Psychology Department, Lomonosov Moscow State University. A former student of Alexander Luria, one of the founders of cultural-historical psychology and neuropsychology, Dr. Akhutina has been head of the laboratory of neuropsychology for 25 years. She heads the research group of developmental neuropsychology. Her scientific publications are in neurolinguistics, child neuropsychology, and remediation of learning disabilities. Her most important topic is how to go from neuropsychological assessment of children to effectively overcoming their learning disabilities. She is an author of *Overcoming Learning Disabilities: A Vygotskian-Lurian Neuropsychological Approach* (Cambridge University Press, 2012).

Amy Banasik, M.S., CCC-SLP, Staff Research Associate, University of California, Davis

Amy Banasik, Staff Research Associate, UC Davis MIND Institute, is a speech and language clinician and language intervention specialist in the Laboratory on Language Development in Neurodevelopmental Disorders at the UC Davis MIND Institute.

Laura Barquero, Ph.D., Research Associate, Education and Brain Research Laboratory, Vanderbilt University, Nashville, Tennessee

Dr. Barquero is a research associate in the Vanderbilt Education and Brain Research Laboratory at Vanderbilt University. Her research interests include using functional neuroimaging to explore responsiveness to intervention in children and adolescents who experience difficulty with reading.

Lauren Bullard, M.S., Doctoral Candidate in Human Development, University of California, Davis

Lauren Bullard is a doctoral candidate in human development at the University of California, Davis. She is a graduate student researcher in the language development lab at the UC Davis MIND Institute. Her research interests include investigating factors that contribute to language development in children with intellectual and developmental disorders, parent–child interactions, and familial well-being. Ms. Bullard received her bachelor of arts degree in psychology from the University of New Mexico in Albuquerque.

Ferenc Bunta, Ph.D., Associate Professor of Communication Sciences and Disorders, University of Houston, Texas

Dr. Bunta is an associate professor of communication sciences and disorders at the University of Houston. His research focuses on bilingual and cross-linguistic phonological acquisition in both typical children and their peers with communication disorders (e.g., children with hearing loss who use cochlear implants). His work has been funded by the National Institute of Deafness and Other Communication Disorders, the U.S. Department of Education, and the Spencer Foundation.

Olga V. Burenkova, Ph.D., Postdoctoral Fellow, Texas Institute for Measurement, Evaluation, and Statistics (TIMES), University of Houston, Texas

Dr. Burenkova is a postdoctoral fellow, Texas Institute for Measurement, Evaluation, and Statistics (TIMES), University of Houston, and a researcher in the Laboratory of Translational Sciences of Human Development, St. Petersburg State University, Russia. A 2009 graduate of Lomonosov Moscow State University in neurobiology, she received her doctorate in 2014 from the P.K. Anokhin Research Institute of Normal Physiology, with research on the epigenetic mechanisms of the influence of early-life adversity on the behavioral development of mice. Her current work in Dr. Grigorenko's lab at the University of Houston is focused on the molecular bases of cognitive development and the impact of early adversity on mental health and development in humans.

Brian Castelluccio, Ph.D., Postdoctoral Fellow in Clinical Neuropsychology, Brown University, Providence, Rhode Island

Dr. Castelluccio is a postdoctoral fellow in clinical neuropsychology at the Warren Alpert Medical School of Brown University. As an affiliate of the Connecticut Institute for the Brain and Cognitive Sciences, his research has been interdisciplinary in nature, spanning cognitive neuroscience, psycholinguistics, genetics, and clinical psychology. The focus of his work has been on the neural underpinnings of language differences in autism spectrum disorder.

Jessica A. Church, Ph.D., Assistant Professor of Psychology and Psychiatry, University of Texas at Austin

Dr. Church is an assistant professor of psychology and psychiatry at the University of Texas at Austin. She heads the Austin neuroimaging team that evaluates functional brain data collected as a part of the Texas Center for Learning Disabilities.

Paul T. Cirino, Ph.D., Professor of Psychology, University of Houston, Texas

Dr. Cirino is a professor of psychology at the University of Houston. He is a developmental neuropsychologist and is the lead on the cognitive projects of the Texas Center for Learning Disabilities.

Laurie Cutting, Ph.D., Professor, Peabody College of Education and Human Development, Vanderbilt University, Nashville, Tennessee

Dr. Cutting, Patricia and Rodes Hart Endowed Chair Professor, Peabody College of Education and Human Development, Vanderbilt University, holds faculty appointments in special education, psychology, radiology, and pediatrics at Vanderbilt University, is a senior scientist at Haskins Laboratories, and has an adjunct faculty position at Johns Hopkins School of Medicine, Department of Neurology. Her research focuses on the area of educational neuroscience—in particular, the neurobiological and behavioral underpinnings of reading, oral language, and dyslexia.

Inge-Marie Eigsti, Ph.D., Professor of Psychological Sciences, University of Connecticut, Mansfield

Dr. Eigsti is Professor of Psychological Sciences at the University of Connecticut, Mansfield. Her program of research focuses on the neurobiological and behavioral circuitry of language acquisition and processing in autism spectrum disorder. Her research also examines special expertise, also called savant skills, in autism. The neurobiological underpinnings of such skills may illuminate broader principles of learning.

Sara Elhasan, Undergraduate Student in Public Health, Sociology, and Health Psychology, Wayne State University, Detroit, Michigan

Sara Elhasan is an undergraduate student at Wayne State University, Detroit, Michigan, studying public health, sociology, and health psychology. She is a member of the NIH-funded President M. Roy Wilson ReBUILDetroit (Building Infrastructure Leading to Diversity) Scholars program, the Ronald E. McNair Scholars program, and Irvin D. Reid Honors College. Sara is also a recent alumna of the Centers for Disease Control Undergraduate Public Health Scholars program. Her research interests include health policy and health disparities, primarily in immigrant and minority health.

Julian (Joe) Elliott, Ph.D., Professor of Educational Psychology, Durham University, Durham, North East England

Dr. Elliott, Principal of Collingwood College and Professor of Educational Psychology, Durham University, initially taught adolescents in mainstream and special schools prior to practicing as a local authority educational (school) psychologist. After holding an academic position at the University of Sunderland, he served as Dean of Education and Lifelong Learning, then became a Chair at Durham University in 2004. A Chartered Psychologist and Fellow of the British Psychological Society, he is registered to engage in clinical practice by the Health Professions Council. Dr. Elliott is an Academician of the Academy of Social Sciences and an appointed member of the United Kingdom's 2014 Research Excellence Framework (REF) Education Panel and its immediate successor, the 2021 REF Education Panel. His research interests—stimulated and informed by his experiences as a school teacher, clinician, teacher trainer, and university lecturer—include reading disability/dyslexia, achievement motivation, behavior management, cognitive education, comparative education, and psychological assessment.

Simon E. Fisher, Ph.D., Director, Max Planck Institute for Psycholinguistics, Nijmegen, the Netherlands

Dr. Fisher is Director, Max Planck Institute for Psycholinguistics, Nijmegen, and a professor of language and genetics, Donders Institute for Brain, Cognition and Behaviour, Radboud University, Nijmegen, the Netherlands. He directs research at the Department of Language and Genetics at the Max Planck Institute for Psycholinguistics in Nijmegen that seeks to understand the functional links between genes, brains, and human cognitive traits. This program builds on prior work at Oxford University, where he developed genomic approaches for studying speech, language, and reading disorders. His research adopts a multidisciplinary viewpoint, integrating data from genomics, psychology, neuroscience, developmental biology, and evolutionary anthropology.

Jack M. Fletcher, Ph.D., ABPP (Clinical Neuropsychology), Professor of Psychology, University of Houston, Texas

Dr. Fletcher is a Hugh Roy and Lillie Cranz Cullen Distinguished University Professor of Psychology at the University of Houston, where he also serves as Associate Vice President for Research. Dr. Fletcher directs a Learning Disability Research Center grant funded by the National Institute of Child Health and Human Development.

David J. Francis, Ph.D., Chair of Quantitative Methods, University of Houston, Texas

Dr. Francis is Hugh Roy and Lillie Cranz Cullen Distinguished University Chair of Quantitative Methods, University of Houston, where he also serves as the founding director of the Texas Institute for Measurement, Evaluation, and Statistics, and as a codirector of the Center for Advanced

Computing and Data Science. Dr. Francis obtained a doctoral degree in clinical neuropsychology from the University of Houston in 1985 and was awarded an honorary doctorate from Moscow City University for Psychology and Education in 2007. He is a Fellow of Division 5 of the American Psychological Association (APA), an Inaugural Fellow of the American Educational Research Association (AERA), and a Fellow of the Association for Psychological Science (APS). He has done extensive research on validity in the identification and classification of learning disabilities and since early 2000 has been focusing on the education of English language learners.

Jonathan Grainger, Ph.D., Research Professor in Cognitive Psychology, Aix-Marseille University, Marseille, France

Dr. Grainger, Senior Scientist at the Centre National de la Recherche Scientifique (CNRS) and Research Professor in cognitive psychology at Aix-Marseille University, Marseille, France, founded and directed (2000–2012) the cognitive psychology research department (LPC) at Aix-Marseille University. He received a prestigious midcareer award from the CNRS in 2011 and the Sir Frederic Bartlett lectureship from the Experimental Psychology Society (United Kingdom) in 2016, and he has served as President of the European Society for Cognitive Psychology. He has received two European Research Council advanced grants to pursue his research on reading. His research focuses on the basic mechanisms involved in the processing of orthographic information by skilled readers.

Svenja Gusewski, M.S., CF-SLP, Doctoral Student in Communication Sciences and Disorders, University of Texas, Dallas

Svenja Gusewski is a doctoral student in communication sciences and disorders at the University of Texas, Dallas. She received her B.S. in speech pathology from the University of Valencia in Spain and her M.S. in communication disorders from the University of Texas, Dallas. She has worked in a variety of settings with bilingual children in Germany, Spain, and the United States. Her research focuses on dual language development of Spanish-speaking preschoolers and its impact on later academic achievement.

Lindsey Hiebert, M.S., CCC-SLP, Doctoral Student in Communication Sciences and Disorders, University of Texas at Dallas

Lindsey Hiebert is a doctoral student in communication sciences and disorders at the University of Texas at Dallas. She received a B.A. in Spanish from the University of Nebraska, Omaha, and an M.S. in speech-language pathology from Northern Arizona University, Flagstaff. She worked as a speech-language pathologist for 6 years in a variety of settings (schools, home health, skilled nursing, and outpatient) in Arizona. Her clinical experience has inspired her research on first language loss and its impact on dual language development in bilingual children.

Tiffany P. Hogan, Ph.D., Professor of Communication Sciences and Disorders, Massachusetts General Hospital Institute of Health Professions, Boston, Massachusetts

Dr. Hogan is Professor of Communication Sciences and Disorders at the Massachusetts General Hospital Institute of Health Professions in Boston. She studies the genetic, neurological, and behavioral links between oral and written language development, with a focus on co-morbid speech, language, and reading disorders. Her research is funded by the National Institute on Deafness and Other Communication Disorders and the Department of Education's Institute of Education Sciences. Dr. Hogan teaches graduate courses in literacy assessment and intervention, phonological disorders, and professional issues in academia.

Shiva Khalaf, Ph.D., Postdoctoral Researcher, Texas Institute for Measurement, Evaluation, and Statistics (TIMES), University of Houston, Texas

Dr. Khalaf is a postdoctoral researcher at the Texas Institute for Measurement, Evaluation, and Statistics (TIMES) at the University of Houston. Her research focus is on applying advanced statistical models to examine the language development of bilingual children and to investigating problems related to English language learners with and without disabilities.

Aleksei A. Korneev, Ph.D., Senior Research Associate, Laboratory of Neuropsychology, Psychology Department, Lomonosov Moscow State University, Russia

Dr. Korneev, Senior Research Associate in the Laboratory of Neuropsychology at Lomonosov Moscow State University, is a member of a research group that focuses on developmental neuropsychology. His areas of interest include the development of writing and reading skills in typically developing children and children with learning disabilities, as well as designing and developing computer-based methods of neuropsychological assessment. He is also a specialist in methods of statistical processing of psychological data.

Ghene't Lee-Yong, B.A., Research Analyst, Education and Brain Research Laboratory, Vanderbilt University, Nashville, Tennessee

Ms. Lee-Yong holds a bachelor's degree in cognitive studies from Ashford University, San Diego, California. She is a research analyst in the Vanderbilt Education and Brain Research Laboratory at Vanderbilt University. Her research interests include neuroscience and early childhood development.

Ekaterina Y. Matveeva, Ph.D., Senior Research Associate, Laboratory of Neuropsychology, Psychology Department, Lomonosov Moscow State University, Russia

Dr. Matveeva, Senior Research Associate in the Laboratory of Neuropsychology at Lomonosov Moscow State University, is a member of a research group that focuses on developmental neuropsychology. She conducts research in the neuropsychological analysis of cognitive development and learning disabilities, in particular the development of writing and reading skills.

Joan Mele-McCarthy, D.A., CCC, Executive Director, The Summit School, Edgewater, Maryland

Joan Mele-McCarthy is Executive Director of The Summit School, a school designed for students who have dyslexia and other learning differences. Prior to this position, she served as Special Assistant to the Assistant Secretary for Special Education/ Rehabilitation Services in the U.S. Department of Education and worked on policy issues related to the connections between special education and general education and to English language learners and disabilities. She also has served on university faculties in departments of communication sciences and disorders, owned/directed a private practice that provided direct intervention and school consultation, and worked in public schools. Her work is focused on language-based learning differences and special education policy.

Jeremy Miciak, Ph.D., Research Assistant Professor, Department of Psychology, University of Houston, Texas

Dr. Miciak is Research Assistant Professor in the Department of Psychology at the University of Houston. Dr. Miciak directs the Assessment and Recruitment Core for the Texas Center for Learning Disabilities.

Robin Morris, Ph.D., Professor of Psychology, Georgia State University, Atlanta

Dr. Morris, Regents Professor of Psychology, Associate Dean for Research and Graduate Studies in the College of Arts and Sciences, and Chair of Psychology, Georgia State University, serves as the executive officer for entrepreneurship, overseeing the university's strategic efforts for student start-ups, campus activities centered around entrepreneurship, and related degree programs. He has served as Associate Provost for Strategic Initiatives and Innovation, and he is the past Vice President for Research. He currently holds faculty research appointments in the Center for Research on Atypical Development and Learning and GSU/Georgia Tech Center for Advanced Brain Imaging and is an associate faculty in the Neurosciences Institutes. Dr. Morris has published widely and has federal grant awards from the NIH, National Science Foundation, Department of Defense, and the U.S. Department of Education.

Sarah Nelson, M.S., CCC-SLP, Doctoral Student in Human Development, University of California, Davis

Sarah Nelson is a doctoral student in the Human Development Graduate Group at the University of California, Davis. Her research focuses on factors related to language and cognitive development in youth with neurodevelopmental disorders. She is particularly interested in the ways in which parenting and the family environment influence language development in children with fragile X syndrome.

Vivian Nguyen, BCBA, Behavioral Health Professional, MIND Institute, University of California, Davis

Vivian Nguyen, Behavioral Health Professional, UC Davis MIND Institute, is a member of the Laboratory on Language Development in Neurodevelopmental Disorders at the UC Davis MIND Institute, where she is involved in research focusing on parent-implemented interventions for children and adolescents with developmental disabilities.

Courtenay Norbury, Ph.D., Director, Literacy, Language and Communication (LiLaC) Lab, University College London, England

Courtenay Norbury is Director of the Literacy, Language and Communication (LiLaC) Lab and a Fellow of the Royal College of Speech and Language

Therapists. She obtained her Ph.D. in experimental psychology at the University of Oxford, working with Professor Dorothy Bishop on the overlapping language profiles that characterize autism spectrum disorder and specific language impairment. Professor Norbury's current research focuses on language disorders in a range of neurodevelopmental conditions and how language interacts with other aspects of development. She is leading a population study of language development and disorder from school entry. She is also a founding member of the Raising Awareness of Developmental Language Disorder (RADLD) campaign (https://www.youtube.com/RADLD).

Benjamin Powers, D.B.A., Headmaster, The Southport School, Southport, Connecticut

Benjamin Powers is a practitioner, researcher, and advocate who works with students with dyslexia and attention-deficit/hyperactivity disorder (ADHD). Having completed his B.A. in Russian language, he holds an executive M.B.A. from Rochester Institute of Technology and a doctorate in business administration from Grenoble Ecole de Management, fusing his interests in dyslexia and entrepreneurship; his doctoral research focused on the self-esteem and self-efficacy perceptions of adolescents with dyslexia and ADHD to understand the affect those personal-level variables have on social-emotional well-being and career intentions. Additional interests include developing collaborative, community-based, and scalable implementation models across learning disability/ADHD, bilingual, bidialectal, and underserved communities. He is the headmaster of The Southport School, an affiliated research scientist at Haskins Laboratories, a research affiliate at Grenoble Ecole de Management, and the codirector of the Academic Centers of Excellence for The Dyslexia Foundation.

Kenneth R. Pugh, Ph.D., President and Director of Research, Haskins Laboratories, New Haven, Connecticut

Dr. Pugh is President and Director of Research, Haskins Laboratories, a Yale University and University of Connecticut affiliated interdisciplinary institute dedicated to the investigation of the biological bases of language, and he holds positions at the University of Connecticut, Yale University, and the Yale University School of Medicine. Dr. Pugh directs the Yale Reading Center; is a member of the Scientific Advisory Boards for the International Dyslexia Association and the Rodin Remediation Academy in Stockholm; and has served as a peer reviewer at the National Institutes of Health and as a panel member at the National Research Council of the National Academies. His research in cognitive neuroscience and psycholinguistics focuses on the neurobiology of typical and atypical language and reading development.

Mabel L. Rice, Ph.D., Professor of Advanced Studies, University of Kansas, Lawrence

Dr. Rice, Fred & Virginia Merrill Distinguished Professor of Advanced Studies, University of Kansas, directs the cross-disciplinary Child Language Doctoral Program and the Merrill Advanced Studies Center. Her research focuses on children with and without language impairments, twins as well as single-born. She has directed longitudinal studies since the late 1980s, encompassing an age span of 2 years into adulthood, including children's siblings and parents, and bridging disciplines (speech-language pathology, linguistics, psychology, pediatrics, genetics, public health, and education) and international boundaries (including work with colleagues in Australia, Norway, Scotland, South Korea, and the Czech Republic). A researcher with the National Institutes of Health–wide Pediatric HIV/AIDS Cohort Study, she has been continuously supported by NIH. She is a Fellow of the American Speech-Language-Hearing Association (ASHA), the American Association for the Advancement of Science, the American Psychological Association, and the American Association for Psychological Science, and she is a member of the Education Board of the American Health Council. Her interests include the linguistic bases of reading and possible shared inherited traits.

Raúl Rojas, Ph.D., CCC-SLP, Associate Professor, Communication Sciences and Disorders, University of Texas, Dallas

Dr. Rojas, Associate Professor and Director of the Bilingual Language Laboratory, is a faculty member in the Communication Sciences and Disorders Program within the School of Behavioral and Brain Sciences at the University of Texas, Dallas. He is a faculty affiliate of the Callier Center for Communication Disorders and the Center for Children and Families. His research focuses on child language from a longitudinal and processing perspective, specifically bilingual language development in typically developing children and in children with language impairments. Dr. Rojas has provided bilingual (Spanish–English) speech-language pathology services in multiple settings, including schools and early intervention programs.

Jenny Saffran, Ph.D., Professor, Department of Psychology, University of Wisconsin, Madison

Dr. Saffran, Vilas Distinguished Achievement Professor, Department of Psychology, University of Wisconsin, directs the Infant Learning Lab at the Waisman Center, University of Wisconsin, Madison. Her research there, which has garnered numerous national awards, is focused on how infants learn about language and other complex aspects of their environment. She has expanded her interests in recent years to include language learning in infants and young children with developmental disabilities, including autism and specific language impairment. In 2015, Dr. Saffran was elected as a Fellow of the American Academy of Arts and Sciences. Her current research focuses on the learning mechanisms underlying language acquisition in both typically and atypically developing infants and young children.

Kristi L. Santi, Ph.D., Associate Professor of Educational Leadership and Policy, University of Houston, Texas

Dr. Santi is Associate Professor of Educational Leadership and Policy at the University of Houston. Her research centers on students with disabilities, including early reading instruction (K–3), language acquisition, and English language learners with and without disabilities. Dr. Santi also conducts research in the areas of coaching teachers in the K–12 setting and factors influencing successful transition of students in special populations from high school to college.

Margaret J. (Maggie) Snowling, Ph.D., President and Professor of Psychology, St. John's College, Oxford, United Kingdom

Dr. Snowling, President, St. John's College, Professor of Psychology, University of Oxford, United Kingdom, and clinical psychologist, researches children's reading and language at the interface of psychology and education. She is committed to widening access to higher education. She has received the British Psychological Society Presidents' Award (2003) and the International Dyslexia Association Orton Award (2005), and she is Past-President of the Society for the Scientific Study of Reading. She served on Sir Jim Rose's Expert Advisory Group on Provision for Dyslexia, advised the Phonics Screening Check in England, and served on the Education for All: Fast Track Initiative (Washington, D.C., 2011). Dr. Snowling holds honorary doctorates from Goldsmiths London (2010), University College London (2014), and Warwick University (2016); is Fellow of the British Academy, the Academy of Medical Sciences, and the Academy of Social Sciences; and was appointed Commander of the British Empire (CBE, 2016)—all for services to science and the understanding of dyslexia.

Robyn Tempero Feigles, B.A., Staff Research Associate, MIND Institute, University of California, Davis

Robyn Tempero Feigles, Staff Research Associate, UC Davis MIND Institute, is an experienced behavioral tester and clinician-in-training in the Laboratory on Language Development in Neurodevelopmental Disorders at the UC Davis MIND Institute.

Richard K. Wagner, Ph.D., Professor of Psychology, Florida State University, Tallahassee

Richard Wagner, a Robert O. Lawton Distinguished Research Professor of Psychology and W. Russell and Eugenia Morcom Chair at Florida State University, is a cofounder and current Associate Director of the Florida Center for Reading Research. He holds a master's degree in school psychology from the University of Akron, has worked as a school psychologist, and holds a Ph.D. in cognitive psychology from Yale University. His research focuses on dyslexia and the normal acquisition of reading. Dr. Wagner is currently principal investigator of a Multidisciplinary Learning Disability Center funded by the National Institute of Child Health and Human Development (NICHD). Dr. Wagner has helped Arkansas and California develop guidelines to implement dyslexia legislation. He also has coauthored tests commonly used in evaluating children for dyslexia and other learning disabilities, including the Comprehensive Test of Phonological Processing, Second Edition (CTOPP-2) (PRO-ED, 2013), the Test of Word Reading Efficiency, Second Edition (TOWRE-2) (PRO-ED, 2012), and the Test of Preschool Early Literacy (TOPEL) (PRO-ED, 2007).

Jason Zevin, Ph.D., Associate Professor of Psychology and Linguistics, University of Southern California, Los Angeles

Dr. Zevin is Associate Professor of psychology and linguistics at the University of Southern California, and he is affiliated with Haskins Laboratories as a senior scientist. He uses a combination of computational modeling, neuroimaging, and other techniques to study the processing of written and spoken words and other aspects of language.

The Dyslexia Foundation and the Extraordinary Brain Series

In the late 1980s, The Dyslexia Foundation (TDF) was founded by William H. "Will" Baker in collaboration with notable researchers in dyslexia. The concept began in the late 70s, then came to fruition in 1982, when, through the generosity of the Underwood and Baker families, the first Dyslexia Research Laboratory under the direction of Drs. Albert Galaburda and Norman Geschwind at Beth Israel Hospital, Harvard Medical School, Boston, Massachusetts, was established to investigate the neural underpinnings of dyslexia. In 1987, top researchers from cognition, neuroscience, and education were convened in a scientific symposium in Florence, Italy, where ideas were presented and discussed, with sufficient time to disagree, identify research challenges, and brainstorm solutions—and the concept of a dyslexia symposium series was born. In the fall of 1989, Baker established the National Dyslexia Research Foundation (later renamed TDF), to focus specifically on research. In 1990, the new foundation sponsored a second symposium in Barcelona, Spain. With it, the symposium series was designated as the Extraordinary Brain Series (EBS)!

The EBS symposia began as think tanks of researchers who were encouraged to discuss, disagree, and explore new possibilities. Many have called these symposia the best research meetings they have ever attended because of the depth of discussion and exchange of ideas afforded by a 5-day think tank. Each symposium resulted in a volume to share the research presented and the ideas that grew out of the deliberations. Educators from independent schools for students with learning differences, interested in hearing the latest research and witnessing these cutting-edge discussions, began to attend and contribute as TDF sponsors to the meetings. Hearing their cry for bringing current research to their classrooms, in a then-novel outreach activity, TDF instituted 1-day annual educational meetings held on the campus of Harvard Medical School, where educators and allied health practitioners could hear about current research directly from researchers. In 2007, at the 10th EBS symposium in Brazil, educators were asking so many questions and were so eager to share their research needs with the researchers present that these educators were given a forum during the meeting, and the research-to-practice efforts of TDF moved to a new, higher level. Since that time, educators and practitioners are heard and participate in each EBS symposium, and the interactions among them and researchers have been rich and rewarding. Although it had been part of the TDF philosophy to include not only senior, established researchers but also promising early-stage researchers as participants in the symposia, this has also accelerated. At the 11th symposium in Taiwan, in 2010, Taiwanese researchers invited their graduate students and postdoctoral fellows to display posters of their work during the meeting. Since that time, those invited to present or moderate sessions at EBS symposia are also invited to bring junior colleagues, postdoctoral fellows, and graduate students and have them present posters—displaying the posters and giving a very brief explanation of their work during one special session at the symposium.

Over the three decades of the Foundation's and EBS's existence, major strides have been made in not only dyslexia and reading research (many researchers have commented that their best new ideas and great new collaborations have grown out of their participation in EBS symposia), but these meetings have also provided a safe venue for exchanging and developing research-to-practice ideas, mentoring many new and emerging researchers, and providing content for the continuing and expanding 1-day research-to-practice meetings for educators and practitioners, which are live-streamed in real time and archived for later viewing.

This volume celebrates the 16th symposium in the Extraordinary Brain Series. The volumes make the thoughts of scholars across various disciplines accessible to all researchers and practitioners as they tackle various aspects of the behavior, neurobiology, and genetics of dyslexia and of learning to read and write. Following is a listing of TDF symposia and the related volumes to date:

I. June 1987, Florence, Italy. Symposium Director: Albert M. Galaburda.

Galaburda, A. M. (Ed.). (1989). *From reading to neurons.* Cambridge, MA: Bradford Books/MIT Press.

II. June 1990, Barcelona, Spain. Symposium Director: Albert M. Galaburda.

Galaburda, A. M. (Ed.). (1993). *Dyslexia and development: Neurobiological aspects of extra-ordinary brains.* Cambridge, MA: Bradford Books/Harvard University Press.

III. June 1992, Santa Fe, NM. Symposium Director: Paula Tallal.

Chase, C., Rosen, G., & Sherman, G. F. (Eds.). (1996). *Developmental dyslexia: Neural, cognitive, and genetic mechanisms.* Mahwah, NJ: Lawrence Erlbaum Associates.

IV. June 1994, Kauai, Hawaii. Symposium Director: Benita Blachman.

Blachman, B. R. (Ed.). (1997). *Foundations of reading acquisition and dyslexia: Implications for early intervention.* Mahwah, NJ: Lawrence Erlbaum Associates.

V. June 1998, Kona, Hawaii. Symposium Director: Drake Duane.
Duane, D. (Ed.). (1999). *Reading and attention disorders: Neurobiological correlates.* Baltimore, MD: York Press.

VI. June 2000, Crete, Greece. Symposium Director: Maryanne Wolf.
Wolf, M. (Ed.). (2001). *Time, fluency, and dyslexia.* Baltimore, MD: York Press.

VII. June 2002, Kona, Hawaii. Symposium Director: Barbara Foorman.
Foorman, B. (Ed.). (2003). *Preventing and remediating reading difficulties: Bringing science to scale.* Baltimore, MD: York Press.

VIII. October 2002, Johannesburg, South Africa. Symposium Director: Frank Wood.
Multilingualism and dyslexia. No publication.

IX. June 2004, Como, Italy. Symposium Director: Glenn Rosen.
Rosen, G. (Ed.). (2006). *The dyslexic brain: New pathways in neuroscience discovery.* Mahwah, NJ: Lawrence Erlbaum Associates.

X. June 2007, Campos do Jordão, Brazil. Symposium Directors: Ken Pugh and Peggy McCardle.
Pugh, K., & McCardle, P. (Eds.). (2009). *How children learn to read: Current issues and new directions in the integration of cognition, neurobiology and genetics of reading and dyslexia research and practice.* New York, NY: Psychology Press, Taylor & Francis Group.

XI. January 2010, Taipei, Taiwan. Symposium Directors: Peggy McCardle, Ovid Tseng, Jun Ren Lee, and Brett Miller.
McCardle, P., Miller, B., Lee, J. R., & Tseng, O. J. L. (Eds.). (2011). *Dyslexia across languages: Orthography and the brain-gene-behavior link.* Baltimore, MD: Paul H. Brookes Publishing Co.

XII. June 2010, Cong, Ireland. Symposium Directors: April Benasich and Holly Fitch.
Benasich, A. A., & R. H. Fitch (Eds.). (2012). *Developmental dyslexia: Early precursors, neurobehavioral markers, and biological substrates.* Baltimore, MD: Paul H. Brookes Publishing Co.

XIII. June 2012, Tallinn, Estonia. Symposium Directors: Brett Miller and Laurie Cutting.
Miller, B., Cutting, L. E., & McCardle, P. (Eds.). (2013). *Unraveling reading comprehension: Behavioral, neurobiological, and genetic components.* Baltimore, MD: Paul H. Brookes Publishing Co.

XIV. June 2014, Horta, Faial Island, The Azores. Symposium Directors: Carol Connor and Peggy McCardle.

Connor, C. M., & McCardle, P. (Eds.). (2015). *Advances in reading intervention: Research to practice to research.* Baltimore, MD: Paul H. Brookes Publishing Co.

XV. June 2016, Saint Croix, U.S. Virgin Islands. Symposium Directors: Albert Galaburda, Fumiko Hoeft, and Nadine Gaab.

Galaburda, A. M., Gaab, N., Hoeft, F., & McCardle, P. (Eds.). (2018). *Dyslexia and neuroscience: The Geschwind-Galaburda Hypothesis 30 years later.* Baltimore, MD: Paul H. Brookes Publishing Co.

XVI. May 2018. St. Petersburg, Russia. Symposium Directors: Elena Grigorenko & Yury Shtyrov.

Grigorenko, E. L., Shtyrov, Y., & McCardle, P. (Eds.). (2020). *All about language: Science, theory, and practice.* Baltimore, MD: Paul H. Brookes Publishing Co.

Preface

This volume is one of two, both based on Extraordinary Brain Series (EBS) Symposia, and thus both resulting in EBS edited volumes. Although it was unprecedented to hold two such symposia within months of one another, it turned out to be a wonderful convergence of ideas and information on the underpinnings of reading and dyslexia. The first symposium (and eponymous volume, coedited by Elena Grigorenko, Yury Shtyrov, and Peggy McCardle), *All About Language: Science, Theory, and Practice* (Paul H. Brookes Publishing Co., 2020), focuses on the evolution and development of language in all its forms—spoken and written—and how typical and atypical language underlie and relate to reading and reading difficulties. The meeting was held in Russia and addressed some of the issues of diagnosis; access to special education services in Russia, the United States, the United Kingdom, and other countries; and education policy. The second volume, *Dyslexia: Revisiting Etiology, Diagnosis, Treatment, and Policy* (Paul H. Brookes Publishing Co., in press), coedited by Julie Washington, Don Compton, and Peggy McCardle, similarly examines how reading develops, what happens when it does not develop typically, and how best to identify and treat those cases, as well as how local and national policies and legislation can help or hinder those trying to do so. This symposium was held in South Africa and looked beyond the United States, with presenters (and thus authors) from other countries or whose work involves international collaborations. The two meetings had seemingly different foci, but both were asking similar questions about how best to understand, treat, and implement proven interventions for those who struggle with reading. Each symposium brought together a group of scholars and clinicians in a think-tank setting to take stock of what is known and what needs to be known. These two groups were largely nonoverlapping, but their timely (almost) co-occurrence allows us to gain access to both sets of information in a very useful complementarity via these two volumes.

The complementarity of these two volumes should enhance our thinking as a field as we move to gain a fuller, more complete understanding of the total picture of reading difficulties, the reading process, the language skills that underlie it, and the individual differences that add to the complexity of this task. EBS symposia (and volumes) bring together scientists from different disciplines and areas of research and generally seek to integratively address the neurobiology, genetics, and behavior of reading and reading disabilities, thinking about how skills are learned, why they might not be, and what influences are in play across development and how they change the course of development (be it typical or atypical) as well as how those influences change our interventions (i.e., what we do about teaching individuals to read). It is increasingly clear that the context—the environment, physical, social, linguistic, cultural, and economic—affects learning. The environment includes language exposure—in the home, community, and school—whereas school instruction requires knowledge that teachers often do not have upon entering the profession. Thus, ensuring that researchers share their reliable findings with educators and other clinicians, and that they seek to answer the questions most pressing for those educators and clinicians, is also an essential goal of every EBS symposium. The volumes contain chapters addressing these issues (with nontechnical summaries to begin each), and the volumes' integrative section commentaries seek to pull together across chapters the common threads of each thematic section. The final chapter in each volume offers suggestions for the way forward.

Acknowledgments

Many dedicated organizations and individuals contributed to this volume. First, the sponsors: University of St. Petersburg, particularly the Laboratory of Translational Developmental Science and the Laboratory of Behavioural Neurodynamics; the Russian Federal P220 program (grant contracts No. 14.Z50.31.0027 to ELG and No. 14.W03.31.0010 to YS); The Dyslexia Foundation (TDF), co-sponsor of the symposium and initiator of the Extraordinary Brain Symposium; the Way Out Foundation (Russia); and the Association for Children and Parents with Dyslexia (Russian Federation).

We also must acknowledge the authors, who traveled to St. Petersburg, Russia, to present their own work and thoughts and engage in deep discussions with symposium participants, and who then wrote and revised chapters for this volume, often meeting stringent deadlines. Some of the coauthors and authors of the integrative commentaries were not in attendance at the meeting but contributed very meaningfully to the volume, and we thank them for their willingness to participate in this work. In addition, we acknowledge the practitioners (teachers, educators, administrators, and clinicians), researchers, graduate students, and postdoctoral fellows who also traveled and not only listened attentively and thought deeply but also discussed, questioned, and commented, helping to inform this volume.

We and TDF offer heartfelt thanks to the following individuals, schools, and businesses that generously supported EBS XVI: Wilson Language Training, Jemicy School, AIM Academy, The Howard School, The Schenck School, The Southport School, Westmark School, Athena Academy, Brehm Preparatory School, Carroll School, Curry Ingram Academy, Marburn Academy, The New Community School, The Summit School, and five individuals and two foundations that wish to remain anonymous.

We are also grateful to the many junior colleagues from St. Petersburg State University who organized and supported the symposium and shared the beauty of the city with the participants. Special thanks to Irina Golovanova, Ekaterina Nikolaeva, Irina Ovchinnikova, Ekaterina Perikova, Olga Titova, and Marina Zhukova.

Finally, thanks go to the flexible, helpful, and very capable editorial staff at Paul H. Brookes Publishing Co., especially Astrid Pohl Zuckerman, Tess Hoffman, MaryBeth Winkler, and Nicole Schmidl, who were willing to take on not just one but two EBS volumes at the same time! Thank you for your diligence, excellent help, and patience on this and the EBS XVII book. We loved working with you!

Coeditors,
Elena Grigorenko, Yury Shtyrov, and Peggy McCardle

CHAPTER 1

All About Language

Science, Theory, and Practice
An Overview and Introduction to the Volume

(Неделя языка: наука, теория, практика)

Elena L. Grigorenko, Yury Shtyrov, and Peggy McCardle

This volume is the collaborative outgrowth of Extraordinary Brain Symposium XVI, which was held in St. Petersburg, Russia, from May 28 to June 1, 2018.[1] The meeting (and thus the volume) included various language-related topics with targeted speakers in language evolution, genetic and environmental etiology, typical development, language disorders, bi- and multilingualism, and various types of literacy, as well as very rich and spirited discussion of these. There were also sessions addressing key language, learning, and learning disability research, practice, and policy issues, which were open to the public and geared toward teachers, parents, and other advocates. In addition to a scientific exchange of ideas among leading scientists, the symposium included a round table of practitioners—participating educators from independent schools, representatives of the Russian educational authorities, and social entrepreneurs and charitable organizations interested in special education. We have sought to include aspects of all of these activities within this volume, and to enhance the accessibility of the information in all sections, each chapter includes a summary of its contents in less technical language, allowing readers to preview chapters prior to delving into them.

Language, in the forms we know it (including 7,472 known spoken languages as well as written, digital, and other varieties), is a hallmark of our species and a backbone of human society. It changes as humans change, both ontogenetically and phylogenetically, and, although most individuals master it, they vary in their language capacity. Human language represents a complex, hierarchically organized symbolic system employed to communicate—that is, to receive and transmit information. These (spoken, written, digital, gestural, and other) systems of symbols are complex, yet they are learnable, although at different developmental periods and at different speeds. It is assumed that the acquisition of spoken language unfolds first, followed by written, then followed by digital language, with the latter two

---

The symposium was supported primarily by two laboratories led by Elena Grigorenko and Yury Shtyrov, both established at the St. Petersburg University, Russia, within the framework of so-called "Mega-grant projects" aimed at giving a major boost to Russian sciences (http://www.p220.ru/en/) and by philanthropic organizations, including The Dyslexia Foundation (United States), the Association for Children and Parents with Dyslexia (Russian Federation), and the Way Out Foundation (Russian Federation).

requiring explicit instruction, whereas spoken language requires only (or primarily) reliable input and imitable human models. These different types of communicative ability and literacy emerge as a child develops into an adult. Although language/literacy acquisition usually unfolds seamlessly when bracketed within a typical developmental trajectory, assuming exposure to normative social and educational environments (i.e., family, school, and digital technology), numerous children demonstrate impairments in acquiring different forms of language, either within one or across two or three of its modes.

The chapters in this volume sample the current state of knowledge regarding the evolution and manifestation of human language. There is a large body of research literature that allows students of language to appreciate both its ontogenetic and phylogenetic development and the multiple sources of individual differences in its (a)typical acquisition. This acquisition begins in utero and continuously extends into the infinity of human life because there is no known age threshold for when language learning, in any or all of its forms, is destined to stop, although there is a great deal of information on the differential parameters of language learning at different stages of the life span. The rate of language learning in all its forms is different during different developmental periods; the earliest acquisition stages are characterized by a growth spurt, followed by a gradual increase in sophistication and expansion of literacy. In general, it is assumed that language learning encompasses increasingly complex linguistic representations, sophisticated communication skills, erudite reasoning, and deepened conceptual knowledge. From the very beginning, however defined, language acquisition follows the powerful laws of exposure and practice in which more leads to enhancements and less leads to stagnation or even attrition.

Although language has always been at the center of humanity's scientific thought, the last two decades of research have been marked by major advances in understanding how children acquire the formal properties of the ambient languages to which they are exposed, with researchers investigating evolutionary, biological, sociocultural, cognitive, affective, and all other relevant mechanisms that underlie different forms of literacy acquisition. Still, numerous essential questions remain unanswered regarding the extent to which the different types of language unfold and the universality and specificity of the mechanisms within and across these different domains, within and across different developmental periods, and within and across different cultures and societies.

All these questions were the focal point of an interdisciplinary group of scholars attempting to integrate the diversity of research findings into coherent theories that, on the one hand, inspire and shape future research and, on the other hand, are of vital interest to practitioners, including speech-language pathologists, pediatricians, and educators faced with the tasks of evaluating the language learning trajectories and deficits in particular individuals and devising clinical and educational interventions that may facilitate the acquisition of literacy in all its forms. Given the theoretical and practical importance of this field of research, opportunities for scholars and practitioners to exchange knowledge and collectively enhance research opportunities are of immense significance. This volume, like the symposium that it draws from, is conceived to provide one such opportunity. The volume is structured in six sections. Each of the first five sections ends with integrative commentary by a known scholar in that topical area, whereas the sixth section (Chapter 16) integrates the research findings presented throughout the volume. Section I sets the stage for our broadly conceived discussion of all aspects of language by addressing the biological underpinnings of language phylogeny and ontogeny. Burenkova and Fisher address language development from a genetic perspective, and Pugh addresses it from a neuroscience one, both chapters citing recent breakthroughs and future directions. These are contextualized by Zevin's integrative commentary in his discussion of *emergentism,* which he defines as "a synthesis between the impulse to delineate and describe distinct language functions, and the impulse to engage with the messiness of their biological substrate."

Sections II–IV address typical and atypical development in oral and written language (i.e., speaking, listening, and reading). The section on typical development (Section II) includes information on how infants learn and build a body of words (Saffran), what eye tracking can tell us about reading development (Akhutina and colleagues), and how children process orthographic units (Grainger). An integrative commentary by Hogan cross-references this section's chapters by focusing the discussion on three key themes—the power of statistical learning, the utilization of innovative methodologies (e.g., eye tracking, computational modeling, infant behavioral learning paradigms), and general and specific characteristics of language acquisition in different languages. She concludes the commentary by stressing the importance of early assessment of language development "to determine individual variation to inform quality, evidence-based spoken and written language instruction."

In Section III, Rice addresses atypical language development via a large longitudinal twin study, offering thoughts on possible causal pathways to specific language impairment, whereas Norbury discusses stability and change over time in the manifestation of Developmental Language Disorders. In addition, Eigsti and Castelluccio examine what can be learned about neural plasticity from the study of language in children with autism spectrum disorder. Common themes of these chapters are addressed in Snowling's integrative commentary. She takes the discourse in these chapters to a higher level, pointing out the importance of remediating language difficulties and the development of robust and long-term interventions "that prevent an intergenerational downward spiral from language difficulty to social disadvantage and poor mental health."

Section IV focuses on reading difficulties, with chapters addressing the role and importance of executive function in both reading development and disorders (Cirino and colleagues) and how students with reading difficulties respond to intervention (Cirino and colleagues as well as Morris). There is also a discussion of what research has shown us regarding the identification of reading disabilities in children learning English as a second language (Francis and colleagues) and the relationships of reading to oral language during development (Cutting and colleagues). Wagner's commentary on these chapters and related recent work integrates these various themes, highlighting both the amazing progress the science of reading has achieved and the amount of work that still needs to be done to ensure fair opportunities for all emergent readers in all languages and of all backgrounds.

Section V addresses real-world applications of the research presented in the previous sections. Abbeduto and colleagues highlight how technology can be used to make interventions more accessible, emphasizing a community-based approach. Elliott describes what we know about identification, assessment, and treatment and how the presently acquired knowledge and experience (that varies across cultures and countries) can benefit those nations and communities seeking to provide or enhance the provision of special education and evidence-based instruction. In their commentary, Mele-McCarthy and Powers address how policy guides practice and stress the importance of research guiding policy, focusing on how districts, states, and nations can move toward education equity for all students.

In our own final chapter, we bring together our own thoughts, the thoughts of the chapter authors, and the thoughts of those who were present in the St. Petersburg discussions in May 2018 on the directions that research should take if we are to be able to integrate what we know of typical and atypical development in all aspects of language—both oral and written, as they clearly are intimately related. We comment on the current landscape of the science of human language and its various modes and acknowledge that although much more detailed and refined than ever before, our understanding of the ontogeny and phylogeny of human language is still far from complete.

SECTION I

Biological Underpinnings of Language

CHAPTER 2

Genetic Insights Into the Neurobiology of Speech and Language

Olga V. Burenkova and Simon E. Fisher

SUMMARY

The biological bases of speech and language are considered here from the perspective of molecular genetics. We describe how the mutations of a gene causing a disorder can be used as a tool to understand intermediate levels of explanation, bridging gaps between genetics and behavioral/cognitive traits, by parsing the interactions and relationships between the different levels. To illustrate the value of this approach, we discuss representative studies of *FOXP2*—the first and most intensively investigated gene to have been implicated in an inherited speech and language disorder. This regulatory gene has a deep evolutionary history and is proposed to be important for the development of cortico-striatal and cortico-cerebellar brain systems involved in the learning, planning, and execution of movements. We broaden our focus to consider the roles of other genes, including upstream and downstream elements of *FOXP2*-dependent networks. The chapter concludes with a discussion of future challenges and opportunities for researchers seeking to understand the neurogenetic mechanisms underlying speech and language. We argue that dramatic rapid advances in affordable DNA genotyping and sequencing must be coupled with sophisticated methods for assessing gene function at multiple levels as well as robust approaches for characterizing behavioral phenotypes in order to successfully trace connections from molecules to minds.

INTRODUCTION

The capacity to acquire complex speech and language skills is one of the unique features of being human. Our understanding of the biological bases of this important suite of abilities is still limited, however, and we are far from having a complete picture. In this chapter, we consider the potential of genetic approaches for addressing questions about human traits. We argue that a molecular perspective holds great promise for yielding novel insights into the neurobiology of speech and language.

Olga V. Burenkova is supported by grant No. 14.Z50.31.0027 (PI: Elena L. Grigorenko) from the Government of the Russian Federation. Simon E. Fisher is supported by the Max Planck Society. The chapter does not necessarily reflect the position or policies of the funding agencies, and no official endorsement should be inferred.

Language acquisition is an apt example of the interplay between genes and environment, as eloquently described by Charles Darwin (1871):

> [L]anguage is an art, like brewing or baking. . . . It certainly is not a true instinct, as every language has to be learnt. It differs, however, widely from all ordinary arts, for man has an instinctive tendency to speak, as we see in the babble of our young children; whilst no child has an instinctive tendency to brew, bake, or write. (p. 55)

Preschool-age children have a vocabulary of thousands of words that they can assemble into meaningful sentences using grammatical rules (Shipley & McAfee, 2015), and they are able to communicate these sentences to others through rapid coordinated sequences of movements of the articulatory apparatus. Such linguistic proficiency typically develops without the need for any kind of formal tuition. Yet, environmental input is clearly essential; without exposure to language, children do not become language users (Curtiss, 1977, 1980). Thus, language may be best conceptualized as a biocultural hybrid, dependent on the tight intertwining of genetic predispositions and environmental inputs.

RARE GENETIC MUTATIONS CAN DISRUPT SPEECH AND LANGUAGE DEVELOPMENT

Unfortunately, not every child who is exposed to language-rich environments during development goes on to become a proficient user of spoken language. In some cases, this may be related to an obvious cause, such as deafness, physical problems, or general cognitive difficulties. A small but significant proportion of children, however, display impaired speech and/or language skills in the absence of a known explanation (Graham & Fisher, 2015). Unexplained developmental speech and language disorders of this kind tend to cluster in families, suggestive of a role for genetic factors. Moreover, levels of concordance for these disorders are higher in identical twins than in nonidentical twins, providing evidence of high heritability (Bishop, Laws, Adams, & Norbury, 2006). Therefore, it is reasonable to consider the potential involvement of genetic mechanisms in explaining why aspects of speech and/or language development go awry in a subset of children.

Since the late 1990s, the existence of such etiological mechanisms has been confirmed by molecular genetics data. Genetic mapping of a rare speech and language disorder inherited by three successive generations of a large British family (the KE family) identified a susceptibility locus (originally named *SPCH1*) on chromosome 7 (Fisher, Vargha-Khadem, Watkins, Monaco, & Pembrey, 1998). In-depth studies of this locus uncovered a point mutation in one copy of the *FOXP2* gene that segregated with the disorder in all the affected members of the KE family, as well as identifying a chromosomal rearrangement disrupting the gene in an independent unrelated case with similar problems (Lai, Fisher, Hurst, Vargha-Khadem, & Monaco, 2001). In the years that followed discovery of these first mutations, additional rare heterozygous disruptions of *FOXP2* have been identified in different cases and families around the world, including other chromosomal rearrangements as well as several different point mutations (summarized by Graham & Fisher, 2015). The affected individuals typically show disruptions of speech and language development and sometimes also show problems affecting other aspects of cognition and/or behavior (MacDermot et al., 2005; Reuter et al., 2017).

So far, the majority of insights into the consequences of mutation of human *FOXP2* have come from a series of clinical and neuropsychological studies of the KE family. Childhood apraxia of speech, also known as developmental verbal dyspraxia, is the most prominent feature of the disorder in this family (Forrest, 2003) and is characterized as difficulty in learning and producing coordinated sequences of the complex orofacial movements underlying speech. The underlying problems persist into adulthood, despite intensive speech therapy (Vargha-Khadem, Watkins, Alcock, Fletcher, & Passingham, 1995). Speech motor deficits of the affected individuals are accompanied by impairments in a wide range of language-related skills: affecting spoken and written modalities, the expression and reception of language, and the comprehension and production of grammar (Gopnik & Crago, 1991; Vargha-Khadem et al., 1995; Watkins, Dronkers, & Vargha-Khadem, 2002). Some members of the KE family show reduced performance on tests of nonverbal cognition (Vargha-Khadem et al., 1995), but it has been argued that this does not represent a core feature because low nonverbal IQ does not cosegregate with the *FOXP2* mutation (Watkins, Dronkers et al., 2002).

Identification of additional families and cases carrying different heterozygous *FOXP2* mutations has broadened the clinical spectrum associated with disruptions of this gene (Reuter et al., 2017). At the same time, such reports have confirmed that speech apraxia is a consistent core feature, and the *FOXP2*-associated disorder is more selective than intellectual disability syndromes, often with more dramatic consequences for verbal cognition than for nonverbal skills. Further investigations are under way to perform deep phenotyping on multiple affected cases carrying distinct *FOXP2* mutations.

THE GAP BETWEEN GENES AND BEHAVIOR

It is now well established that disruption of one copy of *FOXP2* is enough to yield impairments of a person's speech and language skills. Crucially, this does not mean that *FOXP2* should be viewed as a gene for speech or a gene for language. Despite such popular misconceptions, it is important to recognize that genes are unable to directly specify behavioral/cognitive processes and outputs (Fisher & Vernes, 2015). There is a very large mechanistic gap between DNA-based information at the genetic/genomic level and the distal aspects of cognition and behavior that we are able to characterize at the phenotypic level. As with other cognitive traits, it will be essential to fill this gap if we are to fully understand the biological bases of our capacity for speech and language.

Even if the specific details are still to be determined, we already know of many general principles that help govern how different levels of description connect to each other across the genotype-phenotype divide. Briefly, the genes that we understand most about are those that encode proteins, forming the molecular machinery that ensures the functioning of all cells, including neurons (electrically active brain cells). The DNA sequences of such genes specify the amino acid sequences of a huge array of different proteins with distinct properties (determined by their three dimensional shape), including enzymes that catalyze biological reactions, factors that underpin structural features of cells, and signaling molecules that get sent to other cells.

By working together in combination, proteins contribute to multiple key aspects of neuronal development and function (Fisher & Vernes, 2015). For example, they influence the proliferation of neural precursors in early development, their differentiation into distinct types of neurons with specialized properties, and the migration of these neurons to their final positions in the central nervous system. Proteins are also involved with the mechanisms by which extensions grow out from neurons, developing into dendrites and axons, and with the ways that growing axons navigate toward their targets (axon guidance). Such processes support the wiring up of the complex sets of connections between different neurons, leading to the formation of neural circuits. Even after a neural circuit is established, the synaptic connections in that circuit change their strength (to facilitate learning); this plasticity is also mediated by changes in the expression of genes and proteins, meaning that your genome is actively contributing to brain function throughout your life. Ultimately, complicated assemblages of neural circuits built by a combination of gene expression, experience, and stochastic (random) factors form an integrated system (i.e., the brain that enables diverse forms of complex behaviors).

FOXP2 AS A MOLECULAR WINDOW

This brings us back to *FOXP2* and the new opportunities provided by its discovery. When we find that mutation of a certain gene causes a disorder involving a particular profile of cognitive and/or behavioral impairments, it offers novel routes for deciphering the intermediate levels between genotype and phenotype that were previously described. If that disorder is characterized by disproportionate effects on aspects of speech and language, as has been argued for *FOXP2*-associated deficits, then the implicated gene could provide a valuable molecular window into the neurobiological pathways that are important for these human capacities. The following paragraphs illustrate the strategy with some selected examples from the literature on *FOXP2*, considering molecular-, cellular-, and systems-level analyses as well as placing the gene in its deeper evolutionary context. For more details, the interested reader is referred to in-depth review articles on this topic that have been published over the years (e.g., Fisher & Marcus, 2006; Fisher & Scharff, 2009).

FOXP2 is a regulatory gene encoding a transcription factor protein (also given the name FOXP2) that modulates the expression levels of other genes (so-called downstream targets) by binding to particular stretches of DNA (Spiteri et al., 2007; Vernes et al., 2007). The etiological mutation that was originally found in the KE family results in an arginine-to-histidine substitution at a critical residue within the DNA-binding domain of the FOXP2 protein (Lai et al., 2001), and experimental studies demonstrate that this prevents the transcription factor from binding to its usual target sites, impeding regulation of downstream genes (Vernes et al., 2006). Other rare *FOXP2* variants found in cases of speech apraxia have also been shown in cell-based experiments to disrupt the functioning of the encoded proteins (Estruch, Graham, Chinnappa, Deriziotis, & Fisher, 2016).

As a transcription factor, the FOXP2 protein represents a hub in a larger regulatory network, but the upstream and downstream elements of this network are only partially known at this stage. Following the discovery of the *FOXP2* gene, multiple studies sought to define downstream targets and had some success (Spiteri et al., 2007; Vernes et al., 2007, 2011). These investigations revealed that the FOXP2 protein regulates many genes in neuronal cells and brain tissue, but there is enrichment for targets involved in neurotransmission, neurite outgrowth, axon guidance, synaptic plasticity, and other aspects of brain development. A number of downstream targets of FOXP2 have received special attention, such as *CNTNAP2* (Vernes et al., 2008), *DISC1* (Walker et al., 2012), *MET* (Mukamel et al., 2011), and *SRPX2* (Roll et al., 2010), because they have been linked to major neurodevelopmental disorders, such as autism, schizophrenia, and epilepsy. Less is understood about the relevant upstream pathways, such as how transcription factors regulate the expression of *FOXP2* itself, although new studies have begun to examine this using cell-based techniques (Becker, Devanna, Fisher, & Vernes, 2018). In recent years, factors that may help to modulate the activity of the *FOXP2* protein have also been revealed, including the attachment of Small Ubiquitin-like Modifier (or SUMO) proteins to one particular site of this transcription factor (Estruch, Graham, Deriziotis, & Fisher, 2016; Usui et al., 2017). In addition, other transcription factor proteins such as FOXP1 and TBR1, which interact with FOXP2 in regions of the brain with shared expression, have been implicated in neurodevelopmental disorders with connections to speech and language (Deriziotis et al., 2014; Sollis et al., 2016).

AN EVOLUTIONARY PERSPECTIVE

Although *FOXP2* appears to play important roles in the development of proficient speech and language skills, this gene is not uniquely human and, to the contrary, has a deep evolutionary history (Fisher & Marcus, 2006; Fisher & Scharff, 2009). *FOXP2* is a highly conserved gene found in similar form in many diverse vertebrates—for example, zebrafishes (Bonkowsky & Chien, 2005; Shah, Medina-Martinez, Chu, Samaco, & Jamrich, 2006), crocodiles (Haesler et al., 2004), birds (Haesler et al., 2004; Teramitsu, 2004), rodents (Campbell, Reep, Stoll, Ophir, & Phelps, 2009; Ferland, Cherry, Preware, Morrisey, & Walsh, 2003; Lai, Gerrelli, Fisher, & Copp, 2003), nonhuman primates (Takahashi et al., 2008), and humans (Lai et al., 2003). Given the high levels of conservation, both in terms of protein sequence and neural sites of expression (see next), multiple investigations have been carried out in nonhuman animal models to reveal functions of versions of *FOXP2* in other species. For instance, rodent studies suggest that it may help modulate the plasticity of neural circuits responsible for sensory-motor integration (Fisher & Scharff, 2009; Kurt, Fisher, & Ehret, 2012; Middleton & Strick, 2000), a process that is important for human speech, when the motor control of vocal output and the auditory processing of speech signals must be integrated. Other reports have implicated the gene in auditory-guided vocal learning in songbirds, such as the zebra finch (Haesler et al., 2007; Murugan, Harward, Scharff, & Mooney, 2013), and in mouse ultrasonic vocalization (Castellucci, McGinley, & McCormick, 2016; Chabout et al., 2016; Shu et al., 2005) and motor skill behaviors (French et al., 2018; Groszer et al., 2008). Furthermore, the fruit fly (*Drosophila melanogaster*) homolog, *FoxP,* has been linked to perceptual decision making, operant self-learning, and courtship song production (DasGupta, Ferreira, & Miesenböck, 2014; Lawton, Wassmer, & Deitcher, 2014; Mendoza et al., 2014). The observations of conserved neural functions of versions of *FOXP2* found in distantly related species support a framework in which our unique capacity for acquiring spoken language was built on neurogenetic systems that are evolutionarily ancient (Fisher, 2017; Fisher & Marcus, 2006).

IMPACTS OF *FOXP2* PATHWAYS ON CELLS AND SYSTEMS

What has been learned about the impact of *FOXP2* and mutated versions of this gene on cellular properties? Several etiological *FOXP2* mutations lead to the disruption of the nuclear localization of the encoded protein (Estruch, Graham, Chinnappa et al., 2016; Vernes et al., 2006). At the cellular level, the transcription factor has been reported to modulate neurite outgrowth in mouse models (Vernes et al., 2011) and affect the density of dendritic spines in zebra finches (Schulz, Haesler, Scharff, & Rochefort, 2010). Effects of this kind could potentially influence the development of neural connections in circuits that express the gene. Indeed, it was subsequently shown that mutations of the mouse gene (matching those found in cases of speech disorder) impair the normal functioning of striatal circuits during the acquisition of motor skills (French et al., 2012) and auditory-motor association learning (Kurt et al., 2012), in ways that could conceivably stem from abnormal synaptic plasticity in brain structures underlying motor-skill learning, in the striatum (French et al., 2012; Groszer et al., 2008) and cerebellum (Groszer et al., 2008). Thus, studies at the cellular level and in vivo suggest that (among other effects) the *FOXP2* gene is involved in the development and plasticity of neuronal connections in circuits in which it is expressed.

At the systems level, versions of *FOXP2* found in different species (including humans) show comparable neural expression patterns, with consistent enrichment in certain subpopulations, such as deep layers of the cerebral cortex (Campbell et al., 2009; Lai et al., 2003; Takahashi et al., 2008), medium spiny neurons of the basal ganglia (Lai et al., 2003; Takahashi et al., 2008), specific nuclei of the thalamus (Lai et al., 2003; Shah et al., 2006; Teramitsu, 2004), and Purkinje cells of the cerebellum (Bonkowsky & Chien, 2005; Lai et al., 2003; Shah et al., 2006). It is intriguing to note that these structures of the brain, as fundamental elements of cortico-striatal and cortico-cerebellar systems, are substrates for experience-dependent plasticity during motor-skill learning (Doyon, Penhune, & Ungerleider, 2003). Cortico-striatal projections form a main output of the cerebral cortex and represent the major input to the basal ganglia and striatum among them (Wickens & Arbuthnott, 2010). Voxel-based morphometry of magnetic resonance imaging (MRI) data from the KE family revealed reduced grey matter density in cortical regions (including the inferior frontal gyrus) and the striatum, as well as parts of the cerebellum, in the affected family members compared with unaffected members and a group of age-matched controls (Watkins, Vargha-Khadem et al., 2002). Moreover, parts of the striatum, as well as Broca's area, exhibited altered activation in the affected family members during language-based tasks in functional neuroimaging studies (Liégeois et al., 2003; Vargha-Khadem et al., 1998). It is also known that when brain trauma or stroke result in damage to the striatum and Broca's area, speech and language problems can occur (Jarvis, 2004; Lieberman, 2002). Affected KE family members with *FOXP2* mutation have been directly compared with patients with aphasia resulting from a left hemisphere stroke, and similar impairments were observed for a range of speech and language tests (Watkins, Dronkers et al., 2002).

Overall, the findings are consistent with an emerging broad consensus in the field acknowledging that cortico-striatal and cortico-cerebellar systems make important contributions to speech and language development. The functional relevance of *FOXP2*-dependent networks for different parts of these systems is only beginning to be teased apart, (e.g., through selective inactivation in cortex, striatum, and cerebellum in animal models) (French et al., 2018). It is also important to realize that *FOXP2* plays additional roles outside the central nervous system, including in skeletal anatomy (Xu et al., 2018); this is a commonly encountered intrinsic feature of regulatory gene action, known as *pleiotropy*.

NEW TECHNOLOGIES ARE TRANSFORMING MOLECULAR GENETICS

We have illustrated how genetics can offer powerful windows into neurobiology by highlighting a representative selection of studies of *FOXP2*, the first and most intensively investigated gene related to speech and language disorder. Crucially, *FOXP2* is likely to be only one of many genes that interact with each other in complex molecular networks to form the biological underpinnings of our sophisticated linguistic capacities (Graham & Fisher, 2015). As DNA-based technologies advance, there are enhanced opportunities to move beyond *FOXP2* to discover additional genetic loci that are disrupted in cases of developmental speech and language disorders (Deriziotis & Fisher, 2017). For instance, whole genome sequencing approaches are uncovering additional genes implicated in childhood apraxia of speech, with one study identifying rare or de novo causative mutations in *CHD3, SETD1A, WDR5, KAT6A, SETBP1, TNRC6B,* and *ZFHX4* (Eising et al., 2018). Several of these disrupted genes were previously implicated in neurodevelopmental disorders. For example, *KAT6A* mutations are associated with intellectual disability and language delay in combination with subtle facial features (Tham et al., 2015), *ZFHX4* mutations have been linked to intellectual disability and specific facial features (Palomares et al., 2011), and *TNRC6B* mutations have been identified in children with autism spectrum disorder (Iossifov et al., 2014). *SETBP1* is especially interesting because heterozygous deletion has been linked to cognitive problems, motor delay, facial dysmorphism, and delayed expressive language development (Filges et al., 2011), whereas common variants of this same gene have been associated with complexity of linguistic output in an isolated Russian population in which language disorders are unusually prevalent (Kornilov et al., 2016). Moreover, the genes implicated by the speech apraxia genome sequencing study are mainly regulatory genes with functional connections to each other and showing significant coexpression in the developing human brain (Eising et al., 2018). These and other studies demonstrate that the genetic mechanisms underlying speech and language are highly complex and involve the interplay of many different genes with distinct modes of action (Deriziotis & Fisher, 2017).

As illustrated by the *SETBP1* example previously described, it is not only through rare disruptive mutations that we can discover potential connections between genotype and phenotype. Investigations have also searched for association of common gene variants with various common forms of speech, language, and/or reading disorders; the interested reader is referred to other articles for in-depth discussion of this area (Carrion-Castillo, Franke, & Fisher, 2013; Deriziotis & Fisher, 2017; Graham & Fisher, 2015). In contrast to rare disruptive mutations, each common genetic variant has (at most) subtle effects on the function of encoded proteins, and, hence, a single variant only explains a tiny proportion of risk of a disorder, meaning that large sample sizes are needed to have power for a reliable screening study. Association studies using common gene variants are not limited to disorders but are routinely being extended to look for interindividual differences in neuroimaging and behavioral/cognitive measures in healthy participants (Bearden & Thompson, 2017; Deriziotis & Fisher, 2017; Hoogman et al., 2014). Recruiting new cohorts with a specific focus on language-related skills could be a promising approach. Advanced genetic screening technology, however, needs to be matched with improved sophistication of phenotyping, including the standardization of phenotype assessment batteries between different languages and the possibility to scale up for systematic robust testing of thousands of people.

CONCLUSION

The appearance of rapid and affordable large-scale genotyping techniques and next-generation sequencing has fueled dramatic changes in all strands of biology, including human neuroscience, with almost unlimited possibilities for generating new data. But it should not be overlooked that these data require rigorous and careful analysis to detect biologically adequate relationships between particular genomic variants and complex human phenotypes against the broader genomic background. In this regard, DNA sequence analysis is only a first step in the multilevel approach described in this chapter, including the thorough analyses of protein, cellular, physiological, and behavioral levels (Fisher & Vernes, 2015). Efforts should be made to integrate findings from these diverse fields of inquiry. Studies utilizing whole-genome genotyping and/or sequencing, whole-brain imaging, and the comprehensive analysis of cognitive measures are essential steps in that regard, studies that may nevertheless require large cohorts of participants to avoid false positive results. The establishment of new research consortia and networks (e.g., GenLang, http://www.genlang.org) is aimed at facilitating such interdisciplinary integrative studies for understanding the biology of human language.

REFERENCES

Bearden, C. E., & Thompson, P. M. (2017). Emerging global initiatives in neurogenetics: The Enhancing Neuroimaging Genetics through Meta-analysis (ENIGMA) Consortium. *Neuron, 94*(2), 232–236. http://doi.org/10.1016/j.neuron.2017.03.033

Becker, M., Devanna, P., Fisher, S. E., & Vernes, S. C. (2018). Mapping of human FOXP2 enhancers reveals complex regulation. *Frontiers in Molecular Neuroscience, 11,* 47. http://doi.org/10.3389/fnmol.2018.00047

Bishop, D. V., Laws, G., Adams, C., & Norbury, C. F. (2006). High heritability of speech and language impairments in 6-year-old twins demonstrated using parent and teacher report. *Behavior Genetics, 36*(2),173–184.

Bonkowsky, J. L., & Chien, C. B. (2005). Molecular cloning and developmental expression of FoxP2 in zebrafish. *Developmental Dynamics, 234*(3), 740–746. http://doi.org/10.1002/dvdy.20504

Campbell, P., Reep, R. L., Stoll, M. L., Ophir, A. G., & Phelps, S. M. (2009). Conservation and diversity of Foxp2 expression in muroid rodents: Functional implications. *Journal of Comparative Neurology, 512*(1), 84–100. http://doi.org/10.1002/cne.21881

Carrion-Castillo, A., Franke, B., & Fisher, S. E. (2013). Molecular genetics of dyslexia: An overview. *Dyslexia, 19*(4), 214–240. http://doi.org/10.1002/dys.1464

Castellucci, G. A., McGinley, M. J., & McCormick, D. A. (2016). Knockout of Foxp2 disrupts vocal development in mice. *Scientific Reports, 6,* 23305. http://doi.org/10.1038/srep23305

Chabout, J., Sarkar, A., Patel, S., Radden, T., Dunson, D., Fisher, S. E., & Jarvis, E. (2016). A Foxp2 mutation implicated in human speech deficits alters sequencing of ultrasonic vocalizations in adult male mice. *Frontiers in Behavioral Neuroscience, 10,* 197. http://doi.org/10.3389/fnbeh.2016.00197

Curtiss, S. (1977). *Genie: A psycholinguistic study of a modern-day "wild child."* London, England: Academic Press.

Curtiss, S. (1980). A critical period for the acquisition of grammar: Evidence from feral and isolated children. *UCLA Working Papers in Cognitive Linguistics, 2,* 21–36.Darwin, C. (1871). *The descent of man, and selection in relation to sex.* London, England: John Murray.

DasGupta, S., Ferreira, C. H., & Miesenböck, G. (2014). FoxP influences the speed and accuracy of a perceptual decision in Drosophila. *Science, 344*(6186), 901–904. http://doi.org/10.1126/science.1252114

Deriziotis, P., & Fisher, S. E. (2017). Speech and language: Translating the genome. *Trends in Genetics, 33*(9), 642–656. http://doi.org/10.1016/j.tig.2017.07.002

Deriziotis, P., O'Roak, B. J., Graham, S. A., Estruch, S. B., Dimitropoulou, D., Bernier, R. A., . . . Fisher, S. E. (2014). De novo TBR1 mutations in sporadic autism disrupt protein functions. *Nature Communications, 5,* 1–12. http://doi.org/10.1038/ncomms5954

Doyon, J., Penhune, V., & Ungerleider, L. G. (2003). Distinct contribution of the cortico-striatal and cortico-cerebellar systems to motor skill learning. *Neuropsychologia, 41*(3), 252–262. http://doi.org/10.1016/S0028-3932(02)00158-6

Eising, E., Carrion-Castillo, A., Vino, A., Strand, E. A., Jakielski, K. J., Scerri, T. S., . . . Fisher, S. E. (2018). A set of regulatory genes co-expressed in embryonic human brain is implicated in disrupted speech development. *Molecular Psychiatry,* 1–14. http://doi.org/10.1038/s41380-018-0020-x

Estruch, S. B., Graham, S. A., Chinnappa, S. M., Deriziotis, P., & Fisher, S. E. (2016). Functional characterization of rare FOXP2 variants in neurodevelopmental disorder. *Journal of Neurodevelopmental Disorders, 8,* 44. http://doi.org/10.1186/s11689-016-9177-2

Estruch, S. B., Graham, S. A., Deriziotis, P., & Fisher, S. E. (2016). The language-related transcription factor FOXP2 is post-translationally modified with small ubiquitin-like modifiers. *Scientific Reports, 6,* 1–17. http://doi.org/10.1038/srep20911

Ferland, R. J., Cherry, T. J., Preware, P. O., Morrisey, E. E., & Walsh, C. A. (2003). Characterization of Foxp2 and Foxp1 mRNA and protein in the developing and mature brain, *Journal of Comparative Neurology, 460*(2), 266–279. http://doi.org/10.1002/cne.10654

Filges, I., Shimojima, K., Okamoto, N., Rothlisberger, B., Weber, P., Huber, A. R., . . . Yamamoto, T. (2011). Reduced expression by SETBP1 haploinsufficiency causes developmental and expressive language delay indicating a phenotype distinct from Schinzel-Giedion syndrome. *Journal of Medical Genetics, 48*(2), 117–122. http://doi.org/10.1136/jmg.2010.084582

Fisher, S. E. (2017). Evolution of language: Lessons from the genome. *Psychonomic Bulletin and Review, 24*(1), 34–40. http://doi.org/10.3758/s13423-016-1112-8

Fisher, S. E., & Marcus, G. F. (2006). The eloquent ape: Genes, brains and the evolution of language. *Nature Reviews Genetics, 7*(1), 9–20. http://doi.org/10.1038/nrg1747

Fisher, S. E., & Scharff, C. (2009). FOXP2 as a molecular window into speech and language. *Trends in Genetics, 25*(4), 166–177. http://doi.org/10.1016/j.tig.2009.03.002

Fisher, S. E., Vargha-Khadem, F., Watkins, K. E., Monaco, A. P., & Pembrey, M. E. (1998). Localisation of a gene implicated in a severe speech and language disorder. *Nature Genetics, 18*(2), 168–170. http://doi.org/10.1038/ng0298-168

Fisher, S. E., & Vernes, S. C. (2015). Genetics and the language sciences. *Annual Review of Linguistics, 1,* 289–310. http://doi.org/10.1146/annurev-linguist-030514-125024

Forrest, K. (2003). Diagnostic criteria of developmental apraxia of speech used by clinical speech-language pathologists. *American Journal of Speech-Language Pathology, 12,* 376–380. http://doi.org/10.1044/1058-0360(2003/083)

French, C. A., Jin, X., Campbell, T. G., Gerfen, E., Groszer, M., Fisher, S. E., & Costa, R. M. (2012). An aetiological Foxp2 mutation causes aberrant striatal activity and alters plasticity during skill learning. *Molecular Psychiatry, 17*(11), 1077–1085. http://doi.org/10.1038/mp.2011.105

French, C. A., Vinueza Veloz, M. F., Zhou, K., Peter, S., Fisher, S. E., Costa, R. M., & De Zeeuw, C. I. (2018). Differential effects of Foxp2 disruption in distinct motor circuits. *Molecular Psychiatry*. Advance online publication. http://doi.org/10.1038/s41380-018-0199-x

Gopnik, M., & Crago, M. B. (1991). Familial aggregation of a developmental language disorder. *Cognition, 39*(1), 1–50. http://doi.org/10.1016/0010-0277(91)90058-C

Graham, S. A., & Fisher, S. E. (2015). Understanding language from a genomic perspective. *Annual Review of Genetics, 49,* 131–160. http://doi.org/10.1146/annurev-genet-120213-092236

Groszer, M., Keays, D. A., Deacon, R. M. J., de Bono, J. P., Prasad-Mulcare, S., Gaub, S., . . . Fisher, S. E. (2008). Impaired synaptic plasticity and motor learning in mice with a point mutation implicated in human speech deficits. *Current Biology, 18*(5), 354–362. http://doi.org/10.1016/j.cub.2008.01.060

Haesler, S., Rochefort, C., Georgi, B., Licznerski, P., Osten, P., & Scharff, C. (2007). Incomplete and inaccurate vocal imitation after knockdown of FoxP2 in songbird basal ganglia nucleus area X. *PLoS Biology, 5*(12), 2885–2897. http://doi.org/10.1371/journal.pbio.0050321

Haesler, S., Wada, K., Nshdejan, A., Morrisey, E. E., Lints, T., Jarvis, E. D., & Scharff, C. (2004). FoxP2 expression in avian vocal learners and non-learners. *Journal of Neuroscience, 24*(13), 3164–3175. http://doi.org/10.1523/JNEUROSCI.4369-03.2004

Hoogman, M., Guadalupe, T., Zwiers, M. P., Klarenbeek, P., Francks, C., & Fisher, S. E. (2014, July). Assessing the effects of common variation in the FOXP2 gene on human brain structure. *Frontiers in Human Neuroscience, 8,* 473. http://doi.org/10.3389/fnhum.2014.00473

Iossifov, I., O'Roak, B. J., Sanders, S. J., Ronemus, M., Krumm, N., Levy, D., . . . Wigler, M. (2014). The contribution of de novo coding mutations to autism spectrum disorder. *Nature, 515*(7526), 216–221. http://doi.org/10.1038/nature13908

Jarvis, E. D. (2004). Learned birdsong and the neurobiology of human language. *Annals of the New York Academy of Sciences, 1016,* 749–777. http://doi.org/10.1196/annals.1298.038

Kornilov, S. A., Rakhlin, N., Koposov, R., Lee, M., Yrigollen, C., Caglayan, A. O., . . . Grigorenko, E. L. (2016). Genome-wide association and exome sequencing study of language disorder in an isolated population. *Pediatrics, 137*(4), e20152469. http://doi.org/10.1542/peds.2015-2469

Kurt, S., Fisher, S. E., & Ehret, G. (2012). Foxp2 mutations impair auditory-motor association learning. *PLoS ONE, 7*(3), 3–7. http://doi.org/10.1371/journal.pone.0033130

Lai, C. S., Fisher, S. E., Hurst, J. A., Vargha-Khadem, F., & Monaco, A. P. (2001). A forkhead-domain gene is mutated in a severe speech and language disorder. *Nature, 413*(6855), 519–523. http://doi.org/10.1038/35097076

Lai, C. S. L., Gerrelli, D., Fisher, S. E., & Copp, A. J. (2003). FOXP2 expression during brain development coincides with adult sites of pathology in a severe speech and language disorder. *Brain, 126*(Pt 11), 2455–2462. http://doi.org/10.1093/brain/awg247

Lawton, K. J., Wassmer, T. L., & Deitcher, D. L. (2014). Conserved role of Drosophila melanogaster FoxP in motor coordination and courtship song. *Behavioural Brain Research, 268,* 213–221. http://doi.org/10.1016/j.bbr.2014.04.009

Lieberman, P. (2002). On the nature and evolution of the neural bases of human language. *Yearbook of Physical Anthropology, 45,* 36–62. http://doi.org/10.1002/ajpa.10171

Liégeois, F., Baldeweg, T., Connelly, A., Gadian, D. G., Mishkin, M., & Vargha-Khadem, F. (2003). Language fMRI abnormalities associated with FOXP2 gene mutation. *Nature Neuroscience, 6*(11), 1230–1237. http://doi.org/10.1038/nn1138

MacDermot, K. D., Bonora, E., Sykes, N., Coupe, A.-M., Lai, C. S. L., Vernes, S. C., . . . Fisher, S. E. (2005). Identification of FOXP2 truncation as a novel cause of developmental speech and language deficits. *American Journal of Human Genetics, 76*(6), 1074–1080. http://doi.org/10.1086/430841

Mendoza, E., Colomb, J., Rybak, J., Pflüger, H. J., Zars, T., Scharff, C., & Brembs, B. (2014). Drosophila FoxP mutants are deficient in operant self-learning. *PLoS One, 9*(6), e100648. http://doi.org/10.1371/journal.pone.0100648

Middleton, F. A., & Strick, P. L. (2000). Basal ganglia and cerebellar loops: Motor and cognitive circuits. *Brain Research Reviews, 31*(2–3), 236–250. http://doi.org/10.1016/S0165-0173(99)00040-5

Mukamel, Z., Konopka, G., Wexler, E., Osborn, G. E., Dong, H., Bergman, M. Y., . . . Geschwind, D. H. (2011). Regulation of MET by FOXP2, genes implicated in higher cognitive dysfunction and autism risk. *Journal of Neuroscience, 31*(32), 11437–11442. http://doi.org/10.1523/JNEUROSCI.0181-11.2011

Murugan, M., Harward, S., Scharff, C., & Mooney, R. (2013). Diminished FoxP2 levels affect dopaminergic modulation of corticostriatal signaling important to song variability. *Neuron, 80*(6), 1464–1476. http://doi.org/10.1016/j.neuron.2013.09.021

Palomares, M., Delicado, A., Mansilla, E., De Torres, M. L., Vallespín, E., Fernandez, L., . . . Lapunzina, P. (2011). Characterization of a 8q21.11 microdeletion syndrome associated with intellectual disability and a recognizable phenotype. *American Journal of Human Genetics, 89*(2), 295–301. http://doi.org/10.1016/j.ajhg.2011.06.012

Reuter, M. S., Riess, A., Moog, U., Briggs, T. A., Chandler, K. E., Rauch, A., . . . Zweier, C. (2017). FOXP2 variants in 14 individuals with developmental speech and language disorders broaden the mutational and clinical spectrum. *Journal of Medical Genetics, 54*(1), 64–72. http://doi.org/10.1136/jmedgenet-2016-104094

Roll, P., Vernes, S. C., Bruneau, N., Cillario, J., Ponsole-Lenfant, M., Massacrier, A., . . . Szepetowski, P. (2010). Molecular networks implicated in speech-related disorders: FOXP2 regulates the SRPX2/uPAR complex. *Human Molecular Genetics, 19*(24), 4848–4860. http://doi.org/10.1093/hmg/ddq415

Schulz, S. B., Haesler, S., Scharff, C., & Rochefort, C. (2010). Knockdown of FoxP2 alters spine density in Area X of the zebra finch. *Genes, Brain, and Behavior, 9*(7), 732–740. http://doi.org/10.1111/j.1601-183X.2010.00607.x

Shah, R., Medina-Martinez, O., Chu, L.-F., Samaco, R. C., & Jamrich, M. (2006). Expression of FoxP2 during zebrafish development and in the adult brain. *International Journal of Developmental Biology, 50*(4), 435–438. http://doi.org/10.1387/ijdb.052065rs

Shipley, K. G., & McAfee, J. G. (2015). *Assessment in speech-language pathology: A resource manual* (5th ed.). Boston, MA: Cengage Learning.

Shu, W., Cho, J. Y., Jiang, Y., Zhang, M., Weisz, D., Elder, G. A., . . . Buxbaum, J. D. (2005). Altered ultrasonic vocalization in mice with a disruption in the Foxp2 gene. *Proceedings of the National Academy of Sciences of the United States of America, 102*(27), 9643–9648. http://doi.org/10.1073/pnas.0503739102

Sollis, E., Graham, S. A., Vino, A., Froehlich, H., Vreeburg, M., Dimitropoulou, D., . . . Fisher, S. E. (2016). Identification and functional characterization of de novo FOXP1 variants provides novel insights into the etiology of neurodevelopmental disorder. *Human Molecular Genetics, 25*(3), 546–557. http://doi.org/10.1093/hmg/ddv495

Spiteri, E., Konopka, G., Coppola, G., Bomar, J., Oldham, M., Ou, J., . . . Geschwind, D. H. (2007). Identification of the transcriptional targets of FOXP2, a gene linked to speech and language, in developing human brain. *American Journal of Human Genetics, 81*(6), 1144–1157. http://doi.org/10.1086/522237

Takahashi, K., Fu-Chin, L. I. U., Oishi, T., Mori, T., Higo, N., Hayashi, M., . . . Takahashi, H. (2008). Expression of FOXP2 in the developing monkey forebrain: Comparison with the expression of the genes FOXP1, PBX3, and MEIS2. *Journal of Comparative Neurology, 509*(2), 180–189. http://doi.org/10.1002/cne.21740

Teramitsu, I. (2004). Parallel FoxP1 and FoxP2 expression in songbird and human brain predicts functional interaction. *Journal of Neuroscience, 24*(13), 3152–3163. http://doi.org/10.1523/JNEUROSCI.5589-03.2004

Tham, E., Lindstrand, A., Santani, A., Malmgren, H., Nesbitt, A., Dubbs, H. A., . . . Nordgren, A. (2015). Dominant mutations in KAT6A cause intellectual disability with recognizable syndromic features. *American Journal of Human Genetics, 96*(3), 507–513. http://doi.org/10.1016/j.ajhg.2015.01.016

Usui, N., Co, M., Harper, M., Rieger, M. A., Dougherty, J. D., & Konopka, G. (2017). Sumoylation of FOXP2 regulates motor function and vocal communication through Purkinje cell development. *Biological Psychiatry, 81*(3), 220–230. http://doi.org/10.1016/j.biopsych.2016.02.008

Vargha-Khadem, F., Watkins, K., Alcock, K., Fletcher, P., & Passingham, R. (1995). Praxic and nonverbal cognitive deficits in a large family with a genetically transmitted speech and language disorder. *Proceedings of the National Academy of Sciences of the United States of America, 92*(3), 930–933. http://doi.org/10.1073/pnas.92.3.930

Vargha-Khadem, F., Watkins, K. E., Price, C. J., Ashburner, J., Alcock, K. J., Connelly, A., . . . Passingham, R. E. (1998). Neural basis of an inherited speech and language disorder. *Proceedings of the National Academy of Sciences of the United States of America, 95*(21), 12695–12700. http://doi.org/DOI 10.1073/pnas.95.21.12695

Vernes, S. C., Newbury, D. F., Abrahams, B. S., Winchester, L., Nicod, J., Groszer, M., . . . Fisher, S. E. (2008). A functional genetic link between distinct developmental language disorders. *New England Journal of Medicine, 359*(22), 2337–2345. http://doi.org/NEJMoa0802828 [pii]\r10.1056/NEJMoa0802828

Vernes, S. C., Nicod, J., Elahi, F. M., Coventry, J. A., Kenny, N., Coupe, A. M., . . . Fisher, S. E. (2006). Functional genetic analysis of mutations implicated in a human speech and language disorder. *Human Molecular Genetics, 15*(21), 3154–3167. http://doi.org/10.1093/hmg/ddl392

Vernes, S. C., Oliver, P. L., Spiteri, E., Lockstone, H. E., Puliyadi, R., Taylor, J. M., . . . Fisher, S. E. (2011). FOXP2 regulates gene networks implicated in neurite outgrowth in the developing brain. *PLoS Genetics, 7*(7). http://doi.org/10.1371/journal.pgen.1002145

Vernes, S. C., Spiteri, E., Nicod, J., Groszer, M., Taylor, J. M., Davies, K. E., . . . Fisher, S. E. (2007). High-throughput analysis of promoter occupancy reveals direct neural targets of FOXP2, a gene mutated in speech and language disorders. *American Journal of Human Genetics, 81*(6), 1232–1250. http://doi.org/10.1086/522238

Walker, R. M., Hill, A. E., Newman, A. C., Hamilton, G., Torrance, H. S., Anderson, S. M., . . . Evans, K. L. (2012). The DISC1 promoter: Characterization and regulation by FOXP2. *Human Molecular Genetics, 21*(13), 2862–2872. http://doi.org/10.1093/hmg/dds111

Watkins, K. E., Dronkers, N. F., & Vargha-Khadem, F. (2002). Behavioural analysis of an inherited speech and language disorder: Comparison with acquired aphasia. *Brain, 125*(3), 452–464. http://doi.org/10.1093/brain/awf058

Watkins, K. E., Vargha-Khadem, F., Ashburner, J., Passingham, R. E., Connelly, A., Friston, K. J., . . . Gadian, D. G. (2002). MRI analysis of an inherited speech and language disorder: Structural brain abnormalities. *Brain, 125*(3), 465–478. http://doi.org/10.1093/brain/awf057

Wickens, J. R., & Arbuthnott, G. W. (2010). Gating of cortical input to the striatum. In H. Steiner & K. Y. Tseng (Eds.), *Handbook of basal ganglia structure and function: A decade of progress* (pp. 341–351). Amsterdam, The Netherlands: Elsevier.

Xu, S., Liu, P., Chen, Y., Chen, Y., Zhang, W., Zhao, H., . . . Guo, X. (2018). Foxp2 regulates anatomical features that may be relevant for vocal behaviors and bipedal locomotion. *Proceedings of the National Academy of Sciences of the United States of America, 115*(35), 8799–8804. http://doi.org/10.1073/pnas.1721820115

CHAPTER 3

Mapping the Literate Brain

Where We Are and What Must Come Next

Kenneth R. Pugh

SUMMARY

Neurocognitive research has accrued considerable information on genetic and neurobiological differences in typically and atypically developing learners, and this represents a good beginning, but research on the brain bases of reading disability (RD) is still largely descriptive or correlational. Causal models that can explain the brain bases of RD have yet to be fully developed, and progress therein requires 1) a new generation of prospective longitudinal studies that begin tracking children at very early preliterate developmental stages and utilize appropriate measures of gene-brain-cognitive pathways across development, 2) state-of-the-art learning and/or treatment studies that can yield sensitive measures of what works for whom and why, and 3) technical advances in measurement in the areas of genetics and neuroimaging and the application of sophisticated data-analytic tools to make sense of complex gene-brain-behavior relations in next-generation longitudinal or treatment studies. Some provocative new research designs discussed include the use of neuroimaging to actually guide learning approaches and gain insight into how the neurodevelopment of an individual relates to interactions with other brains as we in the field of neuroscience consider how to deliver on the promise of neuroscience to the classroom or clinic.

INTRODUCTION

Reading disability (RD) is the most common neurodevelopmental disorder of childhood, estimated to affect 10%–15% of otherwise typically developing children (Fletcher, Lyon, Fuchs, & Barnes, 2018). RD is often a lifelong disorder, with considerable morbidity in adolescence and adulthood in several domains (Beitchman et al., 1996, 2001). RD is often also a heritable, brain-based developmental challenge that has been reliably associated with differences, relative to typically developing readers, in functional, structural, and neurochemical indices of brain organization (Pugh, Mencl, Jenner et al., 2000; Pugh, Mencl, Shaywitz et al., 2000, Pugh et al., 2013, 2014). These neurobiological anomalies are thought to impede the development of adequate phonological processing skills, and these early phonological deficits, in turn, are thought to impede orthographic (O), phonologic (P), and semantic (S) learning and binding that are needed to create high-quality representations of written words in memory that will support fluent word reading (Harm & Seidenberg, 2004; Perfetti & Hart, 2002).

In this chapter, I take stock of the current cognitive neuroscience research on typical and atypical reading development in children and adults and consider where we are with respect to an ambitious promise made by neuroscience to education: the promise of a brain-informed understanding of the causes of RD that will enrich theory and guide clinical/educational best practices. I consider where we are, where we need to go next, and how we might get there in a timely manner. The aim is not to do an exhaustive review of the multiple research literatures that have arisen in the field, but instead to focus on approaches that I think are promising, along with examples of illustrative research findings.

We take as given that a deeper understanding of gene-brain-cognitive pathways in typical and atypical language and literacy development is a good thing, and as this relatively new field of cognitive neuroscience matures, more precise insights into the neurobiology of learning and development will lead to plausible approaches to better informed instruction and remediation. But obstacles to progress include limits on sensitivity of current neurocognitive measures and data analytic approaches as well as practical limits on the scale and scope of extant prospective longitudinal and/or treatment studies needed to answer big and tough questions. As we consider the overarching goal of neuroscience-guided instructional practices that can address the issue of finding what works best for whom and why, we must examine progress and failures to date with both humility and conservatism. We must remain open to new approaches and novel interdisciplinary partnerships (including mutually respectful partnerships among researchers, educators, and clinicians) that will support progress in both theory and practice in RD research.

At this writing, neurocognitive research has actually accrued considerable information on neurobiological differences in typically and atypically developing learners, and this represents a good beginning. Yet, this body of research on the brain bases of RD, although fairly robust across labs and languages, is still largely descriptive or correlational. Causal models that link biomarkers in RD to specific reading-related cognitive deficits (e.g., noisy sensorimotor processing; deficient phonological awareness, phonological working memory, rapid naming, or grapheme-to-phoneme decoding skills) have yet to be fully developed and will require three things: 1) a new generation of prospective longitudinal studies that begin tracking children at very early preliterate developmental stages and utilize state-of-the-art gene-brain-cognitive measures across development, 2) sufficiently powered dynamic learning and/or treatment studies that can yield sensitive measures of what works for whom and why, and 3) technical advances in measurement in both genetics and multimodal neuroimaging and the incorporation of sophisticated multivariate data-analytic tools (many developed in other scientific domains) to help make sense of complex gene-brain-behavior relations in relevant longitudinal or treatment studies of children at risk for RD.

Although we mainly know how students with RD differ from typically developing readers in brain circuits and not so much why they do—causal models remain elusive—there is genuine value in the current knowledge when it comes to generating neural targets for reading remediation. Knowing which brain pathways are anomalous in RD allows the field to address questions such as 1) Does effective treatment for a certain type of learner at a certain age normalize brain circuits, or does it instead simply improve the function of compensatory brain circuits often relied upon by untreated RD? or 2) Can we discriminate between more or less effective treatments in general by their impact on fragile brain pathways?

Although brain imaging research on treatment and neuroplasticity in RD is exciting and has yielded a few provocative (and replicable) findings thus far (see next), it must be noted that very little of what is called best practice for teaching or remediating reading has been informed (or modified) by neuroscientific findings. Many years of behavioral research on core deficits and carefully controlled studies of treatment efficacy drive the content of evidence-based treatments at present (see Lovett, Steinbach, & DePalma, in press; guidance from university centers aimed at improving instruction and intervention and providing teacher support [e.g., Florida Center for Reading Research [http://www.fcrr.org] and Texas Center for Learning Disabilities [http://www.texasldcenter.org]). We would be hard-pressed to demonstrate how any of this has been modified by current neuroimaging, but for those of us committed to a biological understanding of learning, language, and literacy (and their disorders), it is critical that we quickly get to a point where brain-informed models actually guide educational or clinical practice instead of merely being along for the ride. This is the challenge that will occupy the field for some time, in my estimation, and it is therefore a topic to which stakeholders should pay close attention. I consider next the current state of the field and where we might go next.

BUILDING A LITERATE BRAIN

First, I present a general update on what is now known about the literate brain and the ways in which typically developing and RD learners differ from one another with regard to neurostructure, neurofunction, and neurochemistry (Pugh et al., 2013, 2014). To begin, consider the complex and intimate relationship between language by ear and language by eye. The human brain contains extensive specialization for spoken language (speech perception/production) primarily, but not exclusively, in left hemisphere (LH) frontal temporal networks (or hubs); thus, in a colloquial sense, it can be said that the human brain is wired for expressive and receptive language. The developing child does not need to be taught how to perceive or produce language in anything like formal instruction; rather, the child's brain requires intensive language input from caregivers to train these brain systems for speaking and listening, systems that have evolved over a great expanse of time in our species (Dehaene, 2009). Humans are not, however, wired for reading and writing; written language is a relatively recent cultural invention that requires direct instruction and practice. Learning to read requires extensive reorganization of hubs that are involved in visual pattern recognition, language, associative learning, and attentional control; this reorganization has been termed *neuronal re-cycling* by Dehaene (2009).

With the advent of formal literacy instruction in school, the beginning reader transforms the preliterate brain, with all of its specialized machinery for speech and language, into one that contains a distributed reading neurocircuitry; this new specialization allows fluent and automatic word reading in typically developing children (Pugh et al., 2013). What do we know thus far about this neurocircuitry and how it comes online? Converging functional brain imaging evidence (with tools such as functional magnetic resonance imaging [fMRI], electroencephalography [EEG], and magnetoencephalography [MEG]) since the late 1990s indicates that the acquisition of skilled word reading (fluent decoding) takes place in a largely LH neurocircuitry with temporoparietal (TP), occipitotemporal (OT), and inferior frontal (IFG) hubs and with important contributions from subcortical hubs (e.g., pulvinar/thalamus, basal ganglia) during initial learning and routinization (Preston et al., 2010, 2016; Pugh et al., 2013) and right hemisphere (RH) pathways associated with attentionally controlled processing early on (Shaywitz et al., 2002; Turkeltaub, Gareau, Flowers, Zeffiro, & Eden, 2003).

For both children and adults with RD, marked differences are observed relative to typically developing readers with regard to brain activation and functional connectivity (the process by which distributed hubs/networks work in concert with one another to support decoding; Pugh, Mencl, Shaywitz, et al. 2000). Neurofunctional differences are reliably observed across these LH hubs during brain imaging studies of language- and reading-related processing tasks across varied writing systems (Paulesu et al., 2001). Structural MRI studies of RD have further identified anomalies in brain structure, such as reduced grey matter volumes in those same LH hubs showing functional anomalies (e.g., Blackmon et al., 2010), and diffusion tensor imaging (DTI) has shown reduced white matter connectivity for key tracts that support interregional communication among these LH hubs (Klingberg et al., 2000). Thus, both neurofunction and neurostructure are measurably different in children and adults with RD.

RESEARCH ON EARLY READING DEVELOPMENT AND THE EMERGENCE OF READING DISABILITY

Although typically developing/RD differences appear to be robust across studies and languages in adults and older children, less work has focused on the earliest stages of learning to read. Haskins Labs has made a priority of using gene-brain-behavior designs in pediatric longitudinal studies in which the aim is to identify critical factors that presage persistent reading struggles from the beginnings of literacy learning (Jasińska et al., 2017; Landi et al., 2013; Preston et al., 2016; Pugh et al., 2013, 2014).

In one report by our team (Pugh et al., 2013) with beginning readers (age 7) in a sample ranging from RD to typically developing, we employed a brain-behavior analysis to identify the learning circuit and found that behavioral measures of phonological awareness, pseudoword decoding, and rapid auditory processing jointly reveal a strong positive correlation between neural responses in known reading areas including left TP, OT, and IFG, as well as frontal and parietal control networks, visual cortex, and subcortical networks including thalamus/pulvinar during print tasks. This study indicated that a learning circuit for emergent readers reflects not only tight coupling of LH language with visual regions but also implies a strong role for frontal lobe executive function (EF) systems, parietal control, and cortical (cingulate, precuneus) and subcortical (pulvinar) attentional systems in learning to read. At-risk learners showed reduced activation across this entire network; thus, functional anomalies are detectable at the earliest stages of reading acquisition.

In the same cohort, our team also employed a longitudinal analysis to examine the relevance of early print-speech convergence in emergent readers (age 7) and its links to reading outcomes 2 years later (Preston et al., 2016). Our focus was the degree to which LH circuits for speech overlap with early reading (print-speech convergence). This notion that good reading demands leveraging LH specialized language hubs for word reading was motivated by our longstanding theoretical stance at Haskins Labs regarding the relationship between spoken and written language, which stresses how good reading is parasitic on speech systems (Liberman, 1992), and by ongoing neurocognitive research from our team indicating that individual differences in reading abilities, longitudinal outcomes in children, and print comprehension in adults closely depend upon the ability to reorganize speech-sensitive networks in the LH perisylvian cortex to become available for print processing (Frost et al., 2009; Preston et al., 2016; see also McNorgan, Randazzo-Wagner, & Booth, 2013).

In an initial report on our sample of emergent readers at age 7, our team found that reading readiness (as indexed by tests of phonological awareness) was strongly correlated with the degree to which hubs in the LH relevant basic speech and spoken word processing are coactivated by print (Frost et al., 2009). In other words, children on a good trajectory have begun to modify circuits that have evolved for speech perception and production to process and support reading. Reinforcing the importance of this print-speech integration and the development of skilled reading, we followed these children for 2 years, and we next looked at the relation between print-speech integration at age 7 and reading outcomes at around age 9 (Preston et al., 2016). Findings indicated that the extent to which beginning readers engaged common LH language regions for both print and speech at age 7 strongly predicts performance on standardized reading tests 2 years later (above and beyond patterns of activation for either print or speech alone). In other words, neural integration of the visual and spoken modalities early in learning was the best predictor of reading success in our study. This finding, in conjunction with new cognitive data implicating early speech perception/production skills as predictors of RD/deficits in preliterate children later on (Van den Bunt, 2017, 2018) points to the importance of a language-based focus in initial reading instruction and/or remediation of its disorders.

Another study from this same longitudinal cohort reflects new work from our lab (and others) that seeks to go beyond an initial focus on neurofunctional or neurostructural differences alone to a deep focus on the neurochemistry of learning and plasticity (and how this might provide insights into learning disabilities). In our larger at-risk cohort, we (Pugh et al., 2014) employed a type of MRI protocol called magnetic resonance spectroscopy (MRS). MRS allows us to measure levels of expression of a variety of important neurochemicals associated with brain metabolism, learning, and plasticity in the individual brains. We found that both glutamate and choline levels in the occipital cortex were elevated in 7-year-old children at high risk for persistent reading difficulties relative to typically developing peers. Higher levels of glutamate and choline were robustly and negatively correlated with reading ability (the higher the glutamate or choline concentrations in this brain region, the lower the reading—and reading-related phonological—scores on standard assessments). More important, the glutamate measures at age 7 also predicted reading outcomes 2 years later at age 9; children who appeared to be overexpressing glutamate had poorer reading outcomes (Del Tufo et al., 2018; Pugh et al., 2014). Subsequent analyses of MRS and fMRI data have also shown important relations between these elevated glutamate levels in RD and a breakdown in functional connectivity between the visual regions (where we sampled neurochemistry) and other critical hubs in the LH language and reading circuitry (Pugh et al., unpublished data).

What might all this imply for the field's understanding of the neurobiological basis of RD? Glutamate is a major excitatory neurotransmitter, whereas GABA is the major inhibitory neurotransmitter; in balance, these neurotransmitters modulate excitatory and inhibitory levels of populations of neurons that form the critical hubs discussed thus far, and the relative excitatory or inhibitory activity of these hubs, in turn, controls learning and memory consolidation of new learning (see Hancock, Pugh, & Hoeft, 2017, for background and context). Thus, we can generally say that adequate learning and plasticity in reading (or any other domain) depend on the balance of these important neurotransmitters, and atypical levels appear to be associated with reading problems in the study. Our team has proposed a novel theoretical account that posits a link between this glutamate finding and other findings in RD, including the often reported findings (Hornickel, Anderson, Skoe, Yi, & Kraus, 2012) that RD seems to be characterized by elevated noise or variability at both the brain and behavioral levels of analysis (Hancock et al., 2017). We speculate that elevated glutamate (or abnormal glutamate/GABA ratios) underpins a kind of nonoptimal, noisy processing system in RD that can be framed as a neural noise deficit.

At a more detailed level of analysis, our team posits that neural noise leads to disruption in synchronous activity in relevant sensorimotor or language networks, and this results in abnormal neuro-oscillatory activity and concomitant learning deficits. This model links human and animal models of glutamatergic and GABA-ergic function and, among other things, the relation between elevated glutamate (or glutamate/GABA ratios) and hyperexcitability profiles. (It should be noted that some neurochemical studies have shown similar patterns of elevated glutamate in attention-deficit/hyperactivity disorder [Carrey, MacMaster, Gaudet, & Schmidt, 2007] and have been seen as evidence of hyperexcitability in these populations that can overlap with RD.) This neural noise model applied to RD generates testable hypotheses regarding both critical gene-brain pathways and learning and plasticity deficits and, thus, may address the need for deeper mechanistic models. Although ours was the first pediatric study of excitatory and inhibitory neurotransmitter levels in typically developing children and children with RD, other studies have focused on other neurochemical alterations in RD in older samples. Consistent with these previous adult studies of RD, we also observed elevated choline levels in children with RD relative to typically developing children in our study (Bruno, Lu, & Manis, 2013; Laycock et al., 2008). The finding of elevated choline in RD is not well understood at this juncture but appears quite robust across samples and ages. It may well be a reflection of abnormalities in white matter tracts that connect different brain hubs needed for reading (possibly indicating abnormalities in myelination of major axonal tracts; see Bruno et al., 2013, for details on this speculative account).

What does all this mean? The promise of this deeper dive into the neurochemistry of learning and plasticity is that an increased focus on how reading deficits in RD are mediated by the neurochemicals that underlie learning and plasticity might well provide a critical lens into the neurobiological bases of typical or atypical language and reading development and, thus, a key link in the development of more precise gene-brain-cognitive accounts of RD etiology. To push this forward and provide a critical test of the neural noise account of RD, we (Pugh, Hoeft, and colleagues) are currently engaged in new National Institutes of Health–funded studies expanding on the initial findings, with a focus on how neurochemical factors across a number of important brain regions impede or support the kinds of learning on which good reading relies. And this work, if fruitful, might hold some promise for the classroom or clinic. Although you cannot fix reading problems with medication (you need to teach decoding!), if the learner with RD has a demonstrable abnormality in excitatory/inhibitory neurochemical levels, then it might be the case that we could help prepare the brain for learning/remediation by bringing these levels into a more aligned state. We are not nearly there yet, but the prospect is exciting and drives the studies we are currently doing.

Finally, in another set of analyses from this longitudinal project, our team has examined the interrelations among genes that might confer risk for dyslexia, functional and structural brain data, and reading-related tests (Landi et al., 2013). The COMT Val/Met polymorphism is associated with reading-related skills and consistent patterns of functional neural activation (Jasińska et al., 2017). For instance, in one study (Landi et al., 2013), we examined genetic variation on a gene (*COMT*) that has been associated with learning and cognition differences, brain activity during reading, and reading test scores, and the results indicated that individuals with a specific allele that has been associated with cognitive difficulties in previous work showed both atypical brain activity for print in canonical LH circuits and lower performance on reading-related tasks. These studies are preliminary but provocative, and they do suggest that we can hope to integrate these three levels of analysis (genes, brain, behavior) to help make sense of typical or atypical development in children in the reading and language domains.

RESEARCH CONCLUSIONS ON THE NEUROBIOLOGY OF THE READING BRAIN

It is fair to conclude that extant studies of neurofunction and neurostructure (and more recently of neurochemistry) have taught us a lot about how the RD brain looks different from the typically developing brain; the findings of reduced and unstable LH activation and functional connectivity in RD have been seen across a fairly large number of studies and across multiple languages at this juncture (Richlan, Kronbichler, & Wimmer, 2011). Moreover, our team's developmental neuroimaging studies of emergent readers suggest that one can detect some of these differences at the onset of formal literacy instruction (Pugh et al., 2013); the work further suggests both important links to speech competence (Frost et al., 2009; Preston et al., 2016) and a potentially deep grounding for causal models in measures of brain chemistry (Pugh et al., 2014). Examples of other exciting new studies include those by Gaab and colleagues (in press) at Harvard that focused on examining neurofunctional and neurostructural factors that predict reading difficulties in very young preliterate children that seem to be atypical even prior to learning to read; this has implications both for causal theory and early detection going forward.

Nevertheless, although these kinds of neurobiological findings are reliable, they do not in and of themselves explain why RD manifests with these brain differences. As noted earlier, the field really needs causal brain-based models if neuroscience is to eventually deliver on its promise of improved understanding of RD. This must be the next stage of studies, and it will require integrated genetics, brain imaging, and learning measures in prospective longitudinal studies that start early and allow us to identify biomarkers early on. Despite our inability to explain these brain differences, however, neurobiological findings can provide a robust biomarker or neurophenotype for RD. Describing which brain pathways matter most for skilled reading can, in turn, lead us to explore brain targets for treatment or remediation (and a means of assessing how brain plasticity gives insights into why some children respond to a given treatment and others do not). Thus, some 2 decades into the cognitive neuroscience enterprise, we are looking at fairly consistent and replicable (including across languages) structural, functional, and emerging neurochemical descriptive accounts of RD. These descriptive accounts do not, in and of themselves, provide sufficient insight into causal mechanisms, but, more important, they do provide neural targets for treatment and learning and plasticity research, as is discussed in the next section.

THE NEUROBIOLOGY OF TREATMENT EFFECTS IN READING DISABILITY

Research findings have resulted in a greater appreciation of the heterogeneous developmental trajectories of individuals with RD and the variability in their response to treatment at the behavioral level of analysis (cf. Torgesen, 2000). As a result, there is recognition of the need for rigorous research on how to improve outcomes for individuals with RD. The promise of neuroscience is exquisite sensitivity to individual differences at multiple levels of analysis, such that neuromechanistic accounts of RD might inform our understanding of the causes of individual differences in treatment response (i.e., changes in children's reading after behavioral interventions). That is one major aim for the field; this section reviews recent findings that represent a critical first step in this enterprise.

Converging evidence from extant pre- to postimaging in treatment studies indicates that effective phonological remediation of RD (reinforcing grapheme to phoneme decoding) in children involves some degree of normalization of LH neurocircuitry and greater approximation to the integrated LH organization that characterizes typically developing readers. In one MEG study, children with severe dyslexia underwent phonics-based remediation (Simos et al., 2002). After intervention, the most salient change observed on a case-by-case basis was a robust increase in the apparent engagement of the LH TP region and a moderate reduction in activation of the RH TP areas. Similarly, a number of fMRI studies have revealed postintervention LH TP increases (Shaywitz et al., 2004; Temple et al., 2003). In a large-scale research study involving a team from Syracuse University, Yale School of Medicine, and our Haskins group (Shaywitz et al., 2004), young treatment participants with RD showed reliable gains on reading measures and reliably greater activation increases in LH reading-related sites relative to RD controls. The RD treatment group returned a year later for follow-up fMRI scans; progressive LH increases in OT, TP, and inferior frontal regions, along with decreasing RH activation patterns, were again observed. Critically, most of the studies to date suggesting some degree of LH normalization of the reading circuitry with effective treatment have focused only on the consequences of treatment response, not the online changes that drive growth during treatment. There is still an acute need, therefore, to increase our current, poorly developed understanding of the neurocognitive mechanisms on which treatment response depends and the neurobiological pathways by which it occurs. Treatment responsiveness is a good target domain for cognitive neuroscience, given its exquisite sensitivity to brain mechanisms that underpin individual differences (Pugh et al., 2013, 2014). One step in this direction is to examine the issue of variation in response, which is discussed in the next section.

TREATMENT RESPONSE AND THE PROMISE OF NEUROSCIENCE

Progress has been made in early identification and intervention for basic reading problems in young children. However, in any evidence-based treatment, significant numbers of children will fail to adequately respond. Estimates vary depending on factors such as length of treatment, age, and criterion used, but one can anticipate that in any sample there will be considerable variation in outcome. This phenomenon of treatment resistance has been amply demonstrated and remains a problem of substantial theoretical and clinical import in the literature on RD. As noted, functional neuroimaging studies suggest that the attainment of fluent skilled reading depends on the establishment and coordination of a predominantly LH brain circuitry, with TP, OT, frontal, and subcortical components (Pugh et al., 2013) and on convergence of print and speech patterns (Preston et al., 2016). Unfortunately, there have been few characterizations at cognitive or neurobiological levels of analysis of why and how trajectories of treatment resistance develop in RD. There is a need to attack questions regarding individual differences in treatment responsiveness; our team is currently engaged in such research. Our team is currently immersed in two ongoing NIH projects that use neuroimaging to better understand treatment responsiveness. This use of neuroscience seems most promising, given the exquisite sensitivity of neurocognitive measures to individual differences.

CURRENT COGNITIVE NEUROSCIENCE RESEARCH ON THE PUZZLE OF READING DISABILITY: A SUMMARY

So where are we as a field at this point? Bowers (2016) rightly noted that, for the most part, current brain research on RD and its treatment mainly documents how TD and RD groups differ. Brain studies of treatment and remediation of RD are all derived from years of good behavioral science and education research and usually simply show how the treatments affect the brain. Although several solid treatment studies are getting results in terms of learning (Connor, Kim, & Yang, in press; Lovett et al., in press), we have not as of yet delivered on a big promise that neuroscientific understanding can guide treatment (such that treatment is tailored to the individual brain). There is still work still to do to deliver on the promises made. Some exciting new directions are considered next.

TOWARD A COGNITIVE NEUROSCIENCE FOUNDATION FOR READING ACQUISITION, READING DISABILITY, AND BRAIN-INFORMED INSTRUCTION/REMEDIATION

Interdisciplinary neuroscience is yielding new discoveries every day. Our understanding of the biological bases of language and cognition lurches forward with each new set of tools or perspectives. This move toward biology is the natural next step across many fields, and there is no realistic possibility that education or cognitive psychology will revert to a state in which mapping into the brain does not matter. A deeper understanding of neuromechanisms will eventually inform educational and clinical practices, even though, as noted earlier, we have yet to see neuroscience findings directly drive teaching and remediation approaches (Bowers, 2016). Many of the ways that brain-based accounts might affect the classroom or clinic are not even imaginable at this juncture, but the exquisite sensitivity to individual differences that gene-brain-cognitive measurement affords promises better understanding of what works for whom and why down the road.

Yet, even as we in the field try to go from extant studies using brain imaging as a measure of how treatment affects the brain (and why it fails to do so for some), we also need to move toward brain-based learning approaches. Indeed, there have been some provocative new areas of research in recent years that appear promising and that our team is exploring with our clinical and education partners. One is brain-guided learning and treatment, which has been implemented in autism treatment studies (cf. LaMarca, Gevirtz, Lincoln, & Pindea, 2018) and is a major area for neuroimaging technical development at present. In this context, the learner is given varied experiences and learning/treatment contexts with concurrent brain imaging measures. The promise is that the responses of the brain to learning opportunities might give us a clear sign we are doing something useful for that learner long before this learning translates into behavioral improvement. This becomes a kind of neurofeedback paradigm, and although we are in the early days of this research, there is real enthusiasm that this is the next step beyond simply monitoring the effects of treatment to guiding the content with brain understanding.

The growing focus on measuring the brain in its social context is another new use of neuroimaging with promise for education and clinical practice. For instance, Hirsch and colleagues (2018) used a new kind of dual imaging called functional near infrared spectroscopy (fNIRS) to examine brain activity between two individuals as they interact in conversation; they showed that communication involves a kind of synchrony between the two brains, with correlated activation patterns in the language areas of the speaker and listener. New research with larger groups of individuals interacting while wearing EEG caps shows how an individual entrains to the environment or other individuals and how this entrainment to the outside world affects learning and approaches to learning (Dikker et al., 2017). Entrainment between the learner and teacher in different social contexts can be examined in this way; this can push the envelope. We can begin to gain insights into how the social context creates either an optimal or nonoptimal state for the individual learner. Again, there is much work to be done, but the promise of contextualized brain imaging is profound and logical.

In closing, here is a new direction for research. To promote these kinds of new uses (brain-guided learning and study of the social brain) in the real-world classroom context, we at Haskins Labs have put together novel partnerships with educators and other stakeholders that will allow us to explore these new domains, test the claim that we can use brain understanding to better individuate the learning environment, and tailor this environment to the ways in which the brain optimally learns or changes. The Haskins Global Language & Literacy Innovation Hub is an international interdisciplinary collaborative that brings together researchers, clinicians, educators, and education technology specialists to improve language and literacy outcomes for at-risk children across diverse languages and environments. We leverage decades of NIH-funded research at the labs and with our global partners. In addition, recent advances in developmental neuroscience and education technology provide the impetus and foundation to explore new approaches to long-standing challenges in speech, language, and literacy research, including 1) improving sensitivity of early language assessment and intervention (birth to 7), 2) delivering on the promise of neuroscience-informed reading instruction and/or remediation of reading disorders, and 3) scaling evidence-based learning and remediation practices to the global arena using education technology (e.g., Edtech). Partnerships are key; with the support of the Haskins Training Institute, we are providing opportunities for a new generation of international researchers, clinicians, and educators to work with these emergent tools and technologies. The goal of this collaborative and many others around the world is to forge new models and explicate the complex interrelationships between nature and nurture and genes and environment in order to improve learning and remediation in areas that affect the most important products of speech and language development—reading and literacy. This kind of multidisciplinarity and a willingness to push the envelope by using these new approaches to brain-guided and socially contextualized learning models promises a future full of fascinating discoveries and, frankly, a more mature state for the educational neuroscience vision. We have come some distance in mapping reading and its disorders into the brain; next, we must provide the needed research foundational to developing causal models.

REFERENCES

Beitchman, J. H., Brownlie, E. B., Inglis, A., Wild, J., Ferguson, B., & Schachter, D. (1996). Seven-year follow up of speech/language impaired and control children: Psychiatric outcome. *Journal of Child Psychology and Psychiatry, 37,* 961–970.

Beitchman, J. H., Wilson, B., Johnson, C. J., Atkinson, L., Young, A., Adlaf, E., . . . Douglas, L. (2001). Fourteen-year follow-up of speech/language-impaired and control children: Psychiatric outcome. *Journal of the American Academy of Child and Adolescent Psychiatry, 40*(1), 75–82.

Blackmon, K., Barr, W. B., Kuzniecky, R., DuBois, J., Carlson, C., Quinn, B. T., . . . Mikhly, M. (2010). Phonetically irregular word pronunciation and cortical thickness in the adult brain. *Neuroimage, 51*(4), 1453–1458.

Bowers, J. S. (2016). The practical and principled problems with educational neuroscience. *Psychological Review 123*(5), 600–612. doi:10.1037/rev0000025

Bruno, J. L., Lu, Z. L., & Manis, F. R. (2013). Phonological processing is uniquely associated with neuro-metabolic concentration. *Neuroimage, 67,* 175–181.

Carrey, N. J., MacMaster, F. P., Gaudet, L., & Schmidt, M. H. (2007). Striatal creatine and glutamate/glutamine in attention-deficit/hyperactivity disorder. *Journal of Child and Adolescent Psychopharmacology, 17,* 11–17.

Connor, C. M., Kim, Y-S. G., & Yang, D. (in press). Personalizing literacy instruction for diverse learners and children with severe literacy difficulties. In J. L. Washington, D. L. Compton, & P. McCardle (Eds.), *Dyslexia: Revisiting etiology, diagnosis, treatment, and policy.* Baltimore, MD: Paul H. Brookes Publishing Co.

Dehaene, S. (2009). *Reading in the brain: The new science of how we read.* London, England: Penguin Publishing Group.

Dehaene, S., Cohen, L., Morais, J., & Kolinsky, R. (2015). Illiterate to literate: Behavioural and cerebral changes induced by reading acquisition. *Nature Reviews: Neuroscience, 16*(4), 234–244.

Del Tufo, S. N., Frost S. J., Hoeft F., Cutting L. E., Molfese P. J., Mason G. F., . . . Pugh, K. R. (2018). Neurochemistry predicts convergence of written and spoken language: A proton magnetic resonance spectroscopy study of cross-modal language integration. *Frontiers in Psychology, 9,* 1507. doi:10.3389/fpsyg.2018.01507

Dikker, S., Wan, L., Davidesco, I., Kaggen, L., Oostrik, M., McClintock, J., . . . Poeppel, D. (2017). Brain-to-brain synchrony tracks real-world dynamic group interactions in the classroom. *Current Biology, 27*(9), 1375–1380.

Fletcher, J. M., Lyon, G. R., Fuchs, L. S., & Barnes, M. A. (2018). *Learning disabilities: From identification to intervention* (2nd ed.). New York, NY: Guilford Press.

Frost, S. J., Landi, N., Mencl, W. E., Sandak, R., Fulbright, R. K., Tejada, E. T., . . . Pugh, K. R. (2009). Phonological awareness predicts activation patterns for print and speech. *Annals of Dyslexia, 59*(1), 78–97.

Gaab, N., Turesky, T. K., & Sanfilippo, J. (in press). Early identification of children at-risk for developmental dyslexia and reading impairments: Neurobiology, screening, evidence-based response to screening, and the use of educational technology. In J. L. Washington, D. L. Compton, & P. McCardle (Eds.), *Dyslexia: Revisiting etiology, diagnosis, treatment, and policy.* Baltimore, MD: Paul H. Brookes Publishing Co.

Hancock, R. Pugh, K. R., & Hoeft, F. (2017). Neural noise hypothesis of developmental dyslexia. *Trends in Cognitive Neuroscience, 21*(6), 434–448.

Harm, M. W., & Seidenberg, M. S. (2004). Computing the meanings of words in reading: Cooperative division of labor between visual and phonological processes. *Psychological Review, 111*(3), 662–720.

Hirsch, J., Noah J. A., Zhang, X., Dravida, S., Naples, A., Ono, Y., & McPartland, J. (2018). Dynamic cross-brain neural coupling of face processes reflects the transfer of shared face information. *Society for Neuroscience 13*(9), 907–920.

Hornickel, J., Anderson, S., Skoe, E., Yi, H.-G., & Kraus, N. (2012). Subcortical representation of speech fine structure relates to reading ability. *Neuroreport, 23*(1), 6–9.

Jasińska, K. K., Molfese, P. J., Kornilov, S. A., Mencl, W. E., Frost, S. J., Lee, M., . . . Landi, N. (2017). The BDNF Val^{66}Met polymorphism is associated with structural

neuroanatomical differences in young children. *Behavioural Brain Research, 328,* 48–56. http://doi.org/10.1016/j.bbr.2017.03.014
Klingberg, T., Hedehus, M., Temple, E., Salz, T., Gabrieli, J. D., Moseley, M. E., & Poldrack, R. A. (2000). Microstructure of temporo-parietal white matter as a basis for reading ability: Evidence from diffusion tensor magnetic resonance imaging. *Neuron, 25*(2), 493–500.
LaMarca, K., Gevirtz, R., Lincoln, A. J., & Pindea. J. A. (2018). Facilitating neurofeedback in children with autism and intellectual impairments using TAGteach. *Journal of Autism and Developmental Disorders 48*(6), 2090–2100. https://doi.org/10.1007/s10803-018-3466-4
Landi, N., Frost, S. F., Mencl, W. E., Preston, J. L., Jacobsen, L. K., Lee, M., . . . Grigorenko, E. L. (2013). The COMT Val/Met polymorphism is associated with reading related skills and consistent patterns of functional neural activation. *Developmental Science, 16,* 13–23.
Laycock, S. K., Wilkinson, I. D., Wallis, L. I., Darwent, G., Wonders, S. H., Fawcett, A. J., . . . Nicolson, R. I. (2008). Cerebellar volume and cerebellar metabolic characteristics in adults with dyslexia. *Annals of the New York Academy of Sciences., 1145,* 222–236.
Liberman, A. (1992). The relation of speech to reading and writing. In R. Frost & L. Katz (Eds.), *Orthography, phonology, morphology and meaning* (pp. 167–178). New York, NY: Elsevier.
Lovett, M., Steinbach, K. A., & De Palma, M. (in press). Scaling up evidence-based interventions for reading disorders. In J. L. Washington, D. L. Compton, & P. McCardle (Eds.), *Dyslexia: Revisiting etiology, diagnosis, treatment, and policy.* Baltimore, MD: Paul H. Brookes Publishing Co.
McNorgan, C., Randazzo-Wagner, M., & Booth, J. R. (2013). Cross-modal integration in the brain is related to phonological awareness only in typical readers, not in those with reading difficulty. *Frontiers of Human Neuroscience, 7,* 388.
Paulesu, E., Démonet, J. F., Fazio, F., McCrory, E., Chanoine, V., Brunswick, N., . . . Frith, U. (2001). Dyslexia: Cultural diversity and biological unity. *Science, 291*(5511), 2165–2167.
Perfetti, C., & Hart, L. (2002). The lexical quality hypothesis. *Precursors of Functional Literacy, 11,* 67–86.
Preston, J. L., Frost, S. J., Mencl, W. E., Fulbright, R. K., Landi, N., Grigorenko, E., . . . Pugh, K. R. (2010). Early and late talkers: School-age language, literacy and neurolinguistic differences. *Brain, 133*(Pt 8), 2185–2195. http://doi.org/10.1093/brain/awq163
Preston, J. L., Molfese, P. J., Frost, S. J., Mencl, W. E., Fulbright, R. K., Hoeft, F., . . . Pugh, K. R. (2016). Print-speech convergence predicts future reading outcomes in early readers. *Psychological Science, 27*(1), 75–84.
Pugh, K. R., Frost, S. J., Rothman, D. L., Hoeft, F., Del Tufo, S. N., Mason, G. F., . . . Fulbright, R. K. (2014). Glutamate and choline levels predict individual differences in reading ability in emergent readers. *Journal of Neuroscience: The Official Journal of the Society for Neuroscience, 34*(11), 4082–4089.
Pugh, K. R., Landi, N., Preston, J. L., Mencl, W. E., Austin, A. C., Sibley, D., . . . Frost, S. J. (2013). The relationship between phonological and auditory processing and brain organization in beginning readers. *Brain and Language, 125*(2), 173–183.
Pugh, K. R., Mencl, W. E., Jenner, A. R., Katz, L., Frost, S. J., Lee, J. R., . . . Shaywitz, B. A. (2000). Functional neuroimaging studies of reading and reading disability (developmental dyslexia). *Mental Retardation and Developmental Disabilities Research Reviews, 6*(3), 207–213.
Pugh, K. R., Mencl, W. E., Shaywitz, B. A., Shaywitz, S. E., Fulbright, R. K., Constable, R. T., . . . Gore, J.C. (2000). The angular gyrus in developmental dyslexia: Task-specific differences in functional connectivity within posterior cortex. *Psychological Science, 11*(1), 51–56.
Richlan, F., Kronbichler, M., & Wimmer, H. (2011). Meta-analyzing brain dysfunctions in dyslexic children and adults. *Neuroimage, 56*(3), 1735–1742.
Shaywitz, B. A., Shaywitz, S. E., Blachman, B. A., Pugh, K. R., Fulbright, R. K., Skudlarski, P., . . . Marchione, K. E. (2004). Development of left occipitotemporal systems for skilled reading in children after a phonologically-based intervention. *Biological Psychiatry, 55*(9), 926–933.

Shaywitz, B. A., Shaywitz, S. E., Pugh, K. R., Mencl, W. E., Fulbright, R. K., Skudlarski, P., . . . Gore, J. C. (2002). Disruption of posterior brain systems for reading in children with developmental dyslexia. *Biological Psychiatry, 52,* 101–110.

Simos, P. G., Breier, J. I., Fletcher, J. M., Foorman, B. R., Castillo, E. M., & Papanicolaou, A. C. (2002). Brain mechanisms for reading words and pseudowords: An integrated approach. *Cerebral Cortex, 12,* 297–305.

Temple, E., Deutsch, G. K., Poldrack, R. A., Miller, S. L., Tallal, P., Merzenich, M. M., & Gabrieli, J. D. (2003). Neural deficits in children with dyslexia ameliorated by behavioral remediation: Evidence from functional MRI. *Proceedings of the National Academy of Sciences, 100*(5), 2860–2865.

Torgesen, J. K. (2000). Individual differences in response to early intervention in reading: The lingering problem of treatment resisters. *Learning Disabilities Research & Practice 15*(1), 55–64.

Turkeltaub, P. E., Gareau, L., Flowers, D. L., Zeffiro, T. A., & Eden, G. F. (2003). Development of neural mechanisms for reading. *Nature Neuroscience, 6*(7), 767–773. http://doi.org/10.1038/nn1065

Van den Bunt, M. R., Groen, M. A., Frost, S., Lau, A., Preston, J. L., Gracco, V. L., . . . Verhoeven, L. T. W. (2018). Sensorimotor control of speech and children's reading ability. Scientific Studies of Reading, 22(6),503–516. doi:10.1080/10888438.2018.1491583

Van den Bunt, M. R., Groen, M. A., Ito, T., Francisco, A. A., Gracco, V. L., Pugh, K. R., & Verhoeven, L. (2017). Increased response to altered auditory feedback in dyslexia: A weaker sensorimotor magnet implied in the phonological deficit. *Journal of Speech Language and Hearing Research, 60*(3), 654–667. doi:10.1044/2016_JSLHR-L-16-0201

INTEGRATIVE COMMENTARY 1

Are We Witnessing a Synthesis in the Neurobiology of Language?

Jason Zevin

SUMMARY

From the earliest modern thinking about language and the brain in the late 19th century, there has been a productive tension between two approaches. The first starts from an attempt to break language down into its component parts and then diagram what the brain basis of language might be by extrapolating from the way those parts seem to pull apart from one another or dissociate in observations of people with brain injuries or developmental disabilities. For example, some people seem to have more difficulty with the meanings of words, whereas others have more difficulty with putting words into sentences. Logically, then, there may be distinct processes in the brain that account for these two capacities. This approach is characterized by the creation of diagrams that show how distinct processes send information back and forth. The second approach is to start from an understanding of the brain rooted in biology and consider how complex language phenomena might emerge from such an organ. Freud's idea of a speech field proposes a network of associations among inputs from the senses and resonates with a late 20th-century approach often called emergentism. I describe the paper from Burenkova and Fisher and the paper from Pugh in this context and argue that they are part of a synthesis between the impulse to delineate and describe distinct language functions and the impulse to engage with the messiness of their biological substrate.

INTRODUCTION: LICHTHEIM'S HOUSE AND FREUD'S FIELD

How do we think about language—in all its complexity and in its capacity to evoke far away or imaginary places and events—and its relation to its material substrate? How does language happen in the gooey masses of our brains, in the various tissues that must be coordinated to produce its gestures, and the electrochemical impulses needed to transduce their variable consequences? I will argue that the two chapters in Section I represent a way forward that reflects a synthesis that has been gathering since the late 1990s. Since the first recognizably modern theorizing about language and the brain, there has been a creative tension between two ways of approaching this issue: on the one hand, an attempt to decompose language into parts, more or less on its own terms, with the tools of the psychologist or linguist, and on the other hand, an attempt to understand language as built up from simpler and more disparate biological processes, which need to be understood in their own terms.

Perhaps the clearest example of this tension comes from the critique leveled by Freud (1891) of Lichtheim's diagrammatic approach to understanding the contemporary literature on aphasia. Lichtheim (1885) considered various case reports of individuals who had lost more or less specific language functions as a result of brain injury. His diagrams lay out nodes (e.g., for the storage of acoustic word forms, motor word forms, and concepts), and they describe how destruction or disconnection of these nodes may be used to explain the particular patterns of impaired and spared language capacities. Thus, he explained a pattern wherein understanding of written and spoken language is impaired, whereas the capacity for speaking and writing is spared—what would come to be called Wernicke's aphasia—in terms of damage to cortical areas responsible for storing acoustic word forms. The complementary pattern, famously reported by Broca (1861), in which speech is impaired while comprehension remains intact, could be ascribed to a loss of motor word forms. In this way, by adding nodes to the network (e.g., for representing the visual and motor representations used in reading and writing) and considering how they must be connected in order to accomplish tasks such as repeating words aloud, writing to dictation, and volitional writing and speaking, Lichtheim garnered support for a model of language in the brain based on discrete, localizable centers.

Freud critiqued this approach as being rooted in a category mistake. Following Jackson (1878), he cautioned against imagining psychological constructs such as acoustic word forms as being in any way stored in collections of cells (see Guenther, 2013, & Henderson, 1992, for further discussion). Instead, he advocated considering even apparently simple psychological phenomena as being built up from complex, dynamic interactions among more or less interchangeable units whose function was defined by their connections to one another. He imagined the speech field as being a central network of associations—allowing for some localization (e.g., the specialization of auditory and motor processes by way of their proximity to peripheral sensory efferents and motor afferents)—and ascribed the relatively specific losses of function observed in the aphasia literature to disconnections of various functional assemblies from the broader associative network.

The tension between the two tendencies represented in late 19th-century theorizing about language and the brain has been remarkably durable. In the mid-twentieth century, important progress was made by carefully cataloging dissociations between specific linguistic functions in people with aphasia. This depended in part on better techniques for visualizing brain injuries in vivo, but, perhaps more important, it was due to developments in linguistic theory. In particular, the notion of deep structure—abstract, symbolic, grammatical representations that differ in kind from the perceptual, motor, or conceptual processes involved in producing the surface forms of language (Chomsky, 1965)—provided a new and more sophisticated way of thinking about linguistic functions than was available to researchers in the previous century. Geschwind (1970), whose reworking of the Lichtheim-Wernicke model still serves as a first approximation in undergraduate neuroscience textbooks, and Lenneberg (1967), whose monograph on recovery of language function after pediatric stroke is still a touchstone for research on critical periods, both drew critically on this approach. In contrast, by the turn of the 21st century, a vital program of research would be built on a consideration of how brains seem to work at a more granular level (Elman, Bates, & Johnson, 1998)—often using computer simulations that captured some aspects of learning in biological systems (Elman, 1990, 1991; Rumelhart & McClelland, 1986). The contributions from Burenkova and Fisher and from Pugh in this volume can be read not only as sympathetic to this latter tendency, but also reflect a synthesis that has emerged in the last few decades.

WHAT WOULD A GENE FOR LANGUAGE EVEN BE?

Modern notions of the innateness of language focus on the distinction between deep and surface structure developed by generative linguists. From this view, language acquisition looks little like the acquisition of other skills or behaviors as understood by learning theorists. Abandoning classical learning theory allowed generative linguists to think about the problem of language acquisition in original and interesting ways. In particular, imagining a language acquisition device that is sensitive to the abstract or deep structure of linguistic forms allowed generative theorists to deal with language at a level of description that is difficult to build up from the physical or surface structure of language in spoken, signed, or written form. Pigeons trained to peck to a light at a particular wavelength will also peck to slightly shorter and slightly longer wavelengths, demonstrating generalization based on simple physical similarity (Guttman & Kalish, 1956). As Chomsky (1959) famously argued, this kind of mechanism provides no straightforward means to do the kind of generalization that is important for linguistic functions such as distinguishing grammatical from ungrammatical sentences. Generalization from the many grammatical English sentences we may have encountered to a nonsensical, but grammatical, string such as "Colorless green ideas sleep furiously," is argued to depend on an appreciation of the systematic way grammatical sentences are produced and not on any notion of similarity that depends on surface forms.

Early studies of developmental language disability were initially understood in the context of this nativist view. That children could have difficulties with language acquisition, that these difficulties seemed to be particular to grammatical processing, that they appeared to be heritable, and so forth fit well with the idea that language acquisition required specific innate capacities whose development might be independent of other cognitive skills (Van der Lely, 2005). Indeed, this profile was initially referred to as *specific language impairment,* emphasizing this theoretical point, potentially to the detriment of children with atypical language development (Reilly et al., 2014).

Similarly, the identification of the *FOXP2* gene via careful study of the KE family was initially heralded as the discovery of a language gene (Yong, 2009). Burenkova and Fisher's thoughtful discussion of this literature lays out the problems inherent in thinking about the function of a gene (e.g., coding for proteins, regulating the functions of other genes) in terms of a complex cognitive function (e.g., syntax, speech production). This argument is similar in its outline to Freud's critique of Lichtheim. Genes cannot code for syntactic structures any more than neurons can contain acoustic word forms. An understanding of how a mutation can give rise to language disability will depend on a description of the gene's role in biological processes in the brain. In the case of *FOXP2,* a promising avenue is that it may be important for plasticity, perhaps specifically for sensory-motor learning.

Knowledge of sensory-motor representations of linguistic gestures and their sensory consequences (e.g., distinguishing /p/ from /b/), their distribution (e.g., knowing that an /s/ can follow a /p/, but not a /b/, in the same English syllable), and the transformations they can undergo (e.g., the second vowel in *repetitive* is related to the second vowel in *repeat,* and the same process works for *provoke/provocative, profane/profanity*) is the subject of phonology. As such, phonology provides an interface between the kind of formal, hierarchical representations that generative theory identifies as the computational level of description for language and its implementation as kinetic, sequential operations of the body. This is perhaps clearest in theories such as articulatory phonology (Browman & Goldstein, 1992), which provides a framework for thinking about speech as a special case of motor control for goal-directed action. From this perspective, it is not hard to see how a mutation that interferes with sensory-motor learning and motor performance might lead to a much broader pattern of language disability. That is, difficulty producing or recovering gestural information, particularly over the course of development, interferes with an individual's capacity to appreciate more abstract, deep structure.

Simulation models of language disability provide a demonstration of how this might work (Joanisse, 2004). In a neural network trained to produce present and past tense forms of verbs, interfering with phonological representations produces a pattern that captures important features of performance in the same task in children with language disabilities (Joanisse & Seidenberg, 1998). More important, although the representations in this simulation were not intended to be particularly realistic, they captured aspects of the similarity space for the phonemes of English that were important for generalization. So, correctly forming the past tenses for *bathe, bake,* and *bait* requires appreciating whether the last sound in the root form is voiced or unvoiced and/or is produced with a tongue tip gesture.

READING AND THE BRAIN

Informal histories of research on the brain basis of reading often begin with the description by Déjerine (1892) of selective word blindness, but, in fact, Lichtheim (1885) included both reading and writing in his diagrams of the language system. Coltheart (1981) picked this tradition up in earnest and developed a multicomponent model of reading on the basis of dissociations observed in the neuropsychological literature on acquired dyslexias. Although this dual route model does not imagine an innate mechanism for reading—text as a technology is too new, phylogenetically speaking—it does involve distinct mechanisms for rule-based decoding (critical for recognizing pseudowords, such as *glorp*) and a separate store for whole word knowledge (critical for recognizing words that do not follow the rules, such as *pint* and *have*) (Coltheart, Rastle, Perry, Langdon, & Ziegler, 2001). Evidence for the independence of these routes came first from observations of patients with complementary patterns of relative deficit and spared performance; surface dyslexics, who are impaired at exception word reading with a relatively spared capacity for pseudoword reading, and phonological dyslexics, who show the opposite pattern.

Much like Lichtheim's (1885) diagrams, the dual route model would be critiqued for transposing psychological constructs into the brain wholesale. And, much like Freud (1891), critics of this model would assert that the various patterns of acquired dyslexia could be better explained in terms of a field of associative units organized by their connections to periphery (representations of written and spoken words) and conceptual (semantic) representations and shaped by experience mapping from one to the other (Plaut, McClelland, Seidenberg, & Patterson, 1996; Seidenberg & McClelland, 1989). Rather than attempt to cleanly dissociate pseudoword from exception word reading (a distinction that is only sensible for a handful of relatively deep orthographies, such as English, that have large numbers of words whose pronunciations are at odds with the larger statistical patterns of the writing system), these models demonstrate how deficits in representations of conceptual or phonological knowledge interfere with performance in different ways.

As Pugh reviews in his contribution to this collection, the ability to use print to make contact with existing representations of spoken language has a long history in research on reading disability. The notion that the development of literacy depends on reorganizing hubs that are critical for speech and language processing is broadly consistent with simulation models in which representations that support reading skill are built up from experience.

Here again, the phonology plays a key role in ways that can be demonstrated in simulation models. Adding noise to phonological representations in such a model specifically interferes with its capacity to generalize to pseudowords (Harm & Seidenberg, 1999, 2004). As with the models of language impairment, noisy phonological representations prevent the model from appreciating the relevant similarity space, which, in turn, interferes with learning to map from written to spoken forms of words. That is, if a child has difficulty picking up the pronunciations of *head* and *bread,* which share the same vowel, then learning subtle statistical regularities about how the pronunciation of *ea* is probabilistically conditioned by the word body *-ead* will be more challenging than it would be for a typically developing child. Similarly, speakers of nonmainstream varieties of English may have difficulties with particular mappings in which their variety has greater ambiguity (Washington et al., 2013). This raises a more general concern about how inequality in the distribution of educational resources concords with language differences that may create additional difficulties in learning to read. Many people around the world learn to read in a language or language variety that is different from what is spoken at home, often due to a history of migration, colonization, or other forces determining the concentration of political and economic power in the hands of people whose everyday language use is closer to the official language of instruction for literacy.

CONCLUSION

I have been describing these arguments in a way that gives the advantage to the Freudian critique of Lichtheim in part because of my own sympathies, in part because of a tendency to view science as making progress over time so that more recent theories appear more correct than earlier ones, and in part because of the two chapters discussed. But in the spirit of another late 19th-century German theorist, I would rather like to suggest that the more emergentist models reflect a synthesis, rather than a complete break from the initial thesis that the brain's organization for language is somehow isomorphic with the abilities we can observe in the lab. Of course, we cannot know what a fundamentally emergentist science of the brain and language or dyslexia might have looked like if it did not have a diagrammatic counterpoint to push against. For a variety of reasons—technical, philosophical, and sociological—diagrammatic models were resurrected and took off in the 1960s and 1970s, setting the terms of the debate for the following decades. For example, Shotter (1997) argued that the information processing paradigm drew much of its appeal from its metaphorical grounding in the familiar environment of the white-collar office, with its organizational charts and sharp divisions between executive functions and functions carried out by hourly employees. He noted, for example, Minsky's (1988) use of bureaucratic metaphors throughout his classic artificial intelligence treatise *Society of Mind.* Even emergentist theorists, inspired as they may have been by more organic forms of organization and control, measured their success by their ability to account for patterns of acquired and developmental language disability initially mapped out on the charts laid out by diagram makers.

As a new generation of scientists addresses these issues, they have the benefit of more sophisticated metaphors for how the brain works and more sophisticated tools for trying out their models in silica. Network theory, deep learning, and big data are part of our world in the same way that filing cabinets and physical inboxes and outboxes were part of Marvin Minsky's. This bodes well for a new cycle of emergentist thinking about language and the brain. And yet there is nagging doubt that without some sort of human-readable diagram, we will not be able to understand our own theories.

REFERENCES

Broca, P. (1861). Remarques sur le siège de la faculté du langage articulé, suivies d'une observation d'aphémie (perte de la parole). *Bulletin et Memoires de la Societe Anatomique de Paris, 6,* 330–357.
Browman, C. P., & Goldstein, L. (1992). Articulatory phonology: An overview. *Phonetica, 49,* 155 180.
Chomsky, N. (1959). A review of B.F. Skinner's *Verbal Behavior. Language, 35,* 26–58.
Chomsky, N. A. (1965). *Aspects of the theory of syntax.* Cambridge, MA: The MIT Press.
Coltheart, M. (1981). Disorders of reading and their implications for models of normal reading. *Visible Language, 15,* 245–286.
Coltheart, M., Rastle, K., Perry, C., Langdon, R., & Ziegler, J. (2001). DRC: A dual route cascaded model of visual word recognition and reading aloud. *Psychological Review, 108*(1), 204–256.
Déjerine, J. (1892). Contributionà l'étude anatomopathologique et clinique des différents variétés de cécité verbale. *Mémoires de la Société de Biologie, 4,* 61–90.
Elman, J. L. (1990). Finding structure in time. *Cognitive Science, 14,* 179–211.
Elman, J. L. (1991). Distributed representations, simple recurrent networks, and grammatical structure. *Machine Learning, 7,* 195–225.
Elman, J. L., Bates, E. A., & Johnson, M. H. (1998). *Rethinking innateness: A connectionist perspective on development.* Cambridge, MA: The MIT Press.
Freud, S. (1891). *On aphasia.* Madison, CT: International Universities Press.
Geschwind, N. (1970). The organization of language and the brain. *Science, 170,* 940–944.
Guenther, K. (2013). The disappearing lesion: Sigmund Freud, sensory-motor physiology, and the beginnings of psychoanalysis. *Modern Intellectual History, 10,* 569–601.
Guttman, N., & Kalish, H. I. (1956). Discriminability and stimulus generalization. *Journal of Experimental Psychology, 51,* 79–88.
Harm, M. W., & Seidenberg, M. S. (1999). Phonology, reading, and dyslexia: Insights from connectionist models. *Psychological Review, 163,* 491–528.
Harm, M. W., & Seidenberg, M. S. (2004). Computing the meanings of words in reading: Cooperative division of labor between visual and phonological processes. *Psychological Review, 111,* 662–720.
Henderson, V. W. (1992). Sigmund Freud and the diagram-maker school of aphasiology. *Brain and Language, 43,* 19–41.
Jackson, J. (1878). On affections of speech from disease of the brain. *Brain, 1,* 304–330.
Joanisse, M. F. (2004). Specific language impairments in children: Phonology, semantics, and the English past tense. *Current Directions in Psychological Science, 13,* 156–160.
Joanisse, M. F., & Seidenberg, M. S. (1998). Specific language impairment: A deficit in grammar or processing? *Trends in Cognitive Sciences, 2,* 240–247.
Lenneberg, E. L. (1967). *Biological foundations of language.* New York, NY: Wiley.
Lichtheim, L. (1885). On aphasia. *Brain, 7,* 433–484.
Minsky, M. (1988). *Society of mind.* New York, NY: Simon and Schuster.
Plaut, D. C., McClelland, J. L., Seidenberg, M. S., & Patterson, K. (1996). Understanding normal and impaired word reading: Computational principles in quasi-regular domains. *Psychological Review, 103,* 56–115.

Reilly, S., Tomblin, B., Law, J., McKean, C., Mensah, F. K., Morgan, A., . . . Wake, M. (2014). Specific language impairment: A convenient label for whom? *International Journal of Language and Communication Disorders, 49,* 416–451.
Rumelhart, D. E., & McClelland, J. L. (1986). *Parallel distributed processing: Explorations in the microstructure of cognition. Volume 1: Foundations.* Cambridge, MA: The MIT Press.
Seidenberg, M. S., & McClelland, J. L. (1989). A distributed, developmental model of word recognition and naming. *Psychological Review, 96,* 523–568.
Shotter, J. (1997). Cognition as a social practice: From computer power to word power. In D. M. Johnson & C. E. Erneling (Eds.), *The future of the cognitive revolution* (pp. 317–334). New York, NY: Oxford University Press.
Van der Lely, H. K. (2005). Domain-specific cognitive systems: Insight from grammatical-SLI. *Trends in Cognitive Sciences, 9,* 53–59.
Washington, J. A., Terry, N. P., Seidenberg, M. S., Stone, C., Silliman, E., Ehren, B., & Apel, K. (2013). Language variation and literacy learning: The case of African American English. In C. A. Stone, E. R. Silliman, B. J. Ehren, & K. Apel (Eds.), *Handbook of language and literacy: Development and disorders* (pp. 204–221). New York, NY: Guilford.
Yong, E. (2009). *Revisiting* FOXP2 *and the origins of language.* Retrieved from http://blogs.discovermagazine.com/notrocketscience/2009/11/11/revisiting-foxp2-and-the-origins-of-language/

SECTION II

Typical Language Development (Spoken and Written)

CHAPTER 4

Building a Lexicon

Jenny Saffran

SUMMARY

How do infants come to understand their native language? Early exposure to the sounds of language helps infants figure out how their language works, including which sounds are words and what those words might mean. Infants understand far more than they can say, and they make sense of what they hear in surprisingly subtle ways. Infants and children with developmental disabilities show differences in their learning trajectories in ways that may help to explain some of their successes and challenges in native language learning. In sum, understanding learning itself may help us to better understand the apparently miraculous act of acquiring a native language (or two, for bilingual infants).

INTRODUCTION

Infants go from being linguistic generalists to acquiring detailed information about their native language (or languages) over the course of the first year of postnatal life. They shift from exhibiting general preferences for speech over nonspeech, and infant-directed speech over adult-directed speech, to exhibiting preferences for patterns particular to their own experiences. These feats of learning are even more extraordinary when one considers who is doing the learning: infants, who are often described as preverbal or prelinguistic.

In this chapter, I will consider the learning abilities that facilitate infants' transition from tracking sounds to skilled language comprehension. In particular, I will ask how it is that tracking patterns of sounds facilitates learning words. I will then review recent studies from my lab that are focused on how toddlers begin to understand the meanings of words. I will raise issues throughout about potential downstream consequences of individual differences in these abilities, particularly as they may relate to atypical developmental trajectories.

DISCOVERING SOUND PATTERNS THAT MIGHT BE WORDS

Starting in the mid-1990s, researchers began to investigate the learning abilities that might be responsible for infants' rapid acquisition of native linguistic information. Much of this work focused on infants' detection of regularities in the input, including structural and prosodic patterns (e.g., Morgan & Demuth, 1996). In one such line of research, we tested the hypothesis that infants might be tracking statistical regularities in the input (Aslin, Saffran, & Newport, 1998; Saffran, Aslin, & Newport, 1996). We hypothesized that tracking statistical regularities, such as the probabilities of syllable co-occurrence, would facilitate such processes as detecting words in fluent speech (see Saffran & Kirkham, 2018, for a review). More important, however, these studies did not directly measure whether infants actually treated the high-probability sequences as word-like units. That is, although these studies—and many others—were described as putatively tapping word segmentation processes, they were not actually designed to determine whether infants actually extracted words from continuous speech.

Our subsequent studies were designed to test the hypothesis that statistical learning processes rendered candidate words (Graf Estes, Evans, Alibali, & Saffran, 2007; Hay, Pelucchi, Graf Estes, & Saffran, 2011). We reasoned that if strong statistical properties led infants to detect words in fluent speech, then those units should be treated as better labels for objects than sequences with weaker statistical properties. As in the earlier studies, we exposed infants to sequences of continuous speech, using either artificial languages (Aslin et al., 1998) or unfamiliar natural languages (Pelucchi, Hay, & Saffran, 2009). We then trained the infants on novel label–object pairs, with labels drawn from the continuous speech stream. Crucially, the labels were either words from the fluent speech or equally familiar sequences with weaker statistical properties. The results revealed better label–object mapping when the novel labels were words from the fluent speech. Indeed, the evidence suggests that the statistical properties of fluent speech affect word learning across a range of tasks, including native language word learning, lexical category learning, and discerning phonological properties of the native language (e.g., Graf Estes, Edwards, & Saffran, 2011; Hay, Graf Estes, Wang, & Saffran, 2015; Lany & Saffran, 2010, 2011).

One important implication is that differences in what infants glean from speech input have major downstream effects on learning. The output of one learning process (tracking statistical regularities in native language input) affects other learning processes (mapping candidate words to their meanings). This cascade of learning may help us to understand an array of phenomena, such as the well-documented finding that infants who receive less input are less efficient at language processing and have smaller vocabularies than infants who receive more input.

Infants who receive less and/or poorer quality input (e.g., infants growing up in poverty) have fewer opportunities to extract regularities from their input, hindering downstream word learning. We observed this type of relationship in a study of word learning in the presence of background noise (McMillan & Saffran, 2016). Prior to the word learning task, toddlers heard some of the words embedded in sentences. Simply hearing the sounds of the words facilitated learning when the words were later presented in noise. Prior exposure to the sounds of words helped toddlers facing poor quality word learning input.

Considering individual differences is another way to think about the relationship between facility at tracking the input and downstream outcomes. For example, children with some types of developmental disabilities are at greater risk for language disorders than others. It is interesting to note that children with Developmental Language Disorder (DLD) perform worse on statistical language learning tasks that require tracking of sound sequences than children with typical development (Evans, Saffran, & Robe-Torres, 2009; Haebig, Saffran, & Ellis Weismer, 2017). These differences are also observed for nonlinguistic statistical learning tasks, including sequences of tones and shapes (e.g., Evans et al., 2009; Tomblin, Mainela-Arnold, & Zhang, 2007). Similarly, young adults with developmental dyslexia also show relatively poor performance on nonlinguistic statistical learning tasks (Gabay, Thiessen, & Holt, 2015). Metalinguistic analyses for both DLD and developmental dyslexia suggest difficulties for tasks that require implicitly detecting regularities (Lum et al., 2013, 2014).

More important, not all groups of children with developmental disabilities show challenges in statistical learning. Infants with Williams syndrome, an inherited form of intellectual disability, performed akin to typical infants on a linguistic statistical learning task (Cashon, Ha, Graf Estes, Saffran, & Mervis, 2016). Of note, language attainment is relatively strong for individuals with Williams syndrome, consistent with the view that statistical learning abilities support native language learning processes. Individuals with autism spectrum disorder (ASD) also exhibit age-typical performance on statistical learning tasks, despite well-documented communication challenges for many people with ASD (e.g., Haebig et al., 2017; Mayo & Eigsti, 2012; though see Scott-Van Zeeland et al., 2010). It is possible, though, that this level of performance reflects sampling. Children with ASD who participate in statistical learning studies are usually high functioning because of task demands (see Obeid, Brooks, Powers, Gillespie-Lynch, & Lum, 2016, for a meta-analysis). More generally, examining individual differences both within and across groups will be hugely informative in helping us to uncover relationships between learning abilities and native language outcomes.

DISCERNING INFANTS' LEXICAL REPRESENTATIONS

Turning to the meaning side of words, the situation becomes even more complicated and difficult to study. Even very young infants recognize the word *apple.* But what do they actually think that the word *apple* means? Different adults have different representations of the meanings of words as a function of experience. What does *apple* actually mean, and how can we get at this question with young children?

One way that we have addressed this question is by manipulating object properties to ask what aspects of word meaning are prioritized by different children. To do so, we altered the prototypical colors of highly familiar objects (e.g., a pink cow and a Holstein-colored pig; Perry & Saffran, 2017). Overall, toddlers' word recognition was disrupted by color changes. Even more interesting is the finding that the toddlers who were most disrupted were those whose vocabularies contained a higher proportion of words for non–shape-based categories (e.g., liquids, mass nouns). These data suggest that children may prioritize different aspects of objects in their representations of familiar words, with some children focusing more on shape and others focusing more on other attributes of objects. It is unclear whether intrinsic differences between toddlers' initial prioritizations of properties cause them to more readily learn some words than others or whether idiosyncratic differences in the words toddlers happened to learn first lead to differences in their subsequent interpretations of meaning. Causal direction aside, it is intriguing to find individual differences in lexical access that are predicted by the structure of toddlers' vocabularies.

We can also manipulate early lexical representations in the lab. Consider the object *apple.* We can point to it linguistically by calling out a variety of different dimensions of "appleness:" "Where's the apple?" "Where's the red one?" "Which one can you eat?" Pomper and Saffran (2016) tested the hypothesis that the way we label things sets up expectations for children, such that a switch in the dimension guiding the naming event will slow lexical access. Three-year-old children viewed a sequence of familiar objects, labeled either with their name ("Where's the apple?") or their color ("Where's the red one?"). Halfway through the study, the labeling dimension was switched from name to color or vice versa. Children were slower to shift their gaze to the target object right after the switch, analogous to their performance in executive function tasks like the dimensional change card sort. Notably, this challenge was transient; once children adapted to the new labeling dimension, lexical access sped up again. These data suggest that there are switch costs in language comprehension, such that once a labeling dimension is primed, comprehension is slower when the labeling dimension changes. Indeed, switching may represent a constant challenge in everyday language comprehension.

As little as we know about lexical representations in typically developing children, we know even less about how children with language disorders represent meaning. One group of particular interest is children with ASD, whose delays in lexical comprehension are even greater than those for production (Ellis Weismer, Lord, & Esler, 2010). The types of standardized tasks typically used to assess language comprehension do not help this situation. Examiner-administered measures often require social interaction, which is challenging for many children with ASD, whereas parental report measures underestimate vocabulary knowledge in toddlers with ASD (Venker, Haebig, Edwards, Saffran, & Ellis Weismer, 2016).

Experimental measures using gaze-tracking have potential as an alternate route to investigating language comprehension. For example, Ellis Weismer, Haebig, Edwards, Saffran, and Venker (2016) used an eye-gaze task to assess lexical comprehension when familiar target objects were put into competition with foils that were either semantically or visually similar to the target. Toddlers with ASD performed more poorly overall in recognizing the target objects than a group of typically developing toddlers (matched on the Bayley Scales of Infant and Toddler Development, Third Edition). It is interesting to note that toddlers with ASD with the smallest vocabularies (as measured by parental report) were especially disrupted by perceptual overlap, failing to shift their gaze to a cake when it was labeled in the presence of a similarly colored and shaped hat. These findings speak to the importance of broad samples, which requires developing tasks with minimal demands.

These results, and many others, suggest that we must look beyond how infants learn and process individual words to investigate interactions between words themselves in the nascent lexicon. A line of research focused on the ontogeny of lexical networks addressed the question of whether toddlers connect new lexical entries to one another during learning (Wojcik & Saffran, 2013, 2015). Toddlers were first trained on individual label–object pairs. Crucially, each object was visually similar to another object. We then tested the toddlers using a variant of the Headturn Preference Procedure that we had developed to investigate semantic priming (Willits, Wojcik, Seidenberg, & Saffran, 2013). The results revealed that preferences for pairs of novel words were affected by the visual similarity of the objects to which those words referred, even in the absence of the objects themselves. These results suggest that as young children learn new words, they integrate them into a network of interrelationships.

FINAL THOUGHTS

It is increasingly evident that infants are remarkably good at detecting structure in their world and using that structure to build sophisticated representations, including linguistic ones. Even young learners generate predictions about upcoming events and learn from violations of those predictions (Benitez & Saffran, 2018; Reuter, Emberson, Romberg, & Lew-Williams, 2018; Romberg & Saffran, 2013; Stahl & Feigenson, 2015), and disruptions in these processes may help us to understand atypical developmental trajectories (e.g., Sinha et al., 2014). Far from being preverbal or prelinguistic, infants and toddlers have nuanced linguistic abilities that we are only just beginning to understand. As we continue to uncover the learning processes that underpin successful language acquisition, we will also be in a better position to understand why some children exhibit challenges in learning their native language.

REFERENCES

Aslin, R. N., Saffran, J. R., & Newport, E. L. (1998). Computation of conditional probability statistics by 8-month-old infants. *Psychological Science, 9*(4), 321–324.

Benitez, V., & Saffran, J. R. (2018). Predictable events enhance word learning in toddlers. *Current Biology, 28,* 1–7. https://doi.org/10.1016/j.cub.2018.06.017

Cashon, C. H., Ha, O. R., Graf Estes, K., Saffran, J. R., & Mervis, C. B. (2016). Infants with Williams syndrome detect statistical regularities in continuous speech. *Cognition, 154,* 165–168.
Ellis Weismer, S., Haebig, E., Edwards, J., Saffran, J. R., & Venker, C. (2016). Lexical processing in toddlers with ASD: Does weak central coherence play a role? *Journal of Autism and Developmental Disorders, 46*(12), 3755–3769.
Ellis Weismer, S., Lord, C., & Esler, A. (2010). Early language patterns of toddlers on the autism spectrum compared to toddlers with developmental delay. *Journal of Autism and Developmental Disorders, 40*(10), 1259–1273.
Evans, J. L., Saffran, J. R., & Robe-Torres, K. (2009). Statistical learning in children with specific language impairment. *Journal of Speech, Language, and Hearing Research, 52*(2), 321–335.
Gabay, Y., Thiessen, E. D., & Holt, L. L. (2015). Impaired statistical learning in developmental dyslexia. *Journal of Speech, Language, and Hearing Research, 58*(3), 934–945.
Graf Estes, K., Edwards, J., & Saffran, J. R. (2011). Phonotactic constraints on infant word learning. *Infancy, 16,* 180–197.
Graf Estes, K., Evans, J., Alibali, M. W., & Saffran, J. R. (2007). Can infants map meaning to newly segmented words? Statistical segmentation and word learning. *Psychological Science, 18,* 254–260.
Haebig, E., Saffran, J. R., & Ellis Weismer, S. (2017). Statistical word learning in children with autism spectrum disorders and specific language impairment. *Journal of Child Psychology and Psychiatry, 58,* 1251–1263.
Hay, J., Graf Estes, K., Wang, T., & Saffran, J. R. (2015). From flexibility to constraint: The contrastive use of lexical tone in early word learning. *Child Development, 86,* 10–20.
Hay, J. F., Pelucchi, B., Graf Estes, K., & Saffran, J. R. (2011). Linking sounds to meanings: Infant statistical learning in a natural language. *Cognitive Psychology, 63,* 93–106.
Lany, J., & Saffran, J. R. (2010). From statistics to meanings: Infant acquisition of lexical categories. *Psychological Science, 21,* 284–291.
Lany, J., & Saffran, J. R. (2011). Interactions between statistical and semantic information in infant language development. *Developmental Science, 14,* 1207–1219.
Lum, J. A., Conti-Ramsden, G., Morgan, A. T., & Ullman, M. T. (2014). Procedural learning deficits in specific language impairment (SLI): A meta-analysis of serial reaction time task performance. *Cortex, 51,* 1–10.
Lum, J. A., Ullman, M. T., & Conti-Ramsden, G. (2013). Procedural learning is impaired in dyslexia: Evidence from a meta-analysis of serial reaction time studies. *Research in Developmental Disabilities, 34,* 3460–3476.
Mayo, J., & Eigsti, I. M. (2012). Brief report: A comparison of statistical learning in school-aged children with high functioning autism and typically developing peers. *Journal of Autism and Developmental Disorders, 42*(11), 2476–2485.
McMillan, B., & Saffran, J. R. (2016). Learning in complex environments: The effects of background speech on early word learning. *Child Development, 87*(6), 1841–1855.
Morgan, J. L., & Demuth, K. (1996). Signal to syntax: An overview. In J. L. Morgan & K. Demuth (Eds.), *Signal to syntax: Bootstrapping from speech to grammar in early acquisition* (pp. 1–22). Mahwah, NJ: Lawrence Erlbaum.
Obeid, R., Brooks, P. J., Powers, K. L., Gillespie-Lynch, K., & Lum, J. A. (2016). Statistical learning in specific language impairment and autism spectrum disorder: A meta-analysis. *Frontiers in Psychology, 7,* 1245. doi:10.3389/fpsyg.2016.01245
Pelucchi, B., Hay, J. F., & Saffran, J. R. (2009). Statistical learning in a natural language by 8-month-old infants. *Child Development, 80,* 674–685.
Perry, L., & Saffran, J. R. (2017). Is a pink cow still a cow? Individual differences in toddlers' vocabulary knowledge and lexical representations. *Cognitive Science, 41*(4), 1090–1105.
Pomper, R., & Saffran, J. R. (2016). Roses are red, socks are blue: Switching dimensions disrupts young children's language processing. *PLoS ONE, 11*(6), e0158459. doi:10.1371/journal
Reuter, T., Emberson, L., Romberg, A., & Lew-Williams, C. (2018). Individual differences in nonverbal prediction and vocabulary size in infancy. *Cognition, 176,* 215–219.

Romberg, A. R., & Saffran, J. R. (2013). Expectancy learning from probabilistic input by infants. *Frontiers in Psychology, 3*, 610. doi:10.3389/fpsyg.2012.00610

Saffran, J. R., Aslin, R. N., & Newport, E. L. (1996). Statistical learning by 8-month-old infants. *Science, 274*, 1926–1928.

Saffran, J. R., & Kirkham, N. Z. (2018). Infant statistical learning. *Annual Review of Psychology, 69*, 181–203.

Scott-Van Zeeland, A. A., McNealy, K., Wang, A. T., Sigman, M., Bookheimer, S. Y., & Dapretto, M. (2010). No neural evidence of statistical learning during exposure to artificial languages in children with autism spectrum disorders. *Biological Psychiatry, 68*(4), 345–351.

Sinha, P., Kjelgaard, M. M., Gandhi, T. K., Tsourides, K., Cardinaux, A. L., Pantazis, D., . . . Held, R. M. (2014). Autism as a disorder of prediction. *Proceedings of the National Academy of Sciences, 111*(42), 15220–15225.

Stahl, A. E., & Feigenson, L. (2015). Observing the unexpected enhances infants' learning and exploration. *Science, 348*(6230), 91–94.

Tomblin, J. B., Mainela-Arnold, E., & Zhang, X. (2007). Procedural learning in adolescents with and without specific language impairment. *Language Learning and Development, 3*(4), 269–293.

Venker, C., Haebig, E., Edwards, J., Saffran, J. R., & Ellis Weismer, S. (2016). Early lexical comprehension in young children with ASD: Comparing looking-while-listening and parent report. *Journal of Autism and Developmental Disorders, 46(6)*, 2260–2266.

Willits, J., Wojcik, E., Seidenberg, M., & Saffran, J. R. (2013). Lexical semantic knowledge in 24-month-olds. *Infancy, 18*, 1053–1075.

Wojcik, E., & Saffran. J. R. (2013). Toddlers encode similarity structure when learning novel words. *Psychological Science, 24*, 1898–1905.

Wojcik, E., & Saffran, J. R. (2015). Toddlers encode the lexical structure of novel words from meaningful sentences. *Cognition, 138*, 10–20.

CHAPTER 5

Reading in Grades 2 and 3

Eye Tracking and Neuropsychological Analysis

Tatiana V. Akhutina, Aleksi A. Korneev, and Ekaterina Y. Matveeva

SUMMARY

The present study was designed and conducted to assess primary school students' reading strategies using eye tracking. The first objective was to assess the differences in eye movements for silent reading in Russian for students in the second and third grades. The second objective was to analyze the characteristics of reading and eye movements in third-graders with different levels of executive functions (EF). The sample consisted of 30 second-grade students and 42 third-grade students who read sentences from a corpus specifically developed for reading studies in the Russian language. Results showed that third-graders make fewer fixations when reading, and the total fixation duration is significantly less compared with second-graders. Also, a number of differences in the characteristics of eye movements in third-graders with different levels of EF were found. These differences indicate the important role of EF in the development of the technical components of the reading skill.

Key words: silent reading, eye tracking, neuropsychology, EF, primary school students

INTRODUCTION

In recent decades, the eye-tracking methodology, which allows one to conduct a detailed analysis of one technical component of reading behavior, was actively used in studies of the structure and development of reading skills (Blythe & Joseph, 2011; Radach & Kennedy, 2004; Rayner, 1998). A significant number of studies have observed the development of reading comprehension, investigated the changes in reading strategies, and traced existing strategies of reading and their relationship with the level of cognitive functioning of children.

The dynamics of development of reading technical skills are mostly studied using children reading in English (Zawoyski, Ardoin, & Binder, 2014) or German (Tiffin-Richards & Schroeder, 2015; Vorstius, Radach, & Lonigan, 2014). A large-scale study of silent and oral sentence reading in Grade 1–5 students (Vorstius et al., 2014) showed that children demonstrate significantly reduced fixation duration for the first pass through the text,

This work was supported by the Russian Foundation for Basic Research, project no. 16-06-00374. In addition, we are grateful to Anastasia Lopukhina, Anna Laurinavichiute, and Olga Dragoy (Laboratory of Neurolinguistics of Higher School of Economics) for their help in the organization of this research.

a reduced percentage of repeated fixations on the word, and an increased amplitude of saccades in the period of transition from second to third grade. First fixation duration, rereading time, and number of regressions do not appear to change from second to third grade. A longitudinal study of reading in German in Grades 1–4 (Sperlich, Meixner, & Laubrock, 2016) revealed an equal increase in perceptual span for children with different reading speeds. There are a very limited number of similar studies involving other languages, even major ones, such as Russian. It is important to mention a study carried out by Ivanov, Demidov, and Bezrukikh (2010) that showed decreases in fixation duration and saccade amplitudes between first- and fourth-graders when reading texts of different complexity. The main characteristics of the eye movements of second-grade students are discussed in our previous articles (Korneev, Matveeva, & Akhutina, 2017, 2018). Among other factors, we have confirmed the known effects of word length and word frequency on eye movements during reading. Continuing this line of research, we examined the development of reading skills in primary school students during the second and third grades.

A second important line of research on children's reading skills explores the relationship between characteristics of reading development and cognitive functions (Dehaene, 2009; Fletcher & Grigorenko, 2017). Studies have shown that processing auditory and visual information are particularly important for reading (Bosse, Tainturier, & Valdois, 2007; Lobier, Peyrin, Pichat, Le Bas, & Valdois, 2014; Peyrin, Démonet, N'Guyen-Morel, Le Bas, & Valdois, 2011; Pham & Hasson, 2014; Shaywitz & Shaywitz, 2005). There is evidence that 19%–32% of children with dyslexia demonstrate deficits in phonological processing, whereas 34%–44% have visual attention deficits, 15%–17% exhibit double deficiency, and 17%–22% have no deficits in either auditory or visuospatial information processing (Zoubrinetzky, Bielle, Valdois, 2014). The question arises whether a deficit in EF is the main cause of reading difficulties in the last category of children. Before turning to the role of these functions in reading, it is important to note that the role of the phonological component depends on language; it is more critical in languages with deep orthographies and less important when the orthography is transparent (Melby-Lervåg, Lyster, & Hulme, 2012). Russian belongs to the group of languages with more transparent orthography; thus, the role of phonology should be less significant. This is consistent with data showing that it is not phonological but visuospatial information processing and EF that play the most important roles in viewing time and number of fixations in second-graders' reading skills (Korneev et al., 2018).

Let us consider the role of EF in more detail. Even though it has long been known that EF are involved in the processes of reading, research on the matter has intensified since 2010 (Arrington, Kulesz, Francis, Fletcher, & Barnes, 2014; Britton & Glynn, 2013; Cartwright, 2012; see Titz & Karbach, 2014, for review). The role of EF in understanding discourse is generally established. However, in the literature there are conflicting data on the connection between a deficit of EF and the technique of reading. The most widely used paradigm in studies of reading—the single-word reading paradigm—is insufficient to identify the role of EF in the reading process. But single-word reading does not allow one to analyze the influence of context on written text decoding and reading comprehension. Like Tomasello (2008), we apply a wide definition of *context,* which includes motivation and expectations of the reader and knowledge of the subject matter of the text, as well as the characteristics of the dictionary and structure of text itself. Flexible, purposeful behavior that takes into account the external and internal context is closely related to EF.

Given the ambiguity of the term *executive functions,* we would like to make it clear that we understand them using Luria's (1973) definition—the functions of programming, regulation, and control of activity. In our view, Luria's approach is close to the modern understanding of EF, which proposes the diversity of these functions detected in separate tasks in the presence of one common latent variable (Miyake et al., 2000). Luria developed factor (or syndrome) neuropsychological analysis, which is most suitable for isolating latent variables. For example, a study by Reiter, Tucha, and Lange (2005) showed deficits of verbal and visual working memory, problems with inhibition (in Stroop test), planning (tower of London), and flexibility (letters and numbers choice task) in children with dyslexia. Thus, the analysis of the influence of EF on reading was based on a comparison of reading and performance on separate tests. The Lurian approach involves the allocation of the common denominator from separate tasks, directed at diagnosing one function (i.e., the extraction of the neuropsychological factor). Methods of neuropsychological assessment of 6- to 8-year-old children developed by our team (Akhutina et al., 2016) meet this requirement and contain an algorithm for summarizing the results of separate unidirectional tests.

The unresolved question about the technique of reading in the presence of EF deficits and the principle possibility of its solution using the methods of eye-tracking analysis and the Lurian neuropsychological approach made it possible to establish the second objective of this work—to examine the contribution of EF in the organization of reading techniques in third-grade students.

COMPARISON OF EYE MOVEMENTS OF SECOND- AND THIRD-GRADE STUDENTS

The first study addressed eye movements of second- and third-grade students.

Method

Sample. The sample consisted of 65 primary school students: 30 second-grade students (14 females, 16 males, mean age 8.76 ± 0.38) and 35 third-grade students (14 females, 21 males, mean age 9.53 ± 0.40).

Eye movement recording. All children read sentences from the corpus for the study of Russian reading in primary school students (Korneev et al.,

2017). The corpus consists of 30 sentences including the target word controlled for length (three to eight letters) and frequency (high frequency—above 60 ipm, low frequency—under 30 ipm). The frequency was determined using a subcorpus of children's texts of the *National Corpus of the Russian Language* (http://ruscorpora.ru). The length of sentences was from six to nine words; the target word was never first or last. The monospaced font Ubuntu Mono Normal, size 26 point was used.

Each student was asked to silently read the sentences on the computer screen and be ready to answer questions about their content. Before and in the middle of the session, the eye-tracking device was calibrated. The presentation of the sentence was organized as follows: In the beginning, a fixation point appeared at the left edge of the screen. After the student fixated on it for 500 ms, the point disappeared, and a sentence appeared. The student read it and, at the end of the reading, was instructed to fixate on the area marked with a circle in the lower right corner of the screen. After fixating for 500 ms, the text disappeared, and after a pause of 2 s, the next sentence was presented.

Cognitive functions assessment. All students were tested with a neuropsychological assessment battery designed for children 6–8 years old (Akhutina et al., 2016). It consists of 20 trials and allows testing different components of children's cognitive functions using a special indexing procedure.

Experimental setting. Eye movements were recorded with an EyeLink 1000 device (SR Research), sampling rate 1000 Hz. The student was sitting in front of the screen (diagonal: 22 inch; monitor refresh rate: 200 Hz) at a distance of 90 cm, with the head held stationary with a chin rest.

Analysis of results. Primary processing of eye movement records was carried out using specialized software aimed at distinguishing fixations and saccades (Data Viewer, SR research). Only fixations and saccades that referred to the keywords in the test sentences were included in the further analysis.

The following parameters were calculated for each student: 1) First fixation duration (FFD), 2) Single fixation duration (SFD), 3) Total fixation time on a single word before moving to the next word (gaze duration, GD), 4)) The total duration of the fixations on the word throughout the sample (total viewing time, TT), 5) The total number of fixations on the word (fixation count, FC), 6) The probability of skipping a word (no fixations, SKIPS).

Those fixations shorter than 80 ms or more than 2.5 standard deviations longer than the average duration of fixations over the sample were excluded from the analysis. The data was averaged for word frequency (high and low) and word length.

The influence of frequency, word length, and age (grade) factors was estimated using (generalized) linear mixed models ([G]LMM) with word frequency, length, and class as fixed factors and subject and word as random factors. Statistical analysis was performed using the R software package (version 3.2.5); calculation and evaluation of models was made using lme4 and lmerTest packages.

Auditory processing functions and visuospatial processing functions were calculated on the basis of the neuropsychological assessment generalized indexes of EF. These indexes were calculated on the basis of penalty points and were standardized. Thus, the zero value index corresponds to the average result for the given sample: the positive value means the relative weakness of the function, and the negative value corresponds to above the average level.

Study 1 Results: Eye Movement Analysis in Second- and Third-Grade Students

Average parameters of the fixation duration time (FFD, SFD, GD, and TT) are presented in Figure 5.1, and the results of (G)LMM, estimating the effect of length and frequency factors of words and age (grade) on fixation duration, are presented in Table 5.1.

The figure and table show that the effect of length is observed in relation to SFD, GD, and TT, and the effect of frequency in relation to FFD, GB, and TT. The factor of grade affects the GD and TT.

The probabilities of skipping a word and average fixation count for second- and third-grade students are presented in Figure 5.2, and the results of the statistical analysis of the effect of length and frequency factors of words and age (grade) are presented in Table 5.2.

The table shows that SKIPS are significantly affected by the interaction of frequency and class factors; the number of fixations is affected by word frequency, word length, and grade factors.

To assess the correlation between reading skills and cognitive abilities of a child, we calculated correlations between averaged parameters of eye movements under all conditions—FFD, GD, TT, and FC—and neuropsychological indexes of the levels of EF, auditory processing function, and visuospatial processing function.

Analysis of the structure of correlations between neuropsychological indexes and characteristics of eye movements while reading in second and third grades showed that the most distinct correlations for the second grade are observed between the functions of visuospatial information processing and TT and FC ($r = 0.435$, $p = 0.016$ and $r = 0.431$, $p = 0.003$ respectively). A significant correlation for the third grade is observed between the GD parameter and the neuropsychological index of EF ($r = 0.406$, $p = 0.016$). Thus, it can be assumed that the development of reading skills in the second grade is more dependent on the visuospatial information processing, and EF become more important in the third grade. Let us proceed to describing the role of EF in reading skills in the third grade, which is the aim of the second part of our study.

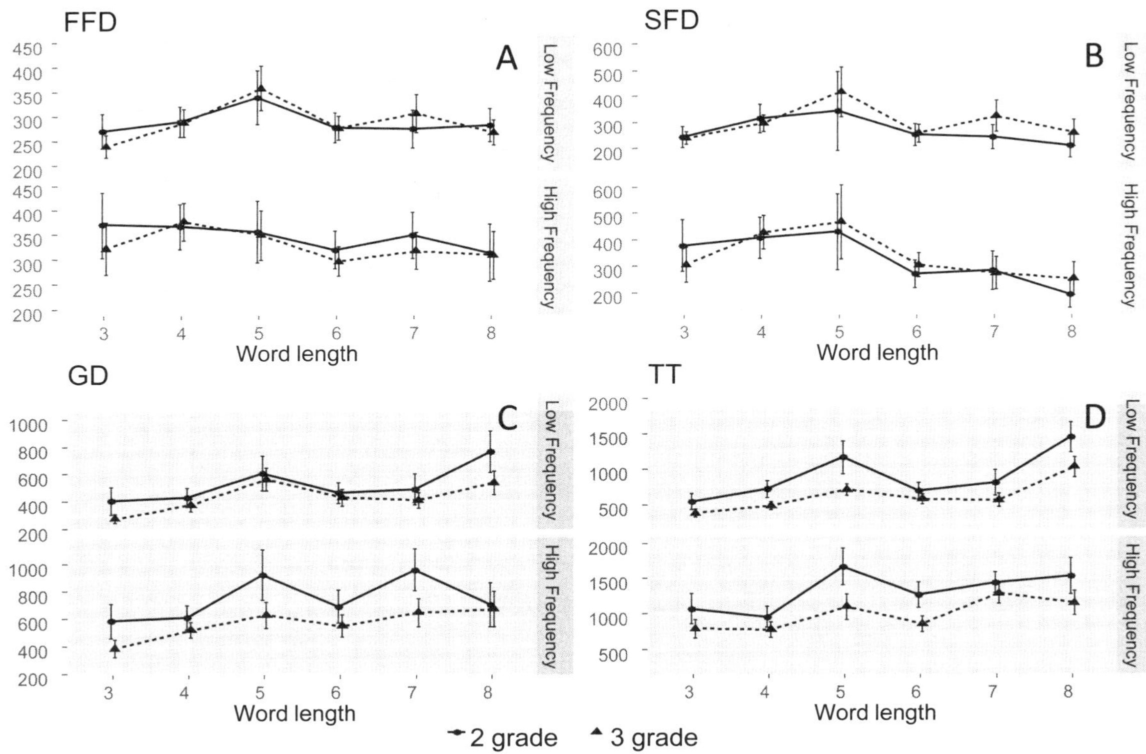

Figure 5.1. Fixation time durations for words of different length and frequency for second- and third-grade students. (A) first fixation duration; (B) single fixation duration; (C) total fixation duration for the first pass through the text; (D) total fixation duration for the whole trial. Error bars—95% confidence interval.

Table 5.1. The effect of fixed factors of length and frequency of words and age (grade) of the participants on the number of fixations

	First Fixation Duration		Single Fixation Duration		Gaze Duration		Total Time	
Fixed effects	Estimate (se)	*p*	Estimate (se)	*p*	Estimate (se)	*p*	Estimate (se)	*p*
Intercept	287.23 (13.603)	< 0.001	266.733 (22.377)	< 0.001	528.597 (41.389)	< 0.001	919.767 (93.813)	< 0.001
Frequency	58.169 (14.436)	< 0.001	56.204 (28.487)	0.054	224.124 (44.789)	< 0.001	420.271 (95.393)	< 0.001
Length	–10.154 (7.254)	0.167	–45.931 (14.219)	0.002	90.748 (22.456)	< 0.001	204.823 (47.706)	< 0.001
Class	–1.632 (16.408)	0.921	26.008 (22.361)	0.247	–99.532 (45.309)	0.031	–294.469 (95.512)	0.003
Frequency X class	–16.008 (15.366)	0.298	–11.544 (25.102)	0.646	–84.531 (38.148)	0.027	–45.983 (49.264)	0.351
Length X class	2.316 (7.756)	0.765	23.094 (12.673)	0.069	–18.249 (19.223)	0.343	–34.647 (24.726)	0.161

Standard errors (se) of coefficients are given in brackets.

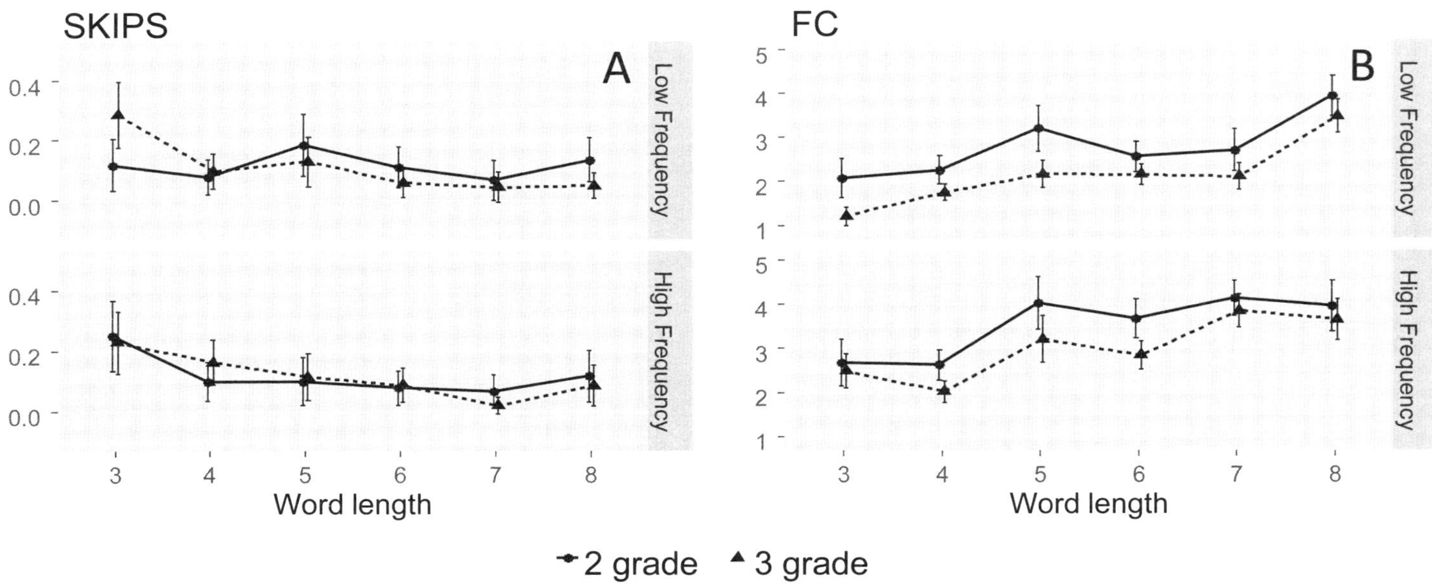

Figure 5.2. The probability of skipping a word (A) and average fixation count (B) when reading words of different length and frequency for second- and third-grade students. Error bars—95% confidence interval.

Table 5.2. The effect of fixed factors of length and frequency of words and age (grade) of the participants on the probability and number of fixations

	SKIPS		Fixations Count	
Fixed effects	Estimate (se)	*p*	Estimate (se)	*p*
Intercept	0.114 (0.021)	< 0.001	2.832 (0.201)	< 0.001
Frequency	–0.003 (0.027)	0.915	0.745 (0.216)	0.001
Length	–0.016 (0.013)	0.247	0.564 (0.108)	< 0.001
Class	–0.011 (0.023)	0.630	–0.637 (0.203)	0.002
Frequency X class	0.01 (0.027)	0.711	0.061 (0.136)	0.652
Length X class	–0.044 (0.014)	0.001	0.04 (0.068)	0.555

Standard errors (se) of coefficients are given in brackets.

CORRESPONDENCE OF THE LEVEL OF EXECUTIVE FUNCTIONS AND OCULOMOTOR ACTIVITY IN THIRD-GRADERS

To increase the representativeness of the sample, we acquired an additional set of data on eye movements during reading and the level of the cognitive abilities in third-graders. In total, 42 third-graders participated in this study (19 females, 23 males, mean age 9.58 ± 0.40). Eye movement recording, cognitive assessments, equipment, and primary data processing procedures were similar to those described in Study 1. Among the analyzed parameters, in addition to those already listed, we included the probability of single fixation on a word (one fixation, OF), multiple fixations—the proportion of cases of two or more fixations per word (multiple fixations, MF) and saccade amplitude (SA), measured in degrees. The sample was divided into two groups to compare reading skills of children with different levels of EF: high EF—children with an index of EF higher than the average for the sample (25 students, 8 females, 17 males, mean age 9.57, referred to later as *High EF group*), and low EF—children whose index of EF was lower than the average for the sample (17 students, 11 females, 6 males, mean age 9.61, referred later as *Low EF group*).

Study 2 Results

(G)LMM analysis, similar to that carried out in Study 1, with the replacement of the grade factor by the EF group factor, showed the presence of significant differences between the two groups in the following parameters of eye movements: GD, TT, OF, MF. The mean values and the estimation of the influence of the parameters included in the model are shown in Figure 5.3 and Table 5.3, respectively.

When analyzing saccade amplitude, we did not take into account the factors of frequency and word length; only the effect of the group was estimated, which was significant (est. = -0.249 (0.076), $p = 0.002$): Low EF group amplitude was smaller than that of the High EF group (1.555 and 1.399 degrees, respectively). Thus, for children of the same age in the third grade,

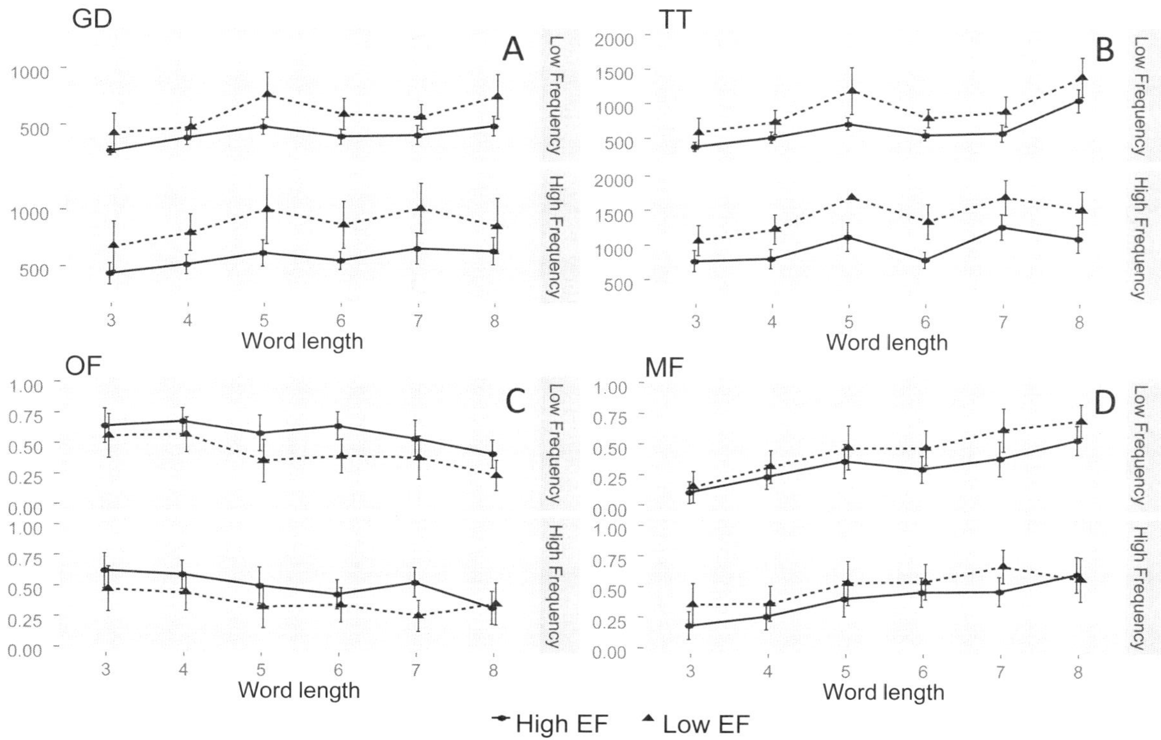

Figure 5.3. Eye movement parameters when reading words of different length and frequency for children with different levels of executive functions. (A) total fixation duration for the first pass; (B) total fixation duration time through the whole trial; (C) probability of a single fixation; (D) probability of two or more fixations. Error bars—95% confidence interval.

Table 5.3. The influence of fixed factors of word frequency, word length, and groups of students on the time of fixation durations

	Gaze Duration		Total Time		One Fixation		Multiple Fixations	
Fixed effects	Estimate (se)	*p*	Estimate (se)	*p*	Estimate (se)	*p*	Estimate (se)	*p*
Intercept	405.296 (41.065)	< 0.001	626.821 (94.068)	< 0.001	0.582 (0.03)	< 0.001	0.321 (0.035)	< 0.001
Frequency	165.338 (40.25)	< 0.001	348.213 (99.744)	0.001	–0.084 (0.037)	0.028	0.073 (0.037)	0.056
Length	61 (20.286)	0.004	162.948 (50.005)	0.003	–0.078 (0.019)	< 0.001	0.127 (0.019)	< 0.001
Class	198.927 (58.833)	0.001	326.386 (107.261)	0.004	–0.169 (0.046)	< 0.001	0.135 (0.051)	0.010
Frequency X class	109.304 (51.06)	0.033	165.314 (62.495)	0.008	0.029 (0.055)	0.597	–0.022 (0.052)	0.678
Length X class	23.229 (25.78)	0.368	55.503 (31.694)	0.080	–0.007 (0.028)	0.801	0.01 (0.026)	0.689

Standard errors (se) of coefficients are given in brackets.

the nature of eye movements when reading differs depending on the level of the EF. This was also confirmed by the analysis of correlations between different indicators of eye movements in the two groups, demonstrating that they are not the same.

No correlations were found between similar parameters in the Low EF group, although there was a distinct correlation in the High EF group between GD and SFD in the High EF group with r = 0.602 (p = 0.002); this correlation was not significant in the Low EF group (r = -0.115; p = 0.660). Saccade amplitudes in the High EF group were negatively correlated with FFD (r = -0.570, p = 0.003) and with the probability of skips (r = 0.451, p = 0.023), whereas these correlations were insignificant in the Low EF group (r = -0.054, p = 0.839 and r = -0.223, p = 0.389, respectively). Saccade amplitude in the High EF group correlated negatively with the time of the first fixation (r = -0.570, p = 0.003); this correlation was not significant in the Low EF group (r = -0.054, p = 0.839). Long fixations correspond to short subsequent saccades when the level of EF is high, and there is no such correspondence when it is low.

The characteristics of the eye movements of children of the Low EF group allow suggesting specificity in reading dynamics, which may be reflected in the deterioration of the performance of the reading probe from the beginning to the end of the procedure. To test this assumption, a comparison was made between eye movements during the first 10 and last 10 sentences. It showed a distinct increase in the number of fixations in the Low EF group (average of 2.91 fixation on a word at the beginning and 3.52 fixation at the end of the experiment), whereas no such effect was observed in the High EF group (an average of 2.6 and 2.56 of the fixation on the word in the beginning and at the end of the experiment). The effect is statistically reflected in the significant interaction of group factor and part of the trial in ANOVA (F[1, 40] = 6.799, p = 0.039).

DISCUSSION

Our results show that students in the second and third grades demonstrated different patterns of eye movements during reading: The number of fixations decreased, and the total time of fixations when reading words of different length and frequency decreased. The average time of the first fixation duration in the analyzed age range and the number of skipped words varied insignificantly, consistent with the results obtained for other languages (Vorstius et al., 2014; see Blythe, & Joseph, 2011, for review). Thus, it can be assumed that the development of reading skills at this stage involves a decrease in the number and optimization of fixations, which may be possible due to the increase in perceptual span noted in children at this age (Häikiö, Bertram, Hyönä, & Niemi, 2009; Sperlich et al., 2016). The average FFD and GD in our study and in other studies of reading in English and German are presented in Table 5.4.

Table 5.4. The mean fixation duration and gaze duration during reading in different studies

Study	Grade	Mean fixation duration	Gaze duration
Our data [Russian]	Second grade	315 ms	637 ms
	Third grade	307 ms	503 ms
Blythe and Joseph (2011) [English]	Second grade	From 260 ms to 300 ms	—
	Third grade	From 253 ms to 316 ms	—
Zawoyski, Ardoin, and Binder (2014) [English]	Second grade	280 ms	430 ms
	Third grade	—	—
Vorstius, Radach, and Lonigan (2014) [German]	Second grade	289 ms	417 ms
	Third grade	282 ms	374 ms
Tiffin-Richards and Schroeder (2015) [German]	Second grade	From 294 ms to 357	From 629 to 1730 ms
	Third grade	—	—

The languages of reading are given in brackets.

In total, average duration of the first fixation amounted to 315 ms in second grade and 307 ms in third grade. This is somewhat longer than previously reported for children of the same age reading in other languages. Still, our findings are comparable with the results of Tiffin-Richards and Schroeder (2015). The total fixation duration for the first pass through the text was also greater in our study than in the studies conducted on German and English (Vorstius et al., 2014; Zawoyski et al., 2014). The data reported by Tiffin-Richards and Schroeder, however, are more comparable with the current results. In general, these data may indicate that the basic characteristics of eye movements while reading may significantly depend on the language in which the child reads, as well as on the stimulus material, particularly the frequency and length of words. The effects of the frequency and length of the word in the second and third grades are consistent with our previous findings in the second-grade sample (Korneev et al., 2017), as well as with the results of other studies conducted on primary school students (Tiffin-Richards & Schroeder, 2015).

Analysis of the characteristics of the eye movements while reading in third-graders as related to EF showed that the relative weakness of these functions increases total duration and the likelihood of multiple fixations on the word. As previously mentioned, the improvement of the technical side of reading happens by decreasing the number of fixations and optimizing their organization. These parameters were shown to be decreased in a group of third-graders with a relative weakness of EF, which slows down the development of reading skills. The nonoptimal reading strategy in the Low EF group is also evidenced by the differences in correlations between the individual parameters in the two selected groups of third-graders. The increase in amplitude of saccades in the High EF group is accompanied by a larger number of skips, and there is no such dependence in the Low EF group (i.e., in these children, the increase in the amplitude does not optimize the reading process). It is also interesting that the correlations between SKIPS and FC in the High EF group are absent ($r = 0.028$), and it is more noticeable in the Low EF group ($r = 0.354$), although it does not reach significance. This tendency to make more fixations and skip more words at the same time is one of the markers of suboptimal strategy of eye movements while reading. It is important to note that this tendency significantly increases by the end of a relatively short experiment in a group of children with weaker EF in comparison with children in the High EF group. In general, we can conclude that lower EF entails changing the characteristics of reading strategy, both at the level of individual words and sentences and at the level of the entire experiment. It stands to reason that these differences, although not very striking per se, when summed up, make the whole reading process more effortful. This, in turn, reduces the motivation of the child and, therefore, results in a general slowdown in the development of reading skills. This assumption is consistent with the results of other studies (Arrington et al., 2014; Britton & Glynn, 2013; Cartwright, 2012). The presence of technical reading difficulties in children with weak EF further explains the frequent joint occurrence of reading difficulties and attention-deficit/hyperactivity disorder, well documented in the literature (e.g., Willcutt et al., 2010). This applies equally to the presence of reading difficulties in children with attention-deficit disorder without hyperactivity and children with processing speed deficiencies (Akhutina, Korneev, Matveeva, & Agris, 2015; Waber, 2010). The well-known presence of mixed forms of dyslexia makes it necessary to include the tasks that prompt the development of EF in assistance programs for children with dyslexia. As Fletcher and Grigorenko (2017) noted with reference to the work of Graham, McKeown, Kiuhara, and Harris (2012), "most effective interventions incorporate a self-regulation component addressing the attention and organizational difficulties experienced by many with LDs" (p. 935).

REFERENCES

Akhutina, T. V., Korneev, A. A., Matveeva, E. Y., Agris, A. R. (2015). Age-related changes of higher mental functions in 7–9-years old children with different types of state regulation deficits. *Psychology Journal of the Higher School of Economics, 12*(3), 131–152.

Akhutina, T. V., Korneev, A. A., Matveeva, E. Y., Romanova, A. A., Agris, A. R., . . . Kuzeva, O. V. (2016). *Metody neiropsikhologicheskogo obsledovaniia detei 6-9 let. [Methods of neuropsychological examination of children 6 years old.].* Moscow, Russia: V. Sekachev.

Arrington, C. N., Kulesz, P. A., Francis, D. J., Fletcher, J. M., & Barnes, M. A. (2014). The contribution of attentional control and working memory to reading comprehension and decoding. *Scientific Studies of Reading, 18*(5), 325–346.

Blythe, H. I., & Joseph, H. S. (2011). Children's eye movements during reading. In S. Liversedge, I. Gilchrist, & S. Everling (Eds.), *The Oxford handbook of eye movements* (pp. 643–662). New York, NY: Oxford University Press.

Bosse, M. L., Tainturier, M. J., & Valdois, S. (2007). Developmental dyslexia: The visual attention span deficit hypothesis. *Cognition, 104*(2), 198–230.

Britton, B. K., & Glynn, S. M. (2013). *Executive control processes in reading.* London, United Kingdom: Routledge.

Cartwright, K. B. (2012). Insights from cognitive neuroscience: The importance of executive function for early reading development and education. *Early Education and Development, 23*(1), 24–36.

Dehaene, S. (2009). *Reading in the brain: The new science of how we read.* London, United Kingdom: Penguin.

Fletcher, J. M., & Grigorenko, E. L. (2017). Neuropsychology of learning disabilities: The past and the future. *Journal of the International Neuropsychological Society, 23*(9–10), 930–940.

Graham, S., McKeown, D., Kiuhara, S., & Harris, K. R. (2012). A meta-analysis of writing instruction for students in the elementary grades. *Journal of Educational Psychology, 104*(4), 879-896.

Häikiö, T., Bertram, R., Hyönä, J., & Niemi, P. (2009). Development of the letter identity span in reading: Evidence from the eye movement moving window paradigm. *Journal of Experimental Child Psychology, 102*(2), 167–181.

Ivanov, V. V., Demidov, A. A., & Bezrukikh, M. M. (2010). Osobennosti dvizhenii glaz u detei mladshego shkol'nogo vozrasta v protsesse chteniya tekstov raznoi slozhnosti. [The characteristics of eye movements in early school students during reading texts of different complexity.]. In V. A. Barabanshchikov (Ed), *Eksperimental'naya psikhologiya v Rossii: traditsii i perspektivy [Experimental psychology in Russia: traditions ant perspectives.]* (pp. 611–616). Moscow, Russia: Izd-vo «Institut psikhologii RAN.

Korneev, A. A., Matveeva, E. Y., & Akhutina, T. V. (2017). Silent reading in Russian primary schoolchildren: An eye tracking study. *Psychology Journal of the Higher School of Economics, 14*(2), 219–235.

Korneev, A. A., Matveeva, E. Y., & Akhutina, T. V. (2018). What we can learn about reading development from the analysis of eye movements. *Human Physiology, 44*(2), 183–190.

Lobier, M. A., Peyrin, C., Pichat, C., Le Bas, J. F., & Valdois, S. (2014). Visual processing of multiple elements in the dyslexic brain: Evidence for a superior parietal dysfunction. *Frontiers in Human Neuroscience, 8*(Article 479), 1–16.

Luria, A. R. (1973). *The working brain.* New York, NY: Basic Books.

Melby-Lervåg, M., Lyster, S. A. H., & Hulme, C. (2012). Phonological skills and their role in learning to read: A meta-analytic review. *Psychological Bulletin, 138,* 322–148.

Miyake, A., Friedman, N. P., Emerson, M. J., Witzki, A. H., Howerter, A., & Wager, T. D. (2000). The unity and diversity of executive functions and their contributions to complex "frontal lobe" tasks: A latent variable analysis. *Cognitive psychology, 41*(1), 49–100.

Peyrin, C., Démonet, J. F., N'Guyen-Morel, M. A., Le Bas, J. F., & Valdois, S. (2011). Superior parietal lobule dysfunction in a homogeneous group of dyslexic children with a visual attention span disorder. *Brain and Language, 118*(3), 128–138.

Pham, A. V., & Hasson, R. M. (2014). Verbal and visuospatial working memory as predictors of children's reading ability. *Archives of Clinical Neuropsychology, 29*(5), 467–477.

Radach, R., & Kennedy, A. (2004). Theoretical perspectives on eye movements in reading: Past controversies, current issues, and an agenda for future research. *European Journal of Cognitive Psychology, 16*(1–2), 3–26.

Rayner, K. (1998). Eye movements in reading and information processing: 20 years of research. *Psychological Bulletin 124*(3), 372–422.

Reiter, A., Tucha, O., & Lange, K. W. (2005). Executive functions in children with dyslexia. *Dyslexia, 11*(2), 116–131.

Shaywitz, S. E., & Shaywitz, B. A. (2005). Dyslexia (specific reading disability). *Biological Psychiatry, 57*(11), 1301–1309.

Sperlich, A., Meixner, J., & Laubrock, J. (2016). Development of the perceptual span in reading: A longitudinal study. *Journal of Experimental Child Psychology, 146* (Supplement C), 181–201.

Tiffin-Richards, S. P., & Schroeder, S. (2015). Word length and frequency effects on children's eye movements during silent reading. *Vision Research, 113*(Part A), 33–43.

Titz, C., & Karbach, J. (2014). Working memory and executive functions: Effects of training on academic achievement. *Psychological Research, 78*(6), 852–868.
Tomasello, M. (2008). *Origins of human communication.* Cambridge, MA: The MIT Press.
Vorstius, C., Radach, R., & Lonigan, C. J. (2014). Eye movements in developing readers: A comparison of silent and oral sentence reading. *Visual Cognition, 22*(3–4), 458–485.
Waber, D. (2010). *Rethinking learning disabilities: Understanding children who struggle in school.* New York, NY: Guilford Press.
Willcutt, E. G., Betjemann, R. S., McGrath, L. M., Chhabildas, N. A., Olson, R. K., DeFries, J. C., & Pennington, B. F. (2010). Etiology and neuropsychology of comorbidity between RD and ADHD: The case for multiple-deficit models. *Cortex, 46,* 1345–1361.
Zawoyski, A. M., Ardoin, S. P., & Binder, K. S. (2014). Using eye tracking to observe differential effects of repeated readings for second-grade students as a function of achievement level. *Reading Research Quarterly, 50*(2), 171–184.
Zoubrinetzky, R., Bielle, F., & Valdois, S. (2014). New insights on developmental dyslexia subtypes: Heterogeneity of mixed reading profiles. *PloS One, 9*(6), e99337.

CHAPTER 6

Orthographic Processing and Reading

Jonathan Grainger

SUMMARY

In languages that use an alphabetic script, the core of the reading process involves orthographic processing (i.e., uncovering the identities of a word's component letters and their positions in the word). Words are the building blocks of the reading process, and orthographic processing is the central pathway to word recognition in skilled readers. I describe a theoretical framework for orthographic processing that distinguishes between two types of positional information for letters—location and order. Based on this distinction, I propose two key ways in which the visual and linguistic processing of letter position information differs from the processing of positional information for other kinds of visual stimuli. I then discuss the possibility that a dysfunction in the processing of letter-specific positional information could result in the types of reading difficulties observed in developmental dyslexia. Finally, I show how this theoretical framework can be extended to the realm of sentence reading, in order to specify how orthographic information can be processed across several words in parallel and how skilled readers encode the location of words along a line of text and infer word order from word location.

INTRODUCTION: WHY FOCUS ON ORTHOGRAPHIC PROCESSING?

When reading, the eyes fixate on most words in the text being read, and typically only once. This implies that readers get a foveal glimpse of most words for about a quarter of a second, and an essential first stage of skilled reading behavior concerns the information processing that is performed during that glimpse. In written languages that introduce extra between-word spacing, words are the buildings blocks of reading, and in those languages that use an alphabetic script, letters are the building blocks of words. Hence, therein lies the importance of understanding orthographic processing (i.e., the processing of information about letter identities and letter positions) in order to understand reading.

Reading is a visual and a linguistic skill, and orthographic processing occupies the key interface between visual and linguistic processing (Grainger, 2018; Grainger, Dufau, & Ziegler, 2016). Figure 6.1 illustrates this point and describes how this interface takes the form of three types of mapping: 1) orthography to semantics via whole-word orthographic representations, 2) orthography to morpho-semantics via morpho-orthographic representations, and 3) orthography to phonology via sublexical spelling–

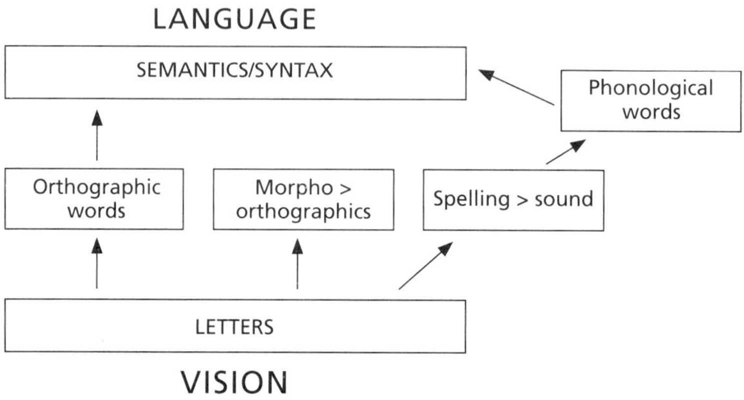

Figure 6.1. Orthographic processing as the interface between visual and linguistic processing during reading. Visual features activate letter representations that provide input to three possible pathways to meaning: 1) via whole-word orthographic representations, 2) via morpho-orthographic representations, and 3) via sublexical spelling-to-sound correspondences. Possible interactions between the different pathways are not shown. (From Grainger, J. [2018]. Orthographic processing: A 'mid-level' vision of reading: The 44th Sir Frederic Bartlett Lecture. *Quarterly Journal of Experimental Psychology, 71*[2], 335–359. Copyright © 2018 by Sage Publications Reprinted by Permission of SAGE Publications, Ltd.)

sound correspondences. This chapter describes the kind of processing that operates at the letter level and focuses on the specific mapping of letter-level information onto whole-word orthographic representations.

LETTER-BASED READING

There is a general consensus today among reading researchers that for written languages that use an alphabetic script, visual word recognition is letter based. Visual feature information is used to obtain information about the word's component letters, and a word's identity is mainly derived from information about these letter identities and their positions. The role for other types of information, such as word shape information that might be gained from the pattern of ascending and descending letters in lowercase text, is thought to be minimal, and there is one key computational argument against a major role for holistic word-shape information in reading—it is more efficient to solve shape invariance at the level of individual letters (N = 26, for the English alphabet) than at the level of whole words ($N \approx$ 30,000). Shape invariance refers to the ability to recognize words (and other kinds of visual objects) independently of the precise visual format in which they are presented—for example,

lowercase vs. UPPERCASE; printed text vs. cursive

The standard explanation for this ability is that individuals identify visual objects via abstract representations that enable different kinds of visual information to make contact with the same object identity. For words written in an alphabetic script, this abstraction occurs at the level of individual letters (see Grainger & Hannagan, 2014, for more detailed coverage of the arguments in favor of letter-based word recognition).

Letter Positions: Location and Order

Grainger and van Heuven (2003) described a theoretical framework for orthographic processing that draws a key distinction between two types of positional information for letters—the location of letters along the horizontal meridian relative to eye fixation (positions defined using gaze-centered coordinates) and the order of letters in a word independently of where the eyes are looking within that word (location-invariant order information). An extension of this framework for the processing of multiple words in parallel is shown in Figure 6.2.

The first level of orthographic processing shown in Figure 6.2 involves the activation of a set of letter identities that are each associated with a specific position along the horizontal meridian relative to where the reader's eyes are fixating. This is achieved by a bank of horizontally arranged letter detectors that are sensitive to visual feature information at a precise location relative to eye fixation. The second level of orthographic processing shown in Figure 6.2 encodes the order of letters in a word on the basis of information made available at the first level, including the presence of between-word spaces represented by the # sign in the figure. In this specific account

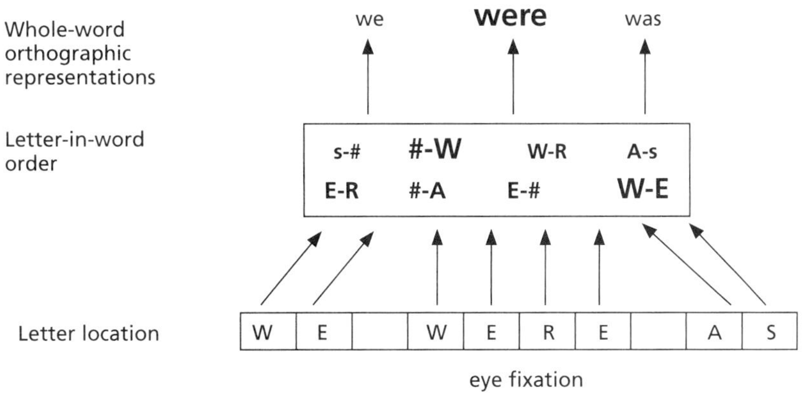

Figure 6.2. Extension of the Grainger and van Heuven (2003) model of orthographic processing to encompass the spatial integration of orthographic information spanning multiple words. Hypothetical differences in activation level in the central layer are represented by differences in size (e.g., "W-E" is strongly activated because it receives input from "we" and "were"). Feedback and lateral connectivity are not shown. (*Source:* Grainger & van Heuven, 2003.)

of orthographic processing, letter order information is encoded using a bag of ordered pairs of contiguous and noncontiguous letters, referred to as *open-bigrams* (Grainger & van Heuven, 2003; Whitney, 2001). That is, each bigram provides order information about contiguous and noncontiguous letter combinations, but the bigrams themselves are unordered. In order to activate an open-bigram representation, an individual only needs to know that a given letter identity occurs to the left or right of another letter identity, and this is precisely the kind of information that is available at the first level of processing in Figure 6.2. A more general model of letter order encoding could take the form of open n-gram coding, such that combinations of different numbers of letters, including single letters, would participate in the overall representation (see Hannagan & Grainger, 2012, for a more detailed discussion).

Letter-Specific Processing

The theoretical framework for orthographic processing previously described postulates certain specificities in the way in which orthographic information is processed compared with other kinds of sequences of visual stimuli (Grainger & Hannagan, 2014). First, the location-specific gaze-centered letter representations that occupy the first level of processing in the model are not hypothesized to exist for other kinds of visual objects, except for digits. Rather, object identification is hypothesized to be mediated by gaze-centered complex features that map onto location-invariant object identities (see Bowers, Vankov, & Ludwig, 2016). I, therefore, hypothesize that during the process of learning to read, letters and digits as independent visual objects adopt a new role as the complex visual features of higher order objects—words and numbers. I further hypothesize that, in order to optimize processing of written words and numbers, a specialized bank of such feature detectors is implemented along the horizontal meridian (for languages with horizontally arranged scripts). It is this specialized system that is thought to underlie observed differences in the processing of horizontally aligned letters and digits compared with other kinds of visual stimuli in experimental tasks that specifically tap into these early processes (e.g., Tydgat & Grainger, 2009).

At the second level of orthographic processing in Figure 6.2, location-invariance is achieved at the level of sublexical orthographic processing by encoding the order of letters in a word independently of the location of that word. The mechanism used to encode for letter order is thought to be specific to written words, and evidence for this has been obtained with a task that requires the processing of location-invariant order information—the same-different matching task. In this task, a first visual stimulus is displayed, typically for 300ms, and is immediately followed by a second stimulus, again typically for 300ms, and participants have to judge as rapidly and as accurately as possible if the two stimuli are the same or not. An interesting dissociation arises when comparing performance to strings of consonants, digits, and symbols with this task. It is harder to decide that two sequences are different when they differ by a transposition of two characters compared with a replacement of the same two characters with different characters (e.g., PGFM-PFGM vs. PTRM-PFGM), and this transposition effect is significantly greater for letters than for either digits or symbols (see Grainger & Hannagan, 2014, for a summary of the evidence). It is the specific way in which location-invariant letter order information is encoded that is thought to generate the larger transposition effects for letters compared with other kinds of stimuli.

Letter-Specific Processing and Reading Disorders

Although educators are understandably concerned about how to help children learn to read independently of whether they have specific difficulties and the origin(s) of such difficulties, reading researchers can use reading disorders to help improve understanding of the basic mechanisms involved in typical reading and learning to read. With this aim in mind, it is cases where one observes a highly selective impairment of learning to read that are important for reading research, with developmental dyslexia being a primary example. Furthermore, reading-specific processing is a natural place to look for the cause of any observed selective impairment in reading. Spelling–sound conversion has long been the dominant explanation here, with the idea that symbol–sound mappings are dysfunctional in children with dyslexia (see Pugh & Verhoeven, 2018, for a summary of the evidence for this and alternative accounts of developmental dyslexia), and this prevents them from using the self-teaching mechanism that is crucial for success in learning in to read (Grainger, Lété, Bertrand, Dufau, & Ziegler, 2012; Share, 1995; Ziegler, Perry, & Zorzi, 2017).

Alternatively, it has been proposed that more elementary visuo-attentional processing is dysfunctional in children with dyslexia (e.g., Valdois, Bosse, & Tainturier, 2004; Vidyasagar & Pammer, 2010) and could, in fact, be the cause of dysfunctional spelling–sound mappings and their consequences (Facoetti et al., 2009). I suggest that both types of dysfunction might be linked to a common source—the processing of location-specific letter identities. Inefficient processing of location-specific letter identities would cause multiple problems downstream on all processes that depend on the efficiency of this initial stage of orthographic processing. The three main categories of reading processes that are concerned by this are shown in Figure 6.1: 1) direct access to whole-word orthographic representations, 2) access to morpho-orthographic representations, and 3) spelling–sound conversion for access to whole-word phonological representations. This account shares certain features with Hawelka and Wimmer's (2005) visual multielement processing deficit hypothesis.

Impaired processing of location-specific letter strings could also be interpreted as revealing a visuo-attentional deficit in children with dyslexia to the extent that the deficit is observed in the processing of letter or digit strings. One key finding here, first reported by Ziegler, Pech-Georgel, Dufau, and Grainger (2010), is that in a character-in-string identification task, children with dyslexia performed at the same level as the control group when the characters were nonalphanumeric symbols but showed a deficit in the processing of letter and digit strings. Furthermore, the study of Boros and colleagues (2016) not only replicated this behavioral pattern, but also revealed underactivation of the middle occipital gyrus in children with dyslexia, a brain region thought to be involved in processing position information in multielement displays (Vidyasagar & Pammer, 2010). In sum, impaired processing of location-specific letter identities in an alphabetic writing system, and possibly of radicals in a logographic writing system, could be the cause of many of the multiple symptoms of developmental dyslexia.

PARALLEL ORTHOGRAPHIC PROCESSING AND SENTENCE READING

The theoretical framework shown in Figure 6.2 describes how location-specific orthographic information processed in parallel across several words is integrated into a single channel for location-invariant orthographic processing and word identification. Grainger et al. (2016) described how the spatial integration of orthographic information into a single processing channel could output a sequence of word identities as the reader's eyes move along a line of text, hence providing the word order information that is crucial for sentence-level processing (see Snell, van Leipsig, Grainger, & Meeter, 2018, for a computational model that implements this basic framework combined with mechanisms for oculomotor control). Recent evidence, however, has forced the conclusion that readers do not identify one word at a time but rather proceed in a much more parallel fashion than has been imagined up to now (Snell, 2018). The novel framework for parallel processing during text reading, motivated by these findings, is shown in Figure 6.3.

In the same way that Grainger et al. (2016) hypothesized two types of positional information for letters in words, here I hypothesize that a similar distinction can be drawn concerning the mechanisms used to encode for the positions of words in a sentence. The location-specific representation of word position is thought to use spatiotopic coordinates that provide a reference frame for representing the location of an object in a visual scene independently of where the viewer's eyes are looking. Adapted to the case of reading, the spatiotopic coordinates for written words are defined as representing a word's location in a line of text that is being read independently of the position of the reader's gaze on that line of text. It is these spatiotopic word representations (i.e., word identities associated with spatiotopic locations) that provide the crucial information about the ordering of word identities to higher level sentence comprehension processes. In other words, I hypothesized that sentence-level syntactic and semantic processing operate on an ordered set of location-invariant word identities that is derived from spatiotopic word representations stored in short-term memory.

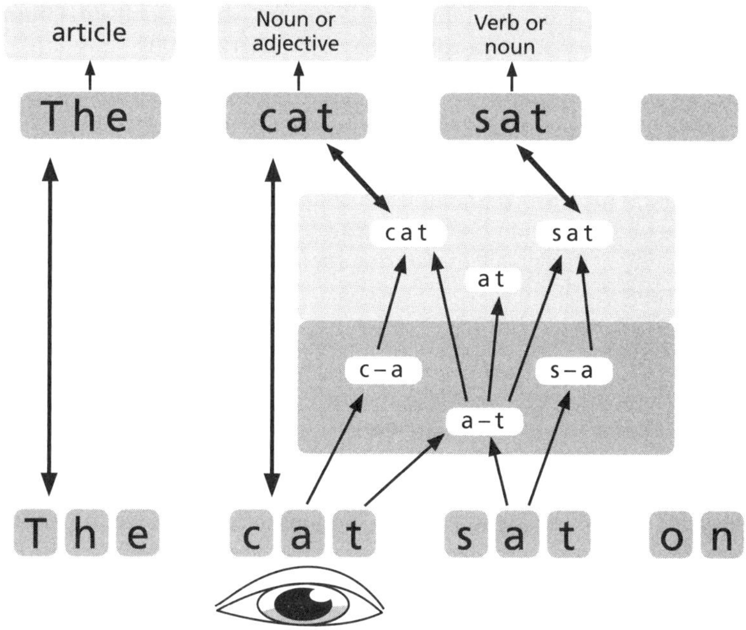

Figure 6.3. "The spatiotopic cat sat on the retinotopic mat"—Snell, Meeter, and Grainger's (2017) model of parallel orthographic processing and reading. Gaze-centered letter detectors (bottom layer) feed forward activation to word-centered sublexical orthographic representations (c-a, a-t, s-a) that, in turn, activate whole-word orthographic representations (cat, at, sat). Activated whole-word orthographic representations are associated with a spatiotopic location that is connected with the retinotopic location of the letter detectors that are the source of activation of the word representation. In this way, different word identities are temporarily bound to distinct spatiotopic locations in short-term memory. (From Snell, J., Meeter, M., & Grainger, J. [2017]. Evidence for simultaneous syntactic processing of multiple words during reading. *PLoS ONE 12*[3], e0173720. https://doi.org/10.1371/journal.pone.0173720; reprinted by permission.)

The development of this theoretical framework was initially motivated by the observation of orthographic parafoveal-on-foveal effects obtained during sentence reading (Angele, Tran, & Rayner, 2013; Dare & Shillcock, 2013; Snell, Vitu, & Grainger, 2017) and with a flanker paradigm (Dare & Shillcock, 2013; Grainger, Mathôt, & Vitu, 2014). In both cases, it was found that the processing of the currently fixated word was influenced by the orthographic overlap between this word and neighboring words in the parafovea. Greater overlap facilitated processing of the fixated word. The model captures these orthographic parafoveal-on-foveal effects via the parallel processing of multiple words and the spatial integration of orthographic information into a single channel (see Figure 6.2).

Most important, however, is that this theoretical framework correctly predicted the existence of a sentence superiority effect. To observe this phenomenon, a short sequence of words is briefly presented (Rapid Parallel Visual Presentation) followed by a backward mask and a postcue for participants to report the identity of the word that had been presented at the postcued location (Snell & Grainger, 2017). In this study, Snell and Grainger tested sequences of four words, three to five letters long, presented for 200ms. They found a robust effect of context, with higher word identification accuracy in syntactically correct sentences compared with ungrammatical scrambled sequences of the same words. This demonstration of a sentence superiority effect was taken as evidence for parallel, cascaded transmission of information from word identities to sentence-level representations, with sentence-level representations improving postcued word identification by facilitating the maintenance in working memory of several word identities and providing feedback to word representations.

CONCLUSIONS

I have presented a theoretical framework for orthographic processing that was initially developed for single-word reading and then expanded to the parallel processing of multiple words during sentence reading. Apart from the strongly parallel and highly interactive nature of the hypothesized processes involved, the key feature of this framework lies in the way positional information is encoded for letters in words and words in sentences. Here, a distinction is drawn between location-specific representations (gaze centered for letters and line centered for words) and location-invariant order information. I have described how this framework accounts for some fundamental phenomena associated with single-word and sentence reading. This theoretical framework holds promise in helping to understand why some children have extraordinary difficulty in learning to read.

REFERENCES

Angele, B., Tran, R., & Rayner, K. (2013). Parafoveal-foveal overlap can facilitate ongoing word identification during reading: Evidence from eye movements. *Journal of Experimental Psychology: Human Perception and Performance, 39,* 526–538.

Boros, M., Anton, J. L., Pech-Georgel, C., Grainger, J., Szwed, M., & Ziegler, J. C. (2016). Orthographic processing deficits in developmental dyslexia: Beyond the ventral visual stream. *NeuroImage, 128,* 316–327.

Bowers, J., Vankov, I., & Ludwig, C. J. H. (2016). The visual system supports on-line translation invariance for object identification. *Psychonomic Bulletin and Review, 23,* 432–438.

Dare, N., & Shillcock, R. (2013). Serial and parallel processing in reading: Investigating the effects of parafoveal orthographic information on non-isolated word recognition. *Quarterly Journal of Experimental Psychology, 66,* 417–428.

Facoetti, A., Trussardi, A. N., Ruffino, M., Lorusso, M. L., Cattaneo, C., Galli, R., . . . Zorzi, M. (2009). Multisensory spatial attention deficits are predictive of phonological decoding skills in developmental dyslexia. *Journal of Cognitive Neuroscience, 22,* 1011–1025.

Grainger, J. (2018). Orthographic processing: A "mid-level" vision of reading. *Quarterly Journal of Experimental Psychology, 71,* 335–359.

Grainger, J., Dufau, S., & Ziegler, J. C. (2016). A vision of reading. *Trends in Cognitive Sciences, 20,* 171–179.

Grainger, J., & Hannagan, T. (2014). What is special about orthographic processing? *Written Language and Literacy, 17,* 225–252.

Grainger, J., Lété, B., Bertrand, D., Dufau, S., & Ziegler, J. C. (2012). Evidence for multiple routes in learning to read. *Cognition, 123,* 280–292.

Grainger, J., Mathôt, S., & Vitu, F. (2014). Tests of a model of multi-word reading: Effects of parafoveal flanking letters on foveal word recognition. *Acta Psychologica, 146,* 35–40.

Grainger, J., & van Heuven, W. (2003). Modeling letter position coding in printed word perception. In P. Bonin (Ed.), *The mental lexicon* (pp. 1–24). New York, NY: Nova Science Publishers.

Hannagan, T., & Grainger, J. (2012). Protein analysis meets visual word recognition: A case for string kernels in the brain. *Cognitive Science, 36,* 575–606.

Hawelka, S., & Wimmer, H. (2005). Impaired visual processing of multi-element arrays is associated with increased number of eye movements in dyslexic readers. *Vision Research, 45,* 855–863.

Pugh, K., & Verhoeven, L. (2018). Introduction to this special issue: Dyslexia across languages and writing systems. *Scientific Studies of Reading, 22,* 1–6.

Share, D. L. (1995). Phonological recoding and self-teaching: Sine qua non of reading acquisition. *Cognition, 55,* 151–218.

Snell, J. (2018). *Readers are parallel processors* (Unpublished doctoral dissertation). Aix-Marseille University, Marseille, France.

Snell, J., & Grainger, J. (2017). The sentence superiority effect revisited. *Cognition, 168,* 217–221.

Snell, J., Meeter, M., & Grainger, J. (2017). Evidence for simultaneous syntactic processing of multiple words during reading. *PLoS ONE, 12,* e0173720.

Snell, J., van Leipsig, S., Grainger, J., & Meeter, M. (2018). OB1-Reader: A model of word recognition and eye movements in text reading. *Psychological Review, 125,* 969–984.

Snell, J., Vitu, F., & Grainger, J. (2017). Integration of parafoveal information during foveal word reading: Beyond the sublexical level? *Quarterly Journal of Experimental Psychology, 70,* 1984–1996.

Tydgat, I., & Grainger, J. (2009). Serial position effects in the identification of letters, digits, and symbols. *Journal of Experimental Psychology: Human Perception and Performance, 35,* 480–498.

Valdois, S., Bosse M. L., & Tainturier, M. J. (2004). The cognitive deficits responsible for developmental dyslexia: Review of evidence for a selective visual attentional disorder. *Dyslexia, 10,* 339–363.

Vidyasagar, T. R., & Pammer, K. (2010). Dyslexia: A deficit in visuo-spatial attention, not in phonological processing. *Trends in Cognitive Sciences, 14,* 57–63.

Whitney, C. (2001). How the brain encodes the order of letters in a printed word: The SERIOL model and selective literature review. *Psychonomic Bulletin and Review, 8,* 221–243.

Ziegler, J. C., Pech-Georgel, C., Dufau, S., & Grainger, J. (2010). Rapid processing of letters, digits, and symbols: what purely visual-attentional deficit in developmental dyslexia? *Developmental Science, 13,* F8–F14.

Ziegler, J. C., Perry, C., & Zorzi, M. (2017). Modelling reading development through phonological decoding and self-teaching: Implications for dyslexia. *Philosophical Transactions of the Royal Society London: B Biological Sciences, 369,* 20120397.

INTEGRATIVE COMMENTARY 2

Typical Language Development (Spoken and Written)

Tiffany P. Hogan

SUMMARY

The chapters in this section describe typical spoken and written language development with an eye toward implications for explaining atypical acquisition. Several themes have emerged. The first is the power of statistical learning for explaining key phenomena in typical and atypical spoken and written language acquisition. A second theme is innovative methodologies, such as eye tracking, computational modeling, and infant behavioral learning paradigms, and their critical role in shedding light on the complex mechanisms driving spoken and written language acquisition. A third theme is that language-specific written and spoken characteristics can mitigate the influence of cognitive-linguistic abilities on acquisition. Future research would include all of these aspects to explicate the complexities of typical and atypical spoken and written language acquisition and their interrelated development over time. It is through well-funded, large-scale, practical yet theory-driven studies that educators can best determine what works for whom to improve spoken and written language acquisition in our increasingly diverse society.

INTRODUCTION

Spoken language acquisition begins in utero and unfolds in a predictable pattern across early childhood. Literate societies use written symbols to represent spoken language, and as such, literacy skills are parasitic to and symbiotic with spoken language development (Cain & Oakhill, 2011). The chapters in this section describe typical spoken and written language development with an eye toward implications for explaining atypical acquisition.

In Chapter 4, Saffran provides compelling evidence that detecting statistical regularities in spoken language is the foundation for early word learning. In support of this claim, children exposed to more spoken language input are better able to detect regularities, whereas those with difficulty learning new words (e.g., children with specific language impairment) are less able to detect these regularities (see Chapter 7). Beyond initial word learning, a lexicon (i.e., mental store of words) grows by cataloging words in interrelational networks that presumably facilitate retrieval (Vitevitch, 2002). Although Saffran's chapter focuses on early statistical learning in spoken language acquisition, there is a parallel line of inquiry into statistical learning in written language acquisition that draws similar conclusions—a child's ability to detect statistical sequences (both visual and auditory) is linked to reading skill, even after controlling for many cognitive and attentional factors. Arciuli (2018) noted that statistical learning influences reading ability both directly and indirectly—directly through sensitivity to cues in written words and indirectly through statistical learning's influence on vocabulary acquisition.

In Chapter 5, Akhutina, Korneev, and Matveeva use eye-tracking data to argue that written language acquisition becomes more efficient between second and third grade, a period of rapid growth in reading acquisition, and visual-spatial processing is related to individual differences in efficiency in second grade. Executive functioning (EF) is more related to individual differences in efficiency in third grade. Phonology, in general, plays a lesser role in languages with transparent orthographies that have straightforward letter-to-sound correspondences, such as Russian. Thus, they conclude that Russian reading acquisition relies more on visual-spatial processing and central EF than on phonology. This work is in line with a strong interest in EF and its impact on spoken and written language acquisition (see Chapter 10).

In Chapter 6, Grainger reviews models of orthographic learning with a focus on important nuances to explain reading acquisition, such as the processing of location-specific letter identities. First, he notes that, during the process of learning to read, letters and digits begin to serve as important individual visual components to characterize words and numbers. Then he points to several studies that led him to conclude that poor orthographic processing may be rooted in difficulty processing location-specific letter identities. Specifically, deficient location-specific letter identities would disrupt the initial formation of orthographic mental representations during early reading acquisition, which would, in turn, disrupt subsequent storage of more complex letter patterns characteristic of more advanced orthographic processing. He ends his chapter by proposing that impaired processing of location-specific letter identities could be the root of atypical reading acquisition in children with dyslexia. This idea is intriguing in light of work showing that children with poor language acquisition do not benefit as much as their typical peers do from orthographic regularities during written word learning (Wolter & Apel, 2010), and evidence shows a more general sequencing deficit in children with dyslexia (Cowan et al., 2017; Majerus & Cowan, 2016).

INTEGRATION, IMPLICATIONS, AND FUTURE DIRECTIONS

Taken together, these chapters highlight the complexities of spoken and written language acquisition. Several themes emerge across chapters. The first is the power of statistical learning for explaining key phenomenon in typical and atypical spoken and written language acquisition. A second theme is innovative methodologies, such as eye tracking, computational modeling, and infant behavioral learning paradigms, and their critical role in shedding light on the complex mechanisms driving spoken and written language acquisition. A third theme is that language-specific written and spoken characteristics can mitigate the influence of cognitive-linguistic abilities on acquisition. For example, in the case of Russian written language acquisition, visual-spatial skills and EF affected reading efficiency more than phonology, presumably because it is a written language with straightforward and consistent letter-to-sound correspondences (i.e., a transparent orthography). That may not be the case for languages that lack such transparency, such as English or Chinese.

Ideally, future research would include all of these aspects to explicate the complexities of typical and atypical spoken and written language acquisition and their interrelated development over time. For example, one well-crafted study could examine phonological, semantic, and orthographic statistical learning from early through middle childhood in children at risk for dyslexia and their typically developing peers to determine the influence of cognitive-linguistic abilities and knowledge in these domains on reading efficiency across languages that vary in orthographic transparency. Variability in home and school environment, digital literacy, and brain function are important additional considerations. Of course, a study of this magnitude would require a large sample size to use the advanced statistical analyses required to unravel these complexities across languages with multidisciplinary teams, including speech-language pathologists who have extensive knowledge in both typical and atypical language development (Hogan, 2018). Moreover, clear and testable hypotheses that consider both spoken and written language processes should serve as a strong, theory-based backbone.

One such example is the well-supported theory of the simple view of reading (Gough & Tunmer, 1986), which states that reading comprehension—the ultimate goal of reading—is the product of one's ability to decode written words and understand the spoken language conveyed by those written words (see Hogan, Adlof, & Alonzo, 2014). Longitudinal studies have confirmed the spoken and written language basis of reading via the simple view (e.g., Foorman, Petscher, & Herrera, 2018). One study conducted by the Language and Reading Research Consortium and Chiu (2018) used structural equation modeling to show that preschool spoken measures comprised one latent construct that explained the majority of the variance in comprehension processes in third grade, whereas phonologically based preliteracy measures (e.g., phonological awareness, letter knowledge, rapid naming) comprised a separate latent construct that explained the majority of the variance in third-grade word reading (Language and Reading Research Consortium & Chiu, 2018). Of note, the preschool language latent constructs—comprehension and preliteracy skills—were correlated, but the most parsimonious model showed only direct effects from each preschool construct to its corresponding third-grade outcome.

It is through well-funded, large-scale, practical yet theory-driven studies that educators can best determine what works for whom to improve spoken and written language acquisition in our increasingly diverse society. In the meantime, synthesizing converging evidence has strong potential to positively affect reading pedagogy. For example, a tutorial (Adlof & Hogan, 2018) reviewed the language basis of dyslexia considering typical spoken and written language development and disorders (see also Snowling & Melby-Lervåg, 2016, for a meta-analysis). One clear practical conclusion from these chapters and the many studies on spoken and written language development is that language skills—both spoken (e.g., oral language comprehension) and written (e.g., word reading and reading fluency)—need to be assessed early and often in school-based assessment frameworks to determine individual variation to inform quality, evidence-based spoken and written language instruction.

REFERENCES

Adlof, S. M., & Hogan, T. P. (2018). Understanding dyslexia in the context of developmental language disorders. *Language, Speech, and Hearing Services in Schools, 49,* 762–773. doi:10.1044/2018_LSHSS-DYSLC-18-0049

Arciuli, J. (2018). Reading as statistical learning. *Language, Speech, and Hearing Services in Schools, 49*(3S), 634–643.

Cain, K., & Oakhill, J. (2011). Matthew effects in young readers: Reading comprehension and reading experience aid vocabulary development. *Journal of Learning Disabilities, 44*(5), 431–443.

Cowan, N., Hogan, T. P., Alt, M., Green, S., Cabbage, K. L., Brinkley, S., & Gray, S. (2017). Short-term memory in childhood dyslexia: Deficient serial order in multiple modalities. *Dyslexia, 23*(3), 209–233.

Foorman, B. R., Petscher, Y., & Herrera, S. (2018). Unique and common effects of decoding and language factors in predicting reading comprehension in grades 1–10. *Learning and Individual Differences, 63,* 12–23.

Gough, P. B., & Tunmer, W. E. (1986). Decoding, reading, and reading disability. *Remedial and Special Education, 7,* 6–10.

Hogan, T. P. (2018). Five ways speech-language pathologists can positively impact children with dyslexia. *Language, Speech, and Hearing Services in Schools, 49,* 902–905.

Hogan, T. P., Adlof, S. M., & Alonzo, C. N. (2014). On the importance of listening comprehension. *International Journal of Speech-Language Pathology, 16*(3), 199–207.

Language and Reading Research Consortium & Chiu, Y. D. (2018). The simple view of reading across development: The prediction of grade 3 reading comprehension by prekindergarten skills. *Remedial and Special Education, 39*(5), 289–303.

Majerus, S., & Cowan, N. (2016). The nature of verbal short-term impairment in dyslexia: The importance of serial order. *Frontiers in Psychology, 7,* 1522.

Snowling, M. J., & Melby-Lervåg, M. (2016). Oral language deficits in familial dyslexia: A meta-analysis and review. *Psychological Bulletin, 142*(5), 498–545.

Vitevitch, M. S. (2002). The influence of phonological similarity neighborhoods on speech production. *Journal of Experimental Psychology: Learning, Memory, and Cognition, 28*(4), 735.

Wolter, J. A., & Apel, K. (2010). Initial acquisition of mental graphemic representations in children with language impairment. *Journal of Speech, Language, and Hearing Research, 53*(1), 179–195.

SECTION III

Atypical Oral Language

CHAPTER 7

Longitudinal Study of Language and Speech of Twins

New Insights Into Possible Causal Pathways

Mabel L. Rice

SUMMARY

Is there an inherited influence on language acquisition? Twin children provide highly informative ways to differentiate biological and environmental effects on language acquisition. Identical/monozygotic (MZ) twins share DNA from conception; fraternal/dizygotic (DZ) twins are related in the same way as other siblings, except they share time in the uterus during the prenatal period with their co-twin and they share time of birth. Even MZ twins can be different due to unique circumstances, such as a bout of meningitis that affects only one of a pair of twins.

This chapter summarizes new evidence from studies of language acquisition in twin children, over four age levels: 2, 4, 6, and 16 years. Key findings are that twins are later in language acquisition in the preschool period compared with single-born children, more so for MZ than DZ twins. The MZ/DZ difference disappears by 6 years and the twinning delay is less evident, indicating the twins are catching up to single-born norms. Language is heritable across many dimensions, although highest for grammar. Heritability increases with age and is higher for comparisons of children with language impairments versus other children. The findings support the likelihood of inherited influence on children's language acquisition.

INTRODUCTION

A long-standing scientific question is whether there is an inherited influence on language acquisition and, if so, that inherited ability is unique to language. The modern era of scientific inquiry can be traced to several sources. Among them is the seminal work of Eric Lenneberg (1967), a linguist and neurologist who published *Biological Foundations of Language.* He explicitly stated that the aim is "to reinstate the concept of the biological basis of language capacities and to make the specific assumptions so explicit that they may be subjected to empirical tests" (p. viii). His ideas were subsequently popularized by Pinker (1994) in his book, *The Language Instinct.* Contempo-

Studies cited in this chapter and preparation of this paper were supported by NIH R01DC005226 (Rice, Zubrick, and Taylor, PIs), NIH R01DC001803 (Rice, PI), NIH P30DC005803 (Rice, PI), and NIH P30HD002528 (Rice, affiliated researcher). I especially thank the children and families who participated in the studies described and the members of the research team.

rary studies under the umbrella term *biolinguistics* bridge evolutionary biology and linguistics (Boecks & Piattelli-Palmarini, 2005); theories proposed by Noam Chomsky (1995) and other scholars inspire ongoing dialogues. Lenneberg cautioned that there was no definitive answer to the fundamental questions in hand about biological bases of language or what would constitute definitive empirical evidence, a caution that remains contemporary.

This chapter picks up on the ongoing relevance of Lenneberg's call for empirical evidence as essential for advancing insights into the possible role of biological influences on children's speech and language. Twin children are the focus of inquiry as potentially highly informative sources of information about the contributions of environment versus biology. The chapter lays out the logic and methods of empirical twin studies as a prelude to a summary of three interrelated twin studies that provides an overarching view of the relative influence of biological similarities from 2 years to 16 years. There is straightforward relevance of the outcomes for identification and treatment of children with dyslexia. The main premise is that language abilities are central to reading abilities, which, in turn, are at the core of the condition of dyslexia. Twin outcomes find the highest estimates of inherited influences at the low end of language abilities. The new perspective here is that this generalization must be updated to be consistent with new findings showing that twins are delayed in their early language acquisition compared with single-born children. Early delays attributable to twinning disappear around 6–8 years of age and must not be confused with the early delays of children likely to persist in the condition of dyslexia throughout childhood and into adulthood. Furthermore, twin studies document the multidimensionality of language and alert us to the need to consider grammar more closely as an inherited ability that could play an important role in children's ability to read language.

THE CASE OF TWINS

Twins are unusual in human births. The twin birth rate in the United States was about 2% of all births from 1915 to the early 1980s. The rate rose to 3.3% from 1980, an increase attributable to older mothers and the advent of assistive reproductive technologies (Martin, Hamilton, & Osterman, 2012). Twin births have two biologically related infants paired in utero during the gestational period and at birth, bringing two infants into the family at the same time. Biologically, there are two kinds of twin pairs. MZ twins, sometimes called *identical,* are developed from a single fertilized egg that splits into two, or, in biological terms, they develop from one zygote, which splits and forms two embryos. DZ twins, sometimes called *fraternal,* develop from two different eggs, each fertilized from its own sperm cell. Children in an MZ twin pair are of the same sex; children in a DZ pair may be of the same sex. Children in a DZ pair can be considered as two siblings who share the same parents and the same birthday (age), whereas children in an MZ pair

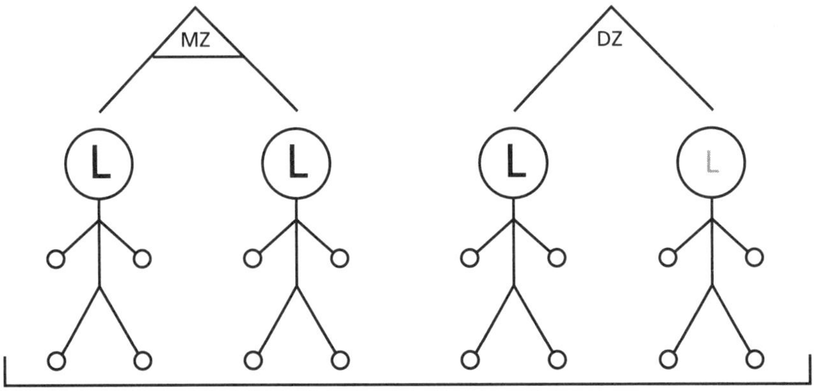

Figure 7.1. Monozygotic twin pair concordant for language phenotype *L*; dyzgotic twin pair discordant for language phenotype.

can be considered as two same-age siblings who share the same parents and the same DNA information. The biological details can be more complex in special cases of some twin pairs, although the generalizations here are generally accepted as the fundamental differences across MZ and DZ twin pairs.

Of interest here is the way in which language abilities are distributed within and across the DZ and MZ twin pairs. The conventional way of depicting the basic logic of the scientific design is shown in Figure 7.1, using symbolic conventions of pedigree displays. In the twin pair on the left, we see two female twins, in which round heads indicate females (males are depicted with square heads). The tent figure over their heads, with a connecting line between the diagonal lines linking the two females, indicates they are an MZ pair. The capitalized *L* inside each head stands for the individual's language ability, known as a behavioral phenotype, a trait thought to be influenced by the interaction of genetics and environment. The large size of the *L* for both females indicates robust abilities that are expected for their age. In comparison, the pair on the right, also both females, are a DZ pair, without the connecting line in the tent above their heads. They do not share the same level of language ability, as indicated by the large black *L* versus the smaller gray *L*, showing that the female on the right has low levels of language ability compared with other children her age.

Informativeness of Studies of Twins and Experimental Methods

Studies of twins can tell us about causal pathways for language acquisition in ways we cannot deduce in studies of single-born children. Scientists have developed methods of studying differences in behavioral phenotypes within and across twin pairs that can be applied to language phenotypes. Under the logic and methods of behavioral genetics (DeFries & Fulker, 1985), twin studies provide discrete estimates of heritability (h^2), environmental effects common to the twin pair (c^2), and environmental effects unique to each twin (e^2). The relationship among the three components is expressed as a formula, $h^2 + c^2 + e^2 = 1.00$, under the assumption that the sources of individual differences in twin children can be attributable to the shared inheritance plus two kinds of shared environmental influences, one common to the twin pair and another unique to each twin (e.g., if one twin contracts meningitis but the other does not).

The DeFries-Fulker method is based on quantitative estimates from calculations of correlations. In contemporary applications, modeling approaches are used that can provide separate estimates for covariates such as maternal education and maternal age (shared by the twin pair) and twin-specific predictors (age at assessment, sex, birth weight, Apgar scores at birth) (Rice, Zubrick, Taylor, Gayán, & Bontempo, 2014; Rice, Zubrick, Taylor, Hoffman, & Gayán, 2018). These quantitative enhancements increase the informativeness of the calculation of heritability and environmental influences.

Another construct that is useful in the study of twins is the notion of concordance, defined as the presence of the same trait in both members of a pair of twins. This is the probability that a pair of individuals will both have a certain characteristic, given that one of the pair has the characteristic (e.g., eye color, language impairment). Concordance is the ratio of the number of twin children in concordant pairs to the total number of twin children in the study. Inherited traits should show higher concordances in MZ than DZ twin pairs. Note that the definition of the trait for this calculation is a categorical one (i.e., a child is scored as having or not having the trait).

The study of twins also allows for empirical documentation of twinning effects, or ways in which twin children differ from single-born children in their development of certain skills. One such possible twinning effect is the widespread assumption that on average, twins' language acquisition starts later compared with single-born children. Although a common assumption, it has not been addressed with scientifically rigorous empirical evidence until recently.

The issue of a possible twinning effect requires differentiation between the calculation of correlations (for heritability estimates) and the determination of actual levels of performance (for how twins perform compared with single-born children of the same age). Recall that heritability estimates focus on the similarity between co-twins in MZ pairs versus DZ pairs, as shown in Figure 7.2, in which Twin 1 is on the Y axis and Twin 2 is on the X axis, and the lines are plots of how well a child scores on a trait, such as vocabulary score. The line for the MZ pairs shows that the two co-twins are very likely to have the same level of vocabulary score, whereas the line for DZ pairs indicates a weaker co-twin relationship. These outcomes would be consistent with a high heritability outcome using the DeFries-Fulker formula.

To sort out the differences between heritability estimates and twinning effects, Figure 7.3 shows two possible outcomes when considering the rela-

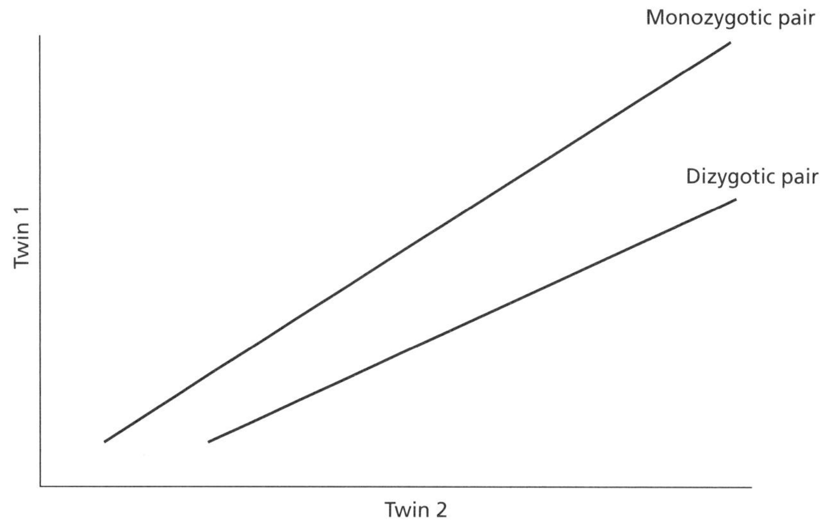

Figure 7.2. Expected outcomes for heritability.

tionship for comparisons of vocabulary standard scores and reading scores. The correlation outcomes for a full sample of children with a range of different abilities is shown to the left. The solid black line indicates a perfect association with a correlation of 1.00; the large dashed line indicates a strong but not perfect association of .80; and the small dashed line indicates a weaker correlation of .30, which could be statistically significant, although a smaller association. Such correlational methods are vitally important to sorting out relationships of reading and other abilities in children.

The other half of Figure 7.3 reports different findings when the question is whether the children at low levels of ability in the full group, defined independently, can have the same association between vocabulary and reading as children at higher levels of ability but at very different levels of standard scores. For example, the full group of children could be sorted into those who have Specific Language Impairment (SLI) versus those who do not. SLI is a language disorder that delays the mastery of language skills in children who have no hearing loss or other developmental delays (affecting 7%–10% of children at school entry) (National Institute on Deafness and Other Communication Disorders Information Clearinghouse, 2011). An alternative term has been proposed, *Developmental Language Disorder (DLD)*, which subsumes SLI but is not synonymous. The boundaries for application of this label have yet to be determined. It may include children with low nonverbal cognitive abilities, hearing loss, autism spectrum disorder (ASD), and other neurological conditions and children learning English as a second language. There is widespread consensus that the classification of children with language impairments should align with the research objectives and

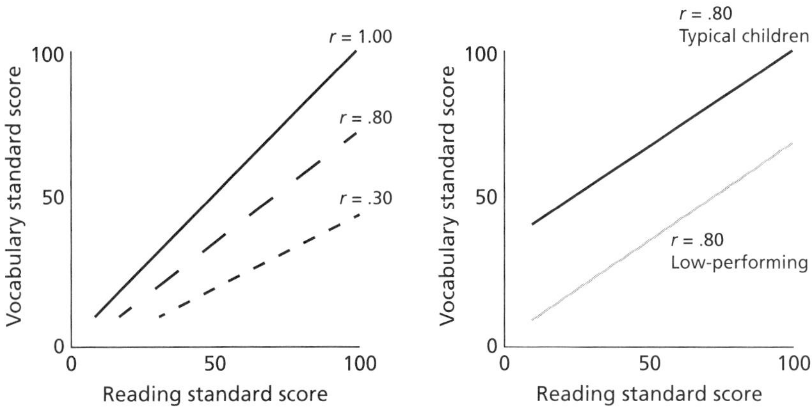

Figure 7.3. Comparing correlational method with method to detect group difference in levels of performance.

methods. SLI is used here because that is the definition followed in the studies cited here. The twin studies exclude children with clinically significant neurological conditions, hearing loss, syndromes such as Down syndrome, ASD, and early multilingual language acquisition as potential confounds in estimates of heritability.

The right half of Figure 7.3 shows a black line for a group of typically developing children and a gray line for children with SLI. Both groups have strong correlations between vocabulary standard scores and reading standard scores, with a correlation of .8 for each group. The distance between the two parallel lines also indicates that the two groups differ in levels of vocabulary standard scores and levels of reading standard scores, such that the typical children score higher relative to their same-age peers than the children with SLI on both traits.

In the context of twin studies, Figures 7.2 and 7.3 show how high heritability could also occur with a twinning effect, although if the focus is only on heritability, then existence of a twinning effect could go undetected or unreported. Figure 7.4 returns to the issue of MZ versus DZ twins. A prominent assumption has been that a possible twinning effect on language acquisition would be due to caregiver demand generated by two infants instead of one (Rutter, Thorpe, Greenwood, Northstone, & Golding, 2003). The expected outcomes for such a simple twinning effect are shown in Figure 7.4. Comparison to single-born children would be possible using percentile scores in which children's scores are calculated relative to the distribution of scores for children their age. Figure 7.4 shows that when the expected (mean) percentile score is 50 for the single-born sample of children of the same age, twin children (whether in MZ or DZ pairs) would perform lower, on average, if a simple twinning effect is operative. However, if a zygosity effect interacts with twinning effects, the two twin pairs would differ.

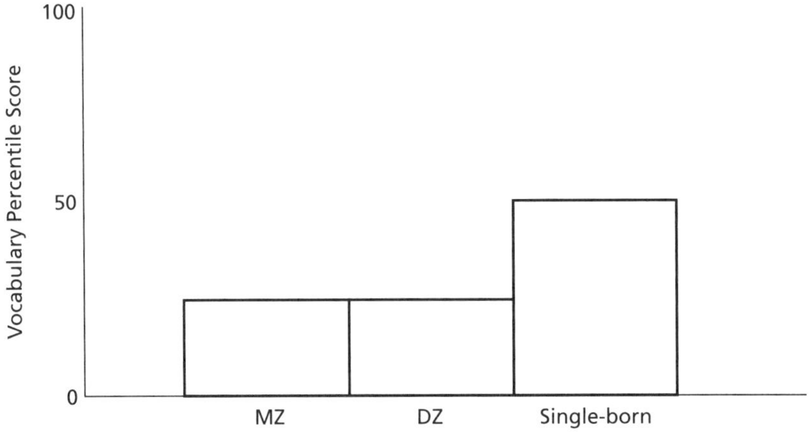

Figure 7.4. Expected outcomes for simple twinning effect. (*Key:* MZ, monozygotic; DZ, dizygotic.)

OVERVIEW: STUDIES OF LANGUAGE ACQUISITION OF TWINS

Empirical studies of twins are challenging. A large sample size is required for the quantitative methods of behavioral genetics. Population-based samples of twins are preferred: "twin clubs" tend to be overrepresented with MZ twin pairs (about one third of a full population-based sample are MZ pairs). For these reasons, twin studies require a strong funding base. The most prominent population-based study is the Twins Early Development Study (TEDS), a longitudinal study of twins born in England and Wales in 1994, 1995, and 1996 (Haworth, Davis, & Plomin, 2012). Language variables were included among a large number of cognitive and behavioral variables.

Important generalizations have emerged about language acquisition from multiple studies affiliated with TEDS: Heritability estimates for language variables range from .24 to .50, with increasing heritability with age and lower levels of performance (Hayiou-Thomas, 2008, 2014). These generalizations hold for a smaller sample of children ascertained by referral (DeThrone, Harlaar, Petrill, & Deater-Deckard, 2012).

Although the TEDS study has provided valuable information about language acquisition in twins, there are notable limitations of the language phenotypes. The measures are general in nature, in keeping with the focus on broad cognitive traits. Until the twins were 16 years old, there were no measures of grammar; speech measures were not included. Individual differences were referenced to a child's rank in the twin sample; no standardized tests with scores referenced to a population-based sample of same-age children were included, presumably due to the longer time needed for test administration. The within-sample ranking, even for a relatively large sample of twins, makes it impossible to detect a possible difference in twin levels of scoring compared with norms for single-born children.

THREE INTERRELATED STUDIES OF TWINS

A prospective cohort study of twins was drawn from a total population sample frame comprising statutory notifications of all births in Western Australia in 2000–2003, plus some twin pairs from the Western Australian Twin Child Health study, born 1997–1998. The population of Western Australia is demographically similar to some states in the Midwestern United States, such as Kansas and the Kansas City area. Standardized English language assessments for language and cognitive abilities are valid for Australian children and can be compared with American or English children. The main cohort of twins was followed longitudinally with direct behavioral assessments at 2, 4, 6, 9, and 14 years. The assessment protocol was designed to collect multiple measures of speech, language, cognition, reading, and social development on age-referenced standardized tests. The first report, referred to here as the 24-month report, is of outcomes from a parent questionnaire of early vocabulary and grammar at 24 months of age (Rice et al., 2014) with a sample of 473 twin pairs (946 children). The second report, referred to here as the 4- and 6-year report is of outcomes at 4 and 6 years with a sample of 628 twin pairs (1256 children). This study provided heritability estimates for 10 phenotypes (nine of speech and language, one of nonverbal IQ) and included an omnibus overall language score, vocabulary, grammar, length of utterances in conversational samples, and speech development (Rice et al., 2018). The third study is a collaboration with the TEDS, carried out with 405 16-year-old twin pairs (810 children) of their ongoing longitudinal sample, referred to here as the 16-year report (Dale, Rice, Rimfeld, & Hayiou-Thomas, 2018). The phenotypes included measures of vocabulary and figurative language and the first grammar task used in a TEDS study—a grammar judgement task developed as a marker with high sensitivity to SLI (Rice, Hoffman, & Wexler, 2009).

Twinning and Zygosity Effects Across Phenotypes at 2, 4, and 6 Years

The first strong empirical documentation of twinning effects emerged from the 24-month report. Outcomes are reported for gender-specific norms because girls generally begin to use words at younger ages than boys, and this was true for the twins in the 24-month report as well as other studies. In this study, twins had lower than expected average language scores compared with population-based age norms. Instead of the expected 50th percentile, the average for the twin sample was 26.63. The mean number of words produced at 24 months in the normative sample is 307, with a standard deviation (*SD*) of 171 (Fenson et al., 2006). The mean for the twin sample was 212.39, or a little more than .5 *SDs* below what is expected, which is a medium effect size. Using the bottom 10th percentile of the gender-specific norms as a definition of Late Language Emergence (LLE), 38% of the twin sample were LLE, indicating more of the twins than expected were at the low end of the number of words produced at 24 months. These differences held up across multiple measures of early words, combined words, and grammar.

A further new finding was that the twinning effect differed for MZ versus DZ twins, revealing a zygosity effect. The modeled number of words for MZ twins was 167.90 (24.16 percentile) compared with 201.80 (29.21 percentile) for DZ twins, showing a statistically significant advantage for DZ twins. As for the twinning effects, the zygosity effect held up across multiple measures, revealing that MZ twins, on average, are somewhat slower to acquire language than DZ twins.

The existence of twinning effects, more pronounced for MZ than DZ twins, early in language acquisition raises the question of whether the twins catch up to single-born children as they age. The 4- and 6-year report addressed this question with multiple measures of speech and language acquisition. The twinning effects were still evident at 4 years but were decreased at 6 years across multiple phenotypes. Neither assessment of nonverbal IQ nor speech abilities showed a twinning effect at 4 years, although the following dimensions of language yielded standard scores below age expectations for single-born children—vocabulary, overall language abilities, syntax, mean length of utterance, and grammatical marking of tense and agreement (finiteness-marking). As at 2 years, the twinning effect was of medium size, with standard scores of about 10 points, or two thirds of an *SD* of 15, below the expected mean of 100 for omnibus language tests and specific tests of grammar. The twinning effect was reduced at 6 years with an across-the-board increase in mean scores and a reduction of the number of measures statistically different from single-born children. Overall, the twins were closing the gap with single-born children in language acquisition, although a statistically significant, but smaller, gap remains at 6 years, a gap that never existed for speech and nonverbal IQ measures.

Zygosity effects were evident at 4 years but disappeared by age 6 years. MZ twins had significantly lower standard scores at 4 years for 6 of the 10 phenotypes, but no significant zygosity differences at age 6 for any phenotype. Thus, the MZ twins, on average, improved their language skills at a faster rate than DZ twins during the 2 years between 4 and 6. In order to close the twinning gap, the twins, especially the MZ twins, improved their language skills at a faster rate than single-born children in this age range to reduce the gap relative to the latter. The outcomes are summarized in Figure 7.5, indicating that twinning effects and zygosity effects are evident during this important preschool period for twins, although the developmental mechanisms are working hard to generate positive momentum to overcome the delay factors.

These early differences between twin language acquisition and single-born expectations for language acquisition raised the question of possible pre- or perinatal effects that could contribute to the differences. A study of

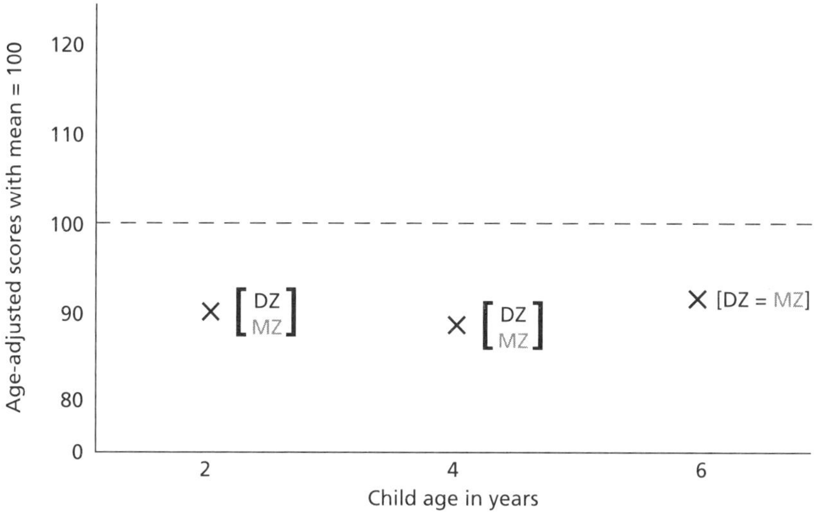

Figure 7.5. Zygosity and twinning effects at 4 and 6 years. (*Key:* MZ, monozygotic; DZ, dizygotic.)

prenatal and perinatal risks for LLE in the otherwise healthy developing twin sample at 2 years found that the same known risk factors for LLE in single-born children contributed to risk for LLE in twins—gestational diabetes, prolonged time to spontaneous respiration, mothers giving birth to two or more children previously, and fetal growth restriction/optimal birth weight. Sociodemographic risk factors, such as low maternal education and socioeconomic area disadvantage, were not associated with increased odds of LLE. Twins may be at greater risk for the conditions that predicted LLE compared with single-born births, highlighting the need for sound pediatric care in the fetal and neonatal periods (Taylor, Rice, Christensen, Blair, & Zubrick, 2018).

Heritability Outcomes at 2, 4, 6, and 16 Years

As expected, heritability increased with age, as shown by concordance calculations as well as calculation of h^2. At 2 years, the concordance rate for LLE was .93 for MZ pairs; .77 for DZ pairs, with an $h^2 = .23$, statistically significant although not high. For the full group, not divided into LLE/non-LLE, for total words produced, $h^2 = .25$; for grammar, $h^2 = .52$ for boys and $h^2 = .43$ for girls; and for combining words, $h^2 = .22$. Heritability estimates obtained from precise direct assessment of language phenotypes were modeled at 4 and 6 years, controlling for maternal education, maternal age, sex, age of assessment, birth weight, and Apgar scores. Conditional model heritability estimates showed consistent increase from 4 to 6 years across all nine phenotypes, and the h^2 values were higher than reported previously, in the range of .44–.92 at 6 years, with the highest estimate for a grammar marker.

The third study is related to the first two studies in the grammar phenotype, evaluated in a different sample of twins, the TEDS sample, at an older age, 16 years. The phenotype was developed from an experimental measure of a grammaticality judgment task with high sensitivity to SLI in children as old as 15 years (Rice et al., 2009), a task related to grammar measures in the 24-month twin study and the 4- to 6-year twin study. The task's focus was on the property of finiteness marking, which is evident in diverse morphemes in English. Although a conventional property of grammar long recognized by linguists (Quirk, Greenbaum, Leech, & Svartvik, 1985), its importance for child grammar was worked out only in the 1990s (Wexler, 1996). The following set of sentences illustrate the property of finiteness, which appears in positions within the sentence in which tense and agreement marking appear:

1. The boy __ walking home.
2. Yesterday Patsy walk__ home.
3. The girl always run __ to the store.
4. Where __ the boy walking?
5. ___ the boy happy?
6. How __ he walk home?

The blanks in the sentences indicate where a finiteness marker should appear. In English, this includes *be* as copula or auxiliary, in the form of *is* or *are;* past tense in regular *-ed* or irregular forms such as *ran,* third person singular *-s* or *z,* and auxiliary *do,* in declarative or interrogative sentences when the sentence location shifts to precede the subject. Finiteness marking is an obligatory feature for a grammatically well-formed sentence. Note that finiteness marking appears across different kinds of surface forms—sometimes as a single word, sometimes as an affix, and sometimes as a word-internal vowel shift as in irregular *run/ran.* Also note that the markers appear in different sites within a sentence, depending on the underlying clause structure.

Early on, children frequently omit these forms where required, as if they consider them to be optional instead of obligatory, hence the term *optional infinitive* to describe this phase. Note that it is about the grammatical function, not the form of the word. For example, the word *do* is omitted only when it functions as an auxiliary, not when it is a main verb, as in "they do their schoolwork every day" (Rice & Blossom, 2013). For children with SLI, this period of optionality is greatly extended. As shown in Figure 7.6, adolescents with SLI continue to judge simple questions with missing finiteness markers as acceptable sentences long after their age peers recognize the grammatical error (Rice et al., 2009). Given that finiteness marking is a core property of many languages (although not all), and children with SLI and other forms of language impairment show extended difficulty with this

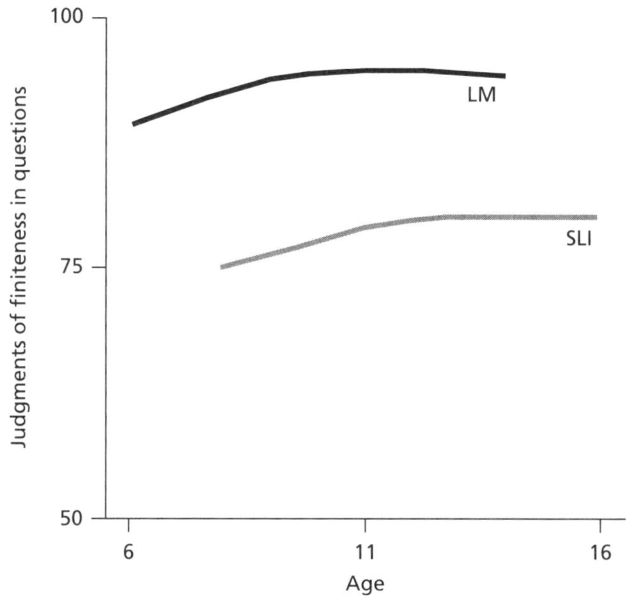

Figure 7.6. Protracted delay in judgements of omitted finiteness markers in questions. (*Key:* LM, younger language matched children at outset; SLI, children with SLI at outset.)

feature (Sterling, Rice, & Warren, 2012), it is hypothesized that this feature is likely to reveal inherited parts of children's language abilities (Wexler, 1996).

The study of twins at 24 months found high heritability using a behavioral phenotype of parent report of children's utterances that used finiteness markers. Precocious emergence of this grammatical feature was heritable. The study of twins at 4 and 6 years used a different assessment, a test of the use of grammatical features in children's sentence production (Rice & Wexler, 2001), and it also found the highest heritability estimates among the various phenotypes assessed. The study of twins at 16 years used a 5-minute assessment comprised of a grammaticality judgment task; after the children heard the sentence they responded whether it was correct (Rice et al., 2009). At the lowest 5th percentile level of performance within the twin sample, the MZ concordance was .43, DZ was .15, and heritability was .74, one of the highest levels reported across many phenotypes in the TEDS study (Dale et al., 2018).

Updated Generalizations

Across the three studies, there is mutually supportive evidence for the grammar marker of language impairment as a likely component of inherited influences on language acquisition. The theoretical rationale is well grounded in linguistic constructs of adult grammar. The pattern of empirical outcomes is consistent with current generalizations about the heritability of language—increasing heritability estimates with age and with lower levels of ability. Important new findings document a twinning effect such that, on average, twins are likely to be somewhat older than single-born children at given stages of language acquisition early on, a delay more pronounced for MZ than DZ twins. The zygosity effect rules out a simple effect caused by the environment of two infants that reduce caregiver time per child, given that would be true for both MZ and DZ twins. The effect is stronger for MZ twins, which, in turn, raises questions about biological differences between MZ and DZ twins that could contribute to the differences. The zygosity effects disappear by age 6, and the twinning effect is greatly moderated by that time as well, suggesting interesting developmental trajectories we have yet to understand. Although there are new findings providing further support of existing generalizations and new evidence of twinning effects, the empirical evidence is not fully definitive. Instead, there remain gaps and limitations that warrant further investigation.

RELEVANCE FOR A BETTER UNDERSTANDING OF DYSLEXIA AND EDUCATIONAL PRACTICES

The outcomes of the twin studies have immediate relevance for four issues central to our understanding of dyslexia and educational practices. The first is the causes of language impairments and the extent to which they are inherited. The chapters in this volume that address genetics and brain function (Chapters 2 and 3) are considering the inheritance issue from the levels of molecular genetics and brain development, all part of the biological underpinnings of human language. Twin studies contribute to growing convergence across these areas of investigation, although the exact underlying neurological mechanisms remain unknown. Studies of twins indicate that although twin children share most developmental generalizations with single-born children, there are definite differences in age of acquisition of early language that must be considered, as well as differences between MZ pairs and DZ pairs that point toward important clues very early in the developmental processes.

The second issue is the need to exercise care in the interpretation of language assessments of young twins. The use of a common criterion to define impairment, such as one *SD* below the age mean on standardized tests, could lead to confusion between a twinning effect on language acquisition that could resolve by age 6 years versus an early manifestation of a language impairment likely to persist. The findings from the studies reported here suggest it would be appropriate to adjust the criterion for levels of impairment in young twins to consider possible twinning effects plus a follow-up period of assessments to track change during the preschool period. This approach would help avoid false positive identification of twins as having language impairments during the preschool period.

Third, we must carefully consider details of the grammar such as finiteness marking used here (and possibly others). Sometimes this part of the grammar is dismissed as unimportant because it is only about the little words. Yet, the little words provide the structural cues in the grammar for the kinds of words to follow, which is very important for the processing of sentences in print as well as spoken language. There is also significant functional effect for children with immature grammar in that teachers can assume a child is socially immature in general or has been treated with special favor as a "baby" in the home, two assumptions that may be untrue and would introduce complications in deciding how to educate a child.

A fourth issue is the likelihood of multiple members of the family showing impairments in language and reading, given the high heritability estimates from twin studies. As educators communicate with parents about a given child's reading abilities, it is important to always keep in mind that one or both parents may have struggled with similar challenges when they were young and may perhaps still have such difficulties.

Lenneberg's (1967) scientific objectives were at the front edge of what was to follow because there are now multiple directions of inquiry into the bases of language acquisition, reading abilities, and methods for adjusting educational settings to best meet the needs of children. It will require all the new sources of information to compile the full picture of biological and environmental influences on children's language acquisition and how that information may enhance our understanding of developmental disorders such as dyslexia, SLI, and DLD.

REFERENCES

Boecks, C., & Piattelli-Palmarini, M. (2005). Language as a natural object, linguistics as a natural science. *Linguistic Review, 22*, 447–466.

Chomsky, N. (1995). *The minimalist program.* Cambridge, MA: The MIT Press.

Dale, P. S., Rice, M. L., Rimfeld, K., & Hayiou-Thomas, M. E. (2018). Grammar clinical marker yields substantial heritability for language impairments in 16-year-old twins. *Journal of Speech, Language, and Hearing Research, 61*, 66–78. doi:10.1044/2017_JSLHR-L-16-0364

DeFries, J. C., & Fulker, D. W. (1985). Multiple regression analysis of twin data. *Behavioral Genetics, 15*, 467–473.

DeThrone, L. S., Harlaar, N., Petrill, S. A., & Deater-Deckard, K. (2012). Longitudinal stability in genetic effects on children's conversational language productivity. *Journal of Speech, Language, and Hearing Research, 55*, 739–753.

Fenson, L., Marchman, V. A., Thal, D. J., Dale, P. S., Reznick, J. S., & Bates, E. (2006). *MacArthur-Bates Communicative Development Inventories user's guide and technical manual* (2nd ed.). Baltimore, MD: Paul H. Brookes Publishing Co.

Haworth, C. M. A., Davis, O. S. P., & Plomin, R. (2012). Twins Early Development Study (TEDS): A genetically sensitive investigation of cognitive and behavioral development from childhood to young adulthood. *Twin Research and Human Genetics, 16*, 117–125.

Hayiou-Thomas, M. E. (2008). Genetic and environmental influences on early speech, language and literacy development. *Journal of Communication Disorders, 41*, 397–408.

Hayiou-Thomas, M. E. (2014). Twin studies of individual differences. In P. J. Brooks & V. Kempe (Eds.), *Encyclopedia of language development* (pp. 647–650). Thousand Oaks, CA: Sage Publications.

Lenneberg, E. (1967). *Biological foundations of language*. New York, NY: Wiley.

Martin, J. A., Hamilton, B. E., & Osterman, M. J. K. (2012). *Three decades of twin births in the United States, 1980–2009*. Retrieved from https://www.cdc.gov/nchs/data/databriefs/db80.pdf

National Institute on Deafness and Other Communication Disorders Information Clearinghouse. (2011). *Specific language impairment*. Retrieved from https://www.nidcd.nih.gov/health/specific-language-impairment

Pinker, S. (1994). *The language instinct*. New York, NY: William Morrow.

Quirk, R., Greenbaum, S., Leech, G., & Svartvik, J. (1985). *A comprehensive grammar of the English language*. New York, NY: Longman.

Rice, M. L., & Blossom, M. (2013). What do children with Specific Language Impairment do with multiple forms of DO? *Journal of Speech, Language, and Hearing Research, 56*, 222–235.

Rice, M. L., Hoffman, L., & Wexler, K. (2009). Judgments of omitted BE and DO in questions as extended finiteness clinical markers of specific language impairment (SLI) to 15 years: A study of growth and asymptote. *Journal of Speech, Language, and Hearing Research, 52*, 1417–1433.

Rice, M. L., & Wexler, K. (2001). *Rice/Wexler Test of Early Grammatical Impairment*. San Antonio, TX: The Psychological Corporation.

Rice, M. L., Zubrick, S. R., Taylor, C. L., Gayán, J., & Bontempo, D. E. (2014). Late language emergence in 24 month twins: Heritable and increased risk for twins. *Journal of Speech, Language, and Hearing Research, 57*, 917–928. doi:10.1044/1092-4388(2013/12-0350)

Rice, M. L., Zubrick, S. R., Taylor, C. L., Hoffman, L., & Gayán, J. (2018). Longitudinal study of language and speech of twins at 4 and 6 years: Twinning effects decrease; zygosity effects disappear; and heritability increases. *Journal of Speech, Language, and Hearing Research, 61*, 79–83. doi:10.1044/2017_JSLHR-L-16_0366

Rutter, M., Thorpe, K., Greenwood, R., Northstone, K., & Golding, J. (2003). Twins as a natural experiment to study the causes of mild language delay: I: Design, twin-singleton differences in language, and obstetric risks. *Journal of Child Psychology and Psychiatry, 44*(3), 326–341.

Sterling, A. M., Rice, M. L., & Warren, S. F. (2012). Finiteness marking in boys with fragile X syndrome. *Journal of Speech, Language, and Hearing Research, 55*, 1704–1715.

Taylor, C. L., Rice, M. L., Christensen, D., Blair, E., & Zubrick, S. R. (2018). Prenatal and perinatal risks for late language emergence in a population-level sample of twins at age 2. *BMC Pediatrics, 18*, 41. https://doi.org/10.1186/s12887-018-1035-9

Wexler, K. (1996). The development of inflection in a biologically based theory of language acquisition. In M. L. Rice (Ed.), *Toward a genetics of language* (pp. 113–144). Mahwah, NJ: Lawrence Erlbaum Associates.

CHAPTER 8

Stability and Change in Developmental Language Disorder

Courtenay Frazier Norbury

SUMMARY

Language development is characterized by growth and longitudinal stability, meaning that while a child's language continues to develop, that child's position relative to peers in terms of language competence is relatively fixed over time. In this sense, Developmental Language Disorder (DLD) is similar to other developmental traits, such as height, that are genetically predisposed but are influenced by a child's experience, occur in all groups of children, and change as children grow, yet are not outgrown and do not simply fade away. DLD is persistent, and there is little evidence that these children can catch up with their peers. Language can be improved and children can increase their language competence over time as they develop. Most important, rate of language change appears consistent across the range of abilities, regardless of other child and environmental characteristics, such as general cognitive ability, behavior, or socioeconomic experiences. Research should focus on optimal points in development for language change, emphasize the considerable time and consistent effort needed to improve language skills in children with DLD, and consider how change in language as a result of intervention might have positive downstream effects on other aspects of child development, such as improved social skills, mental health, and classroom learning.

INTRODUCTION

Concern about the onset and development of spoken language is a common feature of many neurodevelopmental disorders, including autism spectrum disorder (ASD) and reading disorders. Terminology for child language deficits has traditionally been variable and confusing, especially when language deficits occur in the absence of other clinical conditions (Bishop, 2014). An international consortium recommended the term *DLD* to describe cases in which language ability is below chronological age expectations, prognosis is poor, and language deficits yield adverse functional impacts in everyday life (Bishop, Snowling, Thompson, Greenhalgh, & CATALISE, 2017). Unlike Specific Language Impairment, DLD does not require discrepancy between verbal and nonverbal abilities, in part recognizing that selective impairments in language are rare, given the distributed neural networks involved in typical language acquisition and DLD (Krishnan, Watkins, & Bishop, 2016). There is overwhelming evidence that DLD is a multifactorial disorder influenced by complex genetic risk factors that interact with environmental experiences (Bishop, 2014). The long-term consequences of DLD include poor literacy and academic achievement and employment challenges (Conti-Ramsden, Durkin, Toseeb, Botting, & Pickles, 2018). Such findings suggest that some of the environmental risk factors associated with DLD may themselves be genetically influenced (Bishop, 2014).

Intervention typically aims to ensure that a child's language ability is within the range expected for his or her age when measured by a standardized test. There is also an implicit assumption that improving child language will have important cascading impacts on other aspects of development that critically depend on language (e.g., literacy, social skills, educational attainment). Yet, many intervention trials fail to yield improvement on language assessment relative to controls (Bleses et al., 2017), and even when language does improve, transfer to other skills such as literacy is not consistently observed (Fricke et al., 2017).

This chapter considers DLD in the context of two complementary forces in child language development—stability and change (cf. Bornstein, Putnick, & Esposito, 2017). Child, family, and measurement issues that contribute to stability and change are considered. If the goal of clinical and/or educational services is to alter the developmental trajectory of language in DLD, then research efforts must determine the optimal age and intervention dosage required to alter the rate of language learning. Alternatively, although aspects of language are malleable, rate of change is less so, in which case, the goals of intervention may be to optimize language and communication function in order to mitigate negative downstream consequences of DLD.

STABILITY AND CHANGE IN CHILD LANGUAGE DEVELOPMENT AND DISORDER

Longitudinal studies have traditionally focused on individual differences in language growth, or the change in average language scores on standard tests over time. Sometimes studies have focused on specific aspects of language, such as vocabulary (tests of how many words a child knows and how readily the child can define words) or grammar (the rules that govern how words are combined into sentences), whereas other studies use omnibus tests in which they sample a range of language domains in a single test. Regardless of the measure, studies robustly demonstrate that although there is variation in language competence, growth trajectories tend to be parallel, suggesting similar rates of language growth across the distribution (Klem, Hagtvet, Hulme, & Gustafsson, 2016). In other words, children who start off with relatively low levels of language can make just as much progress as children who start with more advanced language skill. Parallel growth trajectories highlight the somewhat paradoxical feature that language has impressive longitudinal stability even though it is always changing (Bornstein & Putnick, 2012). Stability here means that a child's position in the distribution of language scores relative to children of a similar age remains constant. In other words, language is stable if a given child improves language scores by 10 points every year, while all other children in the distribution improve by 10 points as well (Bornstein & Putnick, 2012).

How can language be both changing and stable? It may be helpful to consider another familiar developmental trait that is also influenced by genetic factors but is subject to environmental experience—height. If we were to measure an individual child's height between the ages of 4 and 11, we would definitely see growth—children tend to get taller as they get older. If we asked all children in a given kindergarten classroom to line up in order of relative height, then there would be considerable variation in height, with some relatively tall children and other relatively short children. If we were to repeat this exercise with the same children at age 11, then we would see that all children had grown taller, but the rank height order would remain largely unchanged—the relatively tall children would likely still be the tallest children in the class, and those that were short would still be relatively short, despite growing considerably.

Longitudinal investigations of language that include children at the extremes of the language distribution, including those with DLD, suggest that language behaves in a similar way (Bornstein, Hahn, & Putnick, 2016a; McKean et al., 2017). My own work has included children with additional developmental concerns to assess factors that may increase or disrupt stability. The Surrey Communication and Language in Education Study (SCALES) (Norbury et al., 2016, 2017) is a population study of child language from school entry (ages 4–5 years) to Year 3 (ages 7–8 years). From a population of 7,267 children, a subsample stratified by sex, age, and teacher report of communication was assessed on six core language measures tapping receptive and expressive vocabulary, grammar, and narrative skill (Norbury et al., 2017). Unusually, SCALES includes three groups—children with typical language, children with DLD, and children with a range of developmental conditions that are associated with language, cognitive, and behavioral deficits (including ASD and known genetic conditions).

Language in this population was stable over a 3-year period, yet all three language groups demonstrated language growth (Norbury et al., 2017). The slopes, representing change in language ability from Year 1 to Year 3, were parallel across all three groups. This is encouraging because it indicates that as a group, even children at the bottom of the distribution were improving language skills at the same rate as those with proficient language, despite having additional diagnoses, more severe language deficits, and variable cognitive and behavioral profiles. Parallel rates of growth, however, mean that the language gap between groups is maintained over time; by Year 3, children who started school at the bottom of the language distribution were only just reaching the levels of language competence that children at the top had achieved in Year 1. Similar findings are reported through to adulthood for children with more selective language deficits (i.e., nonverbal cognitive scores within the normal range (Rice, 2013) and within the autism spectrum (Pickles, Anderson, & Lord, 2014).

FACTORS THAT MAINTAIN OR DISRUPT STABILITY

Stability is influenced by a number of factors, including child- and family-level characteristics, contextual factors (e.g., school), and issues of measurement. Children with DLD are very likely to present with co-occurring developmental deficits in motor development, executive function, and literacy, as well as social, emotional, and behavioral challenges (cf. Bishop, 2014). These child-level factors may influence environmental inputs; for example, in SCALES, by age 8, many children with severe language deficits were in special educational provision, had significant peer problems, and had limited levels of literacy (Norbury et al., 2017). DLD was also overrepresented in families from socioeconomically deprived backgrounds (Norbury et al., 2016). Therefore, it is likely that children with DLD elicit different responses from peers, caregivers, and teachers, and the nature of language learning from context changes significantly over time for children with DLD, relative to typically developing peers.

Therefore, one may expect that these additional factors could influence estimates of stability and change. In SCALES, whereas lower child nonverbal cognitive ability; ratings of social, emotional, and behavioral difficulties; and socioeconomic disadvantage were all associated with more severe language deficits, none were associated with rate of growth in language scores over the first 3 years of primary school (Norbury et al., 2017). Similarly, Bornstein and colleagues demonstrated that estimates of stability are similar in groups of children with contrasting early language skills (Bornstein et al., 2016a) and those with environmental and biological risks (Bornstein, Hahn, & Putnick, 2016b; Putnick, Bornstein, Eryigit-Madzwamuse, & Wolke, 2017), even after child cognitive and social skills, home environment, socioeconomic status, and maternal education were taken into account. Such findings lead to the provocative suggestion that similar processes maintain core language whatever the level of language competence (Bornstein et al., 2016a, 2016b).

Child age is one factor that does reliably affect estimates of stability; numerous studies report low estimates of language stability prior to age 4, to the extent that language assessment in the under-3s is not clinically predictive of later language attainment (Bornstein, Hahn, Putnick, & Suwalsky, 2014; Duff, Reen, Plunkett, & Nation, 2015; Pickles et al., 2014). It is unclear what this early instability means—it has been taken as a potential marker of increased neurobiological plasticity and, therefore, may reflect a more optimal time for targeted language intervention (cf. Pickles et al., 2014). Yet, increased stability from school entry may indicate that education introduces more homogeneous environmental experiences that exert greater influence on language growth and attenuate the impact of individual child or family characteristics. Alternatively, developmental variation in stability may also highlight measurement issues and changing assessment practices over time.

Measurement methodology is a crucial consideration as all assessments are subject to measurement error, and accurate estimates of stability and change critically depend on reliable assessments. Stability estimates may vary depending on assessment content (e.g., vocabulary vs. grammar), method variance (e.g., direct assessment vs. parent or teacher report), and the interval between assessments (e.g., reduced stability at longer intervals between tests). Experimental language tasks typically aim to minimize variation in performance between individuals in order to be more reliable at the group level (Hedge, Powell, & Sumner, 2017) and, thus, tend to be less reliable than standardized tests. Reduced reliability will attenuate correlations between tasks over time, and this may be mistakenly interpreted as instability in the underlying construct.

Researchers address these challenges by increasingly employing latent variable techniques, which can incorporate a variety of assessments ostensibly tapping different components of language and can accommodate different assessment methods and respondents (cf. Bornstein et al., 2014). For example, one can combine parent report of everyday language use with direct assessment of receptive vocabulary and expressive grammar to identify an underlying latent construct of language. Latent variables yield more precise statistical estimates because they distinguish shared variance among measures that are common to language and they relegate measurement error to a residual term.

Issues regarding measurement, child, and contextual factors can make it exceedingly difficult to know whether change (or lack of change) in language competence reflects measurement error, changing social and educational contexts, practice effects, real change (developmental or in response to an intervention), or other interactive developmental processes (Bornstein et al., 2017).

WHAT DOES STABILITY MEAN FOR INTERVENTION?

The goal of many special education and clinical (speech-language therapy) services is to accelerate language change for those children at the bottom of the language distribution so that one might normalize a language trajectory, narrow the gap, or demonstrate greater than expected progress on key language indices. Achieving these goals requires us to understand how much natural change can be expected on particular measures over a given period, yet we currently lack sufficient longitudinal data to give us reliable estimates of natural change (Schmitt, Logan, Tambyraja, Farquharson, & Justice, 2017) and, thus, when might be an optimal time to intervene.

Reduced language stability prior to age 3 has suggested a period of enhanced neural plasticity when efforts to change a developmental language trajectory may be most efficacious. Reduced stability in the preschool years, however, may also mean that very early intervention is not warranted or cost effective because many children make considerable progress without any additional support (McGillion, Pine, Herbert, & Matthews, 2017; Wake et al., 2013). Putting all of our eggs in an early intervention basket may result in treating many typically developing children (Norbury, 2015). Yet, the impressive stability of language after school entry can paint a rather bleak picture for children who start school with DLD. The big question is whether greater than expected change in language is possible and what provision is required to realize accelerated language growth.

Universal education provision supports the steady growth of language skills for all children and likely increases language stability over time (Norbury et al., 2017). Language learning itself remains malleable across the life span, and adolescence may be another potential sensitive period for brain development and cognitive change in response to intensive training (Knoll et al., 2016). Yet, even the most promising intervention programs require targeted input over a prolonged period and yield, at best, modest gains in language capacity (Fricke et al., 2017; Hagen, Melby-Lervag, & Lervag, 2017; Haley, Hulme, Bowyer-Crane, Snowling, & Fricke, 2017).

Therefore, a more realistic goal of most school-age therapy services may be to embrace individual differences in language and consider instead how to ensure that children with DLD can fully participate in academic and social activities and how to mitigate potentially negative downstream consequences, such as poor literacy (Snowling, Duff, Nash, & Hulme, 2016); adverse social, emotional, and mental health outcomes (Yew & O'Kearney, 2013); and limited employment options (Conti-Ramsden et al., 2018).

CONCLUSION

Language development is both ever changing and incredibly stable. This appears to be true for typically developing children and those affected by DLD. Similar rates of language growth for children across the spectrum of ability strongly suggest that the core mechanisms that maintain language stability are the same regardless of language competence. One consequence of strong language stability is that DLD is persistent, and narrowing the language gap with peers presents considerable challenges.

Intervention studies tell us that language can be improved, but altering the rate of language learning may also be malleable. Language appears to be less stable in the early years, although it is possible that early instability is more indicative of measurement error than neurobiological plasticity. Nevertheless, early variation in language acquisition is likely to influence the development of later language and cognitive skills, which, in turn, affects future language learning. Thus, changing the nature and intensity of language input could have dramatic impacts on language abilities later in life. It is very unlikely though that we can fully normalize the language trajectories of children with DLD, and we may even question whether it is desirable to do so. On this view, we may accept DLD as the extreme end of normal language variation and focus our intervention efforts on ensuring all children have sufficient language to participate fully in society and develop good social, emotional, and mental health.

REFERENCES

Bishop, D. V. (2014). Ten questions about terminology for children with unexplained language problems. *International Journal of Language and Communication Disorders, 49*(4), 381–415.

Bishop, D. V. M., Snowling, M. J., Thompson, P. A., Greenhalgh, T., & CATALISE. (2017). Phase 2 of CATALISE: A multinational and multidisciplinary Delphi consensus study of problems with language development: Terminology. *Journal of Child Psychology and Psychiatry, 58*(10), 1068–1080.

Bleses, D., Hojen, A., Justice, L. M., Dale, P. S., Dybdal, L., Piasta, S. B., . . . Haghish, E. F. (2017). The effectiveness of a large-scale language and preliteracy intervention: The SPELL randomized controlled trial in Denmark. *Child Development, 89,* e342–e363. doi:10.1111/cdev.12859

Bornstein, M. H., Hahn, C. S., & Putnick, D. L. (2016a). Long-term stability of core language skill in children with contrasting language skills. *Developmental Psychology, 52,* 704–716.

Bornstein, M. H., Hahn, C. S., & Putnick, D. L. (2016b). Stability of core language skill across the first decade of life in children at biological and social risk. *Journal of Child Psychology and Psychiatry, 57*(12), 1434–1443.

Bornstein, M. H., Hahn, C. S., Putnick, D. L., & Suwalsky, J. T. (2014). Stability of core language skill from early childhood to adolescence: A latent variable approach. *Child Development, 85*(4), 1346–1356.

Bornstein, M. H., & Putnick, D. L. (2012). Stability of language in childhood: A multiage, multidomain, multimeasure, and multisource study. *Developmental Psychology, 48*(2), 477–491.

Bornstein, M. H., Putnick, D., & Esposito, G. (2017). Continuity and stability in development. *Child Development Perspectives 11*(2), 113–119. doi:10.1111/cdep.12221

Conti-Ramsden, G., Durkin, K., Toseeb, U., Botting, N., & Pickles, A. (2018). Education and employment outcomes of young adults with a history of developmental language disorder. *International Journal of Language and Communication Disorders, 53*(2), 237–255.

Duff, F. J., Reen, G., Plunkett, K., & Nation, K. (2015). Do infant vocabulary skills predict school-age language and literacy outcomes? *Journal of Child Psychology and Psychiatry, 56*(8), 848–856.

Fricke, S., Burgoyne, K., Bowyer-Crane, C., Kyriacou, M., Zosimidou, A., Maxwell, L., & Hulme, C. (2017). The efficacy of early language intervention in mainstream school settings: A randomized controlled trial. *Journal of Child Psychology and Psychiatry, 58*(10), 1141–1151.

Hagen, A. M., Melby-Lervag, M., & Lervag, A. (2017). Improving language comprehension in preschool children with language difficulties: A cluster randomized trial. *Journal of Child Psychology and Psychiatry, 58,* 1132–1140.

Haley, A., Hulme, C., Bowyer-Crane, C., Snowling, M. J., & Fricke, S. (2017). Oral language skills intervention in pre-school: A cautionary tale. *International Journal of Language and Communication Disorders, 52*(1), 71–79.

Hedge, C., Powell, G., & Sumner, P. (2017). The reliability paradox: Why robust cognitive tasks do not produce reliable individual differences. *Behaviour Research Methods 50*(3), 1166–1186.

Klem, M., Hagtvet, B., Hulme, C., & Gustafsson, J. E. (2016). Screening for language delay: Growth trajectories of language ability in low- and high-performing children. *Journal of Speech, Language, and Hearing Research, 59*(5), 1035–1045.

Knoll, L., Fuhrmann, D., Sakhardande, A., Stamp, F., Speekenbrink, M., & Blakemore, S. (2016). A window of opportunity for cognitive training in adolescence. *Psychological Science, 27,* 1620–1631.

Krishnan, S., Watkins, K. E., & Bishop, D. V. (2016). Neurobiological basis of language learning difficulties. *Trends in Cognitive Science, 20,* 701–714.

McGillion, M., Pine, J. M., Herbert, J. S., & Matthews, D. (2017). A randomised controlled trial to test the effect of promoting caregiver contingent talk on language development in infants from diverse socioeconomic status backgrounds. *Journal of Child Psychology and Psychiatry, 58*(10), 1122–1131.

McKean, C., Wraith, D., Eadie, P., Cook, F., Mensah, F., & Reilly, S. (2017). Subgroups in language trajectories from 4 to 11 years: The nature and predictors of stable, improving and decreasing language trajectory groups. *Journal of Child Psychology and Psychiatry, 58*(10), 1081–1091.

Norbury, C. F. (2015). Editorial: Early intervention in response to language delays—is there a danger of putting too many eggs in the wrong basket? *Journal of Child Psychology and Psychiatry 56I*(8), 835–836. doi:10.1111/jcpp.12446

Norbury, C. F., Gooch, D., Wray, C., Baird, G., Charman, T., Simonoff, E., . . . Pickles, A. (2016). The impact of nonverbal ability on prevalence and clinical presentation of language disorder: Evidence from a population study. *Journal of Child Psychology and Psychiatry, 57,* 1247–1257.

Norbury, C. F., Vamvakas, G., Gooch, D., Baird, G., Charman, T., Simonoff, E., & Pickles, A. (2017). Language growth in children with heterogeneous language disorders: A population study. *Journal of Child Psychology and Psychiatry, 58*(10), 1092–1105.

Pickles, A., Anderson, D. K., & Lord, C. (2014). Heterogeneity and plasticity in the development of language: A 17-year follow-up of children referred early for possible autism. *Journal of Child Psychology and Psychiatry, 55*(12), 1354–1362.

Putnick, D. L., Bornstein, M. H., Eryigit-Madzwamuse, S., & Wolke, D. (2017). Long-term stability of language performance in very preterm, moderate-late preterm, and term children. *Journal of Pediatrics, 181,* 74–79.

Rice, M. L. (2013). Language growth and genetics of specific language impairment. *International Journal of Speech Language Pathology, 15*(3), 223–233.

Schmitt, M. B., Logan, J. A., Tambyraja, S. R., Farquharson, K., & Justice, L. M. (2017). Establishing language benchmarks for children with typically developing language and children with language impairment. *Journal of Speech, Language, and Hearing Research, 60*(2), 364–378. doi:10.1044/2016_JSLHR-L-15-0273

Snowling, M. J., Duff, F. J., Nash, H. M., & Hulme, C. (2016). Language profiles and literacy outcomes of children with resolving, emerging, or persisting language impairments. *Journal of Child Psychology and Psychiatry, 57*(12), 1360–1369.

Wake, M., Tobin, S., Levickis, P., Gold, L., Ukoumunne, O. C., Zens, N., . . . Reilly, S. (2013). Randomized trial of a population-based, home-delivered intervention for preschool language delay. *Pediatrics, 132*(4), e895–e904.

Yew, S. G. K., & O'Kearney, R. (2013). Emotional and behavioural outcomes later in childhood and adolescence for children with specific language impairments: Meta-analyses of controlled prospective studies. *Journal of Child Psychology and Psychiatry, 54,* 516–524.

CHAPTER 9

Language in Autism Spectrum Disorder

What Optimal Outcomes Can Tell Us About Neural Plasticity

Inge-Marie Eigsti and Brian Castelluccio

SUMMARY

Our group has been studying an informative group of individuals who had definitive autism spectrum disorder (ASD) prior to age 5 but by the time of adolescence had lost all symptoms and had IQ and adaptive skills that were at least in the average range. We have found that this group uses unique brain networks to achieve this steep and remarkable developmental trajectory that we termed an "optimal outcome" (OO). Drawing on results from dyslexia, perinatal stroke, and healthy aging, we have proposed a neural model of compensation in which optimal outcomes reflect changes in the distributed integration of task-engaged and resting-state networks. Specifically, domain-general networks involving processes of attentional and cognitive control become involved in language processing in OO, in part via the heightened behavioral rehearsal involved in behavioral intervention. These networks are most malleable early in development; hence, the earliest interventions can have the greatest impact on outcomes.

INTRODUCTION

Autism spectrum disorder (ASD) is a neurodevelopmental disorder characterized by sociocommunicative difficulties and the presence of stereotyped and repetitive behaviors. Diagnostic criteria also include heightened or reduced awareness of sensory cues (American Psychiatric Association, 2013). Among the challenges presented by ASD, perhaps the most striking is its heterogeneity across multiple levels (see Waterhouse, London, & Gillberg, 2016)—behavioral presentation, neuroanatomy, neural function, risk genes, etiology, specificity of treatment, and developmental course. This chapter addresses developmental course via a focus on long-term outcomes in ASD; we propose that this focus may serve to illuminate core mechanisms of ASD. We begin with a brief review of the symptoms of ASD, with a particular focus on language.

LANGUAGE ABILITIES IN AUTISM SPECTRUM DISORDER

Language abilities in ASD are characterized by tremendous heterogeneity. Approximately 30% of affected individuals master fewer than 5–20 productive vocabulary words, a presentation described as "minimally verbal"

(Tager-Flusberg & Kasari, 2013) and associated with significant clinical impairment (Mayo, Chlebowski, Fein, & Eigsti, 2013). Closer to 50% of individuals with ASD were minimally verbal in the mid-1980s. This progress reflects improvements in the timing of diagnosis and an associated increase in the number of individuals who receive early intervention and recognition of milder forms of ASD.

Most people with ASD do attain fluent language abilities, although acquisition is still marked by significant delays (e.g., Eigsti, Bennetto, & Dadlani, 2007; Naigles, 2013). Weaknesses across all linguistic domains have been documented, with the most salient deficits in pragmatics, or the social use of language (Eigsti, de Marchena, Schuh, & Kelley, 2011). The most well-replicated findings include differences in receptive and expressive prosody (Peppe, McCann, Gibbon, O'Hare, & Rutherford, 2007); delays in the use of pronouns (Shield, Meier, & Tager-Flusberg, 2015) and mental state verbs (Bang, Burns, & Nadig, 2013); impairments in use of nonliteral language, such as irony, sarcasm, and metaphor (e.g., Akimoto et al., 2014); and impaired narrative organization and quality (e.g., Canfield, Eigsti, de Marchena, & Fein, 2016).

The salience of these deficits could suggest that all language impairments are secondary to, and explained by, social deficits. Yet, ASD is also characterized by structural language deficits in phonology (Rapin, Dunn, Allen, Stevens, & Fein, 2009), morphosyntax (Brynskov et al., 2017; Eigsti et al., 2007), and semantics (Kamio & Toichi, 2000). Further details on these findings are reviewed elsewhere (Boucher, 2012; Eigsti et al., 2011).

DEVELOPMENTAL COURSE

One productive approach to understanding the early presentation of ASD has capitalized on the increased prevalence of diagnoses (approximately 20%) in infant siblings of children with ASD. "Baby sibling" studies suggest that deficits in pointing, waving, imitation, eye contact, and name response at age 12 months are associated with later ASD diagnosis (Barbaro & Dissanayake, 2013). Other early symptoms include motor delays, atypically high sensitivity to sensory experience, trouble with consonants, attention-shifting delays, and generally lower activity levels (Elsabbagh & Johnson, 2016).

These early markers change over development, forming the constellation of ASD symptoms by age 3 years. The severity and number of symptoms develop along widely varying trajectories. The most common long-term outcome in ASD suggests significant difficulties in the lives of individuals with ASD and their families (Henninger & Taylor, 2013). Adults with ASD struggle more than adults with other disabilities with underemployment (Schall et al., 2015), loneliness and lack of meaningful social relationships (Shattuck et al., 2012), psychiatric comorbidities (Gillberg, Helles, Billstedt, & Gillberg, 2016), and nonindependent living arrangements (Eaves & Ho,

2008). A global study of occupation, friendships, independent living, and physical health and activity showed that only 4% of a group with ASD had *very good* outcomes, 17% had *good* outcomes, and the remainder were *fair* to *very poor* (Eaves & Ho, 2008); psychiatric, behavioral, and health problems were common. Furthermore, these difficulties tend to increase with age in ASD (Howlin, Moss, Savage, & Rutter, 2013).

Some individuals, however, experience more positive outcomes. A longitudinal study following children ages 2–14 indicated the presence of six statistically distinct trajectories, with one (the "bloomers") showing a particularly steep increase in functional skill (Fountain, Winter, & Bearman, 2012). Another study followed children ages 2–19, at which point 9% of participants had overcome the core difficulties associated with ASD and no longer had a diagnosis (Anderson, Liang, & Lord, 2014). A study of 100 males with Asperger syndrome, followed over 19 years, reported a significant decrease in the number of participants meeting criteria for ASD, although a large subgroup had ongoing difficulties in adaptive functioning (Helles, Gillberg, Gillberg, & Billstedt, 2015). The small literature on very good outcomes includes several case studies of children given intensive early applied behavior analysis therapy (Fein, Dixon, Paul, & Levin, 2005; Green, Brennan, & Fein, 2002; Lovaas, Koegel, Simmons, & Long, 1973). These outcomes suggest a very sharp or steep developmental trajectory.

OPTIMAL OUTCOMES IN AUTISM SPECTRUM DISORDER

Our group has done extensive work on OO in ASD (Fein et al., 2013). The primary paper that described the criteria for OO documented overall functioning in a group of 34 individuals ages 8–21, comparing them with age- and IQ-matched individuals with history of typical development (TD) or current ASD. Additional studies have described behavioral functioning in OO that is indistinguishable from or even better than TD. Studies included Vineland-rated social skills (Orinstein et al., 2015), personality and likeability (higher in OO) as coded by naïve raters (Suh et al., 2014), broader autism phenotype measures (Suh et al., 2016), pragmatic language measures (Canfield et al., 2016), academic skills (Troyb, Orinstein, Tyson, Helt et al., 2014), and big five personality traits, with OO participants rated as more extraverted (Orinstein et al., 2015). Restricted and repetitive behaviors that were present in childhood had resolved at the time of study (Troyb, Orinstein, Tyson, Eigsti et al., 2014).

Language is central to long-term educational and occupational functioning. The inclusion criteria for OO required early language delay; however, at the time of the study, standardized language assessments in the OO group did not differ from those in the TD group (Tyson et al., 2014). The exceptions were a vocabulary measure (the Peabody Picture Vocabulary Test–Fourth Edition; Dunn & Dunn, 2007) and a measure of syntax (Clinical Evaluation of Language Fundamentals–Fifth Edition; Wigg, Semel, &

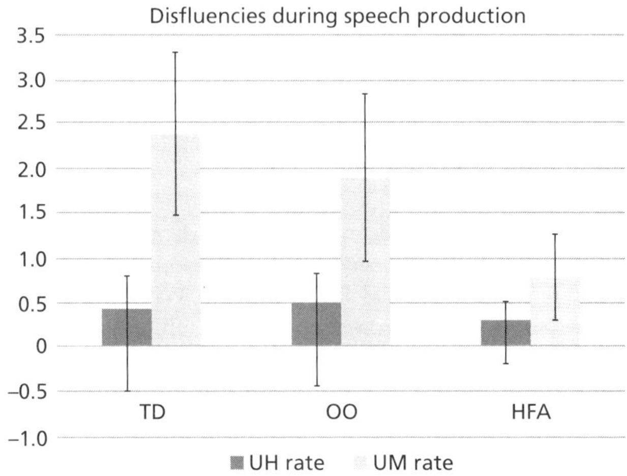

Figure 9.1. Dark bars depict "uh" production per 100 words; light bars depict "um" production per 100 words. The group by category interaction was significant, $p < .01$.

Secord, 2015); OO scores were above average on both measures, but lower than the TD group. In vivo, online, and implicit measures indicate that the OO and TD groups did not differ in most aspects of language production (Canfield et al., 2016; Suh et al., 2014). For example, in a study of speech disfluencies that characterize ASD (more "uhs" than "ums," indicating self-cueing rather than listener-oriented communication), the TD and OO groups both showed the opposite pattern, indicating a focus on their listeners (Irvine, Eigsti, & Fein, 2016) (see Figure 9.1). OO and TD groups focused more on the gestalt of an image and less on details than the ASD group when describing complex images (Fitch, Fein, & Eigsti, 2015). Among the large number of social and communication variables measured, two measures did differentiate the OO from the TD group. The OO group had more idiosyncratic language (Suh et al., 2014) and less coherent narrative structure during a story task (Canfield et al., 2016), which is consistent with Kelley, Paul, Fein, and Naigles's (2006) report on a younger group with OO whose stories had fewer causal links.

Neural Features of Optimal Outcome

This behavioral work shows that OO children who presented with the diagnosis of ASD before age 5 are essentially indistinguishable from children with a typical developmental history when they reach adolescence. What aspects of brain organization or brain function permit such striking plasticity? Early work by our group reported on head circumference data recorded during infant pediatric visits for 24 children with current ASD compared with 15 children with OO and 37 TD controls (Mraz, Dixon, Dumont-

Mathieu, & Fein, 2009). Results showed that both OO and ASD groups had larger head circumference (controlling for height and weight) compared with controls. This echoes a well-replicated finding of increased early (18–24 month) brain volume in children with ASD. In a functional magnetic resonance imaging (fMRI) study of language comprehension (Eigsti et al., 2016), we found greater activation in OO youth in left pars opercularis (BA44, a region involved in phonological, syntactic, and semantic language processing [Price, 2010]). Similarly, a number of other regions had atypical heightened activation in OO—left precentral/postcentral gyri, right precentral gyrus, left inferior parietal lobule, right supramarginal gyrus, left superior temporal/parahippocampal gyrus, left middle occipital gyrus, right middle/superior frontal gyri (including frontal eye fields), and bilateral cerebellum. Behaviorally typical language abilities in OO utilized atypical brain networks, with more recruitment of frontal attentional control systems and right hemisphere language-homologue regions. In other words, typical OO language function reflected atypical OO brain function. Findings were interpreted as compensatory because they showed greater OO activation compared with TD and differences between OO and ASD groups.

Our group has preliminary results from a study of whole-brain connectivity in OO assessed using a psychophysiological interaction approach (Li et al., unpublished data) (see Figure 9.2). Using seeds selected from the most atypical OO regions identified in the fMRI study (Eigsti et al., 2016), including left posterior parietal cortex (2A) and Broca's area (2B), with stringent, whole-brain corrections for multiple comparisons, analyses of functional connectivity indicate that OO connectivity resembled ASD in eight regions (with both groups differing from controls); OO connectivity resembled TD and differed from ASD in one region. There is limited data on brain organization in OO-like samples; one magneto-encephalography study examined auditory response maturation in five children with a possible OO profile (Port et al., 2016). M100 latency and gamma-band activity were associated with autism severity, and the OO-like group's values were intermediate to those in the TD and ASD groups.

To develop a model of neural development that could support the steep developmental trajectories observed in OO, we have reflected on 1) studies of ASD and 2) studies of related disorders in which symptoms remit. Studies of ASD emphasize both under- and overconnectivity (e.g., Muller et al., 2011), particularly in fronto-parietal-striatal (Di Martino et al., 2011) and default mode (e.g., Assaf et al., 2010) networks. Because atypical short- and long-range cortical connectivity predicts ASD symptomatology (Vasa, Mostofsky, & Ewen, 2016) and language (Verly et al., 2014), functional connectivity in OO should reflect the previously documented dramatic behavioral change.

Research in other disorders provides examples of how neural circuitry changes to support dramatic behavioral change. In dyslexia, there is evidence of full normalization of key brain regions of the reading circuit (Ayl-

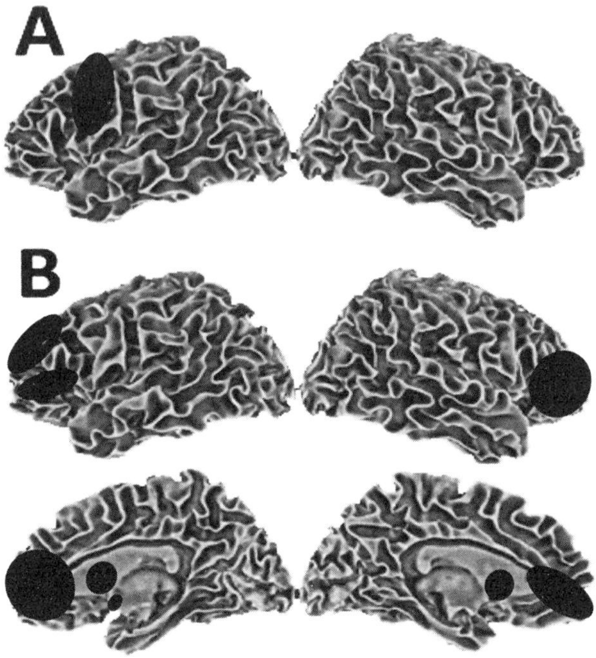

Figure 9.2. Psychophysiological interaction (PPI) comparisons showing A) a dlPFC region detected with PPI during language processing using a posterior parietal cortex seed ($p < .001$ clusterwise, whole-brain corrected) in which OO participants showed abnormal connectivity not seen in either TD or ASD and B) dlPFC, vlPFC, and med PFC regions showing OO connectivity with Broca's. Regions are shown as black ovals.

ward et al., 2003), although most studies also report compensatory changes in regions outside reading and language networks (e.g., Koyama et al., 2013). Preserved or recovered behavioral abilities are associated with strengthening of existing circuits, bilateral activations, and heightened engagement of frontal lobe systems involved in cognitive control in contexts such as stroke recovery (e.g., Foster et al., 2016) and aging (e.g., Sala-Llonch, Bartres-Faz, & Junque, 2015). After brain injury, ipsilateral or contralateral cortical areas beyond normal language processing regions are often recruited (e.g., Voets et al., 2006). Certainly, differences in neural organization may represent either long-term behavioral adaptation to early neural dysfunction (Scheller, Minkova, Leitner, & Kloppel, 2014) or the recruitment of supplemental neural resources (Fassbender & Schweitzer, 2006). Both of these are apparent in our fMRI study of language processing in OO. Recovered function may reflect the development of new connections or the unmasking or strengthening of preexisting connections (Frasnelli, Collignon, Voss, & Lepore, 2011). Distributed network integration (i.e., functional connectivity), in which different brain regions show highly correlated patterns of signal change over time (e.g., Di Martino et al., 2014) is as important as regional brain activity in understanding behavioral functioning. In our connectivity-based neural compensation model, we propose that new brain regions do not learn how to do new things; rather, existing circuits begin to process information in new ways.

There is strong evidence of early (age 6–12 months) differences in neural organization in ASD (Hazlett et al., 2017) and OO (Mraz et al., 2009). Most youth with ASD, including those in our studies, undergo intensive behavioral therapy after they have progressed through critical developmental periods that establish overarching neural configurations and microstructural connections important for language (Werker & Hensch, 2015) and social development (Lloyd-Fox, Széplaki-Köllőd, Yin, & Csibra, 2015). Intensive therapy is unlikely to induce experience-dependent modifications (i.e., wholesale network changes). Rather, we predict that connectivity profiles typical of ASD are reorganized in OO via changes in the interactions of task-specialized brain regions.

Factors That Facilitate Optimal Development in Autism Spectrum Disorder

It is critical to understand early influences on positive outcomes. How can we enable all children to grow up to be happy and healthy, enjoying rewarding activities and relationships? As scientists, we believe that this knowledge will serve to illuminate the mechanisms driving positive outcomes (Mawhood, Howlin, & Rutter, 2000), but we also anticipate that individuals with ASD and their families, and those with related disorders, will benefit from this information.

Early language is the most consistent predictor of better outcomes in ASD (Mawhood et al., 2000; Mayo et al., 2013). Communication at ages 2 and 3 predicts language and other outcomes at age 9 (Luyster, Lopez, & Lord, 2007). Imitation, joint attention, symptom severity, and play have all been found to be predictors of outcomes (e.g., Toth, Munson, Meltzoff, & Dawson, 2006), perhaps in part because they increase response to intervention (Helt et al., 2008).

Predictors of Optimal Outcome Status

There are few prospective studies of the early childhood features that lead to OO. Lord's group reported that earlier intervention and less repetitive behavior and hyperactivity at age 3 (Anderson et al., 2014) correlate with very positive outcomes. Our prospective work indicates that age 2 motor skills (Sutera et al., 2007), and fewer repetitive behaviors, milder social symptoms, and better adaptive skills at 2 (Moulton, Barton, Robins, Abrams, & Fein, 2016), were the best predictors of OO, consistent with retrospective studies showing that earlier intervention (Orinstein et al., 2014) and milder social symptoms (Fein et al., 2013) are associated with OO. There are links between heightened auditory perception and language delays (Eigsti & Fein, 2013), suggesting that attention to acoustic details could negatively affect language acquisition.

There is much more to be done to understand the bewildering heterogeneity of symptoms, causes, and correlates of ASD. Studies of long-term outcomes, including loss of diagnosis, in ASD, however, have the potential to illuminate the mechanisms of disorder. Our neural compensation model, grounded in studies of long-term and particularly positive outcomes in ASD, highlights the centrality of the reorganization of functional connectivity early in development. In future work, this model could be implemented in studies of other disorders such as dyslexia. In the meantime, this research highlights the range of possible outcomes for adults with significant neurodevelopmental disorders.

REFERENCES

Akimoto, Y., Sugiura, M., Yomogida, Y., Miyauchi, C. M., Miyazawa, S., & Kawashima, R. (2014). Irony comprehension: Social conceptual knowledge and emotional response. *Human Brain Mapping, 35*(4), 1167–1178. doi:1110.1002/hbm.22242

American Psychiatric Association. (2013). *Diagnostic and statistical manual of mental disorders* (5th ed). Washington, DC: Author.

Anderson, D. K., Liang, J. W., & Lord, C. (2014). Predicting young adult outcome among more and less cognitively able individuals with autism spectrum disorders. *Journal of Child Psychology and Psychiatry, 55*(5), 485–494. doi:10.1111/jcpp.12178

Assaf, M., Jagannathan, K., Calhoun, V. D., Miller, L., Stevens, M. C., Sahl, R., . . . Pearlson, G. D. (2010). Abnormal functional connectivity of default mode sub-networks in autism spectrum disorder patients. *Neuroimage, 53*(1), 247–256.

Aylward, E. H., Richards, T. L., Berninger, V. W., Nagy, W. E., Field, K. M., Grimme, C., . . . Cramer, S. C. (2003). Instructional treatment associated with changes in brain activation in children with dyslexia. *Neurology, 61,* 212–219.

Bang, J., Burns, J., & Nadig, A. (2013). Brief report: Conveying subjective experience in conversation: Production of mental state terms and personal narratives in individuals with high functioning autism. *Journal of Autism and Developmental Disorders, 43,* 1732–1740.

Barbaro, J., & Dissanayake, C. (2013). Early markers of autism spectrum disorders in infants and toddlers prospectively identified in the Social Attention and Communication Study. *Autism, 17*(1), 64–86. doi:10.1177/1362361312442597

Boucher, J. (2012). Research review: Structural language in autistic spectrum disorder characteristics and causes. *Journal of Child Psychology and Psychiatry, and Allied Disciplines, 53*(3), 219–233. doi:10.1111/j.1469-7610.2011.02508.x

Brynskov, C., Eigsti, I. M., Jørgensen, M., Lemcke, S., Bohn, O.-S., & Krøjgaard, P. (2017). Syntax and morphology in Danish-speaking children with autism spectrum disorder. *Journal of Autism and Developmental Disorders, 47*(2), 373–383.

Canfield, A. R., Eigsti, I. M., de Marchena, A., & Fein, D. (2016). Story goodness in adolescents with autism spectrum disorders and in optimal outcomes from ASD. *Journal of Speech, Language, and Hearing Research, 59,* 533–545. doi:10.1044/2015_JSLHR-L-15-0022

Di Martino, A., Fair, D. A., Kelly, C., Satterthwaite, T. D., Castellanos, F. X., Thomason, M. E., . . . Milham, M. P. (2014). Unraveling the miswired connectome: A developmental perspective. *Neuron, 83*(6), 1335–1353. doi:1310.1016/j.neuron.2014.1308.1050

Di Martino, A., Kelly, C., Grzadzinski, R., Zuo, X. N., Mennes, M., Mairena, M. A., . . . Milham, M. P. (2011). Aberrant striatal functional connectivity in children with autism. *Biological Psychiatry, 69*(9), 847–856.

Dunn, L. M., & Dunn, D. M. (2007). *Peabody Picture Vocabulary Test–Fourth Edition.* Circle Pines, MN: American Guidance Service.

Eaves, L. C., & Ho, H. H. (2008). Young adult outcome of autism spectrum disorders. *Journal of Autism and Developmental Disorders, 38*(4), 739–747. doi:10.1007/s10803-007-0441-x
Eigsti, I. M., Bennetto, L., & Dadlani, M. B. (2007). Beyond pragmatics: Morphosyntactic development in autism. *Journal of Autism and Developmental Disorders, 37*(6), 1007–1023.
Eigsti, I. M., de Marchena, A., Schuh, J., & Kelley, E. (2011). Language acquisition in autism spectrum disorders: A developmental review. *Research in Autism Spectrum Disorders, 5,* 681–691.
Eigsti, I. M., & Fein, D. A. (2013). More is less: Pitch discrimination and language delays in children with optimal outcomes from autism. *Autism Research, 6*(6), 605–613.
Eigsti, I. M., Stevens, M., Schultz, R., Barton, M., Kelley, E., Naigles, L. R., . . . Fein, D. A. (2016). Language comprehension and brain function in individuals with optimal outcomes from autism. *NeuroImage: Clinical, 10,* 182–191.
Elsabbagh, M., & Johnson, M. H. (2016). Autism and the social brain: The first-year puzzle. *Biological Psychiatry, 80*(2), 94–99. doi:10.1016/j.biopsych.2016.02.019
Fassbender, C., & Schweitzer, J. (2006). Is there evidence for neural compensation in attention deficit hyperactivity disorder? A review of the functional neuroimaging literature. *Clinical Psychology Review, 4,* 445–465.
Fein, D., Barton, M., Eigsti, I. M., Kelley, E., Naigles, L. R., Schultz, R. T., . . . Tyson, K. (2013). Optimal outcome in individuals with a history of autism. *Journal of Child Psychology and Psychiatry, 54*(2), 195–205. doi:110.1111/jcpp.12037
Fein, D., Dixon, P., Paul, J., & Levin, H. (2005). Pervasive developmental disorder can evolve into ADHD: Case illustrations. *Journal of Autism and Developmental Disorders, 35,* 525–534.
Fitch, A., Fein, D. A., & Eigsti, I. M. (2015). Detail and gestalt focus in individuals with optimal outcomes from autism spectrum disorders. *Journal of Autism and Developmental Disorders, 45*(6), 1887–1896. doi:1810.1007/s10803-10014-12347-10808
Foster, B. L., He, B. J., Honey, C. J., Jerbi, K., Maier, A., & Saalmann, Y. B. (2016). Spontaneous neural dynamics and multi-scale network organization. *Frontiers in Systems Neuroscience, 10,* 7. doi:10.3389/fnsys.2016.00007
Fountain, C., Winter, A. S., & Bearman, P. S. (2012). Six developmental trajectories characterize children with autism. *Pediatrics, 129*(5), e1112–e1120. doi:10.1542/peds.2011-1601
Frasnelli, J., Collignon, O., Voss, P., & Lepore, F. (2011). Crossmodal plasticity in sensory loss. *Progress in Brain Research, 191,* 233–249. doi:10.1016/B978-0-444-53752-2.00002-3
Gillberg, I. C., Helles, A., Billstedt, E., & Gillberg, C. (2016). Boys with Asperger syndrome grow up: Psychiatric and neurodevelopmental disorders 20 years after initial diagnosis. *Journal of Autism and Developmental Disorders, 46*(1), 74–82.
Green, G., Brennan, L. C., & Fein, D. A. (2002). Intensive behavioral treatment for a toddler at high risk for autism. *Behavior Modification, 26*(1), 69–102.
Hazlett, H. C., Gu, H., Munsell, B. C., Kim, S. H., Styner, M., Wolff, J. J., . . . Piven, J. (2017). Early brain development in infants at high risk for autism spectrum disorder. *Nature, 542*(7641), 348–351.
Helles, A., Gillberg, C. I., Gillberg, C., & Billstedt, E. (2015). Asperger syndrome in males over two decades: Stability and predictors of diagnosis. *Journal of Child Psychiatry and Psychology, 56*(6), 711–718. doi:10.1111/jcpp.12334
Helt, M., Kelley, E., Kinsbourne, M., Pandey, J., Boorstein, H., Herbert, M., & Fein, D. (2008). Can children with autism recover? If so, how? *Neuropsychology Reviews, 18*(4), 339–366.
Henninger, N. A., & Taylor, J. L. (2013). Outcomes in adults with autism spectrum disorders: A historical perspective. *Autism, 17*(1), 103–116. doi:10.1177/1362361312441266
Howlin, P., Moss, P., Savage, S., & Rutter, M. (2013). Social outcomes in mid-adulthood among individuals diagnosed with autism and average nonverbal IQ as children. *Journal of the American Academy of Child and Adolescent Psychiatry, 52,* 572–581.
Irvine, C. A., Eigsti, I. M., & Fein, D. A. (2016). Uh, um, and autism: Filler disfluencies as pragmatic markers in adolescents with optimal outcomes from autism spectrum disorder. *Journal of Autism and Developmental Disorders, 46*(3), 1061–1070.

Kamio, Y., & Toichi, M. (2000). Dual access to semantics in autism: Is pictorial access superior to verbal access? *Journal of Child Psychology and Psychiatry, 41*(7), 859–867.

Kelley, E., Paul, J. J., Fein, D., & Naigles, L. R. (2006). Residual language deficits in optimal outcome children with a history of autism. *Journal of Autism and Developmental Disorders, 36*(6), 807–828.

Koyama, M. S., Di Martino, A., Kelly, C., Jutagir, D. R., Sunshine, J., Schwartz, S. J., . . . Milham, M. P. (2013). Cortical signatures of dyslexia and remediation: An intrinsic functional connectivity approach. *PLoS One, 8*(2), e55454.

Lloyd-Fox, S., Széplaki-Köllőd, B., Yin, J., & Csibra, G. (2015). Are you talking to me? Neural activations in 6-month-old infants in response to being addressed during natural interactions. *Cortex, 70,* 35–48. doi:10.1016/j.cortex.2015.02.005

Lovaas, O. I., Koegel, R., Simmons, J. Q., & Long, J. S. (1973). Some generalization and follow-up measures on autistic children in behavior therapy. *Journal of Applied Behavior Analysis, 6*(1), 131–165.

Luyster, R., Lopez, K., & Lord, C. (2007). Characterizing communicative development in children referred for autism spectrum disorders using the MacArthur-Bates Communicative Development Inventory (CDI). *Journal of Child Language, 34,* 623–654.

Mawhood, L., Howlin, P., & Rutter, M. (2000). Autism and developmental receptive language disorder: A comparative follow-up in early adult life. I: Cognitive and language outcomes. *Journal of Child Psychology and Psychiatry, 41*(5), 547–559.

Mayo, J., Chlebowski, C., Fein, D. A., & Eigsti, I. M. (2013). Age of first words predicts cognitive ability and adaptive skills in children with ASD. *Journal of Autism and Developmental Disorders, 43*(2), 253–264. doi:210.1007/s10803-10012-11558-10800

Moulton, E., Barton, M., Robins, D., Abrams, N., & Fein, D. (2016). Early characteristics of children with ASD who demonstrate optimal progress between age two and four. *Journal of Autism and Developmental Disorders, 46*(6), 2160–2173.

Mraz, K. D., Dixon, J., Dumont-Mathieu, T., & Fein, D. (2009). Accelerated head and body growth in infants later diagnosed with autism spectrum disorders: A comparative study of optimal outcome children. *Journal of Child Neurology, 24*(7), 833–845.

Muller, R. A., Shih, P., Keehn, B., Deyoe, J. R., Leyden, K. M., & Shukla, D. K. (2011). Underconnected, but how? A survey of functional connectivity MRI studies in autism spectrum disorders. *Cerebral Cortex, 21*(10), 2233–2243. doi:10.1093/cercor/bhq296

Naigles, L. R. (2013). Input and language development in children with autism. *Seminars in Speech and Language, 34*(4), 237–248. doi:10.1055/s-0033-1353446

Orinstein, A. J., Helt, M., Troyb, E., Tyson, K. E., Barton, M. L., Eigsti, I. M., . . . Fein, D. A. (2014). Intervention for optimal outcome in children and adolescents with a history of autism. *Journal of Developmental and Behavioral Pediatrics, 35*(4), 247–256.

Orinstein, A. J., Suh, J., Porter, K., De Yoe, K. A., Tyson, K. E., Troyb, E., . . . Fein, D. A. (2015). Social function and communication in optimal outcome children and adolescents with an autism history on structured test measures. *Journal of Autism and Developmental Disorders, 45*(8), 2443–2463. doi:2410.1007/s10803-10015-12409-10806

Peppe, S., McCann, J., Gibbon, F., O'Hare, A., & Rutherford, M. (2007). Receptive and expressive prosodic ability in children with high-functioning autism. *Journal of Speech, Language and Hearing Research, 50*(4), 1015–1028.

Port, R. G., Edgar, J. C., Ku, M., Bloy, L., Murray, R., Blaskey, L., . . . Roberts, T. P. (2016). Maturation of auditory neural processes in autism spectrum disorder: A longitudinal MEG study. *Neuroimage Clinical, 11,* 566–577.

Price, C. J. (2010). The anatomy of language: A review of 100 fMRI studies published in 2009. *Annals of the New York Academy of Sciences, 1191,* 62–88.

Rapin, I., Dunn, M., Allen, D., Stevens, M., & Fein, D. (2009). Subtypes of language disorders in school-age children with autism. *Developmental Neuropsychology, 34,* 66–84.

Sala-Llonch, R., Bartres-Faz, D., & Junque, C. (2015). Reorganization of brain networks in aging: A review of functional connectivity studies. *Frontiers in Psychology, 6,* 663.

Schall, C. M., Wehman, P., Brooke, V., Graham, C., McDonough, J., Brooke, A., . . . Allen, J. (2015). Employment interventions for individuals with ASD: The relative efficacy of supported employment with or without prior Project SEARCH Training. *Journal of Autism and Developmental Disorders, 45*(12), 3990–4001.

Scheller, E., Minkova, L., Leitner, M., & Kloppel, S. (2014). Attempted and successful compensation in preclinical and early manifest neurodegeneration: A review of task FMRI studies. *Frontiers in Psychiatry, 5,* 132. doi:10.3389/fpsyt.2014.00132

Shattuck, P. T., Narendorf, S. C., Cooper, B., Sterzing, P. R., Wagner, M., & Taylor, J. L. (2012). Postsecondary education and employment among youth with an autism spectrum disorder. *Pediatrics, 129*(6), 1042–1049. doi:1010.1542/peds.2011-2864

Shield, A., Meier, R. P., & Tager-Flusberg, H. (2015). The use of sign language pronouns by native-signing children with autism. *Journal of Autism and Developmental Disorders, 45*(7), 2128–2145. doi:10.1007/s10803-015-2377-x

Suh, J., Eigsti, I. M., Naigles, L., Barton, M., Kelley, E., & Fein, D. (2014). Narrative performance of optimal outcome children and adolescents with a history of an autism spectrum disorder. *Journal of Autism and Developmental Disorders, 44,* 1681–1694.

Suh, J., Orinstein, A., Barton, M., Chen, C., Eigsti, I. M., Ramirez-Esparza, N., & Fein, D. (2016). Ratings of broader autism phenotype and personality traits in optimal outcomes from autism spectrum disorder. *Journal of Autism and Developmental Disorders, 46,* 3505–3518.

Sutera, S., Pandey, J., Esser, E. L., Rosenthal, M. A., Wilson, L. B., Barton, M., . . . Fein, D. (2007). Predictors of optimal outcome in toddlers diagnosed with autism spectrum disorders. *Journal of Autism and Developmental Disorders, 37*(1), 98–107.

Tager-Flusberg, H., & Kasari, C. (2013). Minimally verbal school-aged children with autism spectrum disorder: The neglected end of the spectrum. *Autism Research, 6*(6), 468–478.

Toth, K., Munson, J., Meltzoff, A. N., & Dawson, G. (2006). Early predictors of communication development in young children with autism spectrum disorder: Joint attention, imitation, and toy play. *Journal of Autism and Developmental Disorders, 36*(8), 993–1005.

Troyb, E., Orinstein, A., Tyson, K., Eigsti, I. M., Naigles, L., & Fein, D. (2014). Restricted and repetitive behaviors in individuals with a history of ASDs who have achieved optimal outcomes. *Journal of Autism and Developmental Disorders, 44*(12), 3168–3184.

Troyb, E., Orinstein, A., Tyson, K., Helt, M., Eigsti, I. M., Stevens, M., & Fein, D. (2014). Academic abilities in children and adolescents with a history of autism spectrum disorders who have achieved optimal outcomes. *Autism, 18*(3), 233–243.

Tyson, K., Kelley, E., Fein, D., Orinstein, A., Troyb, E., Barton, M., . . . Rosenthal, M. (2014). Language and verbal memory in individuals with a history of autism spectrum disorders who have achieved optimal outcomes. *Journal of Autism and Developmental Disorders, 44*(3), 648–663. doi:10.1007/s10803-013-1921-9

Vasa, R., Mostofsky, S. H., & Ewen, J. B. (2016). The disrupted connectivity hypothesis of autism spectrum disorders: Time for the next phase in research. *Biological Psychiatry: Cognitive Neuroscience and Neuroimaging, 1,* 245–252.

Verly, M., Verhoeven, J., Zink, I., Mantini, D., Peeters, R., Deprez, S., . . . Sunaert, S. (2014). Altered functional connectivity of the language network in ASD: Role of classical language areas and cerebellum. *NeuroImage: Clinical, 4,* 374–382.

Voets, N. L., Adcock, J. E., Flitney, D. E., Behrens, T. E., Hart, Y., Stacey, R., . . . Matthews, P. M. (2006). Distinct right frontal lobe activation in language processing following left hemisphere injury. *Brain, 129*(Pt 3), 754–766. doi:10.1093/brain/awh679

Waterhouse, L., London, E., & Gillberg, C. (2016). ASD validity. *Review Journal of Autism and Developmental Disorders, 3*(4), 302–329.

Werker, J. F., & Hensch, T. K. (2015). Critical periods in speech perception: New directions. *Annual Review of Psychology, 66,* 173–196.

Wiig, E. H., Semel, E., & Secord, W. A. (2015). *Clinical Evaluation of Language Fundamentals–Fifth Edition.* San Antonio, TX: Harcourt Assessment.

INTEGRATIVE COMMENTARY 3

Language and Reading Disorders—Same and Different?

Margaret J. Snowling

SUMMARY

Language and communication are fundamental skills and are at the core of social relationships and foundational for education. Thus, children with language difficulties are at high risk of emotional and behavioral difficulties and difficulty in acquiring literacy and numeracy. It is important to understand the causal mechanisms in order to design theoretically based interventions. This commentary raises a number of issues, which research in developmental disorders of language needs to address, highlighting gaps in the evidence. First, there are highly heritable differences in the rate at which children acquire language, but more needs to be known about how environmental factors might modify these pathways before school entry. From the point of school entry, there is stability in language skills, meaning that if a child enters school with language difficulties, then it is highly likely that these will persist. There needs to be closer investigation of how performance in different domains of language changes and what knock-on effects there are—for some children, there are problems with how speech is used to convey meaning distinctions (phonology); for others, the problem can be in how to put words together in sentences and, in particular, how to correctly use verbs (grammar); a further set of problems centers on how language is used in communication (pragmatics). Differences in the profile of these skills can, in turn, translate into different types of learning problems, with phonological difficulties associated more with dyslexia and difficulties with grammar and pragmatics more strongly associated with poor reading comprehension. We also need to know more about how cognitive strengths and difficulties that accompany individual differences in language profile can exacerbate (or compensate) for these difficulties. The aim of research should ultimately be to develop sustained interventions that prevent an intergenerational downward spiral from language difficulty to social disadvantage and poor mental health.

INTRODUCTION

Language difficulties are arguably the most pervasive of the childhood disorders. They can be observed in the absence of any obvious genetic, medical, or physical cause (Developmental Language Disorder [DLD]) or in conjunction with another developmental disorder, such as autism spectrum disorder (ASD), Down syndrome, or hearing impairment (Bishop, Snowling, Thompson, Greenhalgh, & Catalise-2 Consortium, 2017). By definition, language disorders impair communication; they also have knock-on effects on educational attainment, social relationships, and, in the absence of appropriate interventions, mental health and well-being. For more than half a century, scientists have sought to understand their nature, etiology, and developmental trajectory. The three state-of-the-art papers in this volume highlight contemporary issues relating to the nature and developmental course of children's language difficulties.

Norbury and Rice report recent research findings on DLD (which include children previously defined as having specific language impairment). There are two important messages—language disorders are stable and persistent, and although there are heritable influences on language acquisition, the outcomes for children with DLD depend on gene–environment interactions. Eigsti and Castelluccio, in contrast, discuss the exceptionally variable developmental profiles in ASD and seek neural explanations that explain outcomes.

STABILITY AND PERSISTENCE

Norbury reports data from the United Kingdom's Surrey Communication and Language in Education Study (SCALES) study showing that language skills are stable from ages 4 to 7 years in the population, and the development of language in children with difficulties follows the same trajectory as that of children with typical language skills; the implication, consistent with previous research, is that a child of school age with a language disorder is unlikely to reach a normal level of language proficiency (e.g., Klem, Hagtvet, Hulme, & Gustafsson, 2016; Tomblin, Zhang, Buckwalter, & O'Brien, 2003). There is less certainty regarding the stability of language in the preschool years. Bishop and Edmundson (1987) reported that more than 40% of children with specific language impairment at age 4 resolve their difficulties by age 5½; following this, the classification of these children as "resolved" versus "persistent" language-impaired groups remains broadly similar until adolescence (Stothard, Snowling, Bishop, Chipchase, & Kaplan, 1998). The United Kingdom's Wellcome Language and Reading Project reported that some 25% of children with specific language impairment at age 3½ were in the normal range for language by age 8 (Snowling, Nash, Gooch, Hayiou-Thomas, & Hulme, 2019).

Norbury poses the right question: Is the instability of language development in the preschool years simply a consequence of measurement error? It has to be acknowledged that this could be the case; preschool children do not always cooperate well in assessments. Clinical experience, however, suggests that some children genuinely do have a slow start and then catch up. For instance, late language emergence in twins is a well-documented phenomenon. Rice shows that this delay is greater in monozygotic (MZ) twins (who share 100% of their genes) compared with dizygotic (DZ) twins (who share 50% on average). This is a remarkable finding because co-twins, regardless of their zygosity, typically share the same family environment. Rather than attributing the language delay to the fact that twins (as compared with singletons) share less of the attention of their caretaker (and more of each other's) as has often been supposed, genes are implicated, and genes act through the environment (gene–environment correlation). Rice does not speculate on the mechanisms involved, but it is plausible that DZ twins, by virtue of their genetic differences, create different linguistic environments for themselves and indirectly for each other. This increased linguistic variability could foster more rapid language development for each than is the case for MZ co-twins. Later, differences between twins of different zygosity decrease between 2 and 4 years and disappear by age 6.

Thus, contrary to the notion of stability, the data from twins suggest that language levels are changing, at least in the early years. Rice notes, however, that the heritability of language skills increases across age and is higher for language-impaired children than for typical language learners; this could explain the persistence of language difficulties beyond the early years.

INDIVIDUAL DIFFERENCES IN LANGUAGE TRAJECTORY

Stability is a statistical concept, and, of course, there are outliers. An important question is whether such outliers can tell us anything about language disorders. The Wellcome Language and Reading project followed the development of some 260 children from age 3½ to age 8, including a high proportion (*N* = 73) of children with preschool language difficulties at the first time point (t1). The children underwent language assessments at approximately annual intervals; their performance was defined by a factor score comprising measures of vocabulary and expressive and receptive grammar (Snowling, Duff, Nash, & Hulme, 2016). Children scoring one standard deviation below the typical group were classified as language impaired at each time point. Two groups showed a stable pattern of language skills over the 5 years of the study—a group with persistent language difficulties and the benchmark control group with typical language. We also identified a group with resolving language impairment, classified as having preschool Specific Language Impairment (SLI) at t1 but falling within the normal range by 5½ years. Perhaps more striking is a group whose language was in the typical range at 3½ years but by 5½ years their language was impaired to the same extent as that of children with persistent language impairment—DLD; such a declining language trajectory has also been reported by Dale, Price, Bishop, and Plomin (2003) and others.

It is interesting to consider the factors associated with these different developmental profiles. Scrutiny of our data showed that, consistent with Norbury, the group with persistent difficulties were of lower socioeconomic status (relative to that of the groups with emergent or resolving difficulties). She points out that DLD is associated with a range of adverse social factors and speculates that these may be genetically transmitted via intergenerational processes. They were also of lower nonverbal IQ than the children in the other groups. In the resolving language difficulties group, there were also more boys than girls, suggesting that some boys might be wrongly classified as SLI in the early years because of slow, but gradually normalizing, language acquisition. Finally, about half of the group who showed emergent language difficulties were at family risk of dyslexia. Because phonological difficulties are a marker of the heritable risk of dyslexia (Snowling & Melby-Lervåg, 2016), it is tempting to suggest that these are the cause of declining language skills over time.

LANGUAGE DEVELOPMENT IN AUTISM SPECTRUM DISORDER

Language difficulties are the core of DLD. Language deficits are also observed in ASD, however. Difficulties in social-communication and social interaction—usually accompanied by stereotyped or repetitive behaviors, insistence on sameness, and a restricted range of interests—are central to ASD. Eigsti and Castelluccio emphasize variability in presentation at all levels, including etiology. Insofar as language is concerned, some individuals with ASD are only minimally verbal, whereas others may be verbose; the most frequent difficulties are in the use of language for social purposes or pragmatic skills. Commonly reported are difficulties with turn-taking, using the wrong register when talking, and failing to take into account the context of the conversation. Some individuals also have structural language difficulties, however, which can include problems with phonology, grammar, and/or semantics.

Reflecting the heterogeneity in presentation, the outcomes of children with ASD are also highly variable. Studies of children at family risk of ASD suggest that deficits in social behaviors, such as pointing, waving, eye contact, and imitation at 12 months, presage diagnosis of the disorder at 3 years; it seems likely that these deficits will lead to slower than normal language acquisition. Although prospective studies are rare, language is a key factor in predicting the outcome of affected individuals—optimal outcomes are associated with better performance on standardized language measures. Eigsti and Castelluccio's work indicates other correlates too—better motor skills, milder social impairments, and fewer repetitive behaviors at age 2. They also report that heightened auditory perception has a negative impact on later language. These findings suggest that language development may be moderated by factors outside of the language domain, including the presence of comorbidities (e.g., executive motor and auditory deficits).

DISSOCIATION AMONG LANGUAGE SKILLS

Related to the issue of stability and prognosis is whether language is a single factor. Statistically, a single factor appears to describe data from a diverse range of language measures, but, in clinical samples, dissociations between language domains can be observed—the dissociation between structural and pragmatic aspects of language can be marked in ASD and can also be observed in DLD. The distinction between phonological and grammatical measures is important for understanding the relationships among DLD, ASD, and dyslexia.

According to a framework proposed by Bishop and Snowling (2004), to understand the relationship between reading and language disorders, it is necessary to take into account phonological skills (which are strong predictors of learning to decode) and broader language skills (which are critical in order to understand what you read). Furthermore, there are good theoretical reasons for keeping these two sets of skills differentiated. Rice points out that a particular aspect of grammar—obligatory finiteness marking—is highly heritable (and an inability to use this marker is an aspect of persistence). Furthermore, phonological skills are more highly heritable than nonphonological language abilities (Kovas et al., 2005).

In this view, children with dyslexia have typical levels of language alongside phonological deficits, whereas children with specific reading comprehension impairments (poor comprehenders) show the opposite profile—well-developed phonology in contrast to weak vocabulary and grammatical skills (Hulme & Snowling, 2016). Children with DLD are at risk of problems with reading comprehension by virtue of their language difficulties; dyslexia (defined as a decoding deficit) will impact those for whom phonological skills are also affected. Consistent with this hypothesis, there is accumulating evidence that the main predictor of dyslexia among children with DLD is the status of the language system around the point of formal reading instruction (Bishop & Adams, 1990). Our work shows that the risk of dyslexia in DLD is reduced if phonological difficulties are resolving over time (Snowling et al., submitted). Poor reading comprehension is likely to ensue, however; from the other angle, many poor comprehenders fulfill criteria for DLD (Nation, Clarke, Marshall, & Durand, 2004).

The two-dimensional framework can also be used to consider the reading impairments associated with ASD. As might be expected given the heterogeneity in phenotype, there is much variability in word decoding and reading comprehension skills. In a survey of 54 children with ASD ages 7–11 years, we found that more than 70% of the group scored below average on a measure of reading comprehension, and some 24% could be classified as poor comprehenders (Henderson, Clarke, & Snowling, 2014). Yet, many of the ASD group also had poor reading accuracy. Thus, contrary to earlier beliefs that children with ASD are hyperlexic, this profile is not common. It is indubitable that poor pragmatic skills compromise performance on reading comprehension tests; however, many children with ASD also have decoding deficits.

HIDDEN FACTORS: "THROWING THE BABY OUT WITH THE BATH WATER"

If language skills can dissociate, then why has it been argued that language is a single trait? Statistical models of language development use latent factor scores to capture the shared variance between different measures of linguistic performance and conceptualize this shared variance as language. In turn, such models assume that any residual variance is simply measurement error. There are other ways of modeling such data, however. In a study of the longitudinal predictors of reading, Hulme and Snowling (2016) reported a bifactor model in which seven language measures loaded onto a single latent factor, termed *language;* three of these measures—each requiring phonological processing (word repetition, nonword repetition, and articulation)—were also allowed to load onto a second factor. Together, the shared variance from these measures that did not load with other language measures could be conceptualized as speech. In turn, it was language rather than speech that predicted the foundations of literacy a year later and reading after 2 years. Consistent with this, children with speech-sound disorders are at low risk of reading difficulties unless they also have co-occurring language difficulties (Hayiou-Thomas, Carroll, Leavett, Hulme, & Snowling, 2017).

Similarly, it is important to consider how language-specific and general cognitive skills contribute to performance on measures of language and reading in order to understand the variable reading outcomes in ASD. It seems likely that models of the relationships among language and reading skills will need to include co-occurring deficits, such as deficits in verbal and nonverbal executive functions, which are commonly observed in children with poor language. This is no mean feat. Executive skills typically covary with language skills; when there is collinearity, it is usually language that wins out in predicting literacy. But this does not mean that executive skills and more general cognitive resources are not important—they just do not account for unique variance in the prediction. Thus, we will need more complex developmental models if we are to understand the stability of language over time and how the language problems of some children persist while others resolve.

CAUSES OF LANGUAGE DISORDERS AND RELATED DISORDERS

In their chapters, Rice, Eigsti, and Castelluccio each discuss what might be described as the holy grail of neurodevelopmental disorders, explanations at the biological level. It is clear that genetic factors are involved in both DLD and ASD, but the picture is complex, with multiple genes, gene-gene and gene-environment interactions at play. In turn, such heterogeneity of genetic mechanisms is associated with variations in neural architecture at birth and as the disorder unfolds. The aim of such research is to map these differences to clear and reproducible phenotypes. Eigsti and Castelluccio report preliminary work suggesting that ASD is associated with both typical and atypical neural networks and, as in dyslexia, there is evidence of both normalization over time and compensation, which can include the recruitment of areas beyond those involved in language processing. Yet, as is common in pediatric neuroimaging, current evidence tends to be based on small samples, and the field awaits replication using much larger samples before behavioral findings can be confidently mapped to brain networks and biomarkers of neurodevelopmental disorders identified.

IMPLICATIONS FOR INTERVENTION

Language is the foundation of literacy and, more broadly, education—the curriculum is delivered through language, and language is fundamental to the self-regulation needed to learn effectively. Interventions for language problems are therefore vital if the downward spiral of poor educational achievement and limited career prospects is to be avoided. As argued by Norbury, however, how and when to intervene are not straightforward questions.

Understanding the developmental course of children's language difficulties is the first step to intervention. However, as we have seen, this is a complex matter. The limited evidence base suggests that early intervention is important to improve the outcomes of children with ASD, and symptom severity is one of the best predictors of response to intervention. Given the heterogeneity that Eigsti and Castellucio describe, an alternative reading of the findings is that children with milder forms of ASD are more likely to normalize. In a similar vein, if a substantial number of children with preschool language difficulties resolve their language problems by age 5, then early intervention could be considered a waste of resource.

Notwithstanding these issues, there is a strong argument for early intervention to prepare children for formal education. The findings of longitudinal studies suggest that children who enter school with poor language do poorly in the reading stakes; in turn, literacy is one of the best predictors of educational attainment. Furthermore, language and communication are vital for forming friendships that will be of lasting significance for well-being throughout one's life span. Norbury signals a note of caution about this approach, noting that most evidence-based language interventions have been found to have small effects. But this should not be a counsel of despair. Most current evidence for effective language intervention comes from trials that have delivered between 20 and 30 weeks of daily intervention to children in the early years, amounting to some 50–60 hours of input (e.g., Fricke et al., 2017). This is a very small dose compared with the 3 or 4 years of limited exposure to good language that many of these children have received to date. Rather than accepting that some children have stable and, hence, intractable language problems, the strong influence of gene–environment correlation on language skills is a call to action for education to respond to the challenge of children's poor language with high-quality, sustained language input delivered by parents, teachers, and other family members, where possible. The rationale for evidence-based language intervention is strong and should fuel the future research agenda. Providing language intervention is an imperative not only for learning but also to safeguard the well-being of children with DLD and ASD, help them make friends, and help them form meaningful social relationships.

REFERENCES

Bishop, D. V. M., & Adams, C. (1990). A prospective study of the relationship between specific language impairment, phonological disorders and reading retardation. *Journal of Child Psychology and Psychiatry, 31,* 1027–1050. http://dx.doi.org/10.1111/j.1469-7610.1990.tb00844.x

Bishop, D. V. M., & Edmundson, A. (1987). Language-impaired 4-year-olds: Distinguishing transient from persistent impairment. *Journal of Speech and Hearing Disorders, 52,* 156–173. doi:10.1044/jshd.5202.156

Bishop, D. V. M., & Snowling, M. J. (2004). Developmental dyslexia and specific language impairment: Same or different? *Psychological Bulletin, 130,* 858–888. doi: 10.1037/0033-2909.130.6.858

Bishop, D. V. M., Snowling, M. J., Thompson, P. A., Greenhalgh, T., & Catalise-2 Consortium (2017). Phase 2 of Catalise: A multinational and multidisciplinary Delphi consensus study of problems with language development: Terminology. *Journal of Child Psychology and Psychiatry, 58*(10), 1068–1080. doi:10.1111/jcpp.12721

Dale, P. S., Price, T. S., Bishop, D. V., & Plomin, R. (2003). Outcomes of early language delay: I. Predicting persistent and transient language difficulties at 3 and 4 years. *Journal of Speech, Language, and Hearing Research, 46*(3), 544–560. doi:10.1044/1092-4388(2003/044)

Fricke, S., Burgoyne, K., Bowyer-Crane, C., Kyriacou, M., Zosimidou, A., Maxwell, L., . . . Hulme, C. (2017). The efficacy of early language intervention in mainstream school settings: A randomised controlled trial. *Journal of Child Psychology and Psychiatry, 58*(10), 1141–1151. doi:10.1111/jcpp.12737

Hayiou-Thomas, M. E., Carroll, J. M., Leavett, R., Hulme, C., & Snowling, M. J. (2017). When does speech sound disorder matter for literacy? The role of disordered speech errors, co-occurring language impairment and family risk of dyslexia. *Journal of Child Psychology and Psychiatry, 58*(2), 197–205. doi:10.1111/jcpp.12648

Henderson, L. M., Clarke, P., & Snowling, M. J. (2014). Reading comprehension impairments in autism spectrum disorders. *L'Année Psychologique, 114*(04), 779–797. http://dx.doi.org/10.4074/S0003503314004084

Hulme, C., & Snowling, M. J. (2016). Reading disorders and dyslexia. *Current Opinions in Pediatrics, 28*(6), 731–735. doi:10.1097/MOP.0000000000000411

Klem, M., Hagtvet, B., Hulme, C., & Gustafsson, J. E. (2016). Screening for language delay: Growth trajectories of language ability in low-and high-performing children. *Journal of Speech, Language, and Hearing Research, 59*(5), 1035–1045.

Kovas, Y., Hayiou-Thomas, M. E., Oliver, B., Dale, P. S., Bishop, D. V. M., & Plomin, R. (2005). Genetic influences in different aspects of language development: The etiology of language skills in 4.5-year-old twins. *Child Development, 76,* 632–651.

Nation, K., Clarke, P., Marshall, C., & Durand, M. (2004). Hidden language impairments in children: Parallels between poor reading comprehension and specific language impairment? *Journal of Speech, Language, and Hearing Research, 47,* 199–211.

Snowling, M. J., Duff, F. J., Nash, H. M., & Hulme, C. (2016). Language profiles and literacy outcomes of children with resolving, emerging, or persisting language impairments. *Journal of Child Psychology and Psychiatry, 57*(12), 1360–1369. doi:10.1111/jcpp.12497

Snowling, M J., & Melby-Lervåg, M. (2016). Oral language deficits in familial dyslexia: A meta-analysis and review. *Psychological Bulletin, 142*(5), 498–545. doi:10.1037/bul0000037

Snowling, M. J., Nash, H. M., Gooch, D. C., Hayiou-Thomas, M. E. & Hulme, C. (2019). Developmental outcomes for children at high risk of dyslexia and children with Developmental Language Disorder. *Child Development.* doi:10.1111/cdev.13216 Stothard, S. E., Snowling, M. J., Bishop, D. V. M., Chipchase, B., & Kaplan, C. (1998). Language impaired pre-schoolers: A follow-up in adolescence. *Journal of Speech, Language, and Hearing Research, 41,* 407–418. doi:10.1044/jslhr.4102.407

Tomblin, J. B., Zhang, X., Buckwalter, P., & O'Brien, M. (2003). The stability of primary language disorder: Four years after kindergarten diagnosis. *Journal of Speech, Language, and Hearing Research, 46*(6), 1283–1296. doi:10.1044/1092-4388(2003/100)

SECTION IV

Atypical Reading Development (Dyslexia)

CHAPTER 10

The Role of Executive Functions in Reading Development, Reading Disability, and Intervention Response

Paul T. Cirino, Jessica A. Church, Jeremy Miciak, and Jack M. Fletcher

SUMMARY

In this chapter, we review the concept of executive functions (EF) and evaluate its role for reading ability across the continuum of skill, as well as its potential utility for reading intervention. An understanding of the structure of EF is foundational to identifying any role it might have for reading because EF is construed and measured in many different ways and overlaps with a host of related cognitive skills. The five studies discussed next are all a part of the Texas Center for Learning Disabilities, a multiyear, comprehensive research project designed specifically to better understand cognitive, imaging, and intervention components for struggling readers. We conclude that EF can be conceptualized as having common and specific components, and that when assessed cognitively, EF is related to reading skill, particularly the common component. We also demonstrate that brain areas associated with EF (and with reading) are engaged during reading tasks and during inhibition, but struggling and typical readers only differ in the amount of this activation during reading performance. A demonstration of the utility of EF as incorporated into interventions for struggling readers remains elusive. We consider a number of future directions that might provide clarity in this regard.

INTRODUCTION: WHAT IS EXECUTIVE FUNCTION?

The construct of EF has a long history of research in multiple domains of inquiry. Originally formulated to reflect behavioral impairments in patients with dramatic injuries to the frontal lobes, the construct has evolved and crossed into other disciplines, often with changes in terminology. For example, neuropsychology, cognitive psychology, and developmental and educational psychology are three disciplines that have concepts and research

This research was supported by Award Number P50 HD052117, Texas Center for Learning Disabilities, from the *Eunice Kennedy Shriver* National Institute of Child Health and Human Development to the University of Houston. The content is the sole responsibility of the authors and does not necessarily represent the official views of the *Eunice Kennedy Shriver* National Institute of Child Health and Human Development or the National Institutes of Health.

related to aspects of EF. These disciplines invoke a range of conceptualizations of EF and associated, overlapping terms associated with its measurement that include the following:

- *Neuropsychology:* Cognitive and behavioral functions disrupted by damage to the frontal lobes (planning, problem solving, inhibition, generative fluency, behavioral impulsivity, and personality changes)
- *Cognitive psychology:* Separate but related skills related to the management and control of other cognitive functions (working memory/updating, inhibition, shifting, controlled attention)
- *Developmental/educational psychology:* Strategies used by students to manage goals, problem solve, generate solutions, and monitor performance (attentional control/inhibition, self-regulated learning, metacognition, self-control, planning)

The implicit or explicit idea of the active control of goals is common across these different conceptualizations. We have previously defined *EF* as "a domain-general control process important for managing goal-directed behavior" (Cirino, Ahmed, et al., 2018, p. 176). Still other terms are used in related disciplines—for example, the most common term in cognitive neuroscience appears to be *cognitive control.* The focus of cognitive control in cognitive neuroscience is anchored to the way the brain governs moment-to-moment neural processing via systems of functional networks that are rooted in anterior brain regions with intense interconnectivity with parietal and other regions of the brain. Next, we refer to functional activation of cognitive control networks, but to behavioral tasks as measuring EF. We recognize that cognitive control networks could be described as EF networks, even though some authors (e.g., Stuss, 2011) are much more specific in assigning functions to brain regions. Relatedly, EF can either be construed as a set of cognitive functions each mediated by separable (to some degree) neural circuitry that aligns with the frontal lobes or as a general psychological construct (Stuss, 2006). These two notions are complementary but not the same; our imaging work focuses on the former, whereas our behavioral work focuses on the latter, which we use to relate to and predict other psychological constructs.

Therefore, the broader literature discusses EF and related skills from different perspectives and widely dispersed terminology but with wide variability around its operationalization within and across disciplines. This gives rise to three interrelated issues beyond the lack of linguistic clarity and consistency. First is the task-impurity problem (e.g., Burgess, 1997)—that EF tasks often measure multiple lower level skills and abilities that need to be controlled to isolate the higher order executive component (e.g., requirements for motor functions). Second, it is unclear whether EF is one or many things at either the neural or behavioral level (Miyake et al., 2000). Third, the psychometrics of behavioral or clinical EF tasks tend to be weak, with low reliability, and/or weak intercorrelations with one another, and/or utility at the level of external validity (e.g., Rabbitt, 1997). These issues were encapsulated in the seminal factor analytic study of Miyake and colleagues (Miyake et al., 2000), who found three components of EF—updating, shifting, and inhibition. This work has helped to spawn and guide much research in EF since the early 2000s. This work came primarily from the cognitive perspective, however, and was focused on a relatively small group of undergraduates.

Several notable gaps remained in the literature, some of which were addressed in a large-scale project discussed next. First, most structural studies of the way in which EF is composed had focused either on adults or young children. Second, some EF-related constructs had only been rarely considered, such as behavioral or everyday functioning or self-regulated learning. The range of common constructs, particularly beyond those studied by Miyake et al. (2000), had not been brought together comprehensively. Third, there was relatively little research into the extent to which EF affected academic skills such as reading. A variety of individual smaller studies were available, with few exceptions (e.g., Christopher et al., 2012). EF have been frequently evoked as central concepts for explaining individual differences in academic achievement (e.g., Butterfuss & Kendeou, 2018).

OUR CURRENT WORK IN EXECUTIVE FUNCTIONS

The present chapter reviews a series of studies from our group designed to fill several of these gaps. In doing so, we hope to offer both theoretical and empirical guidance for future work relevant to clarifying the role of EF for reading processes. We specifically address 1) issues with the conceptualization and operationalization of EF (Cirino, Ahmed, et al., 2018), 2) the relation of reading and reading component skills and EF (Cirino, Miciak, et al., 2018), 3) EF correlates of inadequate response to intervention (Miciak, Cirino, Ahmed, Reid, & Vaughn, 2019), and 4) functional neuroimaging studies of the relation of EF to sentence reading and intervention response (Nugiel et al., 2019; Roe et al., 2018).

Sample

The primary source sample for these studies is from a measurement study involving 846 children in Grades 3–5 (8–12 years old; Cirino et al., 2018a). The sample is ethnically diverse (predominantly Latino and African American, but with Caucasian and Asian American representation), roughly equal in gender, and mostly economically disadvantaged. Most of the fourth-grade subsample of these children was selected for participation in a series of reading intervention studies, and, thus, the sample includes a large number of struggling readers (Miciak et al., 2018; Vaughn, Solis, Miciak, Taylor, & Fletcher, 2016). The sample was derived through whole classroom screening for reading comprehension problems and was supplemented with typically developing children for the measurement and neuroimaging studies.

The measurement studies used weighted means to adjust for overrepresentation of children with reading problems.

Executive Function Measurement Study

Cirino, Ahmed, et al. (2018) identified eight EF-related constructs from the neuropsychological, cognitive, and developmental/educational literature: 1) working memory, 2) inhibition, 3) shifting, 4) planning, 5) generative fluency, 6) self-regulated learning, 7) metacognition, and 8) behavioral regulation. The first three are well established and, as noted, are the subject of prior measurement studies (e.g., Miyake et al., 2000), but the remaining constructs are more widely represented across related disciplines. A series of confirmatory latent factor models was derived to test hypotheses regarding the structure of EF, including interrelated versus bifactor models to represent the overlap and shared variance across measures. These models were compared with measurement models (e.g., performance vs. self- or other-report, various subcombinations according to modality or method of administration).

The best fitting model, shown in Figure 10.1, represents a bifactor model with a common EF latent variable and five specific subcomponents: Working Memory as Span and as Manipulate with Planning (WM-S/M and Planning), Working Memory as Updating (WM-U), Generative Fluency, Self-Regulated Learning (SRL), and Metacognition (MCOG). In addition to common EF, the first specific factor (WM-S/M and Planning) represents a combination of a host of complex tasks. These tasks include those that require dual processes, such as processing a sentence for meaning while retaining the last word in a series of statements; those that require observing a sequence and then recalling that sequence in reverse order; and those that require problem solving efficiently while also following a set of rules. The second specific factor (WM-U) requires keeping track of a running sequence for events that reoccur, thus continually updating the most recent event. Fluency requires generating exemplars given either semantic or lexical cues within a time limit. Self-regulated learning indices are self-report measures that reflect on problem-solving strategies and self-perceptions during learning. Metacognition in this context refers to teacher perceptions of a student's ability to initiate, organize, keep in mind, plan for, and monitor performance.

Thus, these results indicate that at a latent variable level where we move beyond test labels and observed measures, a common EF factor (representing the shared relations among all measures), strengthens model fit. Several of the originally proposed constructs do not emerge; for example, there is little independent variance left over for shifting and inhibition beyond the common factor. More specific factors previously described do remain identifiable, although with a range of loadings; for example, working memory/updating, SRL, and metacognition seem more separable from the common EF factor relative to fluency and the working memory/planning specific factors. A key relevance of this work is in providing more clarity to

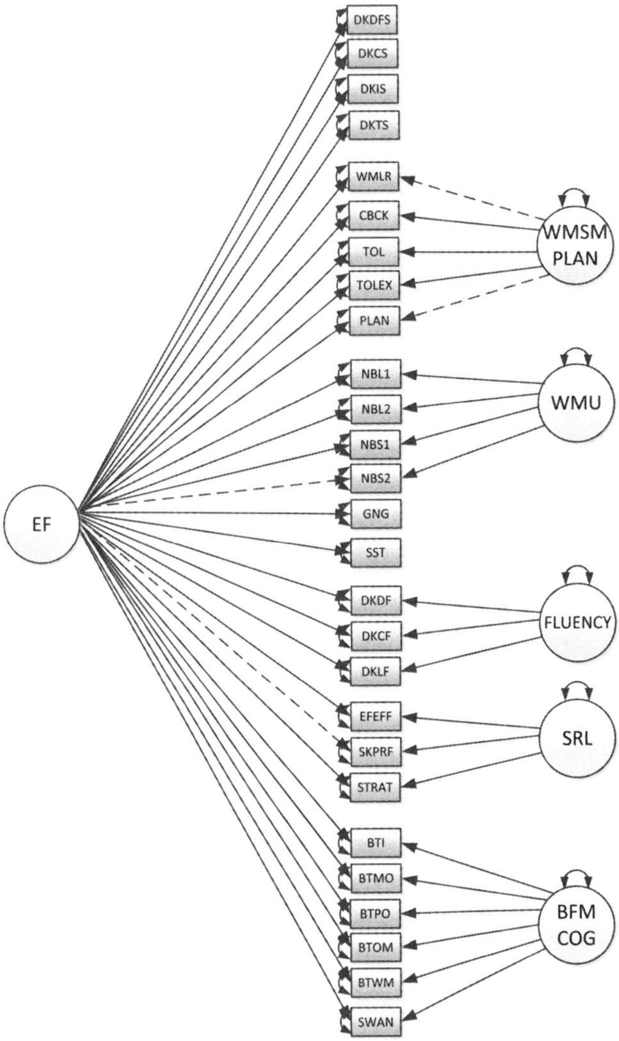

Figure 10.1. Bifactor model with five specific and one general factors. (*Note:* DKDFS = D-KEFS Design Fluency Switching; DKCS = D-KEFS Verbal Fluency Category Switching; DKIS = D-KEFS Color Word Interference Inhibition Switching; DKTS = D-KEFS Trailmaking Test Letter-Number Switching; WMLR = WMTB-C Listening Recall; CBCK = Corsi Blocks Backwards Recall; TOL = Tower of London Accuracy; TOLEX = Tower of London Extra Moves; PLAN = WJ-III Planning; NBL1 = n-back 1 Letter; NBL2 = n-back 2 Letter; NBS1 = n-back 1Shape; NBS2 = n-back 2 Shape; GNG = Go No-Go; SST = Stop Signal Task; DKDF = D-KEFS Design Fluency Filled+Empty Dots; DKCF = D-KEFS Verbal Fluency Categories; DKLF = D-KEFS Verbal Fluency Letters; EFEFF = CLS Effort/Self-Efficacy; SKPRF = CLS Skill/Preference; STRAT = CLS Learning Strategies; BTI = BRIEF Initiate; BTMO = BRIEF Monitor; BTPO = BRIEF Planning/Organization; BTOM = BRIEF Organization of Materials; BTWM = BRIEF Working Memory; SWAN = SWAN Inattention. WM-S/M = Working Memory as Span/Manipulate; WMU= Working Memory as Updating; SRL = Self-Regulated Learning; MCOG = Metacognition. Solid lines = statistically significant at the $p < 0.05$ level; dashed lines = not statistically significant; rectangles = measured variables; circles = latent variables; double-headed arrows = variances; single-headed arrows = loadings) (From Cirino, P. T., Ahmed, Y., Miciak, J., Taylor, W. P., Gerst, E. H., & Barnes, M. A. [2018]. A framework for executive function in the late elementary years. *Neuropsychology, 32,* 176–189; reprinted by permission. Copyright © 2018, American Psychological Association.)

how a comprehensive number of behavioral tasks of EF are related to one another, including relative unity versus diversity. The study sets the stage for future studies to test the relative contributions of these factors to external variables, such as reading outcomes.

Executive Function Prediction of Reading Comprehension Outcomes

Cirino, Miciak, et al. (2018) then took the measurement model and examined it in relation to measures of timed and untimed word reading and different measures of reading comprehension. Demographic variables and covariates that affect performance on measures of EF were also included to assess whether these skills uniquely predict reading skills, including fine motor skills, short-term memory, and language predictors of lower level reading (phonological awareness, rapid naming) and reading comprehension, including the Simple View variables of decoding and listening comprehension (Gough & Tunmer, 1986).

For each dependent variable, controlling for demographic variables and covariates, latent variables from the bifactor model uniquely predicted reading outcomes. It is common to believe that EF is relevant for comprehension but not for lower level reading skills, but the actual evidence is mixed, and larger scale studies more commonly find contributions of EF to a range of reading outcomes (see Cirino, Miciak, et al., 2018). For all reading outcomes in that study, the specific contribution of EF was approximately 3% of the variance above that from the other demographic variable and covariates. In each prediction equation, demographic variables were very strong predictors. In addition, covariates followed expected patterns—phonological awareness was the strongest cognitive predictor of word reading; rapid naming for reading fluency; and Simple View variables for reading comprehension. Thus, the contribution of EF to reading is unique and measurable, even in the context of baseline models with extremely large predictive power. The specific unique effect is relatively small, however, though with large shared variance.

Beyond the unique contribution of EF across reading outcomes, the models also indicated that the ways in which EF contributes to reading varies according to the outcome considered. The contribution of EF to lower level reading skills is direct, with metacognition related to both single-word reading and reading fluency, and common EF, working memory (as span and manipulation, with planning), fluency, and self-regulated learning all additionally uniquely predictive of reading fluency. Direct effects were also noted for reading comprehension, but EF also interacted with Simple View variables.

The most interesting finding was a three-way interaction in the relation of EF, word reading, and listening comprehension. When EF were weakly developed, word reading and listening comprehension interacted with one another to explain reading comprehension. Yet, when EF were strongly developed, there was compensation for poor word reading—reading comprehension may still be successful in the context of low word-reading ability if listening comprehension and EF are higher.

Executive Functions and Inadequate Response to Reading Intervention

Miciak et al. (2019) evaluated whether EF predicted response to reading intervention by treating the assessments in Cirino, Ahmed, et al. (2018) as baseline measures. This study was prompted by a meta-analysis by Stuebing et al. (2015), which found that cognitive variables were generally very weak predictors of intervention response. Yet, none of the studies in that meta-analysis evaluating cognitive and behavioral predictors of intervention response had used assessments of EF other than working memory.

At the end of one school year of intervention (Vaughn et al., 2016), Miciak et al. (2019) defined inadequate response to intervention using a benchmark of a standard score one standard deviation below average (i.e., < 85) on either of two reading comprehension measures. One measure represented a cloze (fill in the missing word) test and the other required reading of text with multiple-choice answers. There were 167 inadequate responders, 64 adequate responders, and 71 typically achieving students. Planned comparisons of each pair of groups on the common EF measure and the five discrete factors revealed that the typical achievers outperformed both the adequate and inadequate responders on general EF and outperformed the

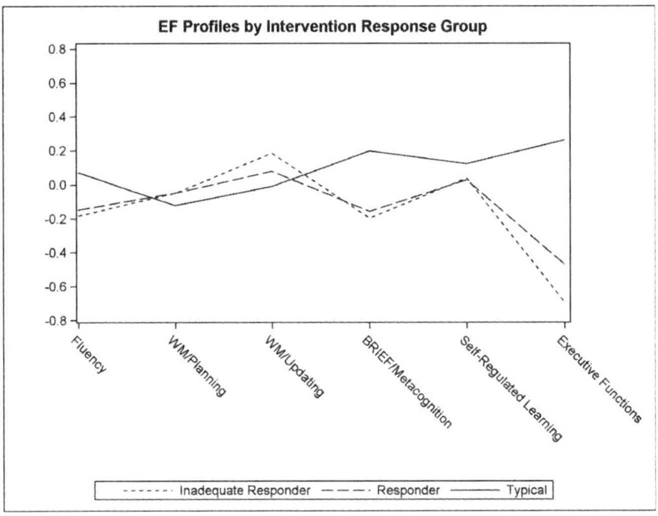

Figure 10.2. Executive function profiles by intervention response group. (*Source:* Miciak, Cirino, Ahmed, Reid, & Vaughn, 2019.)

inadequate responder group on metacognition (see Figure 10.2). No contrasts on the five discrete factors (working memory planning and updating, generative fluency, metacognition, and self-regulated learning) were statistically significant. In addition, all comparisons of the adequate and inadequate responder groups were null, with both groups performing similarly on the general factor and the five discrete factors. No contrasts were significant when level of reading ability was controlled, indicating findings similar to Stuebing et al. (2015) and Fletcher et al. (2011)—cognitive measures do not uniquely discriminate adequate and inadequate responders to intervention nor are they strong predictors of intervention response when baseline performance (pretest) in reading is included. Rather, any cognitive differences reflect the severity of reading impairment (i.e., a continuum of severity) best explained by level of reading ability (Vellutino, Scanlon, Small, & Fanuele, 2006).

Functional Neuroimaging Studies Involving Executive Functions

A subset of the students previously described have been assessed in two studies using functional magnetic resonance imaging (fMRI). The studies we conducted were designed to evaluate the relation of cognitive control brain network activity in struggling readers during performance of reading comprehension at baseline and after intervention (Nugiel et al., 2019; Roe et al., 2018). The fMRI task involved making a sensible/nonsensible decision about sentences modeled after Meyler, Keller, Cherkassky, Gabrieli, and Just (2008). For this task, brain activity was recorded using fMRI while the children read a variety of different sentences and made button-press responses about their sensibility. To test whether struggling readers had reading-specific or more domain-general differences, control-related brain activity during the sentence task was compared with a nonlexical response inhibition task. The stop signal task (Rubia, Smith, Brammer, & Taylor, 2003) is commonly used to measure inhibitory control in behavioral and fMRI studies and compares brain activity for stopping an action to the brain activity during a prepotent motor (button press) "go" task. This task is well established as a measure that engages cognitive control networks in anterior brain regions (Aron, Robbins, & Poldrack, 2014). Critically, no reading was required to perform the task.

Roe et al. (2018) studied struggling ($n = 74$) and nonstruggling ($n = 32$) readers on the two fMRI tasks. The struggling readers demonstrated scores below the 25th percentile on a measure requiring reading fluency and comprehension and, as such, did not meet classic definitions of dyslexia, although some also had poor decoding skills. There was brain activity in both reading and cognitive control regions on the sentence comprehension task. As Figure 10.3 shows, struggling readers had significantly less activation than nonstruggling readers in the left posterior temporal cortex, consistent with Meyler et al. (2008) and what is known about activation of the reading network in poor readers (Dehaene, 2009). Struggling readers showed more

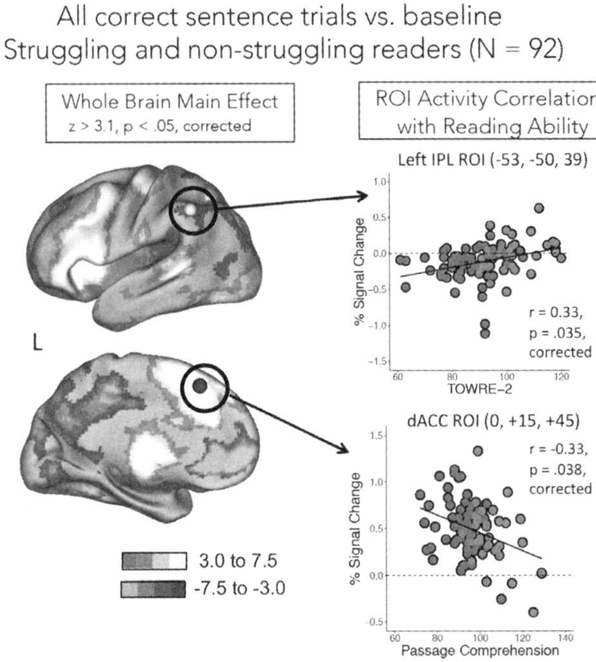

Figure 10.3. A sentence comprehension task produced robust responses in the brains of third- through fifth-graders in both reading-related and executive control-related regions (left). Literature-derived control regions (including the two spheres on the whole brain figure) were tested across the whole sample (right). Struggling readers and nonstruggling readers had brain activity in control-related regions that scaled with reading ability. (*Source:* Roe et al., 2018.)

suppression of activation (relative to fixation) in bilateral inferior parietal regions from the fronto-parietal control network. Also, during sentence reading in the scanner, better reading comprehension ability was associated with less activation of the anterior cingulate, part of the cingulo-opercular network. Struggling readers relied more on cingulate activity in order to perform the sentence comprehension task.

Although multiple analysis approaches found evidence for altered cognitive control-related activity in struggling readers during reading, when the same approaches were applied to the nonlexical inhibition (stop-signal) task, there were no significant group differences in brain activation despite strong activation across participants in the expected cognitive control regions. Altogether, Roe et al. (2018) found that differences in cognitive control in struggling and nonstruggling readers were only present during reading, and, thus, results were not consistent with a more general cognitive control problem, at least to the extent that inhibitory control is a general measure of EF. As in Cirino, Ahmed, et al. (2018), inhibitory control did not emerge as a discrete component of EF, but it was related to the common EF factor.

Nugiel et al. (2019) compared subsets of children who completed the intervention based on their amount of gain across four standard reading measures. At baseline, children were identified as future improvers ($n = 16$) and future nonimprovers ($n = 29$) compared with the 27 typical readers. For those who completed baseline and postintervention fMRI scans, participants were classified as adequate ($n = 14$) and inadequate ($n = 7$) responders. As before, activation patterns on the nonreading inhibitory control task did not differentiate the groups from typical responders, although there was reliable activation of cognitive control regions. In contrast, during the sentence reading task, there was engagement of the right fusiform gyrus before and after intervention related to growth in reading skills (see Figure 10.4). Children with higher activity in the right fusiform improved more. Before intervention, the degree of activation in the default-mode network (precuneus) and the right posterior middle temporal gyrus, associated with the fronto-parietal control network, separated improvers and nonimprovers from typical readers. Changes in left ventral fusiform blood oxygen level dependent (BOLD) activity related to reading improvement was consistent with other intervention imaging studies (Aboud, Barquero, & Cutting, 2018; Barquero, Davis, & Cutting, 2014). Thus, brain control networks were only subtly different between improving and nonimproving subgroups of struggling readers, but again, these control differences were still limited to the reading task and were not seen in the inhibition task.

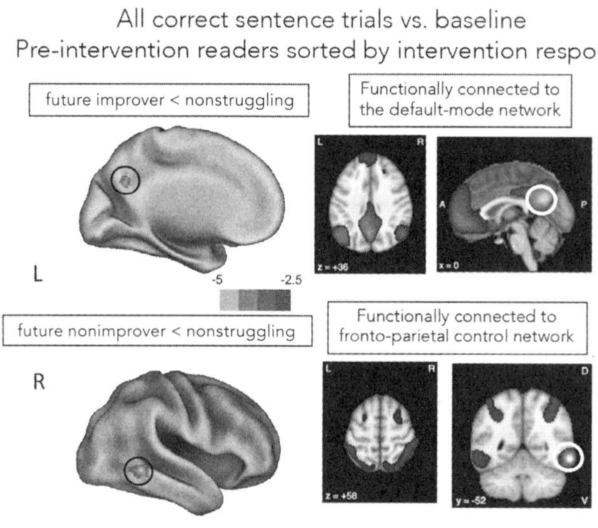

Figure 10.4. Struggling readers who later showed gains (future improvers, $n = 19$) had more negative activity than nonstruggling readers ($n = 28$) in a member of the default mode network, as indicated by Neurosynth (top). Struggling readers who later failed to gain (future nonimprovers, $n = 27$) had less activity than nonstruggling readers in a member of the fronto-parietal control network, as indicated by Neurosynth (http://www.neurosynth.org). (*Source:* Nugiel et al., 2019.)

DISCUSSION

Several main findings are apparent across these studies. First, in this age group, the bifactor framework for EF extends understanding of the ways in which cognitive and behavioral measures of EF relate to one another in the late elementary years (Cirino et al., 2018a). Second, EF is uniquely related to reading achievement even in the context of strong known predictors; this relation is small (~3%), though unique, and variable according to reading outcome. For reading comprehension, EF interacts with Simple View variables involving word reading and listening comprehension (Cirino, Miciak, et al., 2018). Third, although EF are clearly related to the reading process, they are weak predictors of intervention response and not a major attribute of inadequate responders (Miciak et al., 2019). Fourth, brain activation studies show clear involvement of cognitive control brain areas as well as reading-related brain areas during sentence comprehension; control engagement appears related to reading ability and improvement in reading, but only during reading tasks (Nugiel et al., 2019; Roe et al., 2018).

The practical implications of these results are consistent with much of the literature on children who struggle to learn to read. It is common to observe that many of these children have problems with self-regulation and organizational skills. In particular, they have trouble generalizing what they learn across different learning contexts. These problems are even more apparent if the student also meets criteria for attention-deficit/hyperactivity disorder (ADHD). It is not surprising that many reading instructional programs include components that help students organize their behavior and promote generalization across contexts. These specific instructional and intervention components did not arise from the empirical literature on the relation of EF to reading skill, but rather arose from a parallel but implicit understanding that interventionists recognized as an important factor in successful intervention programs. The construct of EF appears to explain these student characteristics, and, at a theoretical level, it makes sense that EF should be involved in the reading process, particularly comprehension (Butterfuss & Kendeou, 2018). Routine measures of EF as captured by cognitive and neuropsychological tests, however, may not be capturing the specific key variance that invariably leads to stronger intervention response or can be used to reliably indicate who does versus does not have a reading disability. As the neuroimaging studies show, differences are much more apparent during reading tasks than an inhibitory control task that engages cognitive control regions.

Therefore, these results do not support assessment of EF as part of a comprehensive evaluation of a child with reading disabilities, as a means of identification, or for deciding the nature of the intervention to be implemented. Such findings are consistent with positions advocating reduced assessment of cognitive skills in favor of assessments of academic skills and instructional response directly related to intervention (Fletcher & Miciak,

2017; see Schneider & Kaufman, 2017, for a different view). Certainly, the results do not support the assertion that routine assessment of EF might parse children into different, individually tailored interventions. In addition, these results are consistent with findings that training EF skills, including working memory, independently of academic content is not likely to generalize to better reading (Jacob & Parkinson, 2015; Melby-Lervåg, Redick, & Hulme, 2016). In examining a different approach, the use of stimulant medication absent reading intervention in students with comorbid reading difficulties and ADHD does not show robust improvement in word reading despite behavioral improvement (Tamm et al., 2017).

As Cirino, Miciak, et al. (2018) suggested, it might be more fruitful to build supports to maximize the child's access to EF to support reading development and intervention response. As a self-regulatory skill, EF can be enhanced by scaffolding to increase motivation, a factor that often fluctuates in children depending on the task and their prior experience with reading. Motivation and self-regulatory factors may fluctuate in a more state-like fashion relative to performance-based EF skills. In addition, reducing the cognitive and linguistic demands in instructional materials and working memory loads may indirectly promote improved reading (see Fletcher et al., 2019; Chapter 5). Thus, perhaps the better question is not how and whether EF skills relate to reading and intervention response, but rather how these domain general skills can be supported and enhanced in the context of high-quality reading intervention.

Limitations

As with any set of research studies, there are several limitations to the generalizability of the results. The studies are largely cross-sectional and restricted to children within a narrow age range (8–12 years). Studies of younger children seem to show stronger relations of EF and general achievement (Diamond, 2013). Although our sample size is large, children were assessed in school, which restricted the number of measures that could be administered. In addition, the neuroimaging studies assessed only one aspect of nonlexical EF—inhibitory control; other EF brain activation tasks might show a different pattern of results. The present results focus on reading, but EF may have effects in other achievement areas as well, such as math, although it is relevant to note that problem solving overlaps with reading comprehension (Fuchs, Fuchs, Compton, Hamlett, & Wang, 2015). Finally, it is possible that more explicit embedding of EF intervention in reading interventions would show effects that are more robust. It would be hard to imagine a successful reading intervention that did not address self-regulation.

FUTURE DIRECTIONS

In the future, additional studies will clarify and expand on these results, but questions remain about how to operationalize and measure EF; definition and operationalization remain elusive and hard to pin down precisely. Conceptual frameworks in attention have a rich history in the cognitive literature and, to a certain extent, the concept of EF can be seen as embedded in the notion of attention and how it is used (Chun, Golomb, & Turk-Browne, 2011). For reading, efforts to isolate and define relevant aspects of the attentional construct may be more tractable and discrete, and in doing so may overlap with concepts involved in the notion of EF. From the attention perspective, EF could be conceptualized as the ongoing allocation of attentional resources (Zelazo, Carter, Reznick, & Frye, 1997), which leads to broader and more direct relations with cognitive neuroscience and neuroimaging. Attention studies frequently focus on posterior brain regions, which lie closer in topography to the posterior brain areas that are dysregulated during reading, than to frontal control regions. One way to unite across control and attention domains is through the idea of linked anterior and posterior brain networks tapped by bottom-up state-dependent components involving arousal and engagement and top-down components involving control regulation. Focusing on EF from an attentional model involving the allocation of resources during skill development may be a fruitful direction for future research.

REFERENCES

Aboud, K. S., Barquero, L. A., & Cutting, L. E. (2018). Prefrontal mediation of the reading network predicts intervention response in dyslexia. *Cortex, 101,* 96–106.

Aron, A. R., Robbins, T. W., & Poldrack, R. A. (2014). Inhibition and the right inferior cortex: One decade on. *Trends in Cognitive Science, 18(4),* 177–185.

Barquero, L. A., Davis, N., & Cutting, L. E. (2014). Neuroimaging of reading intervention: A systematic review and activation likelihood estimate meta-analysis. *PloS One, 9*(1), e83668. Retrieved from https://doi.org/10.1371/journal.pone.0083668

Burgess, P. W. (1997). Theory and methodology in executive function research. In P. Rabbit (Ed)., *Methodology of frontal and executive function* (pp. 81–116). East Sussex, United Kingdom: Psychology Press.

Butterfuss, R., & Kendeou, P. (2018). The role of executive functions in reading comprehension. *Educational Psychology Review, 30*(3), 801–826.

Christopher, M. E., Miyake, A., Keenan, J. M., Pennington, B., DeFries, J. C., Wadsworth, S. J., . . . Olson, R. K. (2012). Predicting word reading and comprehension with executive function and speed measures across development: A latent variable analysis. *Journal of Experimental Psychology: General, 141*(3), 470–488.

Chun, M. M., Golomb, J. D., & Turk-Browne, N. B. (2011). A taxonomy of external and internal attention. *Annual Review of Psychology, 62,* 73–101.

Cirino, P. T., Ahmed, Y., Miciak, J., Taylor, W. P., Gerst, E. H., & Barnes, M. A. (2018). A framework for executive function in the late elementary years. *Neuropsychology, 32,* 176–189.

Cirino, P. T., Miciak, J., Ahmed, Y., Barnes, M. A., Taylor, W. P., & Gerst, E. H. (2018). Executive function: Association with multiple reading skills. *Reading and Writing: An Interdisciplinary Journal.* Retrieved from https://doi.org/10.1007/s11145-018-9923-9

Dehaene, S. (2009). *Reading in the brain: The new science of how we read.* London, England: Penguin.

Diamond, A. (2013). Executive functions. *Annual Review of Psychology, 64*(1), 135-168.

Fletcher, J. M., Lyon, G. R., Fuchs, L. S., & Barnes, M. A. (2019). *Learning disabilities: From identification to intervention* (2nd ed.). New York, NY: Guilford Press.

Fletcher, J. M., & Miciak, J. (2017). Comprehensive cognitive assessments are not necessary for the identification and treatment of learning disabilities. *Archives of Clinical Neuropsychology, 32,* 2–7.
Fletcher, J. M., Stuebing, K. K., Barth, A. E., Denton, C. A., Cirino, P. T., Francis, D. J., & Vaughn, S. (2011). Cognitive correlates of inadequate response to intervention. *School Psychology Review, 40,* 2–22.
Fuchs, L. S., Fuchs, D., Compton, D., Hamlett, C., & Wang, A. (2015). Is word-problem solving a form of text comprehension? *Scientific Studies of Reading, 19(3),* 204–223.
Gough, P. B., & Tunmer, W. E. (1986). Decoding, reading, and reading disability. *Remedial and Special Education, 7*(1), 6–10.
Jacob, R., & Parkinson, J. (2015). The potential for school-based interventions that target executive function to improve academic achievement: A review. *Review of Educational Research, 85,* 512–552.
Melby-Lervåg, M., Redick, T. S., & Hulme, C. (2016). Working memory training does not improve performance on measures of intelligence or other measures of "far transfer": Evidence from a meta-analytic review. *Perspectives on Psychological Science, 11*(4), 512–534.
Meyler, A., Keller, T. A., Cherkassky, V. L., Gabrieli, J. D., & Just, M. A. (2008). Modifying the brain activation of poor readers during sentence comprehension with extended remedial instruction: A longitudinal study of neuroplasticity. *Neuropsychologia, 46*(10), 2580–2592.
Miciak, J., Cirino, P. T., Ahmed, Y., Reid, E., & Vaughn, S. (2019). Executive functions and response to interventions: Identification of struggling readers. *Learning Disability Quarterly, 42*(1), 17–31.
Miciak, J., Roberts, G. J., Taylor, W. P., Solis, M., Ahmed, Y., Vaughn, S., & Fletcher, J. M. (2018). The effects of one versus two years of intensive reading intervention implemented with late elementary struggling readers. *Learning Disabilities Research and Practice, 33*(1), 24–36.
Miyake, A., Friedman, N. P., Emerson, M. J., Witzki, A. H., Howerter, A., & Wager, T. D. (2000). The unity and diversity of executive functions and their contributions to complex "frontal lobe" tasks: A latent variable analysis. *Cognitive Psychology, 41,* 49–100.
Nugiel, T., Roe, M. A., Taylor, W. P., Cirino, P. T., Vaughn, S. R., Fletcher, J. M., & Church, J. A. (2019). Executive control brain activity during reading relates to change in reading skill. *Cortex, 111,* 286–302.
Rabbitt, P. (1997). Introduction: Methodologies and models in the study of executive function. In P. Rabbitt (Ed.), *Methodology of frontal and executive function* (pp. 1–38). Hove, United Kingdom: Psychology Press.
Roe, M. A., Martinez, J. E., Mumford, J. A., Taylor, W. P., Cirino, P. T., Fletcher, J. M., . . . Church, J. A. (2018). Control engagement during sentence and inhibition fMRI tasks in children with reading difficulties. *Cerebral Cortex, 28*(10), 3697–3710.
Rubia, K., Smith, A. B., Brammer, M. J., & Taylor, E. (2003). Right inferior prefrontal cortex mediates response inhibition while mesial prefrontal cortex is responsible for error detection. *NeuroImage, 20*(1), 351–358.
Schneider, W. J., & Kaufman, A. (2017). Let's not do away with comprehensive cognitive assessments just yet. *Archives of Clinical Neuropsychology, 32,* 8–20.
Stuebing, K. K., Barth, A. E., Trahan, L., Reddy, R., Miciak, J., & Fletcher, J. M. (2015). Are child characteristics strong predictors of response to intervention? A meta-analysis. *Review of Educational Research, 85,* 395–429.
Stuss, D. T. (2006). Frontal lobes and attention: Processes and networks, fractionation and integration. *Journal of the International Neuropsychological Society, 12,* 261–271.
Stuss, D. T. (2011). Functions of the frontal lobes: Relation to executive functions. *Journal of the International Neuropsychological Society, 17,* 759–765.
Tamm, L., Denton, C. A., Epstein, J. N., Schatschneider, C., Taylor, H., Arnold, L. E., . . . Maltinsky, J. (2017). Comparing treatments for children with ADHD and word-reading difficulties: A randomized clinical trial. *Journal of Consulting and Clinical Psychology, 85,* 434–451.

Vaughn, S., Solis, M., Miciak, J., Taylor, P., & Fletcher, J. M. (2016). Effects from a randomized control trial comparing researcher and school implemented treatments with fourth graders with significant reading difficulties. *Journal of Research on Educational Effectiveness, 9 (Supp. 1),* 23–44.

Vellutino, F. R., Scanlon, D. M., Small, S., & Fanuele, D. P. (2006). Response to intervention as a vehicle for distinguishing between children with and without reading disabilities: Evidence for the role of kindergarten and first-grade interventions. *Journal of Learning Disabilities, 39*(2), 157–169.

Zelazo, P. D., Carter, A., Reznick, J. S., & Frye, D. (1997). Early development of executive function: A problem-solving framework. *Review of General Psychology, 1*(2), 198–226.

CHAPTER 11

Predicting Response to Reading Disabilities Intervention

Robin Morris

SUMMARY

This chapter examines the language, cognitive, and neural attributes of children with developmental dyslexia (DD) that best predict their response to intervention. The chapter first reviews the literature on various types of predictors of response to intervention. It then provides preliminary data from an ongoing reading intervention study of children with DD and related comorbidities that examines a variety of key language, attentional, neurocognitive, and structural brain relations that are being evaluated to assist in distinguishing treatment responders and resistors. It describes a sample of > 80 children with DD (third- and fourth-graders) with a range of language and/or attention impairments who all received an explicit reading intervention program for 70 hours. Degree of intervention response for word and text reading was measured by a child's pre-to-post increase large enough to represent a reliable gain. Although many preintervention language, attention, executive, and related functions are strongly predictive of children's preintervention reading abilities in this sample, many of the same measures do not predict well the rate or overall amount of change following intervention, and those that do account for only small portions of variance (< 10%). The same is true for data from the preintervention structural magnetic resonance imaging (sMRI) measures. A multiple regression example that combined different baseline predictors from various levels of measurement resulted in more positive results and accounted for greater variance. These preliminary results suggest that more sophisticated multilevel modeling of children's preintervention attributes will be needed to account for the range of responses to intervention and the more accurate identification of treatment resisters.

INTRODUCTION

Developmental Dyslexia (DD) is a neurodevelopmental disorder that, unlike more global brain-based conditions such as intellectual disability, is thought to reflect more circumscribed neurobiological anomalies and etiologies. These conditions interact with environmental and educational inputs to interfere with the development of a variety of neurocognitive and language skills necessary for a fully integrated neural system that is finely tuned for fluent reading. DD is the most common neurodevelopmental disorder of childhood, estimated to affect 10%–15% of otherwise typically developing children (Fletcher, Lyon, Fuchs, & Barnes, 2007), and a lifelong disorder (Shaywitz et al., 1999), presenting with considerable learning difficulty into adolescence and adulthood in many domains.

Research findings since the late 1980s have reshaped our understanding of DD, generating new questions about its diagnosis and prevalence, providing new insights into its neurobiological and genetic substrates, and contributing new concepts and methods to evaluate intervention response and predict long-term outcomes. There is now a much greater appreciation of the heterogeneous developmental trajectories of individuals with DD and the variability in their response to treatment. More recently, there has been increasing interest in understanding how neurocognitive and behavioral factors interact with the attributes of current remediation programs to predict a DD reader's response to specific interventions. There has also been increased attention on those readers with DD who continue to exhibit significant treatment resistance even after completion of intense, empirically backed interventions. This interest in DD treatment resisters is in part founded in an implicit belief that those with such relatively intractable impairments are thought to reflect more severe neurobiological system compromise and, therefore, provide the special potential for studying the circumscribed neurobiological anomalies that give rise to the disorder.

All the factors that distinguish treatment responders from resisters are poorly understood. This limitation may be related to study differences in the degree or type of underlying impairments evaluated, including the presence/absence of co-occurring language and/or attentional impairments, the ages at which interventions were undertaken, or the characteristics or quality/intensity of the interventions provided. Yoder and Compton (2004) cautioned that when studying children learning to read, it is important to differentiate those predictors of reading growth from predictors of treatment response, which typically requires the partitioning of overall change into one portion related to treatment effect, typically accounting for less than 50% of the variance in change, versus that portion due to ongoing reading development related to other factors (i.e., school, home reading activities). In addition, there are methodological differences among researchers in their conceptual and measurement frameworks used to evaluate actual treatment response or identify treatment resisters. Although it is understood that historically, and for ease of communication, it has been easier to discuss the hypothesized construct of treatment response as a categorical or dichotomous entity (responder/resister) operationalized by using arbitrary cut-points on test scores, it is also widely recognized that responses to treatment fall along a continuum of measured change that may differ for different components of reading.

Regardless of the challenges of studying individual differences in treatment response, closer investigation of the profiles of DD treatment resisters and responders is a reasoned step toward identifying those critical demographic, neurocognitive, language, and brain-based attributes that may predict such differential outcomes and will ultimately provide guidance in the type of treatment that may be most effective for these struggling readers. Although there is a growing body of evidence regarding the development and functioning of key brain systems that underlie reading and a variety of studies documenting the related neural anomalies associated with DD compared with typically developing readers, there has been less attention to whether some of these structural or functional anomalies give rise to the specific linguistic or nonlinguistic deficits observed in DD or how they may or may not change with intervention. Overall, this complex question requires the systematic integration of knowledge regarding how different types and degrees of brain anomalies may affect the development of critical component skills and automaticity in reading and how the characteristics of various interventions may affect that development.

Phonological awareness and other reading-related processing and language deficits have historically been identified as core deficits in the majority of individuals with DD and have been extensively studied, with such findings having led researchers to evaluate the efficacy of phonologically based reading interventions. In interventions for young children with DD, large effect sizes have been reported (on average > .70) following early intervention programs emphasizing such instruction (Blachman, 1997; Morris et al., 2012). Consensus exists that effective intervention for DD necessitates direct, explicit, and systematic training of reading skills (Fletcher et al., 2007; McCardle, Chhabra, & Kapinus, 2008; Shaywitz, Morris, & Shaywitz, 2008). Despite substantial evidence for effective interventions and normalization of the neurobiological reading circuits in many young DD children, there remain, in virtually every intervention sample, children whose improvement was limited with treatment proven effective for other DD children (Al Otaiba & Fuchs, 2002). Using different definitions of poor treatment response, varying proportions of resisters have been identified with average estimates of 20%–30%, with some much higher percentages depending on the aspects of reading (i.e., fluency) being evaluated (O'Shaughnessy & Swanson, 2000). The outlook is far less positive for older children and adults with DD. It is difficult to close the gap in older individuals with DD (Torgesen et al., 2001) even after intensive additional interventions (Lyytinen, Erskine, Aro, & Richardson, 2006). Improvement in such older readers with DD is rarely complete and may depend on compensatory cognitive and linguistic processes or alternative neural circuits (Hoeft et al., 2011).

There is also neurobiologically centered literature that has developed new concepts and models used to identify those children with DD who may be at risk of being treatment resisters. It has typically been assumed that measurable differences in functional and structural brain organization affect critical perceptual/motor, cognitive, and learning abilities in DD, and these deficits, in turn, limit the development of reading and related skills (Pugh et al., 2008). A successful beginning reader employs a widely distributed cortical system for print processing including temporoparietal, frontal, and right hemisphere (RH) posterior brain areas. As reading skill increases, more lateralized left hemisphere (LH) ventral regions become more critical in the automatic recognition of printed (word) stimuli. In children with DD, this developmental pattern of lateralized dorsal-ventral consolidation is frequently disrupted and can be identified via functional magnetic resonance imaging (fMRI) studies of reading. In these studies, children with DD frequently exhibit weak LH dorsal and ventral functions, if such brain areas are involved in reading at all; an increased use of the anterior components of the system; and, at times, the continued or increased use of RH homologues of the deficient LH posterior circuits (Shaywitz et al., 2002; Simos et al., 2002). Explicit interventions have been shown to normalize the reading system in some children with DD. Response to intervention rests on the notion that the key difference between children is that responders, those who develop a more normal reading network following explicit intervention, are simply less impaired in key neurobiological systems. There also appear to be some partial responders who become more accurate readers who never develop into fluent automatic decoders. This may be possible by using some compensatory neurocognitive systems (frontal and RH activations) or may represent the continued use of those initial RH analogue neural learning systems.

THE NEUROCOGNITIVE BASES OF TREATMENT RESISTANCE IN DEVELOPMENTAL DYSLEXIA STUDY

Because of continued interest in questions related to predicting treatment response, and particularly those relevant to better understand the neurobiological, environmental, or instructional factors involved in treatment resistance, this report provides a preliminary overview of an ongoing study that attempts to identify those neurobiological, language, and neurocognitive factors that best predict treatment resistance in children with DD. The study was designed to make meaningful connections among brain, neurocognitive, and behavioral data in a way that would lead to more viable models of identifying DD readers' responses to an intervention. This focus grew in response to our study findings that documented the value of early interventions for children with DD, with children receiving interventions during first grade responding with greater change, even on follow-up reading evaluations during fourth grade, than those children who received the same interventions during second or third grades (Lovett et al., 2017). Sixty to seventy percent of those children with DD who received the study intervention during the first grade performed in the average achievement ranges on outcome, but only 30%–40% of those children who received intervention during the third grade met this frequently used outcome criterion.

These results are consistent with the broader research evidence that treatment responders tend to show a degree of normalization of their LH reading neurocircuits in younger cohorts (Shaywitz et al., 2004; Simos et al., 2002), whereas there appears to be a tendency for greater frontal or RH contributions to treatment responses, with less normalization, for older DD cohorts (Eden et al., 2004). It is possible that older DD cohorts consist of larger percentages of more significant brain-based neurocognitive impairments due to a natural filtration process by which many children with primarily experiential problems, or milder neurobiological impairments, will have already been remediated at younger ages. Thus, persistent older DD children might have, on average, more profound compromise of the underlying neural and neurocognitive learning systems, resulting in a greater proportion of treatment resisters. Even in older DD readers who show some treatment response, there is the question of whether they are using more alternative or compensatory neural systems (Hoeft et al., 2011).

The present report represents a preliminary report of limited scope of a much larger study of intervention-driven changes in children (third- and fourth-graders) and adolescents (seventh- and eighth-graders) with DD in order to explore some of the ideas and potential that underlie one approach to the study of treatment resistance. Schools identified their poorest readers, with a preference for those who had received at least 1 year of extra reading assistance, who were then referred for screening for DD and entry into the intervention study if they qualified. Children with comorbid attention-deficit/hyperactivity disorder or language impairment were included to address common comorbidities that may affect treatment outcomes. This report focuses only on a sample of around 80 third- and fourth-graders who have enrolled in the study to date and who were identified as meeting low reading criteria for DD (< = 15th percentile on standardized reading measures) along with at least low average or better intellectual abilities. This age group was selected to make sure that their reading problems were more severe and could not be easily attributed to mild developmental delay or disorder or lack of instructional opportunity.

A 70-hour multiple-component intervention for DD, Phonological and Strategy Training (PHAST; Lovett, Lacerenza, & Borden, 2000), was provided to all children in small instructional groups (four to eight children) by highly trained and experienced research teachers. This intervention program has yielded significant positive effect sizes in the treatment of DD relative to a range of control conditions, and effects have been maintained at follow-up (Lovett, Lacerenza, De Palma, & Frijters, 2012; Lovett et al., 2017; Morris et al., 2012). Direct instruction of foundational skills is combined with explicit instruction of reading strategies (word identification and comprehension) in this intervention program. Along with conventional assessments administered before intervention (baseline learner characteristics) and repeated reading assessments following 23, 45, and 70 hours of the intervention, sMRI and fMRI measurements during reading tasks and a series of yoked behavioral reading experiments were also performed to identify those attributes that might best predict treatment outcomes in DD children (see Figure 11.1 for study design overview). In addition, the same

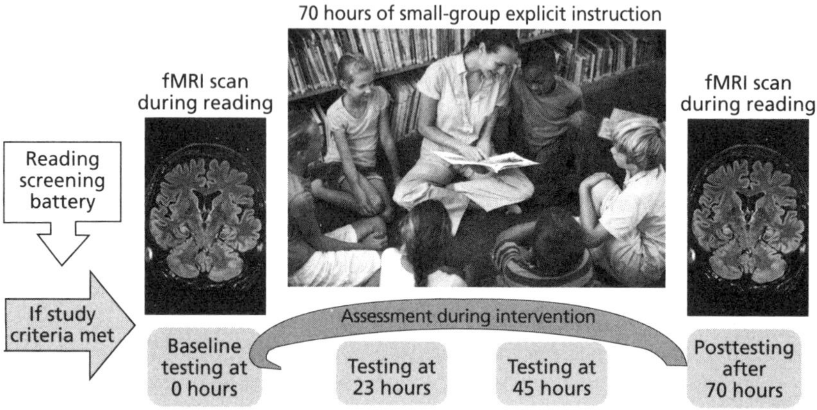

Figure 11.1. Illustration of neurocognitive bases of treatment resistance in developmental dyslexia study framework.

sMRI and fMRI scans were repeated following the 70 hours of intervention (posttreatment) to determine whether those identified as DD responders accomplished better reading skills by relative normalization of their core LH reading circuits or via the development of alternative or compensatory networks.

Measuring Response to Treatment and Identification of Treatment Resisters

Different measures were used to provide the critical data for assessing children's intervention responses. They were chosen in order to provide 1) coverage of the full domain of multidimensional reading skill, including sight-word identification/decoding, fluency, and text reading/comprehension; 2) assessment of directly taught skills and varying degrees of skill transfer in order to help assess treatment implementation and integrity; and 3) repeated measurement to detect growth and change with appropriate sensitivity for use with children given the time available for testing. Accurate and sensitive identification and parameterization of treatment response were the overriding criteria for selection of these measures.

Overall, the study plans to estimate the degree to which each child has responded to treatment. Forming an index of each child's degree of response to the intervention and then classifying them into the categories of treatment responder or resister is a complex and emerging issue within the intervention outcome literature. Some studies have often used relatively simple approaches to classify a DD reader as a responder, such as showing reading score normalization (i.e., attaining the average range on standardized assessments regardless of starting score) or some rationally derived fixed cutoffs in the amount of change observed on a reading measure (i.e., 0.5

standard deviation *[SD]* gain on a measure regardless of how deficient that score may still be), although these approaches can yield different outcomes when they are used for different reading measures. Our research group has been exploring these issues of accurate and statistically and methodologically defensible treatment response criteria and has proposed a set of best options (Frijters, Lovett, Sevcik, & Morris, 2016). This analysis detailed the circumstances in which the use of growth curve models and the reliable change index (RCI) perform most adequately and how best to account for false discovery rates when multiple measures may be used.

In this current report, we illustrate one of these approaches by providing two different examples of composite RCI metrics (Jacobson & Truax, 1991). These metrics account for the psychometric reliability of the outcome measures and observed *SDs,* with the goal of providing a continuous indicator of intervention response across children. In this approach, the RCI analysis establishes whether a child's pre- to postintervention increase on a specific test(s) was large enough to represent a psychometrically reliable gain, such that the change was greater than what would be expected according to the effect of the measure's reliability and sample-specific variability (see Frijters et al., 2016, for more details on this approach). For this report, we provide example data using the RCI for both word identification/decoding measures and the text reading/comprehension outcomes. These represented a composite RCI across multiple measures to increase their measurement reliability in the specific reading domain.

Preintervention Baseline Learner Characteristics of Change

Numerous standardized psychometric and experimental measures were obtained preintervention. These measures were used to characterize the children with DD (baseline learner characteristics) and identify those language- and reading-related abilities known to not only affect reading development, but also to act as potential predictors of response to intervention as identified in previous reviews (Stuebing et al., 2015).

Al Otaiba and Fuchs (2002) performed an early meta-analysis of 23 previous intervention studies that provided characteristics of DD students who were less responsive to interventions. Their review found that almost all studies identified more severe phonological awareness deficits as a primary differentiator between levels of treatment response. They also identified studies that found greater phonological retrieval or rapid naming and working memory or encoding deficits as predictors. Other factors that were predictive in a few studies included low verbal abilities, behavioral or attentional problems, lower socioeconomic status, and the child's age at intervention. Frijters et al.'s (2011) review suggested that phonological awareness appears to show more influence on intervention outcomes in younger children beginning to read, but rapid automatized naming was more predictive on later word reading and reading fluency. Memory and intellectual abilities were also identified. They also documented the importance of evaluating different dimensions of the reading process because children may show different outcomes from an intervention depending on their initial abilities, which is consistent with multidimensional conceptualizations of reading development (Scarborough, 2001). Finally, Stuebing et al.'s (2015) meta-analysis of predictors further documented that phonological awareness, rapid letter naming, verbal working memory, and oral language skills are the best cognitive constructs for differentiating not only DD from typically developing readers but also treatment responders from resisters.

Baseline Learner Predictors of Reliable Change Index

The predictive relationship of our study on children's general language abilities, as represented by a composite factor integrating the three major language measures taken at baseline, and their RCI for the text reading and comprehension measures is shown in Figure 11.2.

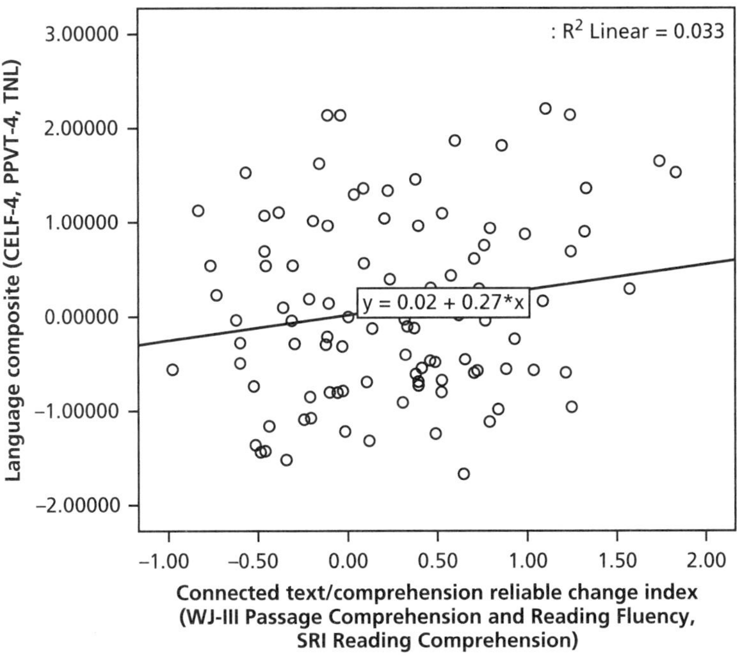

Figure 11.2. Example preliminary scatter plot showing relationship between general language functioning and the amount of change on reading measures of connected text and comprehension. Reliable change scores of .00 and above are considered to represent a significant change on this index. (*Key:* CELF-4, Clinical Evaluation of Language Fundamentals–Fourth Edition [Semel, Wiig, & Secord, 2003]; PPVT-4, Peabody Picture Vocabulary Test–Fourth Edition [Dunn & Dunn, 2007]; TNL, Test of Narrative Language [Gillam & Pearson, 2004]; WJ-III, Woodcock-Johnson–Third Edition [Woodcock, McGrew, & Mather, 2001]; SRI, Standardized Reading Inventory [Newcomer, 1999].)

All reliable change scores of 0 or greater represent statistically significant levels of change on this index. The R^2 of .03 is lower than seen in other studies for like measures, which may be related to the lower reading levels and restricted range of the children in the sample. This result suggests that a child's initial language ability is not the driving factor behind the change taking place during their intervention. Some of the other frequently identified predictors of response to intervention and/or change taken from the literature and their correlations with either word reading/decoding or text reading/comprehension RCI's are provided in Table 11.1.

In this sample to date, only a few of the traditional measures strongly predicted either word reading/decoding or test reading RCI, and the amount of variance accounted for is limited for those that show significant correlations. The baseline basic reading composite scores are negatively correlated, hinting that those children in the sample who start with the lowest basic reading abilities show the largest change index. The visual perceptual zero noise threshold measure also showed a significant negative correlation, but only with the text reading RCI, showing that the better a child's visual perceptual discrimination, the greater their change index. Yet, the receptive vocabulary measure and measures of retention and recall of newly learned verbal information were positive predictors of change in both indices. Overall, this preliminary look at the psychometric data from our current sample of third- and fourth-graders is generally consistent with the available literature on predictors of response to intervention and change.

Baseline Neuroanatomical Predictors of Reliable Change Index

Another approach to identifying such predictors has focused on neurobiological attributes. The brain structures and functioning profiles of children with DD appear to be stable across a large number of studies and appear to be associated with anomalies in related brain structures (Gabrieli, 2009), including reduced grey matter volumes and diffusion tensor imaging (DTI) results, suggesting atypical connectivity or reduced white matter structures that support interregional cortical and subcortical communication among key LH reading system foci (Niogi & McCandless, 2006). These anomalies are thought to be implicated in control and quality of sensorimotor processing, working memory, speeded processing, and a wide range of learning abilities (Graybiel, 2005; Pugh et al., 2008; Stocco, Lebiere, & Anderson, 2010). Although this report would be too extensive and detailed if it documented all the available neurobiological attributes of interest from the current study, their potential value in predicting response to interventions is a key component of the present study. This preliminary report will focus on just a few of the data from MRI structural analysis using measures of structural volume, along with a few examples from DTI analysis, such as fractional anisotropy (FA), for a few LH regions of interest chosen from the

Table 11.1. Correlation of baseline learner characteristics (Time 0) with reliable change index for single word and connected text composites.

Characteristic	Single-word reading/ decoding	Connected text/ comprehension
Age (years)	.09	–.13
Parent annual average income	.19	.10
WASI-II IQ Estimate SS	.02	.15
SWAN Teachers Inattentive Rating	.06	.20
WJ-III Basic Reading W Score	–.26*	–.22*
NEPSY-II Auditory Attention/Response Set Contrast SS	–.03	.18
CELF-4 Core Language Composite Standard Score	.09	.11
PPVT-4 SS	.23*	.32*
TNL Ability Quotient	.04	.19
CTOPP-2 Phonological Awareness Composite SS	.04	.01
Visual Perceptual Zero Noise Threshold	–.11	–.22*
RAN letters SS	–.03	–.06
D-KEFS Color Word Interference SS	.16	.13
D-KEFS Trail Making 4 Letter Number Switching SS	–.06	.01
TNWR	.10	–.01
CVLT-C List A Trials 1–5 T-Score	.16	.19
CVLT-C List A Short Delay Free Recall Total Correct	.25*	.14
CVLT-C List B Free Recall Total Correct	.07	.24*
CVLT-C List A Long Delay Free Recall Total Correct	.24*	.13
Total gray matter volume	.16	.13
Subcortical gray matter volume	.22*	.15
Left thalamus volume	.23*	.25*
Left hemisphere (LH) pars triangularis volume	.15	.09
LH fusiform volume	.18	.15
LH superior temporal volume	.20	–.08
LH middle temporal volume	.11	.04
Corpus callosum—forceps major FA	.12	.11
Corpus callosum–forceps minor FA	.10	–.33*
Left inferior longitudinal fasciculus FA	.03	.07
Left superior longitudinal fasciculus—parietal ending FA	–.01	–.15
Left superior longitudinal fasciculus—temporal ending FA	–.15	.23
Left uncinate fasiculus FA	–.29*	–.32*

Key: SWAN, Strengths and Weaknesses of ADHD–Symptoms and Normal-Behavior Scale (Swanson et al., 2012); WASI-II, Wechsler Abbreviated Scale of Intelligence–Second Edition (Wechsler, 2011); SS, standard score or scaled score; WJ-III, Woodcock-Johnson–Third Edition–Tests of Achievement (Woodcock, McGrew, & Mather, 2001); NEPSY-II, A Developmental NEuroPSYchological Assessment–Second Edition (Korkman, Kirk, & Kemp, 2007); CELF-4, Clinical Evaluation of Language Fundamentals–Fourth Edition (Semel, Wiig, & Secord, 2003); PPVT-4, Peabody Picture Vocabulary Test–Fourth Edition (Dunn & Dunn, 2007); TNL, Test of Narrative Language (Gillam & Pearson, 2004); CTOPP-2, Comprehensive Tests of Phonological Processing–Second Edition (Wagner et al., 2013); RAN, Rapid Automatized Naming Test (Wolf & Denckla, 2005); D-KEFS, Delis-Kaplan Executive Function System (Delis, Kaplan, & Kramer, 2001); TNWR, Test of Nonword Repetition (Dollaghan & Campbell, 1998); CVLT-C, California Verbal Learning Test–Children's Version (Delis et al., 1994); FA, fractional anisotropy.

previous research literature. Although we also obtained two standard fMRI activation paradigms during reading and listening both pre- and postintervention, those data will not be presented due to limited space (see Frost et al., 2009; Malins et al., 2016).

Examples from a few measures (i.e., DTI, FA) of the critical LH's structures were derived at baseline and correlated with either word reading/decoding or text reading RCIs (see Table 11.1). A few of these brain measures in this sample predicted either RCI and accounted for limited variance similar to levels accounted for by the previous psychometric measures. The baseline LH thalamus volume was correlated with both RCIs, consistent with some literature suggesting that subcortical structures and connections may have a relevant role in predicting reading outcomes. Another finding that the left uncinate fasiculus FA measure was correlated with both RCIs may suggest that the quality of this white matter tract connecting the limbic and frontal systems may be an important structure affecting the level of a child's reading change during intervention.

Example Multidomain Predictor Model of Reliable Change Index

Unfortunately, even those individual psychometric and brain baseline measures that significantly predict these different RCIs only accounted for limited variance. At the same time, the data on these children allows for the development of more multidomain, multicomponent prediction equations related to these outcomes. For example, a linear regression focused on predicting the text reading RCI outcome was performed using different types of predictors based on a conceptual model interested in the influence of potential attentional factors on change in reading following intervention (see Table 11.2). The resulting R^2 is .18 (F [6, 74] = 2.71, p <.02), accounting for more significant variance than any of the individual components. What is conceptually of more interest are the individual predictors once many of the covariances among them are accounted for in the model (see part and partial correlations to understand these interrelationships). For example, the thalamus continues to be a significant component of this model, but the visual perception threshold measure is not a significant component, whereas the sustained attention measure is a significant component. Although this is a very limited example, it does show the potential of a mixed-component, conceptually driven modeling approach that better integrates demographic, behavioral ratings, psychometric test data, and brain structure and functioning measures into more complex predictors of a child's potential response to interventions. It is through such approaches that more theoretically driven models can be evaluated and the diverse literatures related to potential predictors of response to interventions can be integrated. Hopefully, such modeling will also allow for more individualized approaches to interventions and ultimately reduce the number of children who can be called treatment resisters.

Table 11.2. Example multiple regression of demographic, behavioral ratings, test scores, and brain volumes (Time 0) with reliable change index for connected text composite

	Coefficients							
	Unstandardized coefficients		Standardized coefficients			Correlations		
Model	B	Standard error	Beta	t	p	Zero-order	Partial	Part
(Constant)	–1.26	1.32		–0.96	0.34			
Age at screening in years	–0.05	0.10	–0.05	–0.49	0.63	–0.09	–0.06	–0.05
SWAN Teacher Inattentive Rating	0.11	0.07	0.17	1.48	0.14	0.20	0.17	0.16
NEPSY-II Auditory Attention/ Response Set Contrast SS	0.05	0.03	0.23	2.05	0.04	0.18	0.23	0.22
Visual perceptual task—zero noise	–0.35	0.25	–0.17	–1.41	0.16	–0.22	–0.16	–0.15
CTOPP-2 Phonological Awareness Composite SS	0.00	0.01	–0.02	–0.18	0.85	0.01	–0.02	–0.02
Left thalamus volume	0.00	0.00	0.26	2.42	0.02	0.25	0.27	0.25
Dependent variable: Connected text/comprehension focused (reliable change across WJ-III passage comprehension, SRI reading comprehension, and WJ-III reading fluency)								

Key: SWAN, Strengths and Weaknesses of ADHD–Symptoms and Normal-Behavior Scale (Swanson et al., 2012); NEPSY-II, A Developmental NEuroPSYchological Assessment–Second Edition (Korkman, Kirk, & Kemp, 2007); CTOPP-2, Comprehensive Tests of Phonological Processing–Second Edition (Wagner et al., 2013); WJ-III, Woodcock-Johnson–Third Edition–Tests of Achievement (Woodcock, McGrew, & Mather, 2001); SRI, Standardized Reading Inventory–Second Edition (Newcomer, 1999).

REFERENCES

Al Otaiba, S., & Fuchs, D. (2002). Characteristics of children who are unresponsive to early literacy intervention: A review of the literature. *Remedial and Special Education, 23,* 300–316.

Blachman, B. (1997). *Foundations of reading acquisition.* Mahwah, NJ: Lawrence Erlbaum Associates.

Delis, D. C., Kaplan, E., & Kramer, J. H. (2001). *Delis-Kaplan Executive Function System (D-KEFS).* San Antonio, TX: Psychological Corporation.

Delis, D. C., Kramer, J. H., Kaplan, E., & Ober, B. (1994). *California Verbal Learning Test–Children's Version (CVLT-C).* San Antonio, TX: Pearson.

Dollaghan, C., & Campbell, T. F. (1998). Nonword Repetition and Child Language Impairment. *Journal of Speech Language and Hearing Research, 41*(5), 1136. doi:10.1044/jslhr.4105.1136

Dunn, L. M. & Dunn, D. M. (2007). *Peabody Picture Vocabulary Test–Fourth Edition (PPVT-4).* Bloomington, MN: PsychCorp.

Eden, G. F., Jones, K. M., Cappell, K., Gareau, L., Wood, F. B., Zeffiro, T. A., . . . Flowers, D. L. (2004). Neural changes following remediation in adult developmental dyslexia. *Neuron, 44*, 411–422.

Fletcher, J. M., Lyon, G. R., Fuchs, L. S., & Barnes, M. A. (2007). *Learning disabilities: From identification to intervention.* New York, NY: Guilford Press.

Frijters, J. C., Lovett, M. W., Sevcik, R. A., & Morris, R. (2016). Four methods of identifying responders to a multiple component reading intervention for struggling middle school readers. *Reading and Writing Quarterly, 26*(4), 539–563.

Frijters, J. C., Lovett, M. W., Steinbach, K. A., Wolf, M., Sevcik, R. A., & Morris, R. (2011). Neurocognitive predictors of reading outcomes for children with reading disabilities. *Journal of Learning Disabilities, 44*(2), 150–166.

Frost, S. J., Landi, N., Mencl, W. E., Sandak, R., Fulbright, R. K., Tejada, E. T., . . . Pugh, K. R. (2009). Phonological awareness predicts activation patterns for print and speech. *Annals of Dyslexia, 58*, 78–97.

Gabrieli, J. D. E. (2009). Dyslexia: A new synergy between education and cognitive neuroscience. *Science, 325*(5938), 280–283.

Gillam, R. B. & Pearson, N. A. (2004). *Test of Narrative Language (TNL).* Austin, TX: PRO-ED.

Graybiel, A. M. (2005). The basal ganglia: Learning new tricks and loving it. *Current Opinion in Neurobiology, 15*, 638–644.

Hoeft, F., McCandliss, B. D., Black, J. M., Gantman, A., Zakerani, N., Hulme, C., . . . Gabrieli, J. D. E. (2011). Neural systems predicting long-term outcome in dyslexia. *Proceedings of the National Academy of Science, 108*(1), 361–366.

Jacobson, N. S. & Truax, P. (1991). Clinical significance: A statistical approach to defining meaningful change in psychotherapy research. *Journal of Consulting and Clinical Psychology, 59*(1), 12–19.

Korkman, M., Kirk, U., & Kemp, S. (2007). *NEPSY–Second Edition (NEPSY-II).* San Antonio, TX: Harcourt Assessment.

Lovett, M. W., Frijters, J. C., Wolf, M., Steinbach, K. A., Sevcik, R. A., & Morris, R. D. (2017). Early intervention for children at risk for reading disabilities: The impact of grade at intervention and individual differences on intervention outcomes. *Journal of Educational Psychology, 109*(7), 889–914.

Lovett, M. W., Lacerenza, L., & Borden, S. L. (2000). Putting struggling readers on the PHAST track: A program to integrate phonological and strategy-based remedial reading instruction and maximize outcomes. *Journal of Learning Disabilities, 33*(5), 458–476.

Lovett, M. W., Lacerenza, L., De Palma, M., & Frijters, J. C. (2012). Evaluating the efficacy of remediation for struggling readers in high school. *Journal of Learning Disabilities, 45*(2), 151–169.

Lyytinen, H., Erskine, J. M., Aro, M., & Richardson, U. (2006). Reading and reading disorders. In E. Hoff & M. Schatz (Eds.), *Handbook of language development* (pp. 454–474). Oxford, England: Blackwell Publishers.

Malins, J. G., Gumkowski, N., Buis, B., Molfese, P., Rueckl, J. G., Frost, S. J., . . . Mencl, W. E. (2016). Dough, tough, cough, rough: A "fast" fMRI localizer of component processes in reading. *Neuropsychologia, 91*, 394–406

McCardle, P., Chhabra, V., & Kapinus, B. (2008). *Reading research in action: A teacher's guide for student success.* Baltimore, MD: Paul H. Brookes Publishing Co.

Morris, R. D., Lovett, M. W., Wolf, M., Sevcik, R. A., Steinbach, K. A., Frijters, J. C. & Shapiro, M. (2012). Multiple-component remediation for developmental reading disabilities: IQ, SES, and race as factors on remedial outcome. *Journal of Learning Disabilities, 45*(2), 99–127.

Newcomer, P. L. (1999). *Standardized Reading Inventory–Second Edition (SRI-2).* Austin, TX: PRO-ED.

Niogi, S. N., & McCandless, B. D. (2006). Left lateralized white matter microstructure accounts for individual differences in reading ability and disability. *Neuropsychologia, 44*, 2178–2188.

O'Shaughnessy, T. E., & Swanson, H. L. (2000). A comparison of two reading interventions for children with reading difficulties. *Journal of Learning Disabilities, 33*(3), 257–277.

Pugh, K. R., Frost, S. J., Sandak, R., Landi, N., Rueckl, J., Constable, R. T., . . . Mencl, W. E. (2008). Effects of stimulus difficulty and repetition on printed word identification: An fMRI comparison of non-impaired and reading disabled adolescents. *Journal of Cognitive Neuroscience, 20,* 1146–1160.

Scarborough, H. (2001). Connecting early language and literacy to later reading (dis) abilities: Evidence, theory, and practice. In S. B. Neuman & D. K. Dickinson (Eds.), *Handbook of early literacy* (pp. 97–110). New York, NY: Guilford Press.

Semel, E., Wiig, E. H. & Secord, W. A. (2003). *Clinical Evaluation of Language Fundamentals–Fourth Edition.* San Antonio, TX: PsychCorp.

Shaywitz, B. A., Shaywitz, S. E., Blachman, B., Pugh, K. R., Fulbright, R., Skudlarski, P., . . . Gore, J. C. (2004). Development of left occipito-temporal systems for skilled reading following a phonologically-based intervention in children. *Biological Psychiatry, 55,* 926–933.

Shaywitz, B. A., Shaywitz, S. E., Pugh, K. R., Mencl, W. E., Fulbright, R. K., Skudlarski, P., . . . Gore, J. C. (2002). Disruption of posterior brain systems for reading in children with developmental dyslexia. *Biological Psychiatry, 52,* 101–110.

Shaywitz, S. E., Fletcher, J. M., Holahan, J. M., Shneider, A. E., Marchione, K. E., Stuebing, K. K., . . . Shaywitz, B. A. (1999). Persistence of dyslexia: The Connecticut longitudinal study at adolescence. *Pediatrics, 104*(6), 1351–1359.

Shaywitz, S. E., Morris, R., & Shaywitz, B. A. (2008). The education of dyslexic children from childhood to young adulthood. *Annual Review of Psychology, 59,* 451–475.

Simos, P. G., Fletcher, J. M., Bergman, M. D., Breier, J. I., Foorman, B. R., Castillo, E. M., . . . Papanicolaou, A. C. (2002). Dyslexia-specific brain activation profile becomes normal following successful remedial training. *Neurology, 58,* 1203–1213.

Stocco, A., Lebiere, C., & Anderson, J. R. (2010). Conditional routing of information to the cortex: A model of the basal ganglia's role in cognitive coordination. *Psychological Review, 117*(2), 541–574.

Stuebing, K. K., Barth, A. E., Trahan, L. H., Reddy, R. R., Miciak, J., & Fletcher, J. M. (2015). Are child cognitive characteristics strong predictors of responses to intervention? A meta-analysis. *Review of Educational Research, 85*(3), 395–429.

Swanson, J. M., Schuck, S., Porter, M. M., Carlson, C., Hartman, C. A., Sergeant, J. A., . . . Wigal, T. (2012). Categorical and dimensional definitions and evaluations of symptoms of ADHD: History of the SNAP and the SWAN Rating Scales. *The International Journal of Educational and Psychological Assessment, 10*(1), 51–70.

Torgesen, J. K., Alexander, A. W., Wagner, R. K., Rashotte, C. A., Voeller, K. K. S., & Conway, T. (2001). Intensive remedial instruction for children with severe reading disabilities: Immediate and long-term outcomes from two instructional approaches. *Journal of Learning Disabilities, 34*(1), 33–58.

Wagner, R. K., Torgesen, J. K., Rashotte, C. A., & Pearson, N. A. (2013). *Comprehensive Test of Phonological Processing–Second Edition (CTOPP-2).* Austin, TX: PRO-ED.

Wechsler, D. (2011). *Wechsler Abbreviated Scale of Intelligence–Second Edition (WASI-II).* San Antonio, TX: NCS Pearson.

Wolf, M. & Denckla, M. B. (2005). *Rapid Automatized Naming and Rapid Alternating Stimulus Tests.* Austin, TX: PRO-ED.

Woodcock, R. W., McGrew, K. S., & Mather, N. (2001). *Woodcock-Johnson III Tests of Achievement.* Itasca, IL: Riverside Publishing.

Yoder, P., & Compton, D. (2004). Identifying predictors of treatment response. *Mental Retardation and Developmental Disabilities Research Reviews, 10*(3), 1080–4013.

CHAPTER 12

Identification of Disabilities in Spanish-Speaking Children in English-Speaking Contexts

David J. Francis, Kristi L. Santi, Shiva Khalaf,
Ferenc Bunta, Raúl Rojas, Svenja Gusewski, and Lindsey Hiebert

SUMMARY

This chapter examines the challenges associated with identifying reading and language disabilities in language minority children (those who speak/hear a home language other than the majority status language of their society). We review the extant literature on disability identification in English language learners (ELs) and examine the problem of identification using data from large-scale longitudinal studies of Spanish-speaking ELs in the United States. In addition to the challenges to identification that have been recognized in the literature, there are special challenges to reliable and valid identification of students with disabilities among language minority students. These complications include heterogeneity in the population and instructional context, most notably in the language of instruction, and complications associated with the language of assessment. Other factors that exert unique complications for this population are the relevance of majority population norms for identifying atypical development relative to age/grade among language minorities, changes in normative values over time, and the role of contextual factors in determining proper developmental expectations.

INTRODUCTION

Scientific inquiry can be hindered by the absence of consistency in definitions and classifications (Blashfield, 1993). In the case of research on students with intellectual and developmental disabilities, progress accelerated in the 1970s and 1980s, which followed an evolving consensus around theoretical frameworks that operationalized disability identification (Hallahan & Mercer, 2002). This consensus led researchers to focus on operational definitions of disabilities and their validation (Morris, Fletcher, & Francis, 1993; Shepard, 1980; Siegel, 1992), including the failure of academic skills to develop at a normative rate (Francis, Shaywitz, Stuebing, Shaywitz, & Fletcher, 1996). Research of this type was conducted on all varieties of disabilities—reading, math, language, attention, and executive function—and has generally shown a lack of discriminant validity between competing operational definitions. The lack of discriminant validity, coupled with regulations that limited students' access to services absent a diagnosis, led to the pursuit of alternative conceptualizations, such as response to intervention (Fletcher, Lyon, Fuchs, & Barnes, 2007) and cognitive process models (Johnson, Humphrey, Mellard, Woods, & Swanson, 2010). Interest in these alternatives has resulted in considerable research focused on their operationalization and validity as a means of disability identification.

Amid this progress, the identification of disabilities among children who are nonnative speakers of the societal language has remained largely underdeveloped. Students who hear a language in their home other than the societal language are termed *language minority children.* In the United States, language minority children whose proficiency in English does not allow them to participate fully in English instruction without language supports are collectively referred to as ELs under federal law. The formal designation of a particular student as an EL involves criteria that vary by state, however, lending some ambiguity to the term as an operational definition. The United States does not report official statistics on language minority students, but it does report on students designated as EL, most recently reported to be 9.5% of school-age children (McFarland et al., 2017). Although the United States has no official language, the language of the majority is English (U.S. Department of Education, National Center for Education Statistics, Common Core of Data, n.d.). In contrast, the European Union (EU) recognizes 23 official languages, and although rates vary considerably across countries, about 4% of EU school-age children are first-generation migrant students (Education, Audiovisual, and Culture Executive Agency, 2012). Federal law in the United States allows for identification of disabilities among ELs using any approach to identification that is allowed with native English speakers, but neither the law nor research has provided guidance on the validity of these operational definitions with language minority students in general, or ELs in particular. This chapter seeks to fill this gap by extending research on IQ-achievement discrepancy and low achievement (LA) to Spanish-speaking ELs. We will specifically investigate the validity of these methods of identification through examination of overlap as well as concurrent validity to nonclassification measures.

To advance understanding of reading and language disability in ELs, a sound theoretical and empirically supported framework for identifying and classifying disabilities in ELs is essential. Most would agree that language disabilities are rooted in the neural substrate underlying language and its development. Similarly, reading disabilities are rooted in the neural substrate for reading, either in that component of the substrate that affects the acquisition of decoding and fluency or the higher order cognitive skills that affect the processing of language presented in text. By definition, reading and language disabilities cannot be the result of a poor learning environment, inadequate instruction, or limited opportunity to learn. Whereas theory on language development, literacy acquisition, and reading disability dictate that a child with a language or reading disability will have his or her learning affected by that disability in any language(s) they speak, read, or write, how these theoretical expectations can be meaningfully incorporated into the identification of disabilities in language minority children has not been widely researched.

IDENTIFICATION OF DISABILITIES IN LANGUAGE MINORITY CHILDREN

Unlike disability identification in language majority students, accurate identification in language minority students must consider the possible moderating influence of language of instruction because students' performance in any domain of skill in a particular language will be affected by the opportunity to learn that skill in that language. Thus, insofar as we seek to develop an empirically and theoretically grounded framework of disability identification for ELs, we expect that language of instruction will significantly moderate the validity of any approach to identification for ELs, such that failure to condition on the language of instruction will lead to significant misidentification of children. At the same time, it is expected that severe low performance in both languages may indicate a disability regardless of the language of instruction. We also predict that students identified under LA and IQ-achievement discrepancy definitions of reading disability will not differ from one another on external measures (i.e., those not used for identification), except to the extent that disabilities identified under discrepancy are more severe conditional on IQ (see Fletcher et al., 2007, for extensive discussion of these issues). Unlike the use of these identification procedures among language majority speakers of English, we further predict that their validity will be significantly affected by the child's history of instruction in English and Spanish.

Methods and Participants

The current study included 3,440 ELs assessed in Grades 1 and 2 from 506 classrooms and 41 schools located in urban California, urban Texas, and south central Texas near the border with Mexico. In this chapter, we examine students' reading performance in the fall of Grade 1 and the spring of Grade 2. The mean age of the participants was 6.7 years (standard deviation [*SD*] = .44) at the beginning of Grade 1. The sample was relatively balanced with respect to gender (51.6% male, 48.4% female).

The primary reading outcome measures were the broad reading cluster scores in English and Spanish from the Woodcock Language Proficiency Battery–Revised (Woodcock, 1991; Woodcock & Muñoz-Sandoval, 1995), which are a combination of measures of decoding skills and reading comprehension. Measures of oral language in English and Spanish included Listening Comprehension, Memory for Sentences, Picture Vocabulary, and Verbal Analogies from the same Woodcock batteries as the reading measures.

To classify children into disability groups, we regressed the broad reading score onto a measure of IQ (viz., the Raven's Progressive Color Matrices). We established four levels of severity based on the probability for standardized residuals in regression (viz., $p \leq .20$, .15, .10, and .05). Students were classified as IQ-achievement discrepant if their achievement fell below expectations and the associated p value for the standardized residual fell below the .20 cut-off. Similarly, students were classified as low achieving in reading based on the percentile score associated with their broad reading cluster score, using the 20th, 15th, 10th, and 5th percentiles as criteria. We classified students using the regression and LA criteria simultaneously, such that children were classified at the most severe threshold met by their performance relative to each set of criteria. For example, if a student met the regression discrepancy (RD) criterion with p (standardized residual) < .18, then that student met the criterion at the ≤ .20 level but not at the ≤ .15 level. Likewise, if a student's achievement score was at the 13th percentile, then the student was classified at the ≤ .15 level for LA but not at the ≤ .10 or ≤ .20 level. In other words, students were classified at the most severe criterion that they met, and classification was carried out independently for the discrepancy criteria and the LA criteria. This approach determines the degree to which the two classes of criteria identify the same or different students.

Results

Results of this study are discussed in the following sections.

Classification and the Language of Instruction Researchers studying language minority children typically hold the language of the assessment constant for examining the impact of important predictors. In the present case, we would examine classifications based on English reading outcomes and then separately examine classifications based on Spanish reading outcomes. Taking that approach with the present sample, when examining English outcomes we would find that only 1,304 of 2,406 students (54%) are classified as typically developing in the fall of Grade 1 (i.e., they meet neither the LA nor the RD at a criterion of .20 or below. More important, that implies that 46% of students are either RD, LA, or both. In fact, of the 1,102 children who were classified as RD, LA, or both, all met the LA criteria, of which 589 (24.5% of the total; 53.4% of those identified) met both the RD and LA criteria. No child met only the RD criteria, which can be seen from the row labeled "Not LA" in Table 12.1. At the same time, we would see that of the 1,102 children who were identified based on English outcomes, 141 had been instructed in English and 961 had been instructed in Spanish. These counts translate into conditional probabilities of 141/787 = .179 and 961/1,619 = .593 for English and Spanish instruction, respectively, because more children in the sample received their instruction in Spanish. If we were to examine classifications based on Spanish outcomes at the same time point, then we would see the opposite picture; the overall rate of identification would be 40% (979/2,441), and the conditional rates of identification would be 567/783 or 72% of children in English instruction and 412/1658 or 24.8% of children in Spanish instruction. These identification rates, particularly the identification rates in English for Spanish instructed students (.593) and Spanish rates for English instructed students (.72), are absurdly high and signify a problem with the approach.

An Alternative Approach to Controlling the Language of Instruction Rather than hold the language of the outcome constant, we instead hold the relationship between the language of instruction and the language of assessment constant, looking first at outcomes in the language of instruction and subsequently at outcomes in the uninstructed language. Thus, we first match the language of instruction and the language of assessment, looking at English language outcomes for children receiving their instruction primarily in English and Spanish language outcomes for children receiving their instruction primarily in Spanish. Subsequently, we examine outcomes not in the language of instruction, namely English outcomes for children instructed in Spanish and Spanish outcomes for children instructed in English.

Complete classification results are presented in Tables 12.1–12.4 following this somewhat novel organizational structure. Specifically, the tables are organized into pairs; Tables 12.1 and 12.2 show results for the fall of Grade 1, and Tables 12.3 and 12.4 show results for the spring of Grade 2. Moreover, Tables 12.1 and 12.3 show results for classifications made in the language of instruction (English outcomes for English-instructed students and Spanish outcomes for Spanish-instructed students), whereas Tables 12.2 and 12.4 show the results when children are classified based on outcomes in the language not matched to the language of instruction (English outcomes for Spanish-instructed students and Spanish outcomes for English-instructed students). Each table shows the cross-classification of students according to the discrepancy and LA criteria at each of the designated levels of severity for a particular grade and time point. Columns of the tables reflect the RD criteria, and the rows of the tables reflect the LA criteria. Any child meeting a more severe criterion also met all lesser criteria. For the purposes of the tables, each student appears only in that cell representing the most severe criteria that the student met.

Each table is structured to provide both the marginal distribution for classifications based on LA and RD criteria. The first section of the table provides the overall classification of students into RD and LA levels of severity collapsing across the two language of instruction groups. The second and third sections of the table provide the results broken out by the language of instruction. As previously stated, classifications are done on outcomes in the language of instruction in Tables 12.1 and 12.3, and the classifications are done on outcomes in the language that is not the primary language of instruction in Tables 12.2 and 12.4.

We predicted that language of instruction was an important factor when it came to classification of disabilities among EL students. There are various ways to examine the information in the tables to see the importance of the language of instruction. If we compare the top portions of Tables 12.1 and 12.2, then we see that 77.4% of children are classified as typically developing, neither RD nor LA on outcomes in the language of instruction (see top section of Table 12.1), whereas only 36.4% of students are seen as typically developing in the language that is not matched to the language of instruction (see top section of Table 12.2). Results vary somewhat based on the language of instruction, regardless of the language of assessment.

Table 12.1. Cross-classification: Regression discrepancy (RD) versus low achievement (LA) in broad reading in the language of instruction for fall semester of Grade 1 (expressed as percentages)

	RD criterion[a]					
LA criterion[b]	Not RD	.20	.15	.10	.05	Total
Combined across English and Spanish language of instruction						
Not LA	77.4%	0.0%	0.0%	0.0%	0.0%	77.4%
Subtotal LA	11.9%	3.7%	3.3%	2.9%	0.9%	22.6%
20	3.2%	0.0%	0.0%	0.0%	0.0%	3.2%
15	2.9%	0.0%	0.0%	0.0%	0.0%	2.9%
10	3.6%	0.4%	0.1%	0.0%	0.0%	4.1%
5	2.2%	3.3%	3.2%	2.9%	0.9%	12.5%
Total	89.2%	3.7%	3.3%	2.9%	0.9%	100.0%
English outcomes within English-instructed programs						
Not LA	82.1%	0.0%	0.0%	0.0%	0.0%	82.1%
Subtotal LA	12.3%	2.2%	2.3%	0.8%	0.4%	17.9%
20	3.6%	0.0%	0.0%	0.0%	0.0%	3.6%
15	3.6%	0.0%	0.0%	0.0%	0.0%	3.6%
10	2.8%	0.4%	0.1%	0.0%	0.0%	3.3%
5	2.4%	1.8%	2.2%	0.8%	0.4%	7.5%
Total	94.4%	2.2%	2.3%	0.8%	0.4%	100.0%
Spanish outcomes within Spanish-instructed programs						
Not LA	75.2%	0.0%	0.0%	0.0%	0.0%	75.2%
Subtotal LA	11.6%	4.4%	3.7%	3.9%	1.2%	24.8%
20	3.0%	0.0%	0.0%	0.0%	0.0%	3.0%
15	2.5%	0.0%	0.0%	0.0%	0.0%	2.5%
10	4.0%	0.4%	0.1%	0.0%	0.0%	4.5%
5	2.1%	4.0%	3.7%	3.9%	1.2%	14.8%
Total	86.8%	4.4%	3.7%	3.9%	1.2%	100.0%

Numerical criteria are mutually exclusive (i.e., children are counted in the table at the lowest criterion that they meet).

a. Student meets RD criterion if the probability of the standardized residual is less than or equal to the criterion probability and greater than the next lower criterion.

b. Achievement score as a percentile is less than or equal to the LA criterion and greater than the next lower criterion.

Specifically, 82.1% of students in English instruction were classified as typically developing compared with 75.2% of students in Spanish instruction. Looking at outcomes in the uninstructed language, only 27.6% of students in English instruction were classified as typically developing in Spanish, whereas 40.6% of students in Spanish instruction were classified as typically developing in English. These results make sense when one considers that children in English instruction are receiving little if any Spanish instruction, whereas children in Spanish instruction are learning to read in English as well as in Spanish. There is simply a primary focus on literacy development in Spanish. As a result, outcomes in the instructed language are not as

Table 12.2. Cross-classification: Regression discrepancy (RD) versus low achievement (LA) in broad reading in the uninstructed language for fall semester of Grade 1 (expressed as percentages)

	RD criterion[a]					
LA criterion[b]	Not RD	.20	.15	.10	.05	Total
Combined across English and Spanish language of instruction programs						
Not LA	36.4%	0.0%	0.0%	0.0%	0.0%	36.4%
Subtotal LA	25.4%	8.9%	9.9%	12.4%	7.0%	63.6%
20	4.1%	0.0%	0.0%	0.0%	0.0%	4.1%
15	5.6%	0.0%	0.0%	0.0%	0.0%	5.6%
10	8.7%	0.9%	0.1%	0.0%	0.0%	9.7%
5	7.1%	8.0%	9.8%	12.4%	7.0%	44.2%
Total	61.8%	8.9%	9.9%	12.4%	7.0%	100.0%
Spanish outcomes within English-instructed programs						
Not LA	27.6%	0.0%	0.0%	0.0%	0.0%	27.6%
Subtotal LA	24.9%	10.5%	12.9%	15.3%	8.8%	72.4%
20	3.4%	0.0%	0.0%	0.0%	0.0%	3.4%
15	5.9%	0.0%	0.0%	0.0%	0.0%	5.9%
10	8.8%	1.7%	0.3%	0.0%	0.0%	10.7%
5	6.8%	8.8%	12.6%	15.3%	8.8%	52.4%
Total	52.5%	10.5%	12.9%	15.3%	8.8%	100.0%
English outcomes within Spanish-instructed programs						
Not LA	40.6%	0.0%	0.0%	0.0%	0.0%	40.6%
Subtotal LA	25.7%	8.1%	8.5%	10.9%	6.2%	59.4%
20	4.4%	0.0%	0.0%	0.0%	0.0%	4.4%
15	5.4%	0.0%	0.0%	0.0%	0.0%	5.4%
10	8.6%	0.6%	0.1%	0.0%	0.0%	9.3%
5	7.2%	7.5%	8.4%	10.9%	6.2%	40.3%
Total	66.3%	8.1%	8.5%	10.9%	6.2%	100.0%

Numerical criteria are mutually exclusive (i.e., children are counted in the table at the lowest criterion that they meet).

a. Student meets RD criterion if the probability of the standardized residual is less than or equal to the criterion probability and greater than the next lower criterion.

b. Achievement score as a percentile is less than or equal to the LA criterion and greater than the next lower criterion.

strong for children in Spanish instruction as for children in English instruction, but at the same time, outcomes in the uninstructed language are superior because there is an effort to develop biliteracy in contrast to the children in English instruction. Thus, it is not terribly surprising to see somewhat higher identification rates in the instructed language and somewhat lower rates of identification in the uninstructed language for Spanish-instructed students when compared with English-instructed students.

Tables 12.3 and 12.4 show the decline in rates of identification as children gain time in instruction. In the language of instruction, identification

Table 12.3. Cross-classification: Regression discrepancy (RD) versus low achievement (LA) in broad reading in the language of instruction for spring semester of Grade 2 (expressed as percentages)

	RD criterion[a]					
LA criterion[b]	Not RD	.20	.15	.10	.05	Total
Combined across English and Spanish language of instruction						
Not LA	91.0%	0.2%	0.0%	0.0%	0.0%	91.2%
Subtotal LA	1.4%	1.8%	1.6%	1.4%	2.5%	8.8%
20	1.1%	0.3%	0.1%	0.0%	0.0%	1.4%
15	0.4%	0.7%	0.3%	0.0%	0.0%	1.4%
10	0.0%	0.8%	0.4%	0.2%	0.0%	1.4%
5	0.0%	0.0%	0.8%	1.2%	2.5%	4.5%
Total	92.5%	1.9%	1.6%	1.4%	2.5%	100.0%
English outcomes within English-instructed programs						
Not LA	90.2%	0.5%	0.0%	0.0%	0.0%	90.8%
Subtotal LA	1.7%	1.8%	2.2%	1.3%	2.2%	9.2%
20	1.3%	0.8%	0.3%	0.0%	0.0%	2.3%
15	0.4%	0.7%	0.9%	0.1%	0.0%	2.1%
10	0.0%	0.4%	0.9%	0.7%	0.0%	2.0%
5	0.0%	0.0%	0.1%	0.5%	2.2%	2.9%
Total	91.9%	2.3%	2.2%	1.3%	2.2%	100.0%
Spanish outcomes within Spanish-instructed programs						
Not LA	91.4%	0.0%	0.0%	0.0%	0.0%	91.4%
Subtotal LA	1.3%	1.7%	1.3%	1.5%	2.7%	8.6%
20	1.0%	0.0%	0.0%	0.0%	0.0%	1.0%
15	0.3%	0.8%	0.0%	0.0%	0.0%	1.1%
10	0.0%	1.0%	0.1%	0.0%	0.0%	1.1%
5	0.0%	0.0%	1.2%	1.5%	2.7%	5.4%
Total	92.7%	1.7%	1.3%	1.5%	2.7%	100.0%

Numerical criteria are mutually exclusive (i.e., children are counted in the table at the lowest criterion that they meet).

a. Student meets RD criterion if the probability of the standardized residual is less than or equal to the criterion probability and greater than the next lower criterion.

b. Achievement score as a percentile is less than or equal to the LA criterion and greater than the next lower criterion.

rates drop to 9% overall, 9.8% for English-instructed students, and 8.6% for Spanish-instructed students, whereas in the uninstructed language, identification rates decline to 35.1% overall, 54.7% among English-instructed students, and 25.3% among Spanish-instructed students. This greater decrease in identification rates in English for students instructed in Spanish is consistent with the fact that students in Spanish instruction are also learning to read in English, albeit at a slower pace than their English-instructed peers, whereas students in English instruction are not generally being taught to read in Spanish. Consequently, identification rates remain excessively high

Table 12.4. Cross-classification: Regression discrepancy (RD) versus low achievement (LA) in broad reading in the uninstructed language for spring semester of Grade 2 (expressed as percentages)

	RD criterion[a]					
LA criterion[b]	Not RD	.20	.15	.10	.05	Total
Combined across English and Spanish language of instruction						
Not LA	64.9%	0.8%	0.0%	0.0%	0.0%	65.7%
Subtotal LA	4.4%	6.1%	6.8%	7.1%	9.8%	34.3%
20	3.2%	0.8%	0.4%	0.1%	0.0%	4.5%
15	1.2%	2.8%	1.6%	0.3%	0.0%	5.8%
10	0.0%	2.6%	2.2%	1.0%	0.05%	5.8%
5	0.0%	0.0%	2.7%	5.7%	9.8%	18.2%
Total	69.3%	7.0%	6.9%	7.1%	9.8%	100.0%
Spanish outcomes within English-instructed programs						
Not LA	46.3%	0.0%	0.0%	0.0%	0.0%	46.3%
Subtotal LA	6.8%	10.0%	9.3%	11.9%	15.7%	53.7%
20	5.1%	0.0%	0.0%	0.0%	0.0%	5.1%
15	1.7%	4.6%	0.0%	0.0%	0.0%	6.3%
10	0.0%	5.4%	1.7%	0.0%	0.0%	7.1%
5	0.0%	0.0%	7.6%	11.9%	15.7%	35.3%
Total	53.1%	10.0%	9.3%	11.9%	15.7%	100.0%
English outcomes within Spanish-instructed programs						
Not LA	74.7%	1.2%	0.1%	0.0%	0.0%	76.0%
Subtotal LA	3.1%	4.1%	5.5%	4.5%	6.1%	24.0%
20	2.2%	1.2%	0.6%	0.1%	0.0%	4.1%
15	0.9%	1.8%	2.5%	0.4%	0.0%	5.6%
10	0.0%	1.1%	2.4%	1.5%	0.1%	5.1%
5	0.0%	0.0%	0.1%	2.5%	6.7%	9.2%
Total	77.8%	5.4%	5.6%	4.5%	6.7%	100.0%

Numerical criteria are mutually exclusive (i.e., children are counted in the table at the lowest criterion that they meet).

a. Student meets RD criterion if the probability of the standardized residual is less than or equal to the criterion probability and greater than the next lower criterion.

b. Achievement score as a percentile is less than or equal to the LA criterion and greater than the next lower criterion.

in Spanish for students instructed in English. These developmental relations make identification based exclusively on English outcomes questionable until after second grade for Spanish-instructed students. Notwithstanding these differences, the similarities in the developmental trends across languages and instructional groups is consistent with theoretical expectations that disabilities are not language specific, suggesting that outcomes in each language carry information about disability status. At the same time, the differences across languages and the apparent interaction with the language of instruction make it clear that using the information from both languages to inform disability identifications must take into account the language of instruction.

Implementing Discrepancy and Low Achievement Unclear from the foregoing discussion is precisely how to establish the LA and IQ-achievement discrepancy criteria. Specifically, when children are instructed in heterogeneous language contexts, using a common regression line to establish the discrepancy criteria and then conditioning on the language of instruction after children have been classified will result in substantial misidentification. If the slope and intercept of the regression line relating achievement to IQ vary depending on the language of instruction, then using a common regression line will overidentify in one instructional group and underidentify in another. This problem is not necessarily resolved by fitting a common regression line for outcomes in the instructed language because the regression line may vary as a function of the language of assessment and the language of instruction. In fact, we find such specificity in the current dataset. In the fall of Grade 1, the slope for IQ in the common regression line was .26 for English outcomes and .28 for Spanish outcomes. Yet, estimated within instructional groups, the slope for IQ for English outcomes was .11 for English-instructed students and .33 for Spanish-instructed students, whereas the slope for Spanish outcomes was .34 for Spanish-instructed students and .13 for English-instructed students. Even the two regressions slopes for outcomes in the instructed language are not comparable to one another (.11 for English outcomes for students instructed in English and .34 for Spanish outcomes for students instructed in Spanish).

In addition to the slope differences just discussed, the intercepts of the regression equations also varied depending on the language of the outcome and the language of instruction. Consequently, the identification of students using IQ-achievement discrepancy must use a regression line that is specific to the language of the outcome and the language of instruction. Although we have not provided direct tests of significance between the regression coefficients in the instructed language (i.e., the .34 for Spanish outcomes for students instructed in Spanish and the .11 for English outcomes for students instructed in English), they are statistically significant given that the slope difference is roughly four times the size of its standard error. Clearly, the language of instruction and the language of assessment must be taken into account at the time of fitting the regression equation; one cannot use a common regression equation and adjust after the fact.

It seems reasonable to suggest that implementation of LA criteria should also use norms that are specific to the language of the outcome and the language of the assessment. Yet, implementing such a strategy is easier said than done because norms do not exist for language minority students, and norms that are specific to a particular instructional method are at least as scarce. Given that language minority students are educationally at risk for a variety of sociodemographic and economic factors, using a more severe criterion (e.g., 5th percentile instead of 20th percentile) would partially mitigate the lack of suitable norms, but it is not obvious how that criterion would need to be adjusted to also take into account the effects of language of instruction on expected performance in each language. Examining the stability of classifications over time may provide guidance on the suitability of different criteria within language of instruction groups as well as how to best incorporate information from both languages into the classification process.

Concurrent Validation As a first step in external validation of the low achievement and discrepancy criteria in the fall of Grade 1, we examined differences between groups on nonreading measures at the same time point (i.e., concurrent validation). For students instructed in Spanish, we looked at both English and Spanish outcomes, and for students instructed in English, we looked only at English outcomes. For validation, we focused exclusively on classifications in the language of instruction. That is, students instructed in Spanish were classified based on their Spanish Broad Reading in fall of Grade 1, and students instructed in English were classified based on their English Broad Reading. To compare classifications, we constructed three groups based on Spanish classifications and three groups based on English classifications. Specifically, students were classified as RD if they met any RD criterion, LA if they met any LA criterion and did not meet any of the RD criteria, and not-reading-impaired if they met none of the LA or RD criteria. English and Spanish classifications were examined separately using a mixed model analogue of profile analysis on four language measures: Listening Comprehension, Memory for Sentences, Picture Vocabulary, and Verbal Analogies. The approach used PROC MIXED in SAS 9.4 to test the Elevation, Flatness, and Shape hypotheses of profile analysis while allowing for imbalance in the design due to missing data. We controlled for clustering within schools by including random intercepts at the school level and employed an arbitrary (i.e., unstructured) residual covariance matrix that allowed the residuals for the four outcomes to freely covary. We did assume a homogeneous covariance matrix for the residuals across the three groups. Because the test of profile shape was significant for all classifications and outcomes ($p < .0001$ for classifications in Spanish and outcomes in English and Spanish; $p = .016$ for English classifications and outcomes in English), we examined simple effects of group (i.e., group differences on each outcome) using a Bonferroni adjusted *p*-value of .05/4 = .0125 because there were four outcomes in each analysis. Significant simple effects were followed up with Bonferroni adjusted pairwise comparisons at $p = .0125/3 = .0042$. Bonferroni adjusted follow-up comparisons between the three groups showed that for both Spanish classifications (Spanish and English outcomes) and English classifications (English outcomes), all four simple effects were statistically significant at $p < .0001$. Thus, for all outcomes and classifications, pairwise comparisons were warranted, focusing on comparison of the LA and RD groups. Table 12.5 provides the differences in least squares means from the multivariate profile analysis for the LA and RD groups, along with an estimate of the *SD* in the population of learners receiving instruction in the language of classification and the effect size based on the mean difference and estimate of the *SD*.

The LA and RD groups differed on some measures in English and in Spanish, but not all. Specifically, we found that LA and RD groups in Spanish differed on measures of Listening Comprehension and Picture Vocabulary ($p < .0001$) in both Spanish and English, and on measures of Verbal Analogies in Spanish ($p = .0004$) and in English ($p = .0023$), but did not differ on Memory for Sentences in Spanish ($p = .3643$) or in English ($p = .8424$). For English classifications and English outcomes, we found that LA and RD differences were generally not statistically significant at the adjusted *p*-value. This difference between the English and Spanish classifications, however, appeared to have been the result of the smaller sample size in the English classifications more so than differences in effect sizes (see Table 12.5), which tended to be larger for the English classifications, ranging from .17 to .38, and ranging from .06 to .35 for the Spanish classifications.

Discussion

We examined IQ-achievement discrepancy and LA as bases for identifying reading problems in Spanish speaking EL students. We examined classifications in two languages at the start of Grade 1 and the end of Grade 2, focusing in particular on the challenges posed by heterogeneity in the language of instruction. We predicted that failure to account for language of instruction would lead to significant misidentification of reading difficulties, and our findings supported this prediction. Overidentification was not found to be a problem of leniency in the criterion nor the language of assessment. The preponderance of students were identified at the most severe criterion that we examined, and overidentification was present regardless of whether identification took place in English or in Spanish. Although identification rates declined by the end of Grade 2, overidentification was still apparent, with 20% of students identified in English and 24% in Spanish when identification is made without consideration for the language of instruction. Identification rates decreased substantially when language of instruction was taken into account by matching to the language in which the outcome was assessed.

Table 12.5. Least squares mean differences between low achievement (LA) and regression discrepancy (RD) and estimated effect sizes

	Listening comprehension			Memory for sentences			Picture vocabulary			Verbal analogies		
Classification language/ outcome language	Mean difference	s_p	d	Mean difference	s_p	d	Mean difference	s_p	d	Mean difference	s_p	d
Spanish–Spanish	4.2	19.15	0.22	0.8	13.30	0.06	4.2	23.45	0.18	4.5	13.13	0.34
Spanish–English	6.1	17.36	0.35	1	12.01	0.08	8.6	26.79	0.32	4.7	16.06	0.29
English–English	6.9	18.97	0.36	3.6	13.40	0.27	3.3	19.27	0.17	4.9	12.76	0.38

In this table, the language of classification is also the language of instruction. The mean difference is estimated from the mixed model taking into account random effects of schools. The estimate of the standard deviation (s_p) is the pooled standard deviation from all three classification groups (NRI, LA, and RD) to give the best estimate of the standard deviation in the population of all English learners receiving their instruction in the language used to classify students. The effect size (d) is the mean difference divided by the estimate of the standard deviation (s_p).

We found that separately focusing on classification in the language of instruction and classification in the uninstructed language had some utility, but patterns of performance over time varied depending on the language of instruction, reflecting the differential emphasis that Spanish language programs place on biliteracy. Although the identification rates vary as children age through the system, it seems quite clear that overidentification occurs whenever the language of instruction is not matched to the language of the assessment used in identification. Moreover, the problem is most pronounced when English-instructed students are assessed in Spanish and when young Spanish-instructed students are assessed in English. As Spanish-instructed students age through the system and have more exposure to literacy instruction, the use of English assessment in identification is less problematic. Precisely how best to use the uninstructed language in the identification of reading problems will require further research, but it seems clear that the recommendation will vary depending on the language of instruction.

Theories of reading disability stipulate that reading disabilities are not language specific, although the precise manifestations of a disability may vary across languages depending on the characteristics of the language and, in particular, the characteristics of the writing system used in that language (Ziegler & Goswami, 2005). Stipulating that reading disabilities are not language specific might be taken to imply that the language of assessment is arbitrary, but nothing could be further from the truth. At the heart of all theories of learning disability is adequate opportunity to learn, and establishing expectations for performance is integral to all identification approaches. Developmental expectations for ELs are complicated by the heterogeneous language learning environments to which students are exposed, including their varied reading instructional environments. Identifying ELs with a reading disability remains challenging because of the need to distinguish performance that is below expectations due to a disability from performance that is below expectations due to limited proficiency in a language, limited opportunity to develop reading proficiency in a language, and/or developmental expectations that are not well calibrated to the particular learner due to the heterogeneity of learners' early literacy experiences. If disabilities are not language specific, then using the uninstructed language to improve identification may be possible, but only if used in conjunction with outcomes in the instructed language. Limited reading proficiency due to limited exposure and/or opportunity to learn to read in a particular language is a significant threat to the valid identification of disabilities for ELs. This threat appears greatest when children are young and/or when the assessment is in the uninstructed language. Having better information regarding developmental expectations for students growing up under different instructional contexts would assist researchers and practitioners in developing more effective approaches and criteria for identifying students with disabilities.

The current work has practical implications for researchers. Intervention studies based on samples with clearly identified risk characteristics will provide additional evidence for specific definitions as studies accumulate over time. We expect this work will show, as in the case of research with monolingual students, that differences between LA and IQ-achievement discrepant students are a function of the IQ differences between these groups. That is, for ELs, as for native English-speaking students, disabilities defined by discrepancy and LA lie on a latent continuum of severity rather than represent latent classes that differ qualitatively from one another. Swanson, Kudo, and Guzman-Orth (2016) undertook a novel approach to address the prevalence and stability of latent classes at risk for reading disabilities for students in K–3 whose first language is Spanish. Their findings aligned with monolingual studies on phonological and cognitive deficits underlying reading disabilities and pointed to the need for more work in the area of identification. Swanson et al. specifically questioned the use of the 25th percentile as the basis for identification, an issue highlighted by other researchers (cf., Francis et al., 2005; Wagner, Francis, & Morris, 2005) and shown to be problematic in the current work.

U.S. policy allows the identification of disabilities in ELs using any of the methods approved for use with native English speakers. Our efforts to empirically examine how such procedures might work in practice clearly indicate that a naïve application of these approaches to ELs would significantly misidentify students. The magnitude of these misidentifications would vary depending on the timing of the identfication and the match/mismatch between the language of assessment and the language of instruction. Although we have not identified a specific approach or set of criteria that would minimize misidentification for individual students, clearly any approach must carefully consider the language of instruction and the language of assessment. Although a case for bilingual assessment can be made, precisely how this information should be combined to improve identification awaits further research.

REFERENCES

Blashfield, R. K. (1993). Models of classification as related to taxonomy of learning disabilities. In G. R. Lyon, D. B. Gray, J. F. Kavanagh, & N. A. Krasnegor (Eds.), *Better understanding learning disabilities: New views from research and their implications for education and public policies* (pp. 17–26). Baltimore, MD: Paul H. Brookes Publishing Co.

Education, Audiovisual, and Culture Executive Agency. (2012). *Key data on teaching languages at school in Europe: 2012.* Retrieved from http://eacea.ec.europa.eu/education/eurydice. doi:10.2797/83967

Fletcher, J. M., Lyon, G. R., Fuchs, L. S., & Barnes, M. A. (2007). *Learning disabilities: From identification to intervention.* New York, NY: Guilford Press.

Francis, D. J., Shaywitz, S. E., Stuebing, K. K., Shaywitz, B. A., & Fletcher, J. M. (1996). Developmental lag versus deficit models of reading disability: A longitudinal, individual growth curves analysis. *Journal of Educational Psychology, 88*(1), 3–17. doi: 10.1037/0022-0663.88.1.3

Francis, D. J., Fletcher, J. M., Stuebing, K. K., Lyon, G. R., Shaywitz, B. A., & Shaywitz, S. E. (2005). Psychometric approaches to the identification of LD: IQ and achievement scores are not sufficient. *Journal of Learning Disabilities, 38*(2), 98–108. doi:10.1177/00222194050380020101

Hallahan, D. P., & Mercer, C. D. (2002). Learning disabilities: Historical perspectives. In R. Bradley, L. Danielson, & D. P. Hallahan (Eds.), *Identification of learning disabilities: Research to practice* (pp. 1–67). Mahwah, NJ: Lawrence Erlbaum Associates.

Johnson, E. S., Humphrey, M., Mellard, D. F., Woods, K., & Swanson, H. L. (2010). Cognitive processing deficits and students with specific learning disabilities: A selective meta-analysis of the literature. *Learning Disability Quarterly, 33*(1), 3–18. doi:10.1177/073194871003300101.

McFarland, J., Hussar, B., de Brey, C., Snyder, T., Wang, X., Wilkinson-Flicker, S., . . . Hinz, S. (2017). *The condition of education 2017 (NCES 2017-144).* Washington, DC: U.S. Department of Education, National Center for Education Statistics.

Morris, R. D., Fletcher, J. M., & Francis, D. J. (1993). Conceptual and psychometric issues in the neuropsychological assessment of children: Measurement of ability discrepancy and change. In I. Rapin & S. Segalovitz (Eds.), *Handbook of neuropsychology* (pp. 341–352). Amsterdam, Netherlands: Elsevier.

Shepard, L. (1980). An evaluation of the regression discrepancy method for identifying children with learning disabilities. *Journal of Special Education, 14*(1), 79–91. doi:10.1177/002246698001400108

Siegel, L. S. (1992). An evaluation of the discrepancy definition of dyslexia. *Journal of Learning Disabilities, 25*(10), 618–629. doi:10.1177/002221949202501001

Swanson, H. L., Kudo, M., & Guzman-Orth, D. (2016). Cognition and literacy in English language learners at risk for reading disabilities: A latent transition analysis. *Journal of Educational Psychology, 108*(6), 830–856. http://dx.doi.org/10.1037/edu0000102

U.S. Department of Education, National Center for Education Statistics, Common Core of Data. (n.d.). *Local education agency universe survey data.* Retrieved from https://nces.ed.gov/ccd/pubagency.asp

Wagner, R. K., Francis, D. J., & Morris, R. D. (2005). Identifying English language learners with learning disabilities: Key challenges and possible approaches. *Learning Disabilities Research and Practice, 20*(1), 6–15.

Woodcock, R. W. (1991). *Woodcock Language Proficiency Battery–Revised.* Itasca, IL: Riverside Publishing.

Woodcock, R. W., & Muñoz-Sandoval, A. F. (1995). *Woodcock Language Proficiency Battery–Revised: Spanish Form.* Itasca, IL: Riverside Publishing.

Ziegler, J. C., & Goswami, U. (2005). Reading acquisition, developmental dyslexia, and skilled reading across languages: A psycholinguistic grain size theory. *Psychological Bulletin, 131*(1), 3–29. doi:10.1037/0033-2909.131.1.3

CHAPTER 13

Relationship Between Spoken and Written Text Over Development

Application of Network Approaches

Laurie Cutting, Ghene't Lee-Yong, and Laura Barquero

SUMMARY

Numerous studies have explored the neurobiology that underlies spoken and written language processes and development. Most of these studies have focused on more simplistic models of language by examining singular regions of the brain that are associated with specific types of tasks. More recently, neurobiological networks involving multiple regions and broader functions have received increasing attention. To gain a full understanding of how brain activity is associated with language skills, both regional and network perspectives should be considered, and this chapter summarizes several studies we conducted. First, we used a meta-analytic database that aggregates brain activation across studies and determined that the brain's reading network overlaps with multiple cognitive networks, most prominently the fronto-parietal (executive control) as well as dorsal and ventral attention networks. Next, as reading is largely dependent on spoken language skills, we collected longitudinal functional magnetic resonance imaging (fMRI) data on children in third and fourth grade during a reading and listening comprehension task. Although there was an expected overlap of written and spoken language activations, listening showed more involvement of the dorsal attention network, and reading included the default mode network, an at-rest network that is understood to be activated for internal narrative and situation model building. Furthermore, we found that dyslexia-affected regions (as defined by meta-analyses) are highly connected to multiple cognitive networks. Relatedly, a reading intervention study showed that the fronto-parietal network interacts with reading specific areas, and this interaction may be predictive of who will respond well to reading intervention, suggesting a role of coordination of reading areas with executive function (EF) in intervention response. Yet, the left occipito-temporal region, which is important for automatic word reading and is predictive of intervention response, is not a highly connected hub region. Hence, both network and regional contributions should be considered in typical and atypical development of language skills.

INTRODUCTION

The capacity for spoken and written language is a core distinguishing feature of humans as compared with other primates (e.g., Pinker & Jackendoff,

2005). Although much is known about the neurobiological origins of spoken and written language, there are aspects of each that are poorly understood, particularly within a developmental context. More specifically, although there have been many studies examining the neurobiological components of written and spoken language, most are within a focal/regional theoretical framework. In contrast, global theories of cognition posit that integration across neurobiological circuits from broad areas across the cortex contributes to specific cognitive functions (Power, Schlaggar, Lessov-Schlaggar, & Petersen, 2013; Yeo et al., 2011). Incorporating both focal and global theoretical contexts in the examination of spoken and written language may be important for understanding both typical and atypical language development.

With regard to written language (reading), existing literature strongly supports that specific brain areas, especially in the left hemisphere, are key, including the left occipito-temporal region (often referred to as the *visual word form area;* VWFA), inferior frontal gyrus, and posterior middle temporal gyrus (Dehaene & Cohen, 2011; Pugh et al., 2000; Richlan, 2012). Although there is a substantial literature on the neurobiology of reading, neurobiological correlates of reading are usually described in terms of specific brain regions. Nevertheless, the brain areas involved in reading are nested within larger functional systems, and new network analysis methods may provide greater insight into how reading difficulty arises. Studies examining how global networks engage when individuals are processing spoken and written language are relatively sparse, and only a handful of studies have examined connectivity in relation to reading, atypical reading in particular (Finn et al., 2014; Koyama et al., 2013). In addition, although existing studies have examined which brain regions are specific to either written or spoken language, and which are common to both within a focal framework, none have investigated this issue within a global brain network framework. Given that written language (reading and writing), in contrast to spoken/oral language, is a *relatively new ability* for humans, it is of particular interest which components of reading at the systems level are unique compared with oral language and how these system-level indices relate to reading development. We posit that although both spoken and written language have typically been studied within a focal framework, examining within the framework of systems-level networks with a focus on key hubs/regions may be an important lens, especially for identification and treatment of dyslexia. Thus, a systems-level framework that incorporates regional-level theoretical frameworks may be revealing in terms of furthering our understanding of typical and atypical language development. In this chapter, findings are highlighted that support the idea that using a global network/systems-level framework may further our understanding about reading development in general, as well as dyslexia more specifically. First, we examine how major networks of the brain map onto spoken and written language networks and the implications for reading development (Bailey, Aboud, Nguyen, & Cutting, 2018). Second, we examine the implications of a network-level framework for dyslexia (Aboud, Barquero, & Cutting, 2018; Bailey et al., 2018). Finally, we examine the linkages between systems- versus region-level frameworks of reading and dyslexia, attempting to reconcile findings that suggest a role for each approach.

HOW MAJOR BRAIN NETWORKS MAP ONTO AREAS LINKED TO READING AND LANGUAGE

Several landmark studies have examined task-independent whole brain connectivity (Power et al., 2011; Yeo et al., 2011); although different studies use various analytical approaches, including Independent Components Analysis or graph theoretical methods, what is of relevance to the current chapter is that their findings illustrate that the entire brain can be segregated into global intrinsic networks, and these networks appear to support separable cognitive functions (Bullmore & Sporns, 2012; Yeo et al., 2011). Figure 13.1 shows different clusters of activation across the brain that covary in separable ways in one well-known study (Yeo et al., 2011). In this study, Yeo et al. segregated the brain into seven distinct intrinsic networks that span across the brain. For example, if examining the visual network specifically, one can see that the visual network spans both traditional visual areas within the occipital lobe as well as more anterior brain regions. Similarly, the fronto-parietal network includes the customary areas thought to be associated with cognitive control as well as those within the temporal regions that are not typically highlighted. Although the number of intrinsic net-

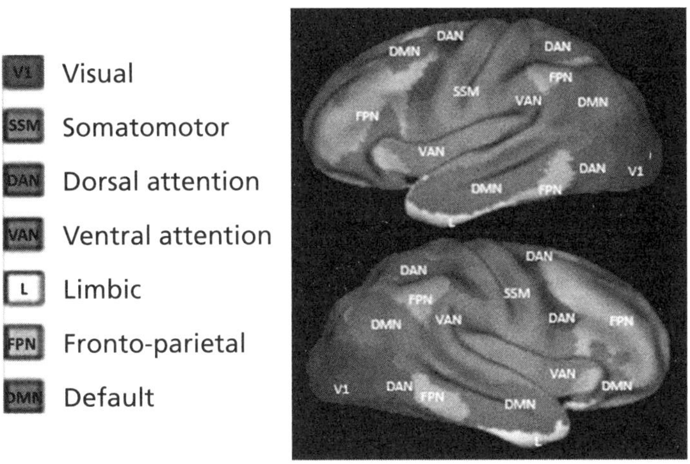

Figure 13.1. The brain is organized into 7 intrinsic networks as revealed by resting-state functional connectivity MRI. (From Yeo, B. T. T., Krienen, F. M., Sepulcre, J., Sabuncu, M. R., Lashkari, D., Hollinshead, M., . . . Buckner, R. L. [2011]. The organization of the human cerebral cortex estimated by intrinsic functional connectivity. *Journal of Neurophysiology, 106,* 1125–1165; adapted by permission.)

works can vary based on user specifications during analysis (e.g., Yeo et al. showed findings from seven networks and then more finely divided those networks into 17 networks), the illustrative point is that the brain clearly organizes itself into intrinsic networks that presumably have distinct roles in cognition, and areas within each network may not be geographically close.

Given the suggestion of distinct cognitive functions being associated with different intrinsic networks, of interest is the degree to which a task that is as cognitively demanding as reading—or listening—differentially maps onto various networks. In Bailey et al. (2018), Neurosynth (a meta-analysis database used to aggregate brain activation from thousands of studies; http://neurosynth.org) was used to examine which intrinsic networks the reading network tapped, focusing on the seven networks in Yeo et al. (2011). Findings revealed that the reading network spanned multiple intrinsic networks. As can be seen in Figure 13.2, reading maps onto all seven of the networks but most prominently the fronto-parietal as well as dorsal and ventral attention networks. These findings reveal that reading places demands on multiple networks, consistent with the idea that reading is a highly cognitively challenging task.

Of particular interest to reading development, however, is understanding more about the tight relationship between spoken and written language, and whether differences in network demands exist across modalities. Previous studies clearly show that spoken and written language are highly overlapping, and the degree to which they overlap predicts reading outcomes (e.g., Pugh et al., 2012; Shankweiler et al., 2008). The theoretical motivation for these studies is the idea that reading is parasitic upon speech, and, thus, regions dedicated to spoken language must become tuned to written language in order to produce a proficient reader (Shankweiler et al., 2008). Yet, whether they tap these major cognitive networks differentially is of interest when trying to understand how spoken and written language overlap and why these overlaps may be important for reading growth. To this end, data collected in third- and fourth-grade children ($N = 45$) on a task that taps both spoken and written language was examined through a network level lens (see Figure 13.3). In the reading part of the task, children viewed visual passages or symbols and were instructed to press a button when a word, phrase, or symbol was repeated. In the listening part of the task, children listened to auditory passages and tones with instructions to press a button for repeated words, phrases, or tones. Univariate analysis of reading and listening revealed, as expected, that there was a high degree of overlap between written and spoken language; however, the degree to which spoken versus written language placed demands across the above seven intrinsic networks varied (see Figure 13.4). Specifically, beyond the expected basic sensory network differences (i.e., reading relying more on the visual network than listening, and listening relying more on the sensory network, which includes auditory cortex, than reading), the dorsal attention network was more involved for listening versus reading, perhaps reflecting the more transitory nature of speech.

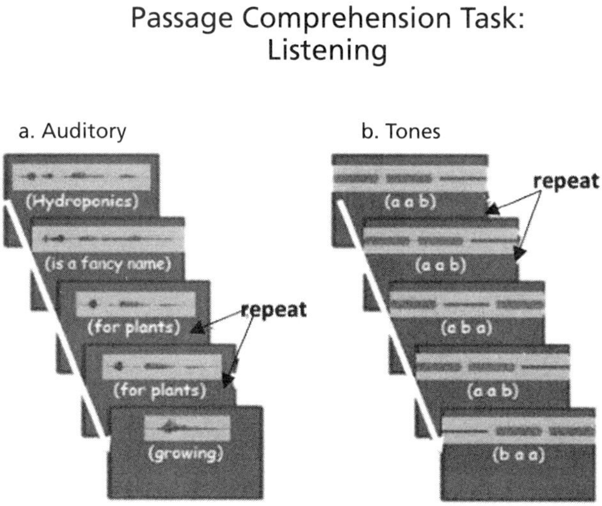

2a See Aboud, Barquero, and Cutting, 2016; Swett et al., 2013

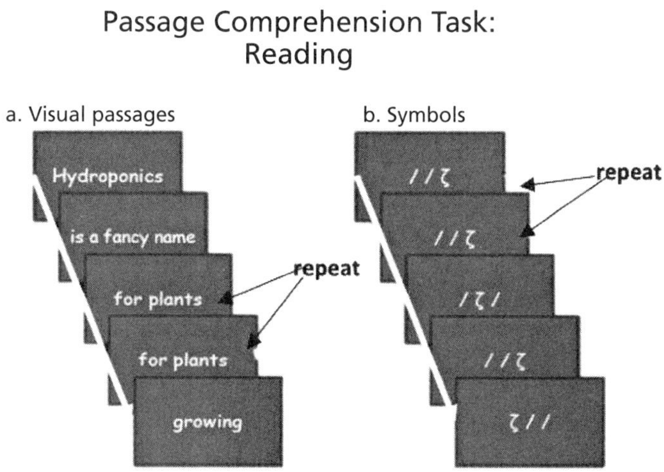

2b See Aboud et al., 2016; Swett et al., 2013

Figure 13.2. Passage comprehension task in Listening and Reading modalities. (From Aboud, K. S., Bailey, S. K., Petrill, S. A., & Cutting, L. E. [2016]. Comprehending text versus reading words in young readers with varying reading ability: Distinct patterns of functional connectivity from common processing hubs. *Developmental Science, 19,* 632–656. doi:10.1111/desc.12422; adapted by permission. From Swett, K., Miller, A.C., Burns, S., Hoeft, F., Davis, N., Petrill, S.A., & Cutting, L.E. [2013.] Comprehending expository texts: The dynamic neurobiological correlates of building a coherent text representation. *Frontiers in Human Neuroscience, 7,* 853. doi:10.3389/fnhum.2013.00853; adapted by permission. This figure is adapted from Swett et al., 2013, under the terms of the Creative Commons Attribution 3.0 License [https://creativecommons.org/licenses/by/3.0/legalcode].)

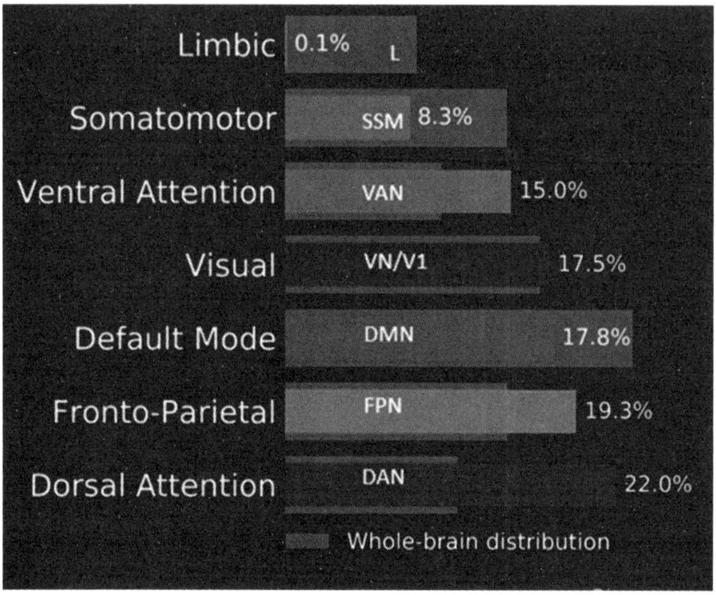

Figure 13.3. Reading is distributed across many intrinsic networks. (From Bailey, S. K., Aboud, K. S., Nguyen, T. Q., & Cutting, L. E. [2018]. Applying a network framework to the neurobiology of reading and dyslexia. *Journal of Neurodevelopmental Disorders, 10*[1], 37. doi:10.1186/s11689-018-9251-z; adapted by permission. This figure is adapted from the article above under the terms of the Creative Commons Attribution 4.0 International License [https://creativecommons.org/licenses/by/4.0/legalcode].)

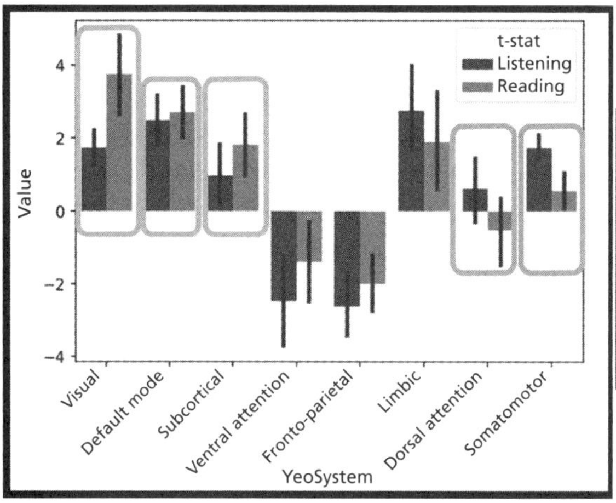

	num_rois	*p*-value	t-stat
Visual	41.0	0.000016	-4.902124
Default mode	60.0	0.000365	-3.782617
Subcortical	22.0	0.002334	-3.461689
Ventral attention	26.0	0.095105	-1.734719
Fronto-parietal	33.0	0.753238	-0.317085
Limbic	10.0	0.070057	2.054890
Dorsal attention	29.0	0.039546	2.159259
Somatomotor	43.0	0.000959	3.551938

Figure 13.4. Reading versus Listening modalities mapping onto intrinsic networks; univariate results by system. (*Sources for networks:* Yeo et al. [2011] & Power et al. [2011].)

Networks more involved in reading versus listening included the default mode network. Given that the default mode network has been associated with building a situation model (Simony et al., 2016; Spreng, Mar, & Kim, 2009; Whitney et al., 2009), it may be that reading places greater demands on the network associated with situation model building. Yet, the passages were carefully matched on a variety of characteristics, so it is not entirely clear why there would be greater demands on building in reading over listening. Further study of the origin of these differences may be fruitful for understanding print/speech overlaps and their importance for reading development.

IMPLICATIONS OF A NETWORK-LEVEL FRAMEWORK FOR DYSLEXIA

What are the implications for dyslexia, given that the previous findings indicate that a network-level framework may be productive for understanding reading development? In Bailey et al. (2018), we observe that areas that are known to be key for reading sit at the juncture of major networks. For example, the temporo-parietal region typically attributed to being important for grapheme-phoneme correspondences (Pugh et al., 2001; Turkeltaub, Gareau, Flowers, Zeffiro, & Eden, 2003) is at the juncture of the ventral attention, default mode, and somatomotor networks. Indeed, previous studies have shown that the more hub-like areas, or the more networks certain nodes (areas) are linked with, the more critical these areas are for cognitive well-being. For example, nodes that are linked to many networks tend to be the regions that are impaired in psychiatric disorders (Power et al., 2013). Yet, no study to date that we are aware of has examined whether areas known to be anomalous in dyslexia are indeed at the nexus of networks.

In Bailey et al. (in press), we took regions from three meta-analyses (Maisog, Einbinder, Flowers, Turkeltaub, & Eden, 2008; Paulesu, Danelli, & Berlingeri, 2014; Richlan, Kronbichler, & Wimmer, 2009) and examined how they mapped onto nodes that were known to be linked to many different networks versus those that were less hub-like. Findings revealed that most of the areas from the dyslexia meta-analyses were regions of the brain known to be highly connected to multiple networks, or have high hubness. These findings suggest that connectivity between networks may be a critical piece toward understanding more about dyslexia—and perhaps response to intervention in dyslexia. Indeed, findings from our lab suggest that the way that the fronto-parietal network in particular interacts with reading-specific areas may be a key piece to predicting who will (or will not) respond to intervention (Aboud et al., 2018). In this study, children with dyslexia received 15 hours of Orton-Gillingham–based intervention (Orton, 1937). Subsequent to intervention, children with dyslexia were categorized as either responders or nonresponders, and both activation levels as well as brain connectivity at baseline (before intervention) between the two groups were examined. Findings were consistent with prior studies that have shown that the brains of those who eventually respond to intervention versus those that do not have neurobiological differences before intervention starts, and these activity patterns predict intervention response (Farris, Ring, Black, Lyon, & Odegard, 2016; Rezaie et al., 2011a, 2011b).

However, of greater interest was whether connectivity indices differed between responders and nonresponders. Several connectivity differences were found, but one intriguing finding was that fronto-parietal connectivity with reading regions was an important predictor of intervention response. In other disorders, specific areas within the fronto-parietal network (including the dorsolateral prefrontal cortex; DLPFC) have been shown to play a facilitatory role. Specifically, Cole and colleagues (Cole et al., 2013; Cole, Repovš, & Anticevic, 2014) have proposed that the DLPFC may serve as a sort of "immune system of the mind" (Cole et al., 2014, p. 652). This idea posits that the DLPFC involvement is suggestive of a healthy EF network, which, in turn, can regulate other neural systems in a goal-directed manner in both typical and pathological states. Poor clinical outcomes may thus reflect both a primary neural deficit as well as a secondary failure of executive systems to direct vulnerable brain areas. The Aboud et al. (2018) findings are consistent with this literature and suggest that readers with a high intervention response have more intact executive support of the reading network than nonresponsive readers.

Larger-scale studies are now underway to fully interrogate these findings in order to understand if connectivity between regions is a key biomarker for predicting intervention response; results from these studies may help clarify some long-standing paradoxical findings in the literature. For example, examination of coordination between networks that support EF and reading may provide insights as to why behavioral indices of EF are linked to reading but nevertheless are robust predictors of intervention response. We would conjecture that the reason for this may be lack of coordination between networks or utilization of EF skills to help coordinate (or compensate for) vulnerabilities in reading networks.

LINKAGES BETWEEN SYSTEMS- VERSUS REGION-LEVEL FRAMEWORKS OF READING AND DYSLEXIA

How do we reconcile this rich literature with the idea that connectivity may be critical for understanding and predicting intervention response in dyslexia, given the long and well-established history of specific areas of the brain being important for skilled and impaired reading (the most prominent of which is the left occipito-temporal region, often referred to as the *VWFA*)? Many studies, including lesion studies, have long supported the idea that there are critical focal areas of the brain for reading, especially for those with dyslexia (Dehaene & Cohen, 2011; Pugh et al., 2001; Shaywitz et al.,

2002). Although the previous findings point to the importance of examining reading and dyslexia within a network framework, there are some key findings that need to be considered. First, in Bailey et al. (in press), we show that a key area associated with reading, the left occipitotemporal region, is not a highly hub-like region—meaning it is not highly connected across networks. Second, in Aboud et al. (2018), we show that the left occipitotemporal region is a baseline predictor of responsiveness to reading, which is consistent with prior findings. These findings together do not negate the importance of key focal regions and suggest that understanding the role of these key regions and their disruption within the context of global networks may allow for convergence between network and regional findings. For example, it may be that intact fronto-parietal connectivity serves as a buffer for focal primary disruption in the left occipito-temporal region (Cole et al., 2013, 2014). How this translates into understanding the origins of dyslexia and foundations for more comprehensive interventions is clearly far from being realized. There may be important differences, however, in focal versus highly hub-like regions in terms of, for example, relationship to genetic versus environmental risk, which is something future studies could explore.

CONCLUSION

Although much advancement has been made in understanding dyslexia and creating interventions, many questions remain regarding the causes of dyslexia and how best to identify risk for dyslexia. It also remains unclear why dyslexia has such a high comorbidity with other developmental disorders. Building on previous findings from studies of brain regions viewed largely in isolation and applying network framing to the study of reading furthers understanding of interconnection differences between regions associated with dyslexia. Such approaches do not replace previous methods of research but instead may help clarify specific vulnerabilities that lead to impaired reading. For example, it may be that anomalies in neural tissue in the left occipito-temporal region, a focal area associated with reading, only become problematic when other systems are unable to coordinate to circumvent this primary deficit. Such approaches may also shed light on mechanisms of comorbidity in dyslexia and why, for example, many individuals with dyslexia also have attention-deficit/hyperactivity disorder. A better understanding of connectivity within neural networks may aid in the development of effective individualized interventions by targeting skills associated with network deficiencies.

REFERENCES

Aboud, K. S., Bailey, S. K., Petrill, S. A., & Cutting, L. E. (2016). Comprehending text versus reading words in young readers with varying reading ability: Distinct patterns of functional connectivity from common processing hubs. *Developmental Science, 19,* 632–656. doi:10.1111/desc.12422.

Aboud, K. S., Barquero, L. A., & Cutting, L. E. (2018). Prefrontal mediation of the reading network predicts intervention response in dyslexia. *Cortex, 101,* 96–106. http://doi.org/10.1016/j.cortex.2018.01.009
Bailey, S. K., Aboud, K. S., Nguyen, T. Q., & Cutting, L. E. (2018). Applying a network framework to the neurobiology of reading and dyslexia. *Journal of Neurodevelopmental Disorders, 10*(1), 37. doi:10.1186/s11689-018-9251-z;
Bullmore, E., & Sporns, O. (2012). The economy of brain network organization. *Nature Reviews Neuroscience, 13*(5), 336–349. http://doi.org/10.1038/nrn3214
Cole, M. W., Repovš, G., & Anticevic, A. (2014). The frontoparietal control system: A central role in mental health. *Neuroscientist, 20*(6), 652–664. http://doi.org/10.1177/1073858414525995
Cole, M. W., Reynolds, J. R., Power, J. D., Repovs, G., Anticevic, A., & Braver, T. S. (2013). Multi-task connectivity reveals flexible hubs for adaptive task control. *Nature Neuroscience, 16*(9), 1348–1355. http://doi.org/10.1038/nn.3470
Dehaene, S., & Cohen, L. (2011). The unique role of the visual word form area in reading. *Trends in Cognitive Sciences, 15*(6), 254–262. http://doi.org/10.1016/j.tics.2011.04.003
Farris, E. A., Ring, J., Black, J., Lyon, G. R., & Odegard, T. N. (2016). Predicting growth in word level reading skills in children with developmental dyslexia using an object rhyming functional neuroimaging task. *Developmental Neuropsychology, 5641,* 1–17. http://doi.org/10.1080/87565641.2016.1158264
Finn, E. S., Shen, X., Holahan, J. M., Scheinost, D., Lacadie, C., Papademetris, X., . . . Constable, R. T. (2014). Disruption of functional networks in dyslexia: A whole-brain, data-driven analysis of connectivity. *Biological Psychiatry, 76*(5), 397–404. http://doi.org/10.1016/j.biopsych.2013.08.031
Koyama, M. S., Di Martino, A., Kelly, C., Jutagir, D. R., Sunshine, J., Schwartz, S. J., . . . Milham, M. P. (2013). Cortical signatures of dyslexia and remediation: An intrinsic functional connectivity approach. *PLoS One, 8*(2), e55454. http://doi.org/10.1371/journal.pone.0055454
Maisog, J. M., Einbinder, E. R., Flowers, D. L., Turkeltaub, P. E., & Eden, G. F. (2008). A meta-analysis of functional neuroimaging studies of dyslexia. *Annals of the New York Academy of Sciences, 1145,* 237–259. http://doi.org/10.1196/annals.1416.024
Orton, S. (1937). *Reading, writing, and speech problems in children.* New York, NY: Norton.
Paulesu, E., Danelli, L., & Berlingeri, M. (2014). Reading the dyslexic brain: Multiple dysfunctional routes revealed by a new meta-analysis of PET and fMRI activation studies. *Frontiers in Human Neuroscience, 8,* 1–20. http://doi.org/10.3389/fnhum.2014.00830
Pinker, S., & Jackendoff, R. (2005). The faculty of language: What's special about it? *Cognition, 95*(2), 201–236. http://doi.org/10.1016/j.cognition.2004.08.004
Power, J. D., Cohen, A. L., Nelson, S. M., Wig, G. S., Barnes, K. A., Church, J. A., . . . Petersen, S. E. (2011). Functional network organization of the human brain. *Neuron, 72*(4), 665–678. http://doi.org/10.1016/j.neuron.2011.09.006
Power, J. D., Schlaggar, B. L., Lessov-Schlaggar, C. N., & Petersen, S. E. (2013). Evidence for hubs in human functional brain networks. *Neuron, 79*(4), 798–813. http://doi.org/10.1016/j.neuron.2013.07.035
Pugh, K. R., Landi, N., Preston, J. L., Mencl, W. E., Austin, A. C., Sibley, D., . . . Frost, S. J. (2012). The relationship between phonological and auditory processing and brain organization in beginning readers. *Brain and Language, 125*(2), 173–183. http://doi.org/10.1016/j.bandl.2012.04.004
Pugh, K. R., Mencl, W. E., Jenner, A. R., Katz, L., Frost, S. J., Lee, J. R., . . . Shaywitz, B. A. (2000). Functional neuroimaging studies of reading and reading disability (developmental dyslexia). *Mental Retardation and Developmental Disabilities Research Reviews, 6,* 207–213.
Pugh, K. R., Mencl, W. E., Jenner, A. R., Katz, L., Frost, S. J., Lee, J. R., . . . Shaywitz, B. A. (2001). Neurobiological studies of reading and reading disability. *Journal of Communication Disorders, 34,* 479–492.
Rezaie, R., Simos, P. G., Fletcher, J. M., Cirino, P. T., Vaughn, S., & Papanicolaou, A. C. (2011a). Engagement of temporal lobe regions predicts response to educational

interventions in adolescent struggling readers. *Developmental Neuropsychology, 36*(7), 869–888. http://doi.org/10.1080/87565641.2011.606404

Rezaie, R., Simos, P. G., Fletcher, J. M., Cirino, P. T., Vaughn, S., & Papanicolaou, A. C. (2011b). Temporo-parietal brain activity as a longitudinal predictor of response to educational interventions among middle school struggling readers. *Journal of the International Neuropsychological Society, 17*(5), 875–885. http://doi.org/10.1017/S1355617711000890

Richlan, F. (2012). Developmental dyslexia: Dysfunction of a left hemisphere reading network. *Frontiers in Human Neuroscience, 6,* 120. http://doi.org/10.3389/fnhum.2012.00120

Richlan, F., Kronbichler, M., & Wimmer, H. (2009). Functional abnormalities in the dyslexic brain: A quantitative meta-analysis of neuroimaging studies. *Human Brain Mapping, 30*(10), 3299–3308. http://doi.org/10.1002/Hbm.20752

Shankweiler, D., Mencl, W. E., Braze, D., Tabor, W., Pugh, K. R., & Fulbright, R. K. (2008). Reading differences and brain: Cortical integration of speech and print in sentence processing varies with reader skill. *Developmental Neuropsychology, 33*(6), 745–775. https://doi.org/10.1080/87565640802418688

Shaywitz, S. E., Shaywitz, B. A., Pugh, K. R., Fulbright, R. K., Constable, R. T., Mencl, W. E., . . . Gore, J. C. (1998). Functional disruption in the organization of the brain for reading in dyslexia. *Proceedings of the National Academy of Sciences of the United States of America, 95*(5), 2636–2641. http://doi.org/10.1073/pnas.95.5.2636

Shaywitz, B. A., Shaywitz, S. E., Pugh, K. R., Mencl, W. E., Fulbright, R. K., Skudlarski, P., . . . Gore, J. C. (2002). Disruption of posterior brain systems for reading in children with developmental dyslexia. *Biological Psychiatry, 52*(2), 101–110.

Simony, E., Honey, C. J., Chen, J., Lositsky, O., Yeshurun, Y., Wiesel, A., & Hasson, U. (2016). Dynamic reconfiguration of the default mode network during narrative comprehension. *Nature Communications, 7,* 1–13. http://doi.org/10.1038/ncomms12141

Spreng, R. N., Mar, R. A., & Kim, A. S. N. (2009). The common neural basis of autobiographical memory, prospection, navigation, theory of mind, and the default mode: A quantitative meta-analysis. *Journal of Cognitive Neuroscience, 21*(3), 489–510. https://doi.org/10.1162/jocn.2008.21029

Swett, K., Miller, A. C., Burns, S., Hoeft, F., Davis, N., Petrill, S. A., & Cutting, L. E. (2013). Comprehending expository texts: The dynamic neurobiological correlates of building a coherent text representation. *Frontiers in Human Neuroscience, 7*(853), 1–14. https://doi.org/10.3389/fnhum.2013.00853

Turkeltaub, P. E., Gareau, L., Flowers, D. L., Zeffiro, T. A., & Eden, G. F. (2003). Development of neural mechanisms for reading. *Nature Neuroscience, 6*(7), 767–773. http://doi.org/10.1038/Nn1065

Whitney, C., Huber, W., Klann, J., Weis, S., Krach, S., & Kircher, T. (2009). Neural correlates of narrative shifts during auditory story comprehension. *NeuroImage, 47*(1), 360–366. http://doi.org/10.1016/j.neuroimage.2009.04.037

Yeo, B. T. T., Krienen, F. M., Sepulcre, J., Sabuncu, M. R., Lashkari, D., Hollinshead, M., . . . Buckner, R. L. (2011). The organization of the human cerebral cortex estimated by intrinsic functional connectivity. *Journal of Neurophysiology, 106,* 1125–1165. http://doi.org/10.1152/jn.00338.2011

INTEGRATIVE COMMENTARY 4

New Directions in the Study of Atypical Reading Development

Richard K. Wagner

SUMMARY

The four chapters in this section address atypical reading development, but each takes a specific approach or focuses on a particular problem related to reading (dis)abilities. The topics covered are how executive function (EF), response to instruction and intervention, and neuroimaging can more deeply inform our understanding of reading disabilities, and the fourth chapter reminds us that in identifying reading disability, we need specific attention to different populations, specifically Spanish-speaking English learners (ELs). Each of the chapters advances knowledge in important ways by taking a multidisciplinary perspective and employing state-of-the-art analytical approaches. Although each contributes to our knowledge in important ways, at best they provide static snapshots of what in reality are dynamic developmental phenomena. Applying more dynamic models to longitudinal, developmental data is an important direction for future research.

INTRODUCTION

The four chapters in this section target different constructs related to reading abilities and disabilities. I discuss each of these constructs in my commentary.

Executive Function

The chapter by Cirino, Church, Miciak, and Fletcher (Chapter 10) considerably advances our knowledge about the nature of individual differences in EF, its measurement, and its relations to important criteria such as reading for comprehension. It does so in part by taking a multidisciplinary perspective that integrates related work in the fields of neuropsychology, cognitive psychology, and developmental/educational psychology.

One of the most important strengths of the measurement study on the nature of EF described in the chapter was that the multidisciplinary perspective was used when selecting constructs and tasks to include in the study. In addition to the more commonly included and studied constructs of working memory, inhibition, and shifting, Cirino et al. included planning, generative fluency, self-regulated learning, metacognition, and behavioral regulation. These constructs were potentially representative of EF as conceptualized by different disciplines. Confirmatory factor analyses supported a bifactor model in which individual differences on the wide variety of EF tasks was explained by a general EF factor, with additional independent specific factors also explaining variance for sets of tasks.

The implicit assumption of much of the research on EF is that individual and developmental differences in EF explain some variance in performance on real-world tasks of importance, including academic tasks such as reading for comprehension and solving math problems. This assumption motivates the research described by Cirino et al. in which EF tasks were included with other predictors to account for individual differences in reading and math. The main finding was that EF accounted for a small amount of independent variance. It is possible, however, that these findings underestimate the importance of EF when reading and solving math problems if EF contributed to individual and developmental differences in performance on other predictors in the model. For example, in the study of predictors of reading comprehension, listening comprehension was included as a predictor in addition to executive functioning. It is possible that performance on the listening comprehension predictor was determined in part by individual and developmental differences in EF, thereby diminishing the apparent effect of EF as an independent predictor in the prediction analyses.

Several issues might be worth considering in future studies of EF. The first is to challenge the implicit assumption of EF as an independent attribute or trait. The alternative conception is that EF is also, or maybe even primarily, domain specific. Something that all executive functioning tasks share is the requirement to do two things at once. How easy or difficult one of those things is will likely affect performance on the other and, consequently, affect overall performance.

Consider Daneman and Carpenter's (1980) reading span task, a measure of working memory that predicts reading comprehension. There have been many variants of this task over the years, but the original one required examinees to read for meaning sentences presented on flash cards, and then they were required to say the last word in each sentence in order when signaled to recall. One variant has examinees verifying a set of statements to ensure reading for comprehension and then asking for recall of the last words in each statement:

1. Birds may sing in the day. T or F
2. Whales make good house pets. T or F
3. The sun rises at night. T or F

The last words in each sentence in order are *day, pets,* and *night.* In addition to the obvious memory component, one has to read the sentences for comprehension, and the difficulty of doing that can influence the amount of attention and cognitive resources left over for remembering the last words in the sentences. For example, imagine taking the test in a second language you do not know nearly as well as your first language. Your performance would likely decline substantially. One can imagine a measurement study of EF analogous to that of Cirino et al. but that incorporates domain as an important dimension in performance. It would be possible to do this by explicitly representing domain in task selection. For example, in addition to reading span, one can give comparable listening span and visuospatial span tasks, thereby measuring EF using similar tasks but from the reading, listening, and visuospatial domains.

In addition to the issue of domain-general versus domain-specific aspects of working memory, a second issue to consider is moving beyond static assessments of relations between EF and important tasks in reading and math domains to dynamic ones. With the development of latent change score modeling (McArdle, 2009), it is now possible to study the codevelopment of constructs that potentially influence the development of one another. The idea is to move beyond studies of the development of EF, language, reading, or math to studies of codeveloping EF, language, reading, and math.

An example addressing the codevelopment of reading and language is Quinn, Wagner, Petscher, and Lopez (2015), who used latent change score modeling to study the codevelopment of vocabulary and reading comprehension. We know that relative status or performance on measures of vocabulary and reading comprehension is positively correlated (i.e., if you score relatively high on measures of vocabulary, then you are likely to score high on measures of reading comprehension). Growth in vocabulary and reading comprehension is also positively correlated (i.e., if you grow relatively fast in vocabulary, then you are likely to grow relatively fast in reading comprehension). But in addition to and independent of correlated status and growth, might vocabulary have a direct influence on the growth of reading comprehension? The idea is that a strong vocabulary might help you comprehend what you read more deeply, and comprehending what you read more deeply over time improves reading comprehension. Alternatively, might reading comprehension have a direct influence on growth in vocabulary? If you are good at reading comprehension, then you might be better at inferring the meanings of new words you come across and also at sharpening your understanding of the meanings of words you already know. Quinn et al. tested four competing models in a longitudinal study from first- through fourth-grade students:

1. Only correlated status and growth but no direct influences
2. A direct influence of vocabulary on the development of reading comprehension in addition to possible correlated status and growth
3. A direct influence of reading comprehension on the development of vocabulary in addition to possible correlated status and growth
4. Direct influences of each on the development of the other in addition to possible correlated status and growth

The results supported the second model: Vocabulary influenced the development of reading comprehension, but reading comprehension did not influence the development of vocabulary. There is a compelling reason to study the codevelopment of EF, language, reading, and math. One can imagine that some aspects of EF influence growth in language processing, reading, and math, and other aspects of EF are influenced by performance in language processing, reading, and math.

Differential Response to Instruction and Intervention

The focus of Chapter 11 by Morris is on understanding differential response to instruction and intervention for students with reading disability. Understanding why some individuals respond to intervention and others do not is obviously a problem of fundamental importance. This chapter makes an important contribution to the research on response to instruction and intervention by addressing two troublesome issues for the field.

The first troublesome issue arises when response to instruction and intervention is used as the primary criterion for identification of individuals with learning disabilities, including reading disability. No single criterion, including one based on response to instruction and intervention results, provides reliable and valid identification of individuals with reading disability (Barth et al., 2008; Fuchs, Fuchs, & Compton, 2004; Waesche, Schatschneider, Maner, Ahmed, & Wagner, 2011; Wagner, Waesche, Schatschnieder, Maner, & Ahmed, 2011). There are two additional problems that arise when either response to instruction and intervention is used as the primary criterion for identification. The first is inability to distinguish between unexpected and expected performance. The concept of being unexpected has been central to nearly all definitions of learning or reading disability: The poor performance is unexpected based on other things known about the individual. This concept has been central to definitions of learning and reading disabilities because for response to instruction and intervention and for reading achievement there is an expected normal distribution of performance. The majority of poor responders' performance is expected in the sense that their level of response is consistent with their performance in other academic domains and with their level of language performance. Mixed in with poor responders and poor performers are individuals whose response or level of performance is unexpected in that it is inconsistent with either performance in other academic domains or language performance. Merely looking at low response does not distinguish an unexpected from an expected response to instruction or intervention. The second problem that arises when response to instruction and intervention is used as the primary criterion for identification is that individuals who have a genuine reading disability but have above average language performance will be missed if their response to instruction and intervention is not low enough to meet the identification cutoff. The study reported by Morris focuses on poor response by individuals whose poor reading is unexpected and, therefore, attempts to distinguish between unexpected and expected poor performance. It did so by pairing low achievement in reading (at or below the 15th percentile) with the requirement of at least low average or better intellectual abilities. Whether that is the best way to distinguish unexpected and expected poor performance has been the subject of considerable discussion, and, in this case, it will miss individuals whose poor performance in reading is unexpected based on their above average language skills but whose absolute level of performance is above the 15th percentile. But for research purposes, any approach that helps avoid the ubiquitous problem for the field of learning disabilities of studying heterogeneous samples is better than ignoring the problem.

The second troublesome issue addressed in the chapter that arises when response to instruction and intervention is used for identification is that different operational definitions of poor response yield largely nonoverlapping groups (Fuchs et al., 2004). Based on Frijters, Lovett, Sevcik, and Morris (2013), the study described by Morris in this chapter used reliable index of change metrics to provide a continuous measure of response that accounts for both the psychometric reliability of the outcome measures and observed standard deviations (Jacobson & Truax, 1991). The result is a measure of response that indicates whether the response was large enough to be reliable relative to what would be expected as a result of measurement error and sample-specific variability.

In practice, a measure of response to intervention may not yield information that is not already available by simply measuring the more reliable level of performance at the end of intervention (Schatschneider, Wagner, & Crawford, 2008). It would be interesting to determine whether this was the case for the present study or whether the use of reliable index of change metrics provided information that was independent of postintervention performance.

Learning Disabilities in English Learners

Chapter 12, by Francis and colleagues, addresses the topic of identification of disabilities in Spanish-speaking children in English-speaking contexts. The critical importance of this topic is that rates of reading disability are likely roughly comparable across different spoken languages and written scripts. Yet, in practice, academic difficulties by children who are nonnative speakers of English may be attributed to their language status, and genuine reading disabilities may be missed.

The chapter reports novel analyses on a valuable large sample of more than 3,000 ELs who were assessed using both English- and Spanish-language assessments. Children were classified using both an IQ-achievement discrepancy and a simple low achievement criterion. As predicted, failing to account for language of instruction resulted in substantial overidentification of students as reading disabled. The pattern was that overidentification occurred whenever the language of instruction did not match the language of assessments used for identification. The challenge is to determine whether the poor performance is attributable to a learning disability, limited proficiency in a language, or mismatches between the languages of instruction and assessment. The chapter convincingly illustrates these issues with the reported study and discusses important implications for both research and practice.

Neurobiology and Reading Development

Chapter 13, by Cutting, Lee-Yong, and Barquero, describes a promising new avenue toward understanding relations between neurobiological variables and the development of language and literacy. Much of the existing literature documents specific regions of the brain that are activated differentially by individuals with reading disability compared with typical reading controls. The new avenue adds much broader networks into the picture. Of particular interest is a study by Bailey, Aboud, Nguyen, and Cutting (2018) in which a meta-analytic database was used to determine the extent to which each of seven major brain networks identified by Yeo et al. (2011) overlapped with the reading network. Although there were relations with all seven major networks, reading appeared to be related more to some than to others.

Much of the literature that relates reading and language to neurobiological variables is based on the assumption that neurobiological variables are more fundamental and are probable causes of observed development and differences in reading and language. Most of the data are correlational, and brain function and even structure may be affected by behavioral performance and experience as much as neurobiological variables. For example, the fact that some brain activation patterns normalize when reading problems are successfully remediated is consistent with the idea that at least some activation patterns are by-products of cognitive functioning rather than causes. The final story is likely to be complicated, with different brain regions and networks acting as causes or by-products of reading and language performance, with roles possibly changing over development.

One way to begin to study the dynamics of these relations over development is to apply the same kinds of latent change score models previously described to longitudinal data in which both imaging and behavioral data are collected multiple times across a developmental time period, similar to the approach described for studying the codevelopment of EF and reading.

CONCLUSION

Collectively, the four chapters advance our understanding of their respective topics by applying multidisciplinary perspectives and sophisticated and state-of-the-art analytic approaches.

Chapter 10 advances our knowledge about the nature of individual differences in EF, its measurement, and its relations to important criteria such as reading for comprehension by including EF constructs and associated tasks from the fields of neuropsychology, cognitive psychology, and developmental/educational psychology. It then applies confirmatory factor analysis to describe the latent dimensions of EF.

Chapter 11 focuses on understanding differential response to instruction and intervention for students with reading disability from the vantage points of theoretically driven models of reading that incorporate cognitive-behavioral, neurocognitive, and neurobiological perspectives. The state-of-the-art methodology they exploit is a sophisticated approach for quantifying response to instruction and intervention called *reliable index of change metrics.*

Chapter 12 addresses the topic of identification of disabilities in Spanish-speaking children in English-speaking contexts. The multidisciplinary perspective here is that of examining learning disabilities across different languages. The state-of-the-art approach is a set of novel analyses on a large sample of ELs who were assessed using both English- and Spanish-language assessments. The key result was the important role of language of instruction on rates of identification.

Chapter 13 uses a multidisciplinary perspective that incorporates language and literacy, specific brain regions, and more general neural networks. The state-of-the-art approach is to examine overlap between reading-related brain regions and independently derived neural networks.

Although each of the chapters contributes to our knowledge in important ways, they can be characterized as providing static snapshots of what in reality are better characterized as dynamic developmental phenomena. A potentially important direction for future research on the topics of each of the four chapters is to move toward applying dynamic models to longitudinal, developmental data. Several examples of a more dynamic approach were provided.

REFERENCES

Bailey, S. K., Aboud, K. S., Nguyen, T. Q., & Cutting, L. E. (2018). Applying a network framework to the neurobiology of reading and dyslexia. *Journal of Neurodevelopmental Disorders, 10,* 9. doi:http://dx.doi.org/10.1186/s11689-018-9251-z

Barth, A. E., Stuebing, K. K., Anthony, J. L., Denton, C. A., Mathes, P. G., Fletcher, J. M., & Francis, D. J. (2008). Agreement among response to intervention criteria for identifying responder status. *Learning and Individual Differences, 18,* 296–307. doi:10.1016/j.lindif.2008.04.004

Daneman, M., & Carpenter, P. A. (1980). Individual differences in working memory and reading. *Journal of Verbal Learning and Verbal Behavior, 19,* 450–466.

Frijters, J. C., Lovett, M. W., Sevcik, R. A., & Morris, R. D. (2013). Four methods of identifying change in the context of a multiple component reading intervention for struggling middle school readers. *Reading and Writing, 26*(4), 539–563.

Fuchs, D., Fuchs, L. S., & Compton, D. (2004). Identifying reading disabilities by responsiveness-to-instruction: Specifying measures and criteria. *Learning Disability Quarterly, 27,* 216–227. dx.doi.org/10.2307/1593674

Jacobson, N. S., & Truax, P. (1991). Clinical significance: A statistical approach to defining meaningful change in psychotherapy research. *Journal of Consulting and Clinical Psychology, 59*(1), 12–19.
McArdle, J. J. (2009). Latent variable modeling of longitudinal data. *Annual Review of Psychology, 60,* 577–605.
Quinn, J. M., Wagner, R. K., Petscher, Y., & Lopez, D. (2015). Developmental relations between vocabulary knowledge and reading comprehension: A latent change score modeling study. *Child Development, 86,* 159–175.
Schatschneider, C., Wagner, R. K., & Crawford, E. C. (2008). The importance of measuring growth in response to intervention models: Testing a core assumption. *Learning and Individual Differences, 18,* 308–315.
Waesche, J. B., Schatschneider, C., Maner, J. K., Ahmed, Y., & Wagner, R. K. (2011). Examining agreement and longitudinal stability among traditional and RTI-based definitions of reading disability using the affected-status agreement statistic. *Journal of Learning Disabilities, 44,* 296–307.
Wagner, R. K., Waesche, J. B., Schatschneider, C., Maner, J., & Ahmed, Y. (2011). Using response to intervention for identification and classification. In P. McCardle, B. Miller, J. R. Lee, & O. J. L. Tzeng (Eds.), *Dyslexia across languages: Orthography and the brain-gene-behavior link* (pp. 202–213). Baltimore, MD: Paul H. Brookes Publishing Co.
Yeo, B. T. T., Krienen, F. M., Sepulcre, J., Sabuncu, M. R., Lashkari, D., Hollinshead, M., . . . Buckner, R. L. (2011). The organization of the human cerebral cortex estimated by intrinsic functional connectivity. *Journal of Neurophysiology, 106,* 1125–1165. http://doi.org/10.1152/jn.00338.2011

SECTION V

Language, Education, Disability, and Society

CHAPTER 14

Using Technology to Bring Treatments to Families Affected by Autism and Related Neurodevelopmental Disorders in Their Communities

Leonard Abbeduto, Lauren Bullard, Sarah Nelson,
Amy Banasik, Robyn Tempero Feigles, Vivian Nguyen, and Sara Elhasan

SUMMARY

This chapter briefly describes the most recent diagnostic criteria and prevalence rates of autism spectrum disorder (ASD), some of the challenges faced by individuals with ASD and their family members, and the economic burden of ASD on society. We also highlight factors related to inequality in access to services. Given these concerns, telehealth is discussed as a promising approach for providing greater access to evidence-based, cost-effective care to all people affected by ASD and related disorders. Two examples of telehealth-delivered parent-implemented interventions for improving language in youth with fragile X syndrome (FXS) by increasing parental verbally responsive behaviors are described. The first of these involved a play-based intervention delivered partly in a clinic and partly into the home via telehealth to biological mothers of young boys with FXS between the ages of 27 and 43 months. The second intervention was delivered solely via telehealth and included mothers and their school-age and adolescent sons with FXS. Given the older age of these participants, shared storytelling using wordless picture books was the intervention context. Improvements in maternal strategy use and child language were seen across the studies. We conclude by considering barriers to the use of telehealth in the United States.

INTRODUCTION

Autism spectrum disorder (ASD) creates barriers to social interaction, effectively isolating the affected individual from other people (Travis & Sigman, 1998). More formally, ASD is defined in the *Diagnostic and Statistical Manual of Mental Disorders, Fifth Edition* (*DSM-5;* American Psychiatric Association, 2013) as having 1) persistent deficits in social communication and social interaction across multiple contexts and 2) restricted, repetitive patterns of behavior, interests, or activities. Moreover, those symptoms must 3) emerge early in development, 4) cause clinically significant impairment in multiple facets of daily functioning, and 5) not be due to intellectual disability or global developmental delay.

ASD has increased dramatically in prevalence in recent years. In 1995, 1 in 2,500 people was diagnosed with ASD. In 2018, the U.S. Centers for Disease Control and Prevention estimated the prevalence of ASD at 1 in 59 children (Baio et al., 2018). There is considerable debate about the causes of this increase in prevalence. Many have argued that much of the increase is attributable to changes in diagnostic practices (Williams, Higgins, & Brayne, 2006). Indeed, there is considerable evidence from educational data that many children who previously would have been diagnosed as having an intellectual disability, emotional disorder, or language disorder are now likely to receive an ASD diagnosis instead (e.g., Shattuck, 2006). At the same time, there is evidence that the increase is not attributable entirely to diagnostic practices. Factors such as exposure to neurotoxins during prenatal development or delays in the age at which people decide to have children may have also led to an increase in the number of true cases of ASD (Matelski & Van de Water, 2016). The relative proportion of the increase in prevalence due to changes in diagnostic practices versus true cases of the disorder, however, remains controversial. What is not controversial is that 1 in 59 children and their families in the United States, and many more worldwide, need help to ameliorate and cope with the behavioral symptoms that are associated with the diagnosis of ASD.

Indeed, despite the existence of several evidenced-based approaches to early intervention that can change the trajectory of development for many children affected by ASD, most individuals do not outgrow the diagnosis and continue to struggle in daily life. As many as 25% develop no meaningful spoken language (Klinger, Dawson, & Renner, 2003). As young adults, more than half do not go on to postsecondary education or have full-time employment (Shattuck et al., 2012; Taylor & Seltzer, 2011), and many never live on their own (Howlin, Goode, Hutton, & Rutter, 2004). The problems extend beyond the diagnostic features of ASD because many affected individuals also have comorbid problems, such as intellectual disability (31%) (Baio et al., 2018) and anxiety (84%) (White, Oswald, Ollendick, & Scahill, 2009).

The burden of ASD on individuals, families, and society is considerable. Medical, educational, and therapeutic costs and productivity losses totaled $268 billion in the United States for 2015 and will reach $1 trillion in 2025 (Leigh & Du, 2015). The burden created by ASD is also differentially experienced across different communities. In the United States, there is evidence of disparities in access to care depending on race, ethnicity, language spoken, and geography (e.g., Bishop-Fitzpatrick & Kind, 2017; Leigh, Grosse, Cassady, Melnikow, & Hertz-Picciotto, 2016).

So, faced with an increasing number of families affected by ASD, poor outcomes for many affected individuals, and a system of help that is underresourced and not equally accessible to all citizens, there is need for change. Indeed, we believe that scientists, clinicians, educators, and health providers must 1) develop more powerful evidence-based diagnostic procedures, evaluation tools, and treatments; 2) make services and support available to all people regardless of race, ethnicity, language, or geography; and 3) create cost-effective services and systems of support. In this chapter, we present one promising approach to addressing these clinical mandates; namely, telehealth-delivered parent-implemented interventions.

TELEHEALTH-DELIVERED, PARENT-IMPLEMENTED INTERVENTIONS FOR IMPROVING LANGUAGE

There is considerable evidence that the ways in which parents (caregivers) interact with, and talk to, children shape the course and pace of language development (Hart & Risley, 1995). Numerous studies have found that adults talk differently to typically developing children than to other adults, and the characteristics of this so-called child-directed language (CDL) function to capture children's attention, adjust to the child's current capabilities and interests, and simplify the task of learning language (Dominey & Dodane, 2004). Moreover, the same features of CDL that facilitate language learning for typically developing children are also facilitative for children with a variety of disorders, including ASD and intellectual disability (e.g., Haebig, McDuffie, & Weismer, 2013; Warren & Brady, 2007). At the same time, however, it is often more difficult for parents and other caregivers to have optimal interactions with children with ASD or other disorders because of the many behaviors that define their disorders, including a lack of interest in people, an inability to engage in normative play with objects, and tantrums in response to change (Mundy, Sigman, Ungerer, & Sherman, 1986). Thus, by teaching parents how to optimize their interactions and language input to their children with ASD or other disorders, we are effectively enlisting parents as therapists.

There are several advantages of training parents to optimize interactions to support language learning. First, and most important, parents spend far more time with their children than any professional therapist ever could; thus, children can potentially receive much higher doses of an intervention (Ingersoll & Gergans, 2007). Second, parents interact with the child in many contexts and in contexts that bring the child into contact with others (e.g., siblings, teachers), offering more opportunities for the child to generalize new learning to everyday life compared with a typical clinic-based, clinician-delivered intervention (Kashinath, Woods, & Goldstein, 2006). Third, parents may feel more competent in their parenting practices, which may have a positive cascade of effects for the parent, the child, and the whole family (Jones & Prinz, 2005). Finally, bringing the parent into the therapeutic process may create more of a partnership with the clinician and thereby greater support for any clinician-delivered treatment. We are not, however, arguing that parent-implemented intervention should replace clinician-delivered treatment; instead, we see the two as complementary and potentially synergistic if designed correctly.

Interventions, whether clinician- or parent-implemented, face a number of logistical challenges when they are conducted in a clinic setting, which is typical. First, travel can be a considerable burden (Statham, Ponder, Richards, Hallowell, & Raymond, 2011), and clinic appointments often require that a parent take time off from work and/or find child care for siblings. Second, travel may be unduly stressful and/or even impossible for children with ASD and/or other disorders because they have difficulty with changes in routine (Larson, 2006). Third, travel—and especially repeated visits to the clinic over a brief period of time, as is often required by a treatment protocol—may not be feasible for many families who live in rural areas or parts of the world with few clinics (Meadan, Meyer, Snodgrass, & Halle, 2013).

We believe that technology, in the form of distance video teleconferencing via programs such as Skype or Zoom, may hold the answer for intervention delivery. In the case of parent-implemented interventions, parents can be trained in the intervention techniques in their own homes through telehealth technology, thereby reducing the financial and psychological burden of travel. Telehealth delivery of such training also may make treatment accessible to families who would not otherwise have access to professional help, such as those from rural or underresourced communities. In addition, training parents in the home instead of the clinic may make them more comfortable and better able to learn. In short, delivering parent-implemented interventions via telehealth may be cost effective and reduce disparities in access to care.

EXAMPLES OF TELEHEALTH-DELIVERED, PARENT-IMPLEMENTED LANGUAGE INTERVENTIONS TARGETING FRAGILE X SYNDROME

We have developed two distance-delivered, parent-implemented language interventions for individuals with FXS, one for young children (McDuffie, Oakes et al., 2016; Oakes, Ma, McDuffie, Machalicek, & Abbeduto, 2015) and the other for older children and adolescents (McDuffie, Machalicek et al., 2016; McDuffie et al., 2018). FXS is the leading inherited cause of intellectual disability and the leading single-gene cause of ASD (Tassone et al., 2012). Nearly two thirds of individuals with FXS meet diagnostic criteria for ASD, and FXS accounts for 3%–6% of cases of ASD (Timothy & Berry-Kravis, 2014; Wang, Berry-Kravis, & Hagerman, 2010). FXS is caused by a mutation in the *FMR1* gene on the X chromosome. The syndrome is more common and typically more severe in males because it is X-linked. Additional phenotypic features of FXS include language impairments (Abbeduto, Brady, & Kover, 2007), attentional problems (Munir, Cornish, & Wilding, 2000), hyperactivity (Farzin et al., 2006), anxiety (Cordeiro, Ballinger, Hagerman,

& Hessl, 2011), and self-injurious behavior (Oakes et al., 2016). Interestingly, the full mutation is passed on to children only from the biological mother, who is herself a carrier of either the full mutation or, more commonly, the premutation (i.e., a less severe alteration of the gene than in the full mutation causing FXS) (Nolin et al., 2003). Even in the case of the premutation, however, women have phenotypic features (e.g., anxiety, depression) that may further complicate their ability to engage in optimal interactions with their children (e.g., Bailey, Raspa, Olmsted, & Holiday, 2008).

In both interventions, the goal was to teach mothers specific strategies to make their interactions with their children with FXS more verbally responsive. Verbally responsive language is a core element of CDL and has the following characteristics: 1) follows the child's lead (i.e., talk and behavior is focused on child's current interests); 2) is affectively positive (i.e., warm, friendly, and inviting intonation); 3) contains contingent responses to the child's utterances and behaviors (i.e., conceptually and socially related responses); 4) includes developmentally appropriate examples of language (i.e., matched to the child's level of linguistic competence); and 5) encourages child communication (e.g., Haebig et al., 2013). Parents are taught specific strategies for increasing their verbal responsivity, sustaining the child's interest in the interaction, and minimizing child challenging behaviors. Again, although clinicians focus on training the parents, the goal is for the parents to use these strategies in their interactions with their sons and daughters throughout the day rather than only when working with the clinicians.

Toddler/Preschooler Intervention

We conducted a series of single-participant analyses for six dyads of boys with FXS and their biological mothers (McDuffie, Oakes et al., 2016). The boys ranged in age from 27 to 43 months at the start of participation, and their expressive language levels ranged from 10 to 20 months. Some of the boys produced few, if any, words, and some produced a limited number of multiword combinations. All the children met criteria for having an intellectual disability. We used a multiple baseline design across participants (collecting baseline data points for all while staggering across participants the point at which the intervention began) so that we could more reliably attribute changes in the dyads' behavior to receipt of the intervention. The instruction to parents was delivered partly in the clinic and partly through distance video teleconferencing into the family home (as described subsequently).

The treatment was delivered in the context of dyadic play and everyday routines (e.g., dressing, bathing, brushing teeth). The primary focus was on helping parents use behaviors that would help increase their children's communication and secondarily increase their children's use of language. Specifically, parents were taught three strategies—follow-in commenting, indirect prompting, and interpreting/expanding. In follow-in commenting, the parent simply described the child's focus of attention (e.g., if the child held up a block, then the parent might be instructed to say, "Oh, a block. A blue block."). In indirect prompting, the parent might be engaged in a repetitive activity with the child, such as chasing, and say, "Ready, set, . . ." and then wait for the child to complete the sequence with "go." In interpreting/expanding, the child might sign MORE and the parent could sign MORE, or the child might say, "milk" while extending the cup and the parent might expand the utterance by saying, "More milk. You want more milk."

Parents were taught these strategies over a period of 17 weeks. The dyads visited the clinic monthly and reviewed a PowerPoint lesson (including video examples) focused on the strategy to be learned, followed by a coaching session. In the coaching session, the parent played with her child as the clinician provided real-time prompting of strategy use along with feedback. Between clinic visits, weekly video teleconferences were conducted in the home during which the clinician coached the parent in real time as she engaged in dyadic play with the child. (This was achieved by providing parents with a laptop computer equipped with a webcam at the outset of the study.) Finally, for each dyad, we conducted pre- and post-treatment assessments of play interactions, independent of coaching or clinician participation.

Most important, although the goal of the intervention was to improve communication and language, it also involved teaching parents ways of preventing or reducing challenging behaviors, such as aggression, escape from task demands, and self-injury. These behaviors are common in children with FXS (Hatton et al., 2002) as well as in those with ASD (Jang, Dixon, Tarbox, & Granpeesheh, 2011). Without addressing challenging behaviors, interactions with the child would be brief, frustrating, and provide little opportunity for the back-and-forth exchanges that are the foundation for verbally responsive language. Thus, clinicians also worked with parents, in the coaching sessions and through feedback on video-recorded routines, to reduce these challenging behaviors (Oakes et al., 2015).

The primary data for evaluating the efficacy of the intervention was collected during an observation-only period of each intervention session. This period involved the parent interacting with the child in dyadic play without benefit of any coaching or clinician feedback. Maternal use of the targeted strategies and child communication were coded from the video recordings of these sessions, with trends over sessions between baseline and treatment being analyzed separately for each dyad. Graphs of these trends can be found in McDuffie, Oakes et al. (2016). Although there was variability across dyads, the general findings were of improvement in maternal use of the targeted strategies and child communication over the course of treatment relative to the baseline sessions, with virtually all dyads showing some improvement.

In terms of maternal behavior, the mean number of follow-in comments, indirect prompts, and interpretations/expansions across mothers and all baseline sessions during the sampling period were 15.3, 0.1, and 2.5, respectively. In comparison, the corresponding means across all mothers and treatment sessions were much larger—33.4, 4.2, and 6.2 over the course of the 16-week intervention. In general, the mothers acquired the skills being taught and used them independently, albeit at variable rates across mothers.

The children all produced more communication acts after treatment than during baseline. In terms of communication acts prompted by maternal behavior, the mean across all children during baseline sessions was 0.1, whereas the frequency of prompted communication acts across all treatment sessions for all children was 2.9. In terms of spontaneous (i.e., unprompted) communication, improvements were seen from baseline to treatment, although the changes were less dramatic and less consistent across children. The mean frequency of spontaneous communication acts across all children during baseline sessions was 2.5, whereas the frequency of such acts across all treatment sessions for all children was 4.2. These increases in communication are important because they lead to longer and more satisfying interactions for both participants, allow the child to practice linguistic and nonlinguistic communication skills, and set the stage for maternal responses that provide the child further information about the language being learned, thereby creating a positive developmental cascade.

In summary, a treatment delivered largely through telehealth technology led to acquisition of the targeted skills by parents and improvements in child communication skills. Moreover, surveys and interviews completed by parents at the end of the study suggested that they found the intervention to be helpful, felt they grasped its basic content, believed that they were helping their children, and found their interactions with their children to be more positive and fulfilling. These positive parental attitudes are promising, suggesting that parents may continue using the targeted strategies even after their participation with the clinicians and the study has ended, with potential ongoing benefits to the children with FXS.

Adolescent Intervention

We developed and tested the efficacy of a parent-implemented language intervention for adolescent males with FXS and their mothers in two studies, one a series of three single-case analyses (McDuffie, Machalicek et al., 2016) and the second a small-scale randomized controlled trial (RCT) (McDuffie et al., 2018). In this intervention, we again taught parents to use strategies to increase their verbally responsive language; however, in light of the older age of the individuals with FXS, we embedded the teaching in the context of shared storytelling using wordless picture books rather than in play with objects. The picture book provided a shared conversational topic for the mother–adolescent dyad. In contrast to the preschool study, the focus was on helping mothers to expand their adolescents' language, especially vocabulary and syntax, and increase the adolescents' participation in the shared storytelling activity.

The intervention was delivered entirely into the family home through video teleconferencing using a laptop computer with a built-in webcam; there was no clinic-based instructional component. The intervention began with two parent education sessions implemented by the clinician. These sessions provided a description of and rationale for the targeted strategies as well as video examples of their use. The intervention continued for 12 weeks with four types of activities each week. First, there was a real-time coaching session as the parent interacted with the adolescent in a shared storytelling activity. The coaching was provided to the mother through either a Bluetooth earpiece or headphones. Second, the mother video-recorded a homework session in which she used the targeted strategies independently in a shared storytelling activity with the adolescent and sent the video to the clinician via a secure cloud-based platform. Third, the mother and clinician discussed the homework in a video teleconference session, with the clinician emphasizing appropriate uses of the strategies and missed opportunities. Finally, the clinician recorded a storytelling session between parent and adolescent without coaching for subsequent analysis of parental strategy use and adolescent language and communicative behavior. The books were digitized and presented on an iPad, with a different book used each week so that the dyad gained practice in the language and routines necessary for shared storytelling and were not simply memorizing a particular story.

Parents were taught three verbally responsive strategies. The first was to use open-ended *wh-* questions. For example, while reading a story with her child, a parent might ask a question designed to elicit a verbal response from the adolescent, thereby drawing him into the storytelling activity and allowing him to practice his language skills (e.g., "What is the boy doing?" "How is the boy feeling?"). The answers, like other verbal contributions from the adolescent, set the stage for the parent to use the second strategy—expansions (the parent providing a fuller, more mature version of the adolescent's utterance, thereby providing him an opportunity to learn new words and syntactic forms for expressing his meaning). For example, if the adolescent responded with "boy run," then the parent would expand by saying, "the boy is running (across the field)." The third strategy was the use of fill-in-the-blank statements; the parent started a sentence using a rising intonation and paused to convey the expectation that the adolescent should complete the sentence (e.g., the parent states "the doggy is being chased by the . . ." and the adolescent completes the sentence by responding with "girl"). Fill-in-the-blank statements allow the adolescent to participate in telling the story in a highly scaffolded way to minimize the linguistic demands on the adolescent and create a high likelihood of communicative success.

We first tested the efficacy of the intervention with three mother–adolescent dyads (McDuffie, Machalicek et al., 2016). The boys were either

10 or 11 years of age and had nonverbal IQs ranging from 40 to 56. The boys all produced three-word or longer utterances at least occasionally according to maternal report. However, on formal testing, all had less severe impairments in expressive vocabulary than in expressive syntax. Two boys had significant symptoms of ASD on formal evaluation. The boys participated with their biological mothers. Using a multiple baseline across participants design, we documented training-related changes on a number of measures for the mothers and the boys, suggesting acquisition of the targeted strategies by mothers and improvements in participation in the talk and vocabulary for the boys. These findings encouraged us to conduct a small-scale RCT (McDuffie et al., 2018).

In the McDuffie et al. (2018) RCT, 20 dyads of 10- to 17-year-olds and their biological mothers were randomized to either the parent-implemented language intervention or a treatment-as-usual group. The former received an intervention that was largely the same as in the single-case studies of McDuffie, Machalicek et al. (2016). The treatment-as-usual group received no intervention from the research team beyond a pre- and post-assessment separated by a delay equivalent to the length of the intervention, although many were receiving some form of speech-language therapy in their schools or privately. The youth with FXS had nonverbal IQs ranging from 36 to 62 and had lower scores on standardized tests of syntax than of vocabulary, although they were substantially delayed on all measures of language relative to age expectations.

The primary pre- and posttreatment assessments included measures of vocabulary (number of different words) and syntax (mean length of utterance, or MLU) in three shared storytelling dyadic contexts—with the mother at home, with the mother at the clinic, and with an examiner at the clinic. All focused on telling the story in a wordless picture book. Books used in the assessments were not those used in treatment, and different books were used across contexts and in pre- and posttreatment assessments. Mothers received no coaching or instruction about how to behave in the assessment contexts, and the examiners followed a script and provided little prompting or scaffolding for the individual with FXS in the assessment context. The aim of these varying contexts was to determine the generalizability of the gains the youth with FXS made in home-based dyadic interactions with their mothers.

The results of this small-scale RCT were generally consistent with the results of the single-case studies. Mothers in the treatment group showed substantial and statistically significant increases in the use of all three targeted strategies over the course of treatment, whereas there was no change from pre- to posttreatment assessments for the treatment-as-usual group. The adolescent treatment group showed a dramatic and statistically significant increase in the number of different words used by the individuals with FXS; no increase over this period was observed in the treatment-as-usual group. There also was an increase in the length of sessions from pre- to posttreatment for the treatment group measured both in time and number of story-related utterances, whereas there was no such change in the treatment-as-usual group. No differences related to treatment condition, however, were observed for the syntax (as measured by MLU) of the individuals with FXS. The same pattern of findings was observed for measures derived from mother–child interactions at home and in the clinic. These data suggest that the intervention promoted growth in both mother and child behavior that was not specific to a single story or setting but more general to the dyadic shared storytelling context.

Yet, gains observed for the youth with FXS in vocabulary in their interactions with their mothers did not generalize to their narratives elicited by the examiner in the clinic context. There was no change from pre- to posttreatment assessments in the number of different words used or in MLU for the adolescents with FXS in the treatment group. We believe that this lack of generalizability reflects the fact that, unlike the scaffolding that parents were providing through their *wh-* questions, expansions, and fill-in-the-blanks, the examiners minimized their participation and provided no scaffolding so as to gauge what each youth with FXS was capable of achieving independently. Thus, the findings suggest that the emerging vocabulary skills observed in the mother–youth with FXS interactions were still forming and not sufficiently strong as to be used without considerable contextual support. In the future, we will explore the possibility that achieving such generalization may require a longer intervention period and/or some practice in shared storytelling with other people besides the mother to more firmly establish a vocabulary that can be used across all contexts in which it is needed.

CONCLUSIONS

We believe from the research we and others have conducted that the use of telehealth technology to deliver treatment and support to families in their homes has the potential to solve the issues of access and equity. Initially, telehealth was met with some skepticism, with health care professionals citing concerns about loss of security, lack of professionalism, and added costs (VisuWell, 2018). These concerns have largely been addressed today; however, gaps in policy have hindered the growth and adoption of telehealth.

The Center for Connected Health Policy (2018) reported that it is difficult to establish a general set of guidelines for everyone to follow given that private payer laws vary greatly among public insurance agencies in each state in the United States. The Center also noted that there are varying degrees of reimbursement offered by Medicare, Medicaid, and private insurance companies and variation in the requirements that must be met in order to cover a specified range of services (Center for Connected Health Policy, 2018). These terms and requirements place restrictions on patient and health care providers in the United States regarding the types of services that can be offered. If insurance cannot cover particular services, then they would realistically only be available to affluent families who already have access to other forms of health care services. If telehealth is to become a legitimate form of health care in the United States and beyond, then it needs to be accessible to everyone, especially those experiencing health inequities. This may be less of an issue in countries with a single-payer health care system if they generally accept the legitimacy and value of telehealth treatment.

There is also an issue within the United States regarding licensure and reimbursement of health care providers across state lines. According to the official Medicaid web site, providers must "practice within the scope of their State Practice Act" (Centers for Medicare and Medicaid Services, 2019, para. 9). They also reported that some states "require providers using telemedicine technology across state lines to have a valid state license in the state where the patient is located," yet another barrier that will hinder the growth and potential of telehealth usage (Centers for Medicare and Medicaid Services, 2019, para. 9). Thus, the spread of telehealth in the United States and other countries will require allowing flexibility on the geographic scope of practice for providers.

In summary, telehealth has the potential to provide evidence-based treatment in a cost-effective and accessible manner. Its wide-scale adoption beyond research settings, however, awaits action by policy makers.

REFERENCES

Abbeduto, L., Brady, N., & Kover, S. (2007). Language development and fragile X syndrome: Profiles, syndrome-specificity, and within-syndrome differences. *Mental Retardation and Developmental Disabilities Research Reviews, 13*(1), 36–46.

American Psychiatric Association. (2013). *Diagnostic and statistical manual of mental disorders* (5th ed.). Arlington, VA: Author.

Bailey, D. B., Raspa, M., Olmsted, M., & Holiday, D. B. (2008). Co-occurring conditions associated with fMR1 gene variations: Findings from a national parent survey. *American Journal of Medical Genetics Part A, 146*(16), 2060–2069.

Baio, J., Wiggins, L., Christensen, D. L., Maenner, M. J., Daniels, J., Warren, Z., . . . Dowling, N. F. (2018). Prevalence of autism spectrum disorder among children aged 8 years: Autism and Developmental Disabilities Monitoring Network, 11 Sites, United States, 2014. *MMWR Surveillance Summaries, 67*(6), 1–23.

Bishop-Fitzpatrick, L., & Kind, A. J. (2017). A scoping review of health disparities in autism spectrum disorder. *Journal of Autism and Developmental Disorders, 47*(11), 3380–3391.

Center for Connected Health Policy. (2018). *State telehealth laws and reimbursement policies report.* Retrieved from https://www.cchpca.org/sites/default/files/2018-10/CCHP_50_State_Report_Fall_2018.pdf

Centers for Medicare and Medicaid Services. (2019). *Telemedicine.* Retrieved from https://www.medicaid.gov/medicaid/benefits/telemed/index.html#.W1F48W_EdaU.link

Cordeiro, L., Ballinger, E., Hagerman, R., & Hessl, D. (2011). Clinical assessment of DSM-IV anxiety disorders in fragile X syndrome: Prevalence and characterization. *Journal of Neurodevelopmental Disorders, 3*(1), 57–67.

Dominey, P. F., & Dodane, C. (2004). Indeterminacy in language acquisition: The role of child directed speech and joint attention. *Journal of Neurolinguistics, 17*(2-3), 121–145.

Farzin, F., Perry, H., Hessl, D., Loesch, D., Cohen, J., Bacalman, S., . . . Hagerman, R. (2006). Autism spectrum disorders and attention-deficit/hyperactivity disorder in boys with

the fragile X premutation. *Journal of Developmental and Behavioral Pediatrics, 27*(2), S137–S144.
Haebig, E., McDuffie, A., & Weismer, S. E. (2013). The contribution of two categories of parent verbal responsiveness to later language for toddlers and preschoolers on the autism spectrum. *American Journal of Speech-Language Pathology, 22*(1), 57–70.
Hart, B., & Risley, T. R. (1995). *Meaningful differences in the everyday experience of young American children.* Baltimore, MD: Paul H. Brookes Publishing Co.
Hatton, D. D., Hooper, S. R., Bailey, D. B., Skinner, M. L., Sullivan, K. M., & Wheeler, A. (2002). Problem behavior in boys with fragile X syndrome. *American Journal of Medical Genetics, 108*(2), 105–116.
Howlin, P., Goode, S., Hutton, J., & Rutter, M. (2004). Adult outcome for children with autism. *Journal of Child Psychology and Psychiatry, 45*(2), 212–229.
Ingersoll, B., & Gergans, S. (2007). The effect of a parent-implemented imitation intervention on spontaneous imitation skills in young children with autism. *Research in Developmental Disabilities, 28*(2), 163–175.
Jang, J., Dixon, D. R., Tarbox, J., & Granpeesheh, D. (2011). Symptom severity and challenging behavior in children with ASD. *Research in Autism Spectrum Disorders, 5,* 1028–1032.
Jones, T. L., & Prinz, R. J. (2005). Potential roles of parental self-efficacy in parent and child adjustment: A review. *Clinical Psychology Review, 25*(3), 341–363.
Kashinath, S., Woods, J., & Goldstein, H. (2006). Enhancing generalized teaching strategy use in daily routines by parents of children with autism. *Journal of Speech, Language, and Hearing Research, 49*(3), 466–485.
Klinger, L. G., Dawson, G., & Renner, P. (2003). Autistic disorder. In E. J. Mash & R. A. Barkley (Eds.), *Child psychopathology* (2nd ed., pp. 409–454). New York, NY: Guilford Press.
Larson, E. (2006). Caregiving and autism: How does children's propensity for routinization influence participation in family activities? *OTJR: Occupation, Participation and Health, 26*(2), 69–79.
Leigh, J. P., & Du, J. (2015). Brief report: Forecasting the economic burden of autism in 2015 and 2025 in the United States. *Journal of Autism and Developmental Disorders, 45*(12), 4135–4139.
Leigh, J. P., Grosse, S. D., Cassady, D., Melnikow, J., & Hertz-Picciotto, I. (2016). Spending by California's Department of Developmental Services for Persons with Autism across demographic and expenditure categories. *PLoS One, 11*(3), e0151970. doi:10.1371/journal.pone.0151970
Matelski, L., & Van de Water, J. (2016). Risk factors in autism: Thinking outside the brain. *Journal of Autoimmunity, 67,* 1–7.
McDuffie, A., Banasik, A., Bullard, L., Nelson, S., Feigles, R. T., Hagerman, R., & Abbeduto, L. (2018). Distance delivery of a spoken language intervention for school-aged and adolescent boys with fragile X syndrome. *Developmental Neurorehabilitation, 21,* 48–63.
McDuffie, A., Machalicek, W., Bullard, L., Nelson, S., Mello, M., Tempero-Feigles, R., . . . Abbeduto, L. (2016). A spoken-language intervention for school-aged boys with fragile X syndrome. *American Journal on Intellectual and Developmental Disabilities, 121*(3), 236–265.
McDuffie, A., Oakes, A., Machalicek, W., Ma, M., Bullard, L., Nelson, S., & Abbeduto, L. (2016). Early language intervention using distance video-teleconferencing: A pilot study of young boys with fragile X syndrome and their mothers. *American Journal of Speech-Language Pathology, 25*(1), 46–66.
Meadan, H., Meyer, L. E., Snodgrass, M. R., & Halle, J. W. (2013). Coaching parents of young children with autism in rural areas using internet-based technologies: A pilot program. *Rural Special Education Quarterly, 32*(3), 3–10.
Mundy, P., Sigman, M., Ungerer, J., & Sherman, T. (1986). Defining the social deficits of autism: The contribution of non-verbal communication measures. *Journal of Child Psychology and Psychiatry, 27*(5), 657–669.
Munir, F., Cornish, K. M., & Wilding, J. (2000). A neuropsychological profile of attention deficits in young males with fragile X syndrome. *Neuropsychologia, 38*(9), 1261–1270.

Nolin, S. L., Brown, W. T., Glicksman, A., Houck Jr, G. E., Gargano, A. D., Sullivan, A., . . . Kooy, F. (2003). Expansion of the fragile X CGG repeat in females with premutation or intermediate alleles. *American Journal of Human Genetics, 72*(2), 454–464.

Oakes, A., Ma, M., McDuffie, A., Machalicek, W., & Abbeduto, L. (2015). Providing a parent-implemented language intervention to a young male with fragile X syndrome: Brief report. *Developmental Neurorehabilitation, 18*(1), 65–68.

Oakes, A., Thurman, A. J., McDuffie, A., Bullard, L. M., Hagerman, R. J., & Abbeduto, L. (2016). Characterising repetitive behaviours in young boys with fragile X syndrome. *Journal of Intellectual Disability Research, 60*(1), 54–67.

Shattuck, P. T. (2006). The contribution of diagnostic substitution to the growing administrative prevalence of autism in U.S. special education. *Pediatrics, 117*(4), 1028–1037.

Shattuck, P. T., Narendorf, S. C., Cooper, B. P., Sterzing, P., Wagner, M., & Taylor, J. L. (2012). Postsecondary education and employment among youth with an autism spectrum disorder. *Pediatrics, 129,* 1042–1049. doi:10.1542/peds.2011-2864

Statham, H., Ponder, M., Richards, M., Hallowell, N., & Raymond, F. L. (2011). A family perspective of the value of a diagnosis for intellectual disability: Experiences from a genetic research study. *British Journal of Learning Disabilities, 39*(1), 46–56.

Tassone, F., Iong, K. P., Tong, T. H., Lo, J., Gane, L. W., Berry-Kravis, E., . . . Hagerman, R. J. (2012). FMR1 CGG allele size and prevalence ascertained through newborn screening in the United States. *Genome Medicine, 4*(12), 100.

Taylor, J. L., & Seltzer, M. M. (2011). Employment and post-secondary educational activities for young adults with autism spectrum disorders during the transition to adulthood. *Journal of Autism and Developmental Disorders, 41*(5), 566–574.

Timothy, W. Y., & Berry-Kravis, E. (2014, July). Autism and fragile x syndrome. *Seminars in Neurology, 34*(3), 258–265.

Travis, L. L., & Sigman, M. (1998). Social deficits and interpersonal relationships in autism. *Mental Retardation and Developmental Disabilities Research Reviews, 4,* 65–72.

VisuWell. (2018). *State legislative changes for telemedicine taking effect in 2018.* Retrieved from https://visuwell.io/news/legislative-changes-telehealth-2018-state

Wang, L. W., Berry-Kravis, E., & Hagerman, R. J. (2010). Fragile X: Leading the way for targeted treatments in autism. *Neurotherapeutics, 7*(3), 264–274.

Warren, S. F., & Brady, N. C. (2007). The role of maternal responsivity in the development of children with intellectual disabilities. *Mental Retardation and Developmental Disabilities Research Reviews, 13*(4), 330–338.

White, S. W., Oswald, D., Ollendick, T., & Scahill, L. (2009). Anxiety in children and adolescents with autism spectrum disorders. *Clinical Psychology Review, 29*(3), 216–229.

Williams, J. G., Higgins, J. P., & Brayne, C. E. (2006). Systematic review of prevalence studies of autism spectrum disorders. *Archives of Disease in Childhood, 91*(1), 8–15.

CHAPTER 15

Identification, Assessment, and Treatment of Reading Difficulties

Learning From Examination of U.S. and U.K. Practices

Julian Elliott

SUMMARY

This chapter concerns developments in Russia regarding the assessment of, and treatment for, reading disability/dyslexia. It notes that specialists and advocates in Russia are looking to developments in Western countries, such as the United States and United Kingdom, to guide their emerging policy and practice. The chapter highlights some of the difficulties involved in emulating Western systems, adding that these are not without significant weaknesses that typically result in a failure to address the needs of many struggling readers. Rather than creating a dyslexia industry that will highlight the needs of a small proportion of children, it is recommended that attention be given to the development of school-based approaches geared to identifying and assisting all children who encounter reading difficulty. The chapter highlights some of the strengths of traditional approaches to teaching and learning in Russia but notes that key proximal processes (involving everyday classroom practices and interpersonal dynamics) may need to be modified if all poor readers are to be helped to thrive. The importance of developing electronic assistive technology (AT) operating in the Russian language is highlighted. Finally, the chapter exhorts Russian educators to be mindful of their rich theoretical heritage and the emphasis this places on highly skilled teacher–student interaction informed by a deep understanding of the child's current and potential development

INTRODUCTION

Specialists in the science of language and literacy gathered in St. Petersburg, Russia. Hosting aspects of the conference were committed advocates for raising public awareness of dyslexia in Russia. This confluence of leading researchers, educational practitioners, and therapists—and in the public meetings, those with personal experience of the challenges and traumas of reading disability—clearly offered opportunities for affecting significant improvements in the identification, assessment, and intervention of complex reading difficulties. So why did I have an abiding sense of unease about the general direction of travel?

In many ways, the difficulties I foresaw mirrored those that I and others have already identified in various other educational contexts (Elliott & Grigorenko, 2014). It seemed, however, that these could be inflated by the particular sociohistorical context of Russian schooling. Paradoxically, the greatest threat came from one of the strengths of the Soviet educational system—a well-developed set of classroom practices that, for many generations of schoolchildren, have been powerful means to development and learning (Alexander, 2001). Although my comments are focused on what Russian educators might learn from scrutiny of the strengths and weaknesses of the U.K. and U.S. systems, the insights offered here also have broader applicability to the nations that have similar, traditionally teacher-centered educational approaches or are just beginning to recognize and develop tailored treatments for reading disabilities and other learning disabilities.

There are many positive opportunities that the work of dyslexia advocates and supporters can offer for struggling readers, including widening recognition that long-term difficulties in decoding text are not a consequence of laziness, low intelligence, or indolent or uncaring parents. Rather, in most cases, the challenges such children face are the consequence of a developmental problem of biological origin. This does not rule out the importance of the environment, however, and the extent of struggling readers' difficulties can be exacerbated or ameliorated by their lifetime experiences. In particular, positive support in the home and, crucially, the understanding and actions of their teachers and peers will have a significant impact on their progress. The challenges I foresee for dyslexia advocates in Russia can be summarized as follows:

- Current practices for identifying and diagnosing dyslexia in the United States and United Kingdom militate against the needs of many struggling readers. Applying these approaches directly to the Russian context and similar education systems may prove even more problematic.
- Traditional approaches to the schooling of children with special educational needs may render it difficult to operate the type of inclusive approach that is necessary if a positive and systemwide approach to helping children with reading difficulties is to operate effectively.
- Some of the most powerful classroom approaches that are hallmarks of the Russian education system can prove problematic for children with reading difficulties.
- The difficulties in successfully intervening with those with the most complex reading difficulties can often result in ready acceptance of alternative approaches that may lack scientific support.

Each of these is considered next.

CURRENT APPROACHES TO IDENTIFYING AND DIAGNOSING DYSLEXIA: RELEVANCE FOR THE RUSSIAN AND OTHER SIMILAR CONTEXTS

The term *dyslexia* will be familiar to many in Russia, particularly educators and psychologists, although understanding will often be unclear. Yet, it would be a mistake to assume that this term's use in other countries was unproblematic.

Since clinical accounts were first published by physicians in Victorian England, many terms have been employed to describe the difficulties that some people encounter in trying to decode text. *Congenital word blindness, visual agnosia for words,* and *specific reading disability* are just some of these, although these have been almost universally replaced by the term *dyslexia.* Nevertheless, achieving a workable and scientifically valid definition of dyslexia has proven highly elusive (Elliott & Grigorenko, 2014; Elliott & Nicholson, 2016). What has compounded the difficulty is that there is often a gulf between formal definitions of dyslexia (which themselves differ greatly) and the way that professionals have chosen to operationalize these in educational and clinical practice.

Many researchers and clinicians use the term *dyslexia* as a synonym for reading disability/reading disorder (i.e., anyone who struggles to decode text is considered to be dyslexic) (Black, Myers, & Hoeft, 2015; Pennington & Bishop, 2009). Participants for scientific studies of dyslexia are typically selected on the basis of their performance on standardized reading tests and the absence of severe or profound difficulties (e.g., visual or hearing impairment, significant intellectual disability). Reflecting this position, one review stated:

> Dyslexia is mainly defined as the low end of a normal distribution of word reading ability. . . . Thus, in order to diagnose the disorder, a somewhat arbitrary cutoff must be set on a continuous variable. (Peterson & Pennington, 2015, p. 285)

In some research, clinical, or educational contexts, not all those who struggle with decoding are considered to be dyslexic (Kuppen & Goswami, 2016; Le Jan et al., 2011). As a consequence, a vast dyslexia test industry has sprung up that offers the promise of scientifically determining which poor readers are dyslexic and which are not. Decisions are primarily based on the results of psychometric testing and the observed presence of certain cognitive difficulties that are more often found in poor readers (in particular, those concerning phonological awareness, rapid naming/processing, and verbal working memory). Other common problems, such as weaker attention/concentration, psychomotor skills, computational abilities, and organizational difficulties, are also often seen as markers of dyslexia. Elliott and Grigorenko (2014) noted, however, such difficulties are more common to all those with poor reading skills, not a subset of individuals with dyslexia.

In the United States, Lyon, Shaywitz, and Shaywitz's (2003) conception of dyslexia has been widely taken up by federal and state agencies and embraced by dyslexia advocacy groups. For these authors, dyslexia can be conceived as a specific learning disability that is neurobiological in origin and is characterized by difficulties with accurate and/or fluent word recognition and by poor spelling and decoding abilities. The difficulties arise from a deficit in the phonological component of language. The reading problems are often unexpected in relation to other cognitive abilities and the provision of effective classroom instruction. Reading comprehension problems and reduced experience may limit vocabulary growth, and background knowledge may arise as secondary consequences of dyslexia. The difficulties and challenges of using such a definition to differentiate between poor readers who have dyslexia and those who do not are discussed in detail in Elliott and Grigorenko (2014), and there is insufficient space to discuss these in this chapter. It should be pointed out, however, that such conceptions are highly problematic for clinical use.

The identification of certain cognitive processes as indicators of dyslexia has led to suggestions by some practitioners in the United Kingdom that dyslexia should be considered as more than a reading difficulty (Cooke, 2001). According to this line of reasoning, one may have dyslexia even if one does not have a serious reading difficulty. Such a perception seems to be most commonly found for adult learners. For example, Ryder and Norwich (2018) found that more than a quarter of their sample of higher education learning disability/dyslexia assessors did not consider past or current difficulties with literacy skills to be necessary for a diagnosis of dyslexia.

At the St. Petersburg meeting, I pondered which of these three broad understandings of dyslexia was most likely to be adopted by Russian educators and clinicians. Should dyslexia be seen as 1) a synonym for reading difficulty, 2) a condition experienced by only some poor readers who present with a particular cognitive profile, or 3) a condition marked by certain cognitive difficulties that might result in impaired reading? Certainly, the third option (rare in Western countries, too) was not a likely one. Given that our Russian colleagues appeared to be primarily informed by developments in the United States and, to a lesser extent, the United Kingdom, my guess was that, either explicitly or implicitly, they are unlikely to assume that all struggling readers in Russian classrooms should be identified as dyslexic. Rather, drawing on a medical model that reflects a long history in the science of defectology, they appear to be looking to the establishment/enlargement of diagnostic services that will test individuals, identify those who are dyslexic, introduce special individualized programs for mainstream schools to implement, and encourage teachers to reframe their understanding of the children concerned in ways that will recognize their potential more fully.

This scenario maps quite closely to developments in the United States where the popularity of the term has fluctuated since the 1930s (Rooney, 1995). Recently, the term has captured political attention and, as a result, dyslexia legislation has mushroomed. As of March 2018, 42 states had statewide dyslexia laws (almost twice as many as in 2013), and it seems likely that very shortly all will have introduced such legislation (Youman & Mather, 2018). Given its current trajectory, the use of this term for diagnostic purposes in U.S. educational settings will almost certainly increase in popularity.

My concern about attempts to emulate models of operation in the United Kingdom and the United States is that, as in these countries, identification and diagnostic procedures will result in only a small proportion of struggling readers being identified and helped. Not only are current assessment approaches often flawed (discussion of the use of psychological testing is addressed next), but this approach will also only select the few at the expense of the many. Unfortunately, the desire of well-meaning advocates to change teachers' understanding and practice for those children identified as dyslexic has the potentially iatrogenic effect of impairing the experiences of those poor readers who fail to get the label. This is highly problematic in countries such as the United States and United Kingdom that have a long tradition of operating inclusive educational practices. This risk is significantly greater in a country such as Russia, which has a long and proud history of providing special schooling for those who struggle in the often highly challenging and demanding mainstream classrooms or, alternatively, transferring them to vocational schools.

The use of cognitive measures to diagnose and intervene in dyslexia remains popular in the United States and United Kingdom, although it is hoped this will not be the case in Russia. As Jack Fletcher stated at the St. Petersburg conference and has written about extensively, the evidence for their utility is demonstrably weak. Historically, psychologists employed IQ tests as key elements in the dyslexia diagnostic process. When IQ was found to be inappropriate for this task (Fletcher, Lyon, Fuchs, & Barnes, 2007; Gresham & Vellutino, 2010; Stuebing, Barth, Molfese, Weiss, & Fletcher, 2009; Stuebing et al., 2002), psychometricians looked to derive profiles on the basis of selected IQ subtests. When this approach was found to be ineffective (Frederickson, 1999; Ward, Ward, Hatt, Young, & Molner, 1995), alternative approaches emphasizing patterns of strength and weakness across different cognitive abilities (Flanagan, Fiorello, & Ortiz, 2010; Naglieri, 1999) were advocated for diagnosing learning disabilities (or specific learning disorders) such as dyslexia. These have also been shown to be unfit for this purpose (Fletcher & Miciak, 2017; Stuebing et al., 2009). Similarly, Fletcher has refuted claims that testing the "new kids on the block"—executive functions—has sufficient value for diagnosing learning disability (see Chapter 10).

There is little empirical support for claims that cognitive assessments can be employed to assist in screening or planning interventions for children with reading difficulties (Burns et al., 2016; Elliott & Resing, 2015) or help us predict which children will most benefit from assistance (Stuebing et al., 2015). We should also note the opportunity costs involved in creating expensive and time-consuming assessment procedures that add little to our understanding of a child's reading difficulty. Research has shown that detailed assessment of the individual's specific literacy skills is the most appropriate means of identifying the forms and content of instruction that will meet his or her particular needs (Connor, Kim, & Yang, in press; Connor, Morrison, Fishman, Schatschneider, & Underwood, 2007). Vellutino, Fletcher, Snowling, and Scanlon stated a generation ago that psychologists and other practitioners should

> Shift the focus of their clinical activities away from emphasis on psychometric assessment to detect cognitive and biological causes of a child's reading difficulties for purposes of categorical labelling in favour of assessment that would eventuate in educational and remedial activities tailored to the child's individual needs. (2004, p. 31)

Such an approach runs counter to the popular Russian use of labels for struggling readers, specifically "delayed psychological development" or, in some cases, "mental retardation." The former term is employed to describe those considered to have selective, rather than generalized, cognitive impairments, whereas the latter describes those with IQ scores between 50 and 79. With the nascent development of a fledgling psychological testing industry in Russia (Kornev, Rakhlin, & Grigorenko, 2010), the resistance of Russian specialists to call for a predominantly educational focus for tackling individuals' reading difficulties is likely to mirror that widely found in Western societies.

Existing nomenclature and, perhaps, the use of the term *teacher-defectologist* (Dmitriev & Tverskaya, 2015) may reinforce teacher perceptions that struggling readers are less intelligent than their peers. As a consequence, parental concern to avoid this is likely to fuel the dyslexia testing industry. Kornev and Isimova (2010) suggested that about 5% of Russian school-age children have dyslexia, a figure that is lower than the range of 5%–20% that has been proposed for children in English-speaking school systems. This may be explained by Russian's transparent orthography, which enables children to make letter–sound associations more easily than in opaque languages such as English. Interestingly, this transparency in Russian orthography operates in the direction of letters to sounds but not in the opposite direction of sounds to letters. As a result, the relative acquisition of spelling is more complex and time consuming for Russian children (Kornev et al., 2010).

THE NEED FOR AN INCLUSIVE APPROACH

The shift in Western classrooms from integration to inclusion in the second half of the 20th century reflected a broad change in philosophy concerning how best to support children with special educational needs. Integration was predominantly concerned with helping children who might otherwise be educated in special education settings to succeed in mainstream classrooms. To some extent, this reflected a desire to enable children to fit into an existing school environment (Avramidis & Norwich, 2002). In contrast, inclusion is concerned with providing an educational environment that enables all children to realize their potential. As such, moving to inclusive schooling requires more comprehensive systemic change than the more piecemeal integration approach. In practice, operating a fully inclusive, effective environment continues to be a challenge in every culture.

There are certainly many struggling readers in Western classrooms who fail to receive the forms of educational support that they require. Perhaps it is for this reason that the dyslexia advocacy movement has become so strong in the United States and the United Kingdom. If schools are unable or unwilling to provide effective instruction to help overcome children's reading difficulties, and if teachers fail to modify classroom tasks to reflect the child's unique abilities and needs, then there will be a need to assess, identify those with the condition, and mandate the resourcing of special provision and accommodations. Such assistance will typically be provided only to those children who have proceeded through a lengthy specialized testing process, and other poor readers will continue to be neglected and, hence, poorly served. Such a solution is likely to reduce the political motivation and funding for systemwide response to instruction models that are designed to identify and support all children struggling with learning in particular domains such as reading.

Concerns that the Soviet education system took little account of individual differences led Russian reformers to call for greater humanization (involving responding to students as individuals with differing goals and potential) in the 1990s. Although the intervening years have led to widespread acceptance of the need to operate more inclusive classrooms (Dmitriev & Tverskaya, 2015), Russia's long and, for many children, highly effective system of whole-class teaching has rendered the creation of inclusive environments a particular challenge (Oreshkina, 2009). Historically, those children who could not thrive in the fast-paced, very public, and highly demanding mainstream classroom were likely to receive some form of special education in one of the diverse range of special schools or, increasingly, onsite in specialized classrooms (Malofeev, 1998). In order to receive such forms of specialized education, struggling readers would have to present with definable cognitive, intellectual, or speech and language difficulties (Kornev et al., 2010). The children in regular schooling settings were considered to be equal and expected to cope with typical classroom demands (Korkunov, Nigayev, Reynolds, & Lerner, 1998). This arrangement permitted teachers to focus on highly skilled teaching to the class group that rarely required them to make significant adjustments on the basis of individual student needs. Indeed, Elliott, Hufton, Illushin, and Willis (2005), conducted a cross-cultural study and noted that a small proportion of the Russian teachers observed or interviewed had a meaningful understanding of the notion of differentiation by task within the classroom. When this concept was explained to them, few saw this as workable at scale within the current Russian education system.

WHY TRADITIONAL RUSSIAN CLASSROOM PRACTICES MAY BE PROBLEMATIC FOR STRUGGLING READERS

The particular strengths of Russian pedagogy were highlighted by Alexander (2001). He conducted a detailed and sophisticated analysis of primary education in Russia and demonstrated that the purpose of classroom talk was predominantly cognitive, rather than social, and extended, probing exchanges between teacher and child led to deeper and more complex understandings than might be typically found in U.S. or U.K. classrooms. Students in the Russian (formerly Soviet) classroom are not perceived as lone individuals who are, in some ways, competing among themselves but, rather, as members of a classroom learning community who listen to and learn from one another. Although such environments are valuable for the majority of students, they may present considerable challenges for those with special educational needs. The very strength of this collective enterprise may become a challenge for those who require a more differentiated approach or who find the public nature of their literacy difficulties to be shameful or humiliating (Riddick, 2010).

As is the case in the United Kingdom and United States, Russian families will be likely to seek a diagnosis of dyslexia if they believe that teachers and peers will consequently be less likely to attribute their child's reading problems to laziness or stupidity and, accordingly, be more prepared to find ways to assist the child to learn. Even if the labeling of dyslexia is successful, the problem is that its usage and potency will reinforce negative perceptions with respect to those other poor readers who are not given a diagnosis of dyslexia. The preferred scenario is one in which teachers are educated to understand that it is wholly inappropriate to make a judgment of a child's intelligence on the basis of his or her literacy skills. Teachers also need to understand that some children's reluctance to make a concerted attempt to improve their reading is the result of a sense of helplessness, following a lengthy period of struggle, and/or a self-worth protection strategy (Covington, 1992).

The behavior of teachers toward poor readers is obviously an important factor in encouraging students to overcome their difficulties, and, in this respect, there are significant cultural differences between Russia and the United States. Elliott et al.'s (2005) comparative study of fourth-graders found that children in the United States overestimated, and Russian children underestimated, their teachers' perceptions of their abilities. It seemed that this phenomenon was a function of the different messages that their teachers communicated. Echoing this conclusion, Alexander (2001) compared the tendency of teachers in the United States to be fulsome in their praise of children's efforts (perhaps being unduly and unhelpfully excessive on some occasions [Elliott, 2002]) with the historic tendency of Russian teachers to use public criticism for what is deemed to be inadequate performance. Such differences are skewed by different grading practices and appear to be the consequence of broader child socialization practices involving contrasting cultural understandings about the importance of praise (Alexander, 2001; Damon, 1995; Muckle, 1990). Interestingly, a similar phenomenon was reported in the former East Germany (Marsh, Koller, & Baumert, 2001), where a high proportion of student lower self-appraisals were seemingly influenced by teachers' public and detailed feedback.

THE SEDUCTIVENESS OF ALTERNATIVE APPROACHES

Attempts to tackle complex reading difficulties included a diverse range of approaches involving colored lenses, fish oil, neurofeedback, and auditory and psychomotor training. Although the supporters of each of these offer claims as to their efficacy, the reality is that only traditional structured educational approaches using training in the alphabetic principle have serious scientific support (Elliott & Grigorenko, 2014).

In St. Petersburg, I observed how noneducational approaches to tackling reading difficulties, endorsed by international proponents, could be persuasive for advocates and practitioners eagerly looking to the West for new ideas and methods. Given the complexity of reforming classroom practices to better assist struggling readers, the attractiveness of an esoteric, recondite, and therapeutic practice, sometimes backed up by claims of support from neuroscience, is easy to understand (Snowling, 2010). Yet, following such a path is inadvisable, and it needs to be understood that only structured educational approaches currently have scientific support. Understandably, other forms of intervention can become particularly attractive to parents and teachers when children fail to make meaningful progress despite receiving the best educational programs (these children are sometimes known as *treatment resisters*) (Wanzek et al., 2013). Yet, alternative approaches, such as perceptual motor training, biofeedback, dietary supplements, and visual and auditory therapies, lack scientific support (see Elliott & Grigorenko, 2014) and should be resisted. For students who do not make adequate progress despite sound teaching, it is important to recognize the potential of AT that can read printed text aloud or convert the individual's speech to computerized text at speed. At the St. Petersburg meeting, I was informed that such tools were not yet available for Russian speakers; hopefully, this position will soon be remedied.

RECOMMENDATIONS FOR A WAY FORWARD

Russian children with formally identified reading difficulties are permitted some modifications at the discretion of their teachers, including dispensation from having to read aloud in front of their peers, the possibility of substituting oral for written assignments, and freedom from penalization for poor spelling (Kornev et al., 2010). Although such accommodations are laudable, it is questionable whether these can be scaled up to apply to all struggling readers (rather than merely those who manage to get a formal label) and whether this can influence the development of inclusive practices.

Meaningful, systemic change will be necessary to ensure that all struggling readers in Russia are identified and given individualized assistance. Watzlawick, Weakland, and Fisch (1974) referred to first-order change in which incremental modifications are made within an established way of operating. Here, meaningful, system-level change will rarely occur. In contrast, second-order change involves qualitative, often discontinuous, transformation that enables us to see and understand phenomena very differently. Modifying an existing quasi-medical diagnostic system to identify and treat children with dyslexia (from what will inevitably be a much larger pool of poor readers) runs the risk of conducting first-order change. Children so identified may benefit from extra services and greater understanding of their needs, but everyday classroom practices and teacher skills will remain largely unchanged in most other respects. Such modifications will fail to serve the needs of the great majority of struggling readers.

To achieve second-order change, a rather different approach is necessary. The educational system itself needs to be modified so that all children who struggle with reading are assessed on the basis of their existing literacy skills and subsequently provided with appropriate instruction. In short, the following steps are recommended to help achieve this:

1. Educate all teachers to understand the nature of various forms of reading and spelling difficulty.
2. Train teachers to identify and address these problems at an early stage of the child's development.
3. Provide opportunities during broader curricular activities to learn and demonstrate learning that do not require engagement with detailed and lengthy texts that are inappropriately matched to the child's literacy skills.
4. Ensure that if the term *dyslexia* is employed, it applies to all struggling readers, not only those who are labeled on the basis of psychometric tests or other forms of psychological assessment.
5. Emphasize the importance of dissociating literacy skills from cognitive ability. In so doing, help teachers understand that the intellectual demands of curricular tasks offered to students with similar levels of reading difficulties may often need to differ.
6. Recognize the threats to the individual when he or she is required to demonstrate literacy-based skills in public settings, such as classrooms and wider school events.
7. Provide evidence-based forms of structured reading and spelling instruction to all students struggling with literacy. Specialized instruction and accommodations may be necessary throughout the student's school years, and continuing difficulties should not prove to be a barrier to higher education (Kornev et al., 2010).
8. Develop the use of AT (e.g., pen scanners, voice recognition software) in the Russian language and encourage its use in mainstream and special school classrooms.
9. Draw on the rich Russian theoretical heritage of social constructivism that has long enriched teachers' understanding of learning, teaching, and development (Zukerman, 2014). Scholars such as Vygotsky,

Elkonin, and Davydov have sensitized generations of Russian educators and, indeed, scholars across the world to the importance of skillful teacher action that can draw on a profound understanding of each child's functioning and potential to support and enhance learning. The growth of an international dyslexia industry is, in part, a consequence of global concerns that educators too often fail to understand and meet the needs of the struggling reader. For many teachers of struggling readers in Russia, the roots of the way forward reside in the confluence of their own rich theoretical traditions and the rapid empirical advances that are found in international research.

REFERENCES

Alexander, R. J. (2001) *Culture and pedagogy: International comparisons in primary education.* Oxford, England: Blackwell.

Avramidis, E., & Norwich, B. (2002). Teachers' attitudes towards integration/inclusion: A review of the literature. *European Journal of Special Needs Education, 17,* 129–147.

Black, J. M., Myers, C. A., & Hoeft, F. (2015). The utility of neuroimaging studies for informing educational practice and policy in reading disorders. *New Directions for Child and Adolescent Development, 147,* 49–56.

Burns, M. K., Petersen-Brown, S., Haegele, K., Rodriguez, M., Schmitt, B., Cooper, M., . . . VanDerHeyden, A. M. (2016). Meta-analysis of academic interventions derived from neuropsychological data. *School Psychology Quarterly, 31,* 28–42.

Connor, C. M., Kim, Y.-S. G., & Yang, D. (in press). Personalizing literacy instruction for diverse learners and children with severe literacy difficulties. In J. A. Washington, D. L. Compton, & P. McCardle (Eds.), *Dyslexia: Revisiting etiology, diagnosis, treatment, and policy.* Baltimore, MD: Paul H. Brookes Publishing Co.

Connor, C. M., Morrison, F. J., Fishman, B. J., Schatschneider, C., & Underwood, P. (2007). Algorithm-guided individualized reading instruction. *Science, 315,* 464–465.

Cooke, A. (2001). Critical response to "Dyslexia, literacy and psychological assessment (Report by a Working Party of the Division of Educational and Child Psychology of the British Psychological Society)": A view from the chalk face. *Dyslexia, 7*(1), 47–52.

Covington, M. V. (1992). *Making the grade: A self-worth perspective on motivation and school reform.* New York, NY: Cambridge University Press.

Damon, W. (1995). *Greater expectations.* New York, NY: Free Press.

Dmitriev, A. A., & Tverskaya, O. N. (2015). Modern approaches to inclusive education of children with disabilities in Russia: Mini review. *Biological Medicine (Aligarh), 7*(4).

Elliott, J. G. (2002). Could do better? The risks of cultivating positive self-esteem. *Human Givens: Radical Psychology Today,* 9(1), 38–43.

Elliott, J. G., & Grigorenko, E. L. (2014). *The dyslexia debate.* New York, NY: Cambridge University Press.

Elliott, J. G., Hufton, N., Illushin, L., & Willis, W. (2005). *Motivation, engagement and educational performance.* London, England: Palgrave Press.

Elliott, J. G., & Nicholson, R. (2016). *Dyslexia: Developing the debate.* London, England: Bloomsbury Press.

Elliott, J. G., & Resing, W. C. M. (2015). Can intelligence testing inform educational intervention for children with reading disability? *Journal of Intelligence, 3*(4), 137–157.

Flanagan, D. P., Fiorello, C. A., & Ortiz, S. O. (2010). Enhancing practice through application of Cattell–Horn–Carroll theory and research: A "third method" approach to specific learning disability identification. *Psychology in the Schools, 47*(7), 739–760.

Fletcher, J. M., Lyon, G. R., Fuchs, L. S., & Barnes, M. A. (2007). *Learning disabilities.* New York, NY: Guilford Press.

Fletcher, J. M., & Miciak, J. (2017). Comprehensive cognitive assessments are not necessary for the identification and treatment of learning disabilities. *Archives of Clinical Neuropsychology, 32*(1), 2–7.

Frederickson, N. (1999). The ACID test—or is it? *Educational Psychology in Practice, 15,* 2–8.
Gresham, F. M., & Vellutino, F. R. (2010). What is the role of intelligence in the identification of specific learning disabilities? Issues and clarifications. *Learning Disabilities Research and Practice, 25*(4), 194–206.
Korkunov, V. V., Nigayev, A. S., Reynolds, L. D., & Lerner, J. W. (1998). Special education in Russia: History, reality, and prospects. *Journal of Learning Disabilities, 31*(2), 186–192.
Kornev, A. N., & Isimova, O. A. (2010). Metodika diagnostiki disleksii u detej. *Metodičeskoe posobie.* Sankt-Peterburg: Izdatel'stvo Politehničeskogo universiteta.
Kornev, A. N., Rakhlin, N., & Grigorenko, E. L. (2010). Dyslexia from a cross-linguistic and cross-cultural perspective: The case of Russian and Russia. *Learning Disabilities: A Contemporary Journal, 8*(1), 51–78.
Kuppen, S. E., & Goswami, U. (2016). Developmental trajectories for children with dyslexia and low IQ poor readers. *Developmental Psychology, 52*(5), 717–734.
Le Jan, G., Le Bouquin-Jeannès, R., Costet, N., Trolès, N., Scalart, P., Pichancourt, D., . . . Gombert, J. E. (2011). Multivariate predictive model for dyslexia diagnosis. *Annals of Dyslexia, 61*(1), 1–20.
Lyon, G. R., Shaywitz, S. E., & Shaywitz, B. A. (2003). A definition of dyslexia. *Annals of Dyslexia, 53,* 1–14.
Malofeev, N. N. (1998). Special education in Russia: Historical aspects. *Journal of Learning Disabilities, 31*(2), 181–185.
Marsh, H. W., Koller, O., & Baumert, J. (2001). Reunification of East and West German school systems: Longitudinal multilevel modelling study of the big-fish-little-pond effect on academic self-concept. *American Educational Research Journal, 38,* 321–350.
Muckle, J. (1990). Portrait of a Soviet school under Glasnost. London, England: Macmillan.
Naglieri, J. A. (1999). *Essentials of CAS assessment.* New York, NY: Wiley.
Oreshkina, M. (2009). Education of children with disabilities in Russia: On the way to integration and inclusion. *International Journal of Special Education, 24*(3), 110–120.
Pennington, B. F., & Bishop, D. V. (2009). Relations among speech, language, and reading disorders. *Annual Review of Psychology, 60,* 283–306.
Peterson, R. L., & Pennington, B. F. (2015). Developmental dyslexia. *Annual Review of Clinical Psychology, 11,* 283–307.
Riddick, B. (2010). *Living with dyslexia: The social and emotional consequences of specific learning difficulties/disabilities.* Oxford, England: Routledge.
Rooney, K. J. (1995). Dyslexia revisited: History, educational philosophy, and clinical assessment applications. *Intervention in School and Clinic, 31,* 6–15.
Ryder, D., & Norwich, B. (2018). What's in a name? Perspectives of dyslexia assessors working with students in the U.K. higher education sector. *Dyslexia, 24*(2), 109–127.
Snowling, M. J. (2010). Dyslexia. In C. L. Cooper, J. Field, U. Goswami, R. Jenkins, & B. J. Sahakian (Eds.), *Mental capital and mental wellbeing* (pp. 775–783). Oxford, England: Blackwell.
Stuebing, K. K., Barth, A. E., Molfese, P. J., Weiss, B., & Fletcher, J. M. (2009). IQ is not strongly related to response to reading instruction: A meta-analytic interpretation. *Exceptional Children, 76,* 31–51.
Stuebing, K. K., Barth, A. E., Trahan, L. H., Reddy, R. R., Miciak, J., & Fletcher, J. M. (2015). Are child cognitive characteristics strong predictors of responses to intervention? A meta-analysis. *Review of Educational Research, 85*(3), 395–429.
Stuebing, K. K., Fletcher, J. M., LeDoux, J. M., Lyon, R. G., Shaywitz, S. E., & Shaywitz, B. A. (2002). Validity of IQ-discrepancy classifications of reading disabilities: A meta-analysis. *American Educational Research Journal, 39,* 469–518.
Vellutino, F. R., Fletcher, J. M., Snowling, M. J., & Scanlon, D. M. (2004). Specific reading disability (dyslexia): What have we learned in the past four decades? *Journal of Child Psychology and Psychiatry, 45,* 2–40.
Wanzek, J., Vaughn, S., Scammacca, N. K., Metz, K., Murray, C. S., Roberts, G., & Danielson, L. (2013). Extensive reading interventions for students with reading difficulties after Grade 3. *Review of Educational Research, 83*(2), 163–195.

Ward, S. B., Ward, T. J., Hatt, C. V., Young, D. L., & Molner, N. R. (1995). The incidence and utility of the ACID, ACIDS and SCAD profiles in a referred population. *Psychology in the Schools, 32,* 267–276.

Watzlawick, P., Weakland, J. H., & Fisch, R. (1974). *Change: Principles of problem formation and problem resolution.* New York, NY: Norton.

Youman, M., & Mather, N. (2018, Spring). Dyslexia laws in the U.S.: A 2018 update. *Perspectives on Language and Literacy,* 37–41.

Zukerman, G. (2014). Developmental education. In A. Yasnitsky, R. van der Veer, & M. Ferrari (Eds.), *The Cambridge handbook of cultural-historical psychology* (pp. 177–202). New York, NY: Cambridge University Press.

INTEGRATIVE COMMENTARY 5

Great Expectations

A Current Perspective on Education, Disability, and Society

Joan Mele-McCarthy and Benjamin Powers

SUMMARY

Many countries endeavor to promote equal educational opportunities for people with disabilities, but there is an ongoing debate about how best to achieve that objective. Inclusive classroom approaches have been identified as one opportunity to provide equitable access to all students by providing comprehensive instruction and support services within mainstream classroom environments; however, inclusion requires merging different educational philosophies and creating a demand on general education teachers to be well versed in special education practices. At the same time, an important—and contentious—question is whether inclusive educational approaches can meet all of the needs of students who struggle academically. Also, effective education policy designed to meet the needs of students with disabilities requires significant systems changes that provide appropriate investments, including financial resources and teacher training, and measures for accountability. It is clear that the practice of inclusive education requires further, thoughtful study to understand its effectiveness and limitations. At the same time, for any equitable access approach to work, we need to develop effective professional development models for educators as informed consumers of education research so they are equipped to identify students at risk for disabilities and are able to implement evidence-based instruction.

INTRODUCTION

The issue regarding disabilities and society is one of recognition of the universal human birthright of equality of all citizens, which includes compassion for all human conditions and regulatory legislation to ensure civil rights for all people. Meaningful civil rights legislation, otherwise known as *entitlement legislation,* is of paramount importance for citizens, as it helps ensure that society does not marginalize people with disabilities; otherwise, the results can have devastating and lifelong impact, including lower levels of educational attainment, employment, and social-emotional functioning and higher levels of incarceration (Brault, 2012; Burgdorf, 2015; Hall, 2009; Moody et al., 2000; National Center for Health Statistics, 2007; Peat, 1997; Sideridis, 2005).

Disability rights legislation promotes the acceptance of people with differing abilities through policies designed to provide equitable access to areas of society that might otherwise be limited, from buildings, mass transportation, and telecommunications to hiring practices and government services (Burgdorf, 2015). In developed countries, such laws also include the requirement of equal access to educational opportunities. Within the legislative framework, the practice of inclusion (a model in which special education students, including those with visible and invisible disabilities, spend most or all of their time in general education classrooms) has been one of the most lauded—and controversial—in the United States and other countries. The practice of inclusion in schools began with demands by parents and advocacy groups for equal access to educational opportunities for students with disabilities; however, given that individual student needs vary, those groups were demanding equity. In other words, instead of equal (i.e., identical) access, those constituencies were asking for equitable (i.e., fair) access.

The concept of equity goes beyond the notions of equality and appropriateness. It extends to the broader context of fairness, whereby individuals receive what they need to be successful in an environment, even if what is needed by some students or groups of learners is more than what is needed for others. Access to services and accommodations through special education legislation, which is entitlement legislation, should provide that equity for students with disabilities so that schools can provide a free appropriate and equitable public education—because what is appropriate for one learner to be successful in school may not be appropriate for another. The two chapters by Abbeduto et al. and Elliott address ways to achieve equity in education for specific subgroups of children with disabilities.

INCLUSION AS A MEANS OF ACHIEVING EDUCATIONAL EQUITY

If inclusive practices are geared toward providing an equitable education for all, then there are specific parameters that should be evident in an inclusive setting. Hornby (2015) contended that inclusion is the most controversial issue in education because it requires merging two different philosophies, those of special education and general education, and the chasm between those two approaches seems to be widening. The ongoing tension and controversy around this debate have implications for both developed and developing countries. Some countries, such as the United States, have implemented an inclusive education policy as a way to serve students with disabilities, yet other countries view inclusive education as a core value for broad reforms to welcome diverse learners into the general education setting (UNESCO, 2001). Elliott (Chapter 15) points out that Russian education reform has voiced the need for more inclusive classrooms (citing Dmitriev & Tverskaya, 2015), but the whole-class instructional approach common to Russian education makes the implementation of inclusion especially challenging.

Despite the political drivers and taking into account good intentions, one of the main obstacles to true and effective inclusion implementation is that it requires the fusion of myriad dynamics—from social and political acceptance to school reform; it also requires a shift to a student-centered focus in the classroom to include equitable educational access (Hornby, 2015). This can be challenging for countries that have an established and long-standing public school system, such as the United States or Russia, because it requires a change in mindset for teachers and education administrators. For those with a populace-driven, democratic political system, these parameters have evolved socio-politically and have been accepted and implemented in education policy (Flourian & Rouse, 2009). True inclusive education policies are also likely to be a challenge in developing countries where the robust provision of public education is not fully established for all students, and especially for students with disabilities.

To be sure, an inclusive educational approach for students with disabilities describes a somewhat utopian view of educational practice. Inclusion may not provide an appropriate education for the diverse population of students with disabilities, however, if the inclusive environment is not appropriate to their needs (see Chapter 15; Terzi, 2014). Furthermore, some suggest that labeling children in school settings may be psychosocially damaging (Hornby, 2015), whereas others, such as Norwich (2014), promote the notion of the dilemma of difference, noting that if children are not identified as having a disability or educational difficulty, then they will not receive appropriate instruction. In this volume, Elliot discusses whether students should be labeled with dyslexia and asserts that identifying only those students who qualify for special education services may leave behind other struggling students. Those assertions invite an important question: Does inclusive education as it exists in classrooms globally truly meet the needs of all students who struggle academically?

The U.S. implemented the No Child Left Behind Act of 2001 (PL 107-110) and the Individuals with Disabilities Education Improvement Act (IDEA) of 2004 (PL 108-446) to promote appropriate instructional environments through evidence-based interventions in a multi-tiered system of support (MTSS). For tiered academic support, MTSS became synonymous with the response to intervention paradigm, designed to provide early identification of students in need of extra support coupled with increasing levels of research-based, differentiated instruction delivered within general education classrooms.

Essentially, educators were advised to address academic challenges through a tiered support system as opposed to identifying those students struggling with academic difficulties with special education labels. In doing so, it was believed that students would have access to high teacher expectations and would not be stigmatized by special education services outside the general education classroom; yet, Kauffman and Badar (2014) asserted that children are still unofficially labeled by teachers and classmates when they struggle academically. More important, the academic outcomes for students with disabilities have not improved to the degree anticipated; reading achievement in fourth and eighth grades has not reached the "basic" level of proficiency in the United States since the shift to inclusive education environments (Farrell, Dyson, Polat, Hutcheson, & Gallannaugh, 2007; National Assessment of Education Progress, 2017). How can education policy and the practice of inclusion minister to the specific academic needs of all students who struggle academically, including those with a disability, while promoting healthy self-esteem, motivation, and resilience? Elliot (Chapter 15) notes that in Russian classrooms, "moving to inclusive schooling requires more comprehensive systemic change than the more piecemeal integration [education in special education settings] approach. In practice, operating a fully inclusive, effective environment continues to be a challenge in every culture."

CHALLENGES TO ENSURING EDUCATION EQUITY

Teacher training and preparedness is a critical factor in providing effective inclusive settings for students with disabilities. The inclusion model creates a demand on general education teachers to be well versed in special education practices for academically struggling students as well as those classified as having autism spectrum disorder (ASD); speech, language, and communication disorders; dyslexia and other reading difficulties; learning disabilities; and behavioral and emotional difficulties (Hanushek & Raymond, 2003; Rosenzweig, 2009). General education teacher training programs in the United States and Europe, however, do not require extensive training in special education foundational theory and practice (Allday, Neilsen-Gatti, & Hudson, 2013; Brownell, Adams, Sindelar, Waldron, & Vanhover, 2006; Cameron & Cook, 2007; Florian & Rouse, 2009; Hornby, 2015; Lee-Tarver, 2006; Wasburn-Moses, 2008), let alone methods courses in teaching reading to struggling readers or those who struggle with written language or math (Allday et al., 2013). Teachers are not well prepared to implement a differentiated inclusive classroom whereby individual student needs are addressed within the context of the general education classroom (see Chapter 15). In some previous work, Elliott and colleagues (Elliott, Hufton, Illushin, & Willis, 2005) found that teachers were ill-prepared for the type of differentiated, individualized instruction that students with special learning needs would require.

In addition to teacher training, funding is another significant issue with inclusion models for special education. It is assumed that the costs to support an inclusion model for special education can be managed and supported in developed countries; in reality, however, the actual cost of well-designed inclusive classroom environments exceeds the cost of self-contained classes or resource rooms (Hornby, 2015).

BEYOND INCLUSION

The two chapters in this section provide valid concerns and applications of child development research that bring our focus in this chapter from overall education policy about inclusive classrooms for all children who struggle academically to practice, or "what to do about Johnny," in the classroom and outside the classroom. Education policy is only as effective as the research on which it is based, and research-based education practice can flow from education policy, or it can inform education policy. It is this latter sequence that is more desirable because it frames the questions asked by education researchers, educators, and parents.

Elliott outlines a list of recommendations designed to implement systems change and, in doing so, a more inclusive education system in Russia. Those recommendations are also pertinent to Western countries, which, despite a longer history of special education implementation and a more tolerant view of inclusive education, still struggle with providing effective targeted, specialized instruction to all students who struggle academically, not just those who are classified as having ASD, dyslexia, and/or a learning disability or a speech and language/communication disorder. As Abbeduto et al. (Chapter 14) suggest, the United States continues to be faced with "a system of help and support that is underresourced and not equally accessible to all citizens."

Abbeduto et al. discuss new opportunities and delivery channels for effective implementation models, such as telehealth. These include parent-delivered interventions for students with disabilities that are being identified and validated; such parent-delivered systems are an especially important focus for students with language impairments, such as dyslexia or ASD. Because those students require specialized instruction, which may not be readily available within their communities, new channels, especially those that can harness technology, are important to develop. Opportunities to employ readily available (and often free) online delivery models hold great promise for professional development, instruction, and intervention; some examples include social media, online forums, and video conferencing. At the same time, it is important to acknowledge that no matter how much easier we make the delivery of specialized instruction, it is only a worthwhile endeavor if the instruction being delivered works (i.e., if it is based on science that has demonstrated that it can be effective).

THE RESEARCH-TO-PRACTICE LINK

Controversies notwithstanding, the policy of inclusive education is built on the acceptance of basic human rights and acceptance of all human conditions and deserves the attention of researchers, policy makers, and constituents (parents of students with disabilities and students themselves) if we are to improve education practice and outcomes. There is a need to determine which components of inclusive education are effective as well as the components that are ineffective. This determination, in turn, will drive research that informs education policy and practice to improve education access, equity, and instruction for all students who struggle in school.

Parallel to the important debate about how to create effective and inclusive models for special education students is the continued call from multidisciplinary groups of researchers, practitioners, policy makers, and related experts in all fields of education to use science to inform teacher training and instruction (Denton, Vaughn, & Fletcher, 2003). How we apply research to practice with greater fidelity, consistency, and efficacy is a fundamental question that we have been unable to address consistently and effectively in the United States. We cannot rely only on occasional, serendipitous conversations between researchers and practitioners, as valuable and productive as they may be; rather, we need to develop effective teacher education models in which teacher candidates, especially those preparing to enter general education classrooms, are educated as consumers of research so they may be better equipped to bridge the research-to-practice gap. Furthermore, part of the ongoing professional development for educators of reading (and all instructional disciplines) must rely on ongoing conversations between the research and the academic communities.

At the same time, we caution that this is only part of the story. There are myriad factors (e.g., amount of instruction, dialect variation) that must be considered (e.g., Saeigh-Haddad, in press; Terry, Connor, Petscher, & Conlin, 2012; Vaughn, Levy, Coleman, & Bos, 2002; Washington & Lee-James, in press). As we continue to consider those factors, however, we acknowledge that there must be agreement on the importance of early instruction and identification of students, which should begin before students enter formalized primary education programs (Catts, Nielsen, Bridges, Liu, & Bontempo, 2015; Morris et al., 1998, 2012). Several studies indicate that the first and second years of preschool are associated with decoding and letter knowledge gains (Skibbe, Connor, Morrison, & Jewkes, 2011); therefore, we suggest that a truly inclusive approach is one that extends the range of preservice educators who receive training to include those teaching in preschools. Preschool educators are likely the first ones to encounter students with learning disabilities, so those educators also need access to training in evidence-based instructional techniques (Kornev, Rakhlin, & Grigorenko, 2010).

For educational systems, such as Russia's, that are at earlier stages in the dyslexia and ASD debates, there are opportunities to learn from the experiences of Western countries, such as the United States and United Kingdom (see Chapter 15). Although there are many important lessons about classroom instruction that could be included, there are three critical determinants of success for students with learning disabilities:

1. Develop effective teacher education/professional development models in which preservice and in-service educators are trained as consumers of education research.

2. Equip general education teachers with the resources to identify students at risk for disabilities.
3. Ensure that students are identified and provided with individualized, evidence-based instruction.

CONCLUSION

The history of educating people with learning disabilities has been one of great expectations in the modern world, which, unfortunately, have all too much in common with a line from the novel *Great Expectations:* "Suffering has been stronger than all other teaching" (Dickens, 1861, p. 489). Through recognition and compassion, building the foundation of equity is possible within society, but such a foundation may only be secured through strong, effective legislation coupled with sound, evidence-based approaches. Otherwise, society risks continued suffering for students who struggle in school and remain in a marginalized status into adulthood. Those countries who are in the nascent stages of building their educational infrastructure to support students with learning disabilities have an opportunity to leverage existing experiences and, perhaps, provide leadership in this critical space.

REFERENCES

Allday, R. A., Neilsen-Gatti, S., & Hudson, T. M. (2013). Preparation for inclusion in teacher education pre-service curricula. *Teacher Education and Special Education, 36*(4), 298–311.

Brault, M. W. (2012). *Americans with disabilities: 2010. Household economic studies, current population reports.* Washington, DC: U.S. Department of Commerce Economics and Statistics Administration, U.S. Census Bureau.

Brownell, M. T., Adams, A., Sindelar, P., Waldron, N., & Vanhover, S. (2006). Learning from collaboration: The role of teacher qualities. *Exceptional Children, 72*(2), 169–185.

Burgdorf, R. L. (2015). *Why I wrote the Americans with Disabilities Act.* Retrieved from https://www.washingtonpost.com/posteverything/wp/2015/07/24/why-the-americans-with-disabilities-act-mattered/?noredirect=on&utm_term=.e9cc88241095

Cameron, D. L., & Cook, B. G. (2007). Attitudes of preservice teachers enrolled in an infusion preparation program regarding planning and accommodations for included students with mental retardation. *Education and Training in Developmental Disabilities, 42*(3), 353–363.

Catts, H. W., Nielsen, D. C., Bridges, M. S., Liu, Y. S., & Bontempo, D. E. (2015). Early identification of reading disabilities within an RTI framework. *Journal of Learning Disabilities, 48*(3), 281–297.

Denton, C. A., Vaughn, S., & Fletcher, J. M. (2003). Bringing research-based practice in reading intervention to scale. *Learning Disabilities Research and Practice, 18*(3), 201–211.

Dickens, C. (1861). *Great expectations* (20th ed.). London, England: Chapman and Hall.

Dmitriev, A. A., & Tverskaya, O. N. (2015). Modern approaches to inclusive education of children with disabilities in Russia: Mini review. *Biological Medicine (Aligarh), 7*(4), BM-134-15.

Elliott, J. G., Hufton, N., Illushin, L., & Willis, W. (2005). *Motivation, engagement and educational performance.* London, England: Palgrave Press.

Farrell, P., Dyson, A., Polat, F., Hutcheson, G., & Gallannaugh, F. (2007). Inclusion and achievement in mainstream schools. *European Journal of Special Needs Education, 22*(2), 131–145.

Florian, L., & Rouse, M. (2009). The inclusive practice project in Scotland: Teacher education for inclusive education. *Teaching and Teacher Education, 25*(4), 594–601.
Hall, S. A. (2009). The social inclusion of people with disabilities: A qualitative meta-analysis. *Journal of Ethnographic & Qualitative Research, 3*(3), 162–173.
Hanushek, E. A., & Raymond, M. E. (2003). Improving educational quality: How best to evaluate our schools? In Y. Kodrzycki (Ed.), *Education in the 21st century: Meeting the challenges of a changing world* (pp. 193–224). Boston, MA: Federal Reserve Bank of Boston.
Hornby, G. (2015). Inclusive special education: Development of a new theory for the education of children with special educational needs and disabilities. *British Journal of Special Education, 42*(3), 234–256.
Individuals with Disabilities Education Improvement Act (IDEA) of 2004, PL 108-446, 20 U.S.C. §§ 1400 *et seq.*
Kauffman, J. M., & Badar, J. (2014). Instruction, not inclusion, should be the central issue in special education: An alternative view from the USA. *Journal of International Special Needs Education, 17*(1), 13–20.
Kornev, A. N., Rakhlin, N., & Grigorenko, E. L. (2010). Dyslexia from a cross-linguistic and cross-cultural perspective: The case of Russian and Russia. *Learning Disabilities: A Contemporary Journal, 8*(1), 51–78.
Lee-Tarver, A. (2006). Are individualized education plans a good thing? A survey of teachers' perceptions of the utility of IEPs in regular education settings. *Journal of Instructional Psychology, 33*(4) 263–273.
Moody, K. C., Holzer, C. E., Roman, M. J., Paulsen, K. A., Freeman, D. H., Haynes, M., & James, T. N. (2000). Prevalence of dyslexia among Texas prison inmates. *Texas Medicine, 96*(6), 69–75.
Morris, R. D., Lovett, M. W., Wolf, M., Sevcik, R. A., Steinbach, K. A., Frijters, J. C., & Shapiro, M. B. (2012). Multiple-component remediation for developmental reading disabilities: IQ, socioeconomic status, and race as factors in remedial outcome. *Journal of Learning Disabilities, 45*(2), 99–127.
Morris, R., Stuebing, K., Fletcher, J., Shaywitz, S., Lyon, G., Shankweiler, D., . . . Shaywitz, B. (1998). Subtypes of reading disability: Variability around a phonological core. *Journal of Educational Psychology, 90*(3), 347–373.
National Assessment of Education Progress. (2017). *NAEP mathematics and reading assessments: Highlighted results at grades 4 and 8 for the nation, states, and districts.* Retrieved from https://www.nationsreportcard.gov/reading_math_2017_highlights
National Center for Health Statistics. (2007). *Health, United States, 2007 health: With chartbook on trends in the health of Americans.* Retrieved from https://www.cdc.gov/nchs/data/hus/hus07.pdf
No Child Left Behind Act of 2001, PL 107-110, 115 Stat. 1425, 20 U.S.C. §§ 6301 *et seq.*
Norwich, B. (2014). How does the capability approach address current issues in special educational needs, disability and inclusive education field? *Journal of Research in Special Educational Needs, 14*(1), 16–21.
Peat, M. (1997). Attitudes and access: Advancing the rights of people with disabilities. *Canadian medical association journal, 156*(5), 657–659.
Rosenzweig, K. (2009). *Are today's general education teachers prepared to meet the needs of their inclusive students?* Retrieved from https://opencommons.uconn.edu/cgi/viewcontent.cgi?referer=https://scholar.google.com/&httpsredir=1&article=1019&context=nera_2009
Saeigh-Haddad, E. (in press). The impact of linguistic distance on dyslexia in dialect speakers: The case of Arabic diglossia. In J. A. Washington, D. L. Compton, & P. McCardle (Eds.), *Dyslexia: Revisiting etiology, diagnosis, treatment, and policy.* Baltimore, MD: Paul H. Brookes Publishing Co.
Sideridis, G. D. (2005). Social, motivational, and emotional aspects of learning disabilities. *International Journal of Educational Research, 4*(43), 209–214.
Skibbe, L. E., Connor, C. M., Morrison, F. J., & Jewkes, A. M. (2011). Schooling effects on preschoolers' self-regulation, early literacy, and language growth. *Early Childhood Research Quarterly, 26*(1), 42–49.

Terry, N. P., Connor, C. M., Petscher, Y., & Conlin, C. R. (2012). Dialect variation and reading: Is change in nonmainstream American English use related to reading achievement in first and second grades? *Journal of Speech, Language, and Hearing Research, 55*(1), 55–69.
Terzi, L. (2014). Reframing inclusive education: Educational equality as capability equality. *Cambridge Journal of Education, 44*(4), 479–493.
UNESCO. (2001). *The open file on inclusive education.* Retrieved from http://unesdoc.unesco.org/images/0012/001252/125237eo.pdf
Vaughn, S., Levy, S., Coleman, M., & Bos, C. S. (2002). Reading instruction for students with LD and EBD: A synthesis of observation studies. *Journal of Special Education, 36*(1), 2–13.
Wasburn-Moses, L. (2008). Teacher candidates' understandings of instructional strategies in a changing field. *Action in Teacher Education, 29,* 66–82.
Washington, J. A., & Lee-James, R. (in press). Intersection of race, poverty, and diagnostic accuracy: Identifying reading disabilities in African American children. In J. A. Washington, D. L. Compton, & P. McCardle (Eds.), *Dyslexia: Revisiting etiology, diagnosis, treatment, and policy.* Baltimore, MD: Paul H. Brookes Publishing Co.

SECTION VI

Finale

CHAPTER 16

Future Directions for Research and Practice

Integrating Language Development With Reading and Learning Disabilities

Elena L. Grigorenko, Yury Shtyrov, and Peggy McCardle

SUMMARY

Language is the hallmark of human cognition that makes us who we are and enables our rich personal, social, cultural, and economic lives and, ultimately, human society and civilization itself. Any deficits of linguistic communication ability, particularly those that affect development and acquisition of linguistic skills (e.g., reading) in childhood, are devastating for the affected individuals and their families and costly for society. Yet, in spite of all the advances made in recent decades by scientists worldwide, the mechanisms that enable oral and spoken language, their evolutionary and ontogenetic underpinnings, and their neural implementation in the brain remain poorly understood, which, in turn, prevents timely diagnosis of communicative deficits and development of efficient interventions. Here, we highlight the need for integrated multidisciplinary studies that combine different fields, approaches, and techniques in an effort to explain and target disabilities. To this end, this volume brings together international leaders working on language, development, reading, and their deficits and amelioration from very different angles, which include neuroscience, behavioral and experimental psychology, genetics, and network analysis as well as policy planning and practice development. Through covering the biological underpinnings of language, typical and atypical development of linguistic skills (most important, reading), and cross-talk between different skills and functions and by giving research-based perspectives on educational policies, we conclude that the field can only advance through coherent, large-scale, multidisciplinary integrative research conducted in partnership with educators.

INTRODUCTION

The authors of this volume have thought deeply about the directions that research should now take by addressing the various language-related topics of language evolution, the genetic and environmental etiology of language and literacy disorders, typical development, and bi- and multilingualism. Future studies would ideally bring together the various strands of research into typical and atypical oral and written language development. The body of research on the phylogenetic and ontogenetic development of these various aspects of language and the multiple sources of individual differences in typical and atypical development should direct us to explorations that consolidate and integrate what we know across these threads. In particular, since the late 1990s, researchers have made advances in understanding how children acquire the formal properties of spoken and written language; we now know much more about the evolutionary, biological, sociocultural, cognitive, and affective mechanisms that underlie different forms of literacy acquisition. Nonetheless, many essential questions remain about the extent to which spoken, written, and digital language unfolds and the universality and specificity of the mechanisms within and across domains and developmental periods and within and across different cultures and societies.

BIOLOGICAL UNDERPINNINGS OF LANGUAGE

Section I of the volume lays the groundwork by explaining the new frontiers of genetic and neurobiological explorations of language and literacy development. In Chapter 2, Burenkova and Fisher indicate that new technologies that are now faster and more affordable have supported and will continue to support and inspire changes in how researchers study the biology and neuroscience of language acquisition, learning in general, and related disorders. They caution that this must be done with a careful, rigorous analysis of the relation between complex phenotypes and particular genomic DNA variants using a multilevel approach suitable for establishing the relevant associations. These authors advocate interdisciplinary studies that integrate whole genome and whole brain analysis with cognitive data from large cohorts, which would most successfully be accomplished through research consortia.

In Chapter 3, Pugh discusses recent and forthcoming progress in understanding the biological bases of language and cognition to eventually inform and potentially guide both instruction and intervention. Pugh argues that "the exquisite sensitivity to individual differences that gene-brain-cognitive measurement affords promises better understanding of what works for whom and why down the road." He lists new, promising approaches currently being explored: 1) brain-guided learning and treatment, a sort of brain imaging biofeedback approach to various learning experiences and contexts, and; 2) use of functional near infrared spectroscopy (Hirsch et al., in press) and electroencephalography (Dikker et al., 2017) for measurements during social conversation and interaction to examine brain synchrony during these exchanges and learn about optimal learning contexts. Pugh emphasizes that these new approaches require multidisciplinary teams of researchers as well as close collaborative partnerships with educators. Zevin's integrative commentary on the Section I chapters offers a historical perspective on the development of current theoretical approaches, arguing that current, more sophisticated metaphors of brain function, better technology for modeling, and the availability of big data enable today's generation of scientists to move farther faster than those of the past. He cautions we may not be able to fully understand the current theories we develop without deep understanding of our paths among past theories and their synthesis.

TYPICAL AND ATYPICAL LANGUAGE DEVELOPMENT

Although the volume organizationally addresses typical and atypical language development in separate sections, there is general agreement across these areas of research on the need to integrate data from both and examine individual differences as we seek to more fully understand the development of language and literacy and what goes awry for those children who experience difficulties in these domains. Early language development is critical because it underlies children's ability to later acquire the abilities to read and write. The three chapters of Section II discuss typical oral and written language development by summarizing the research using various methodologies—infant behavioral learning paradigms (Saffran, Chapter 4), state-of-the-art methods in eye tracking paired with neuropsychological measures (Akhutina, Korneev, & Matveeva, Chapter 5), and computational modeling (Grainger, Chapter 6).

Akhutina and colleagues found not only that ocular fixations decreased with development but that there were also differences in fixation correlated with different levels of executive function (EF). Most important, this mention of the role of EF in language and reading is further developed by Cirino, Church, Miciak and Fletcher (Chapter 10). Relatedly, Cutting, Lee-Yong, and Barquero (Chapter 13) indicate the brain's reading network overlaps prominently with the cognitive regions of the brain responsible for executive control (fronto-parietal network), and based on their own intervention work, they suggest that this network plays a coordinative role for reading and EF in a student's response to intervention. The role of EF is clearly enmeshed with reading and merits close additional research attention.

Whereas Saffran (Chapter 4) discusses the building of an oral lexicon in early childhood, Grainger (Chapter 6) looks at how early readers learn to identify words and the component letters within them, developing word- and then sentence-reading ability; his theoretical framework can guide studies of why some children struggle with learning to read. Hogan points out in her integrative commentary on the Section II chapters that future research should examine data from all of these perspectives and it should take into account the characteristics of language as we seek to understand the interrelatedness of spoken and written language across development. She calls for large-scale, theory-driven studies of how language and literacy unfold over time to guide educators in tailoring practices for the increasingly diverse groups of students they seek to educate (see also Connor, Kim, & Yang, in press; Saeigh-Haddad, in press; Washington & Lee-James, in press).

The importance of individual differences is also highlighted by various contributors to the volume. Saffran outlines how infants build a lexicon, acquiring the complexities of language. She argues that understanding the differences in learning trajectories for those with and without developmental disabilities as they acquire language should help explain the individual differences seen in how children with language difficulties deal with the challenges of learning language and literacy. Rice (Chapter 7) reviews 16 years of longitudinal research on twin pairs learning language and the heritability of specific language impairment and also highlights the importance of what we can learn from examining individual differences. Rice presents evidence that the grammar marker of language impairment may be part of the inherited influences that shape a child's language development. She urges further study of the differences in the documented twinning effect across mono- and dizygotic twin pairs, examining biological differences and development trajectories that could contribute to this difference—especially studies of molecular genetics and brain development, as recommended by Burenkova and Fisher and by Pugh in Section I of this volume. She also calls for adjustable criteria for defining impairment and more attention to the details of grammar, including finiteness marking, in light of the findings on twin pairs. (Criteria that take into account specific student characteristics, including native language, are also called for by Francis and colleagues [Chapter 12] in their discussion of reading disabilities in English language learners [ELs].) Future studies will need to integrate new sources of information if we are to gain a fuller understanding of language-based and language-related developmental disorders.

Norbury (Chapter 8) emphasizes the remarkable stability and persistence of developmental language disorders, which change with development but are not outgrown; they exhibit consistent rates of language change despite environmental influences. She calls for research that focuses on the optimal points for intervention (which may be during more plastic periods) when rate of growth is most malleable and notes that the nature and intensity of language input has the potential to affect other areas such as social skills, mental health, and learning in general. Eigsti and Castelluccio (Chapter 9) focus on early childhood as that optimal point, claiming the potential for overcoming some aspects of language disorder based on information about early brain connectivity. They report on a group of individuals with autism spectrum disorder (ASD) diagnosed prior to age 5 who seemingly normalized by adolescence and argue that early behavioral intervention appears to have retooled a domain-general brain network to assume specific language processing functions. Like others, they call for prospective studies of early childhood, with their call aiming at the symptoms, causes, and correlates of ASD and the early functional brain connectivity that may be key to successful interventions with this group.

Although several authors note the stability of language development rate over time, Snowling's Section III commentary points out that there are highly heritable differences in that rate and we do not have the full story of how the environment affects it in early childhood. She also calls for examining development within different domains of language—phonology, grammar, and pragmatics—and for the development of "sustained interventions that prevent an intergenerational downward spiral from language difficulty to social disadvantage and poor mental health."

LANGUAGE AND THE DEVELOPMENT OF READING

Language is fundamental to and its development precedes reading development, and those factors that affect language development affect the acquisition of reading skills. Four chapters in Section IV of this volume focus on recent and current work on several aspects of reading disability and related constructs (e.g., EF).

In Chapter 10, Cirino and colleagues focus on the concept of EF, universally recognized as one on the key constructs in studies on all developmental disabilities. Although multiple reviews of the content and usage of this concept have been conducted, the authors argue that it is still unclear 1) what developmental fluctuations characterize EF, 2) how the related subconstructs are connected, and 3) how the notion of EF as a family of constructs and various subconstructs can be helpful in explaining individual differences in academic achievement in general and reading achievement in particular. While addressing these questions, the authors concur with the view in the literature of the important role of EF in developmental disorders, but they also state that it is important to ask how EF skills can be supported and enhanced in the context of high-quality reading intervention.

Just as the authors addressing language disorders are seeking optimal times for intervention and ways to predict and maximize successful responses, so too are dyslexia researchers. Morris (Chapter 11) discusses an intervention study of third- and fourth- grade students with language and or attention difficulties. Although many functions measured prior to intervention (language, attention, EF, and other cognitive functions) seem to predict reading abilities, they do not predict either the rate or the amount of change following intervention. He examined the individual predictors and found that sustained attention is an important predictor, and thalamic function also appears to be a significant component of the prediction model. He concludes that a mixed-component model that better integrates demographic, behavioral, and psychometric data with brain structure and function will offer improved predictions of a student's potential response to intervention. Morris calls for more sophisticated multilevel modeling work to more accurately predict the range of intervention responses and identify those who may not respond.

The challenges faced in identifying children with reading and language disabilities are magnified when those children are native speakers of a language other than the language of instruction in the schools, an increasingly common situation in the modern world. This complexity is amplified by the cultural and linguistic heterogeneity of the population and the instructional context (including language of assessment and instruction/intervention). Francis and colleagues (Chapter 12) found that failure to account for the language of instruction in identifying ELs with reading problems often leads to significant mis- and overidentification. This problem is greatest when the languages of assessment and instruction diverge (e.g., students are assessed in Spanish while being instructed in English). How best to use the uninstructed language in identification of reading problems requires further research, although consideration of language of instruction will clearly be part of any recommendation. We must know the effect on ELs who are trying to learn under different instructional contexts to provide effective education, identification, and intervention for them. These authors caution that using the same criteria for ELs that are used to identify disabilities in native English speakers, as allowed under U.S. policy, would significantly misidentify students. How information from bilingual assessments should be used to improve identification is still an open question and one that requires additional research.

Cutting, Lee-Yong, and Barquero (Chapter 13) present an argument based on meta-analytic data on brain activation studies and their own research indicating that specific language and reading functions vary in the brain networks they activate, and these particular networks overlap with regions responsible for specific cognitive functions. In conclusion, they call for research that considers and integrates regional and network analyses in studies of typical and atypical language and literacy skills. This may offer insights into how to best identify those at risk for dyslexia and why comorbidity with other developmental disorders is so commonly found. The approach put forth by Cutting et al. seems timely and quite logical given the example provided by Eigsti and Castelluccio's argument (Chapter 9) that early behavioral intervention in children with ASD appears to rewire a domain-general brain network to assume specific language processing functions.

Wagner's Section IV commentary places each of the four chapters in the larger context of the relevant research, outlining the field with regard to its current accomplishments and its future destinations. In discussing Cirino et al.'s work on EF, Wagner praises their multidisciplinary approach to defining the construct, but he points out that they may actually be underestimating the effect of EF in reading and math because EF may affect performance on other predictors within the model. He suggests studies that challenge the concept of EF as an independent attribute and consider it as primarily domain specific. Wagner suggests using latent change modeling to study the codevelopment of constructs such as language, reading, and math because each may well influence the development of the others, making studies of their dynamic relationships particularly important. Wagner clearly indicates that use of response to instruction and intervention for identification poses challenges (no single measure can do the job, and this approach cannot account for various issues in identifying reading disability). He calls the networks approach described by Cutting and colleagues promising, and he cautions that in viewing these correlational data, we must consider that normalization with successful remediation could also be consistent with some brain activation patterns being the product rather than the cause of changes in cognitive performance, emphasizing the complexity of this work and probable explanations.

PRACTICE AND POLICY

The final section of the volume addresses linking research to practice and policy—at the intersection of language, education, disability, and society. Abbeduto et al. (Chapter 14) describe using a telehealth model for delivering interventions to individuals and families affected by ASD and related disorders. Although some barriers to such approaches exist, these authors argue that most can be overcome, and this use of technology can significantly extend the provision of evidence-based interventions, lowering cost and improving accessibility to care. Elliott (Chapter 15) takes a different approach and argues not only for evidence-based treatment for children with reading disabilities, but that those countries just beginning to establish diagnosis and treatment for reading disabilities, such as Russia, should also learn from the ups and downs of those who went before. He points out that what works for typically developing children, such as the traditional instructional approach in Russia, may need to be modified for children with dyslexia and advocates the exploration of assistive technology. In both of these chapters, it seems clear that the novel implementations of intervention, while using evidence-based interventions but in new contexts, should also be the subject of additional research because conditions of implementation can affect whether an intervention is fruitful. Thus, the need for a research–education partnership is reinforced. In their integrative commentary on Section V, Mele-McCarthy and Powers discuss the concept of inclusion and whether it is a viable approach to achieving educational equity (see Mele-McCarthy, in press). They heartily endorse Elliott's recommendation to learn from those who went before and specifically note the determinants that will help students with learning disabilities—teacher education/professional development, which should include both familiarization with research and information on how best to identify students with learning disabilities, and guidance in using research evidence to instruct those students.

CONCLUSION

The many suggestions offered by the authors of this volume coalesce into a coherent call for multidisciplinary, integrative research conducted in partnership with educators. The integration of genetic, neurobiological, and behavioral data has been the focus of many research teams for several years—

further integrating this with social, economic, cultural, and language/dialect data and across typical and atypical development is crucial. Although this has been incorporated in some studies to a degree, the call is for language and literacy research to routinely integrate consideration of the complexities of student characteristics and environmental context. The use of novel approaches, be they genetic, computational, neural network analyses, or latent change score modeling, will play important roles in studying the several factors at play in an integrated, dynamic way. Large-scale developmental studies are advocated. Such studies are complex and costly, but consortia of research groups and sharing of data (which has become far more common in recent decades) can make such work possible; such approaches require planning in advance of research and would benefit from data repositories. Again, partnerships with schools and educators can greatly facilitate these approaches, with the added benefits that schools can be on the front lines of testing and implementing new interventions, instructional techniques, and delivery mechanisms. Finding the best ways to identify learning disabilities in diverse populations and determining optimal points of intervention for those with certain profiles or individual characteristics is a dream that can be realized, but only through the multifaceted types of integrated research outlined here. Finally, as this volume points out, sustained interventions are needed if we are to not only succeed in remediating language difficulties but also prevent the devastating comorbidities of poor mental health and social and economic hardship that follow the failure to do so.

REFERENCES

Connor, C. M., Kim, Y.-S. G., & Yang, D. (in press). Personalizing literacy instruction for diverse learners and children with severe literacy difficulties. In J. L. Washington, D. L. Compton, & P. McCardle (Eds.), *Dyslexia: Revisiting etiology, diagnosis, treatment, and policy*. Baltimore, MD: Paul H. Brookes Publishing Co.

Dikker, S., Wan, L., Davidesco, I., Kaggen, L., Oostrik, M., McClintock, J., . . . Poeppel, D. (2017). Brain-to-brain synchrony tracks real-world dynamic group interactions in the classroom. *Current Biology, 27*(9), 1375–1380.

Hirsch, J., Noah J. A., Zhang, X., Dravida, S., Naples, A., Ono, Y., & McPartland, J. (in press). Dynamic cross-brain neural coupling of face processes reflects the transfer of shared face information. *Society for Neuroscience*.

Mele-McCarthy, J. (in press). Dyslexia trifecta: Research, education policy, and practice. In J. L. Washington, D. L. Compton, & P. McCardle (Eds.), *Dyslexia: Revisiting etiology, diagnosis, treatment, and policy*. Baltimore, MD: Paul H. Brookes Publishing Co.

Saeigh-Haddad, E. (in press). The impact of linguistic distance on dyslexia in dialect speakers: The case of Arabic diglossia. In J. L. Washington, D. L. Compton, & P. McCardle (Eds.), *Dyxlexia: Revisiting etiology, diagnosis, treatment, and policy*. Baltimore, MD: Paul H. Brookes Publishing Co.

Washington, J., & Lee-James, R. (in press). Intersection of race, poverty, and diagnostic accuracy: Identifying reading disabilities in African American children. In J. L. Washington, D. L. Compton, & P. McCardle (Eds.), *Dyslexia: Revisiting etiology, diagnosis, treatment, and policy*. Baltimore, MD: Paul H. Brookes Publishing Co.

Index

Page numbers followed by *f* and *t* indicate figures and tables, respectively.